Professional Practice in Sport Psychology

Sport psychologists working with athletes, teams and sports performers are only as effective as their professional techniques and competencies will allow. This is the first book to offer a detailed and critical appraisal of the conceptual foundations of contemporary professional practice in sport psychology. The book presents a series of reviews of the most up-to-date academic and professional literature on professional practice, exploring issues that all psychologists face when working with clients in sport, and offers important evidence-based recommendations for best practice. Key topics covered include:

- models of practice and service delivery
- counselling and clinical intervention
- working with teams
- working with young performers
- providing life skills training
- managing career transitions
- working with special populations
- enhancing coach–athlete relations.

With contributions from leading sport psychology consultants in the UK, the US, Canada, Australia and continental Europe, this is a comprehensive and thought-provoking resource that bridges the gap between research and application. It is vital reading for all advanced students, researchers and professionals working in sport psychology.

Sheldon Hanton is a Professor of Sport Psychology in the Cardiff School of Sport at the University of Wales Institute, Cardiff. He has published over 200 peer-reviewed journal articles, edited texts, book chapters and refereed conference papers. He is also the Professional Practice Editor of *The Sport Psychologist*, on the Advisory Board for the *Journal of Sports Sciences* and on the editorial board for the *Journal of Applied Sport Psychology*, the *Journal of Imagery Research in Sport* and *Physical Activity and Qualitative Research in Sport and Exercise.*

Stephen D. Mellalieu is a Senior Lecturer in Applied Sport Psychology in the Department of Sports Science at Swansea University, where he is Director of Postgraduate Studies. He has published over 50 research papers and is currently Associate Editor of the *Journal of Applied Sport Psychology*, a member of the editorial board of *The Sport Psychologist* and regularly reviews for a number of journals in the field of sport psychology.

Professional Practice in Sport Psychology

A review

Edited by Sheldon Hanton and
Stephen D. Mellalieu

Routledge
Taylor & Francis Group
LONDON AND NEW YORK

First published 2012
by Routledge
2 Park Square, Milton Park, Abingdon, Oxon OX14 4RN

Simultaneously published in the USA and Canada
by Routledge
711 Third Avenue, New York, NY 10017

Routledge is an imprint of the Taylor & Francis Group, an informa business

First issued in paperback 2013

British Library Cataloguing in Publication Data
A catalogue record for this book is available from the British Library

Library of Congress Cataloging in Publication Data
Professional practice in sport psychology : a review / edited by Sheldon Hanton and Stephen D. Mellalieu.
p. cm.
1. Sports psychologists. 2. Sports–Psychological aspects. I. Hanton, Sheldon. II. Mellalieu, Stephen D. (Stephen David)
GV706.4.P638 2012
796.01–dc23

2011022370

ISBN: 978-0-415-57996-4 (hbk)
ISBN: 978-0-415-85832-8 (pbk)
ISBN: 978-0-203-85133-3 (ebk)

Typeset in Baskerville
by Wearset Ltd, Boldon, Tyne and Wear

Contents

Illustrations

Figures

Tables

Biographies

Editors

Sheldon Hanton, PhD is a Professor of Sport Psychology in the Cardiff School of Sport at the University of Wales Institute, Cardiff (UWIC). He received his PhD in 1996 from Loughborough University, and is currently the Director of Research for his institution. Sheldon is the Professional Practice Editor of *The Sport Psychologist*, on the Advisory Board for the *Journal of Sports Sciences*, and on the Editorial Board for the *Journal of Applied Sport Psychology*, the *Journal of Imagery Research in Sport and Physical Activity* and *Qualitative Research in Sport and Exercise.* He is also a member of the Economic and Social Research Council's Peer Review College. Professor Hanton lists his interests as stress and anxiety, mental toughness, organisational psychology, sports injury and reflective practice. Sheldon has published over 200 peer-reviewed journal articles, edited texts, book chapters and refereed conference papers. He has advised on 12 PhD completions, examined internationally, and is currently supervising nine Doctoral candidates. Sheldon is an Accredited Sport Scientist with the British Association of Sport and Exercise Sciences, a Registered Olympic Psychologist, and a Certified Consultant and Fellow with the Association for Applied Sport Psychology. He is also a Chartered Psychologist with the British Psychological Society and Registered with the United States Olympic Committee. Sheldon regularly works with elite populations on psychological preparation, and supervises trainee sport psychologists to attain professional status. As a former National High Performance Centre Psychologist, he advised the England Swim Team and consulted at international training camps and competitions.

Stephen D. Mellalieu, PhD is a Senior Lecturer in Applied Sport Psychology in the Department of Sports Science at Swansea University, where he is Director of Postgraduate Studies. He received his PhD in 2000 from the University of Gloucestershire, and has since published over 50 research papers in a wide range of international sport and social psychology journals and texts, together with the supervision of over ten postgraduate research students. His current research interests lie in the areas of stress and performance, psychological skills training, and the organisational environment of elite sport. He is currently Associate Editor of the *Journal of Applied Sport Psychology*, a member of the Editorial Board of *The Sport Psychologist*, and regularly reviews for a number of journals in the field of sport psychology. Stephen is a Chartered Sport and Exercise Psychologist with the British Psychological Society, and a nationally accredited sport and exercise psychologist with the British Association of Sport and Exercise Sciences. He has consultancy experience in a number of Olympic and professional sports, particularly in rugby union, having been a former junior international rugby union player and Director of Coaching for Swansea University RFC. When he is not working, Stephen enjoys spending time with his family and taking part in outdoor pursuits, including surfing, open-water swimming and cycling.

Contributors

Mark B. Andersen, PhD has been a chartered (licensed, registered) practising psychologist for over 20 years, and is a Professor at Victoria University in Melbourne, Australia. He is also a member of the Institute for Sport, Exercise and Active Living. His areas of research interest include the psychology of injury and rehabilitation, the role of exercise in mental health and quality of life, and the practice and supervision of sport psychology service delivery. He has published six edited/authored books, and more than 140 refereed journal articles and book chapters. He is one of the world's experts in the supervision and training of applied sport psychologists. He has been an invited keynote speaker at 14 different professional conferences on four continents. He is one of the few sport psychologists who blends cognitive-behavioural theory, psychodynamic practice and Buddhist philosophy in teaching his students and in working with his clients. Besides his academic duties, he has a small psychotherapy practice in St Kilda, a beach suburb of Melbourne.

Richard Anderson, MSc is a former student within the School of Sport, Exercise, and Health Sciences at Loughborough University. He graduated with a BSc in Sport and Exercise Science in 2007 and gained an MSc in Sport and Exercise Psychology in 2009. Richard is an UEFA A-licence football coach who has worked at several football clubs at youth, university and senior levels. As a tutor on the Football Association's psychology development courses for coaches, he has interest in the application of psychological skills into team environments through the work of the coach.

Mark W. Aoyagi, PhD is Director of Sport and Performance Psychology and Assistant Professor at the University of Denver. Mark is a recognised sport psychology consultant and has worked with several Division I athletic departments as well as professional and Olympic individual athletes. He is a licensed psychologist in the state of Colorado, a Certified Consultant, AASP (Association of Applied Sport Psychology), and is listed in the USOC Sport Psychology Registry. His areas of expertise include peak performance, team effectiveness, and sport as a mechanism for personal growth and social change. Mark is active in several professional organisations, including the American Psychological Association and the Association for Applied Sport Psychology, and has publications and national conference presentations on the topics of sport psychology, team effectiveness, and ethics among others.

Brendan Cropley, PhD is a Lecturer in Coaching Science and Sport Psychology at the University of Wales Institute, Cardiff (UWIC). Having received his PhD from UWIC in 2010 in the area of reflective practice and consultant effectiveness, his current research interests include reflective practice, professional training and development, and the psychology of sports coaching. Brendan gained accreditation as a Sport and Exercise Scientist (sport psychology) from the British Association of Sport and Exercise Sciences (BASES) in 2007, and has since provided a range of support to a variety of both elite and non-elite individual and team sport participants, teams, sports coaches and sports officials. Brendan has also provided supervision to three BASES supervised experience candidates, and is involved in the delivery of professional development workshops focusing on reflective practice for UK Sport and BASES.

Lynne Evans, PhD is a Reader in Sport Psychology and Course Director of the MSc in Sport/Applied Sport Psychology at the University of Wales Institute, Cardiff (UWIC). Lynne's primary area of research is the psychology of sport injuries, which includes both pre-injury (prediction of injury occurrence) and post-injury (athletes' responses to injury) phases. She has published widely in this area. Her teaching complements her research and her professional practice activity incorporating injury, psychological skills, consultant effectiveness, and professional practice issues. Lynne is a British Olympic Association Registered Sport Psychologist, a British Association of Sport and Exercise Sciences Accredited Sport Scientist, and Chartered through the British Psychological Society. In a consultancy capacity, she works with elite sport teams and individual coaches, sports medicine personnel and performers in the areas of performance enhancement and injury.

Kate Goodger, PhD is a full-time applied sport and exercise psychologist with the English Institute of Sport (EIS). As an institute psychologist, she is a member of the GB Canoeing sport medicine and sport science team working with athletes and coaches towards the London 2012 Olympics. Kate also supports the British Olympic Association in a programme developed to assist Olympic sports in their preparations for competing at a home Games. She received her PhD from Loughborough University in 2007, and has research interests in burnout, applied sport psychology and organisational stress. She is a member of the British Psychological Society and is a Chartered Sport and Exercise Psychologist.

Chris Harwood, PhD is a Reader in Applied Sport Psychology within the School of Sport, Exercise, and Health Sciences at Loughborough University. His personal research and teaching interests lie in the area of achievement motivation, optimal performance and talent development environments, and educational consulting, with a particular focus on social psychological issues in youth sport. He has published extensively within these areas in applied sport psychology, and is currently an Associate Editor for the *Journal of Applied Sport Psychology*. Chris is a British Association of Sport and Exercise Sciences High Performance Sport Accredited Practitioner, British Psychological Society Chartered and Health Practitioner Council Registered Sport Psychologist whose areas of consultancy extend to youth and senior athletes, coaches, and parents across variety of team and individual sport organisations. He currently serves as Lead Sport Psychologist for the Lawn Tennis Association.

Nicholas L. Holt, PhD is an Associate Professor in the Faculty of Physical Education and Recreation at the University of Alberta, where he directs the Child and Adolescent Sport and Activity (CASA) lab. Research conducted in the CASA lab focuses on psychosocial aspects of youth sport and physical activity, with a particular focus on peer and parent interactions. He has published over 70 articles/book chapters and edited two books. He currently holds grants from the Social Sciences and Humanities Research Council of Canada and the Canadian Institutes of Health Research to investigate ways in which youth sport can be provided to promote positive development among youth from low-income communities. He was Associate Editor of *The Sport Psychologist* from 2007 to 2011, and is a Certified Consultant with the Association for Applied Sport Psychology. He primarily provides sport psychology consulting services to young athletes, sports clubs, and sport governing bodies.

Martin I. Jones, PhD is a Senior Lecturer in sport psychology in the faculty of applied sciences at the University of Gloucestershire. Martin received his MSc and PhD from Loughborough University, and completed a postdoctoral research fellowship at the University of Alberta, Canada. Martin's research interests are focused on positive youth development through sport, particularly the development of life skills. Martin has written and co-authored several peer-reviewed articles and book chapters, and has presented research findings at international conferences and professional meetings. In addition to his research interests, Martin is a British Association of Sport and Exercise Sciences accredited sport scientist and tennis coach, and has consulted with a variety of athletes, coaches and national governing bodies in Canada and the UK.

Sophia Jowett, PhD is a Reader in Psychology in the School of Sport, Exercise, and Health Sciences at Loughborough University. She received her PhD from the University of Exeter in 2001. Her main research revolves around the affective, cognitive and behavioural aspects of interpersonal relationships. Her research has been funded by the Economic and Social Research Council, the British Academy, the Nuffield Foundation, the GB Sasakawa Foundation, the Hellenic Olympic Committee and the Hellenic Ministry of Culture and Sport. She is Section Editor of the *International Journal of Sport and Exercise Psychology*, and is on the Editorial Board of several other leading journals in the field. A chartered sport psychologist and an associate fellow of the British Psychological Society, Dr Jowett has authored over 60 peer-reviewed journal articles and 110 conference papers focused on interpersonal relationships in the sport domain and the psychosocial aspects of sport coaching.

Göran Kenttä, PhD earned his doctorate in psychology at Stockholm University in 2001. He has a passion to build bridges between the domains of sport psychology research, education and applied work in elite sports. The majority of his research and publications has focused on elite-level athletes and the training process with a stress–recovery perspective. He has an extensive coaching background with various national and club teams in flat water sprint kayaking. Over the years Göran has been involved with both the Swedish Olympic Committees and the Swedish National Sport Federation (NGB), and several Olympic sports, in order to develop strategies for sport psychological support for the elite athletes and coaches. Göran currently holds a research position in Stockholm at The Swedish School of Sport and Health Sciences, and is a director of the Coach Education Program at the university; he is also the past president of the Swedish Sport Psychological Association.

Camilla J. Knight is a PhD student in the Faculty of Physical Education and Recreation at the University of Alberta. She is completing her PhD under the supervision of Dr Nicholas Holt in the Child and Adolescent Sport and Activity (CASA) Research Laboratory. Her research interests are concerned with the psychosocial experiences of children in sport, particularly focused upon the influence of parents. Recent studies have examined athletes' preferences for parental behaviours at youth sport competitions, coaches' perceptions of parental involvement in youth sport, and understanding the experiences of parents involved in youth sport. Camilla has produced a number of parent education materials, including parental dos and don'ts lists, a parental behaviour leaflet, and presentations. She has also consulted with various tennis organisations in Canada and the UK, providing recommendations for improving parental involvement in junior tennis.

Ronnie Lidor, PhD is a Professor of Motor Behaviour and is the Director of the Zinman College of Physical Education and Sport Sciences at the Wingate Institute (Israel). His main areas of research are cognitive and learning strategies, talent detection and early development in sport, and sport development. Dr Lidor has published over 100 articles in peer-reviewed scientific journals, in addition to book chapters and proceedings chapters in English and Hebrew. He is the Senior Editor of several books, among them *Sport Psychology: Linking Theory and Practice* (1999) and *The Psychology of Team Sports* (2003). As a former basketball coach, Dr Lidor has provided psychological consultation to young and adult elite basketball players. His main focus was on attentional techniques used before the execution of free-throw shots.

Jeffrey J. Martin, PhD is a full Professor at Wayne State University in Detroit, Michigan where he has been for the past 20 years. He obtained his PhD in exercise and sport psychology in 1992 at the University of North Carolina at Greensboro. He has published over 95 research articles and book chapters. His major research agenda has been on the psychosocial aspects of disability sport and physical activity, as well as understanding physical activity engagement among minority inner-city children. He has received over $8 million in federal and foundation funding to support his and his colleagues' research programs. He is currently the Editor for *Sport, Exercise, and Performance Psychology*, the official journal of Division 47 of the APA, and was recently inducted into the National Academy of Kinesiology. A Canadian citizen and former professional athlete, Dr. Martin represented Canada in the 1985 and 1987 World Cup Marathons.

Artur Poczwardowski, PhD is an Associate Professor at the University of Denver. Since 1991, Artur has consulted with athletes and teams from numerous sports (e.g. tennis, golf, hockey, judo, squash, team handball, soccer, track and field, diving, rowing, speed skating). He is a Certified Consultant, AASP (Association of Applied Sport Psychology), and is listed in the USOC Sport Psychology Registry. Artur has over 25 publications (in professional journals and as book chapters). He has delivered over 60 professional presentations at national and international levels, and over 25 invited and educational lectures and workshops. His publications and professional presentations focus on sport psychology practice for performance enhancement and psychological well-being, coach–athlete relationships, and coping strategies in elite performers. He served as an Associate Editor for *The Sport Psychologist* (2004–2006), and currently serves on its Editorial Board.

Daniel J. A. Rhind, PhD is a Lecturer in Sport Psychology and Research Methods at Brunel University. He is a Chartered Psychologist, and received his PhD in 2008 from Loughborough University. Daniel's research focuses on the development and maintenance of effective relationships in sport that enhance the psychological well-being and performance of athletes, coaches and referees. He recently published an edited book entitled *Elite Child Athlete Welfare* (Brackenridge and Rhind, 2010, Brunel University Press). Daniel has worked on projects for the Football Association, the Child Protection in Sport Unit and the British Judo Association. He also works as a consultant in elite sport for people with a disability, primarily with those who are blind or visually impaired.

Natalia B. Stambulova, PhD is a Professor of Sport and Exercise Psychology in the School of Social and Health Sciences at Halmstad University, Sweden. Her professional experiences in sport psychology include her work for about three decades as a teacher, researcher and practitioner in the Soviet Union/Russia and, since 2001, in Sweden. Her research and over 100 publications relate mainly to the athletic career topic, with an emphasis on athletes' career transitions and crises. Her particular specialisation in applied work is assisting athletes and coaches to deal with various career/lifestyle issues, and especially with career transitions and crises. She was a keynote speaker at the European Congress of Sport Psychology in 2007. In 2004, she received a Distinguished International Scholar Award of the Association of Applied Sport Psychology.

David Tod, PhD completed his doctorate from Victoria University, Melbourne, Australia under the supervision of Professor Mark Andersen. He currently lectures in the Department of Sport and Exercise Science at Aberystwyth University, Wales. David's research is focused on the professional development and training of applied sport psychologists, and the psychological factors involved in strength and conditioning. David is on the Editorial Boards of *Qualitative Research in Sport and Exercise, Sport and Exercise Psychology Review*, and *The Sport and Exercise Scientist.* Prior to completing his PhD David worked for eight years at the Waikato Institute of Technology (New Zealand), where he offered psychological services to athletes from various sports, including rugby union, rugby league, powerlifting and bodybuilding.

Ross Wadey, PhD is a Lecturer in Sport and Exercise Psychology and the Programme Coordinator of the BSc in Sport Psychology at Roehampton University. He received his PhD from the University of Wales Institute, Cardiff (UWIC), which examined the personality trait of hardiness throughout the sport injury process. Ross's research focuses on the psychology of sport injury and the psychology of sporting excellence. His work provides insights on how to reduce the risk of injury occurrence, attain sport injury rehabilitation outcomes, transform potentially debilitating experiences into opportunities for growth and development, and deliver sustainable performance and ultimately thrive in stressful situations. Ross is a British Psychological Society Chartered Psychologist, and consults with national and international able-bodied and disabled performers from a variety of sports.

Gal Ziv, MPE is a doctoral student at the University of Haifa – Faculty of Education (Israel). His doctoral research involves attentional focusing, gaze behaviour, and the learning of closed, self-paced motor skills. Gal's research interests involve the effects of cognition, attention and gaze on sport performance, physical and physiological demands of beginner and skilled athletes, and the use of tests in early phases of talent development. Gal has published 12 scientific papers in peer-reviewed journals.

Reviewers

Megan Babkes Stellino, EdD. Professor in Exercise Science, College of Natural and Health Sciences: Sport and Exercise Science, University of Northern Colorado, USA.

Katherine Bond, PhD. Principal Lecturer in Sport and Exercise Psychology, Department of Sport and Exercise Sciences, University of Chichester, UK.

Sam Carr, PhD. Lecturer, Department of Education, University of Bath, UK.

Alexander Cohen, PhD. Sport Psychology Program Chair, Argosy University, Atlanta, USA.

Jean Cote, PhD. Professor and Director, School of Kinesiology and Health Studies, Queen's University, Canada.

Tim Holder, PhD. Reader in Applied Sport Psychology, School of Human Sciences, St Mary's University College, Twickenham, UK.

Zoe Knowles, PhD. Senior Lecturer in Sport and Exercise Psychology, School of Sport and Exercise Sciences, Liverpool John Moores University, UK.

Larry Lauer, PhD. Director of Coaching Education and Development, Institute for the Study of Youth Sports, Michigan State University, USA.

David Lavallee, PhD. Professor and Head of School of Sport, University of Stirling, UK.

Chris Lonsdale, PhD. Senior Lecturer in Sport and Exercise Psychology, School of Biomedical and Health Sciences, University of Western Sydney, Australia.

Meghan McDonough, PhD. Assistant Professor in Sport and Exercise Psychology, Department of Health and Kinesiology, Purdue University, USA.

Sunghee Park, MSc. Researcher in Applied Sport Psychology, School of Sport, University of Stirling, UK.

Acknowledgements

We are very grateful to all the authors for their contributions to this book. We appreciate the task was challenging, and we hope you are as pleased with the result as we are – thank you. We are also greatly indebted to all the reviewers who gave up their time to provide comprehensive and insightful feedback on each of the respective chapters. Our appreciation is extended to Routledge for working with us once more, and specifically to all the staff at the Sport and Leisure Section of Routledge Publishing.

Lastly, we would like to give a special mention to our respective families for their ongoing love and support throughout the production of another book and our professional careers in general.

Introduction

Welcome to *Professional Practice in Sport Psychology: A Review*, the third book in our series of reviews within the domain of sport psychology. Some time ago, our intention was to produce a collection of in-depth literature reviews on key subject areas to assist research and practice within the field. Specifically, we wanted to invite collections from established international experts along with exciting emerging researchers that were subject to external peer review, similar to the process for journal publication, but without the constraints on length that journals inevitably face. Our first project, *Literature Reviews in Sport Psychology*, was published five years ago (Hanton and Mellalieu, 2006) and examined many of the common theoretical areas such as motivation, anxiety and emotion. We moved to Routledge for our second offering, and *Advances in Applied Sport Psychology: A Review* was published three years later (Mellalieu and Hanton, 2009). This text synthesized reviews addressing areas such as goal-setting, mental imagery and self-efficacy. Commissioning reviews addressing the area of professional practice for this project was not so straightforward. Inevitably, professional practice texts often focus on service provision, with some excellent examples being how to consult with athletes (e.g. Andersen, 2000, 2005) or the specific techniques and process involved (e.g. Williams, 2009). We hope this text complements the previous work by offering reviews of key professional practice topics which draw on the extant literature in order to derive specific practice-based implications. In doing this we gave the contributors licence to present the key issues in the manner most appropriate for their area of specialisation. By design, the text first addresses the models of practice and delivery before offering chapters with a specific consultancy focus, such as working with young athletes, the disabled, in a team setting, or with injured performers. Athletes experiencing burnout and considering career transition and retirement are then discussed. The final chapters of the book address other issues pertinent for professional practitioners, such as talent identification, the coach–athlete relationship, life skills, counselling, and reflective practice and consultant effectiveness. We hope these reviews present a current synthesis of the research in each area, as well as providing clear professional practice advice from individuals with a wealth of experience in their field of research and consulting.

This book contains 12 chapters. The first chapter, by Mark Aoyagi and Artur Poczwardowski, begins with a review of literature on the models adopted in sport psychology practice and delivery. Specific emphasis is placed upon recent theoretical conceptualisations, clinical insights and empirical support. Models such as psychological skills training, counselling, medical (or clinical), interdisciplinary sport science and supervisory consulting are defined and critically reviewed.

In the second chapter, Camilla Knight and Nick Holt provide a resource for sport psychology consultants interested in working with young athletes. Barriers and opportunities for providing sport psychology services to young athletes are presented. Specific emphasis is placed upon issues related to two main developmental periods: childhood and adolescence. The authors then proceed to discuss developmental milestones and sport psychology research associated with each period, along with implications for sport psychology consultants. Finally, pertinent information regarding delivering sport psychology to young athletes is presented, before considerations of future directions for research in the area.

In Chapter 3, Jeffrey Martin reviews the research related to performance enhancement for athletes with physical disabilities. The chapter includes a discussion of the research on the psychological factors associated with superior performance, psychological skill use among athletes with disabilities, and intervention research involving athletes with disabilities. Using a holistic human development model of professional practice, the author then considers a number of disability sport-specific challenges that athletes with disabilities encounter, and the subsequent implications for sport psychology practice.

Chapter 4, written by Chris Harwood and Richard Anderson, appraises the professional practice literature that has focused on psychological service provision within team settings. Issues are presented in relation to the major pre-consultancy factors and early stage initiatives underpinning trust-building with a team, methods of team-based psychological assessment, the range of services and popular strategies noted by consultants in their intervention work, and methods of evaluating consulting effectiveness that have been documented by consultants.

In the fifth chapter in this volume, Ross Wadey and Lynne Evans discuss the common challenges injured athletes typically experience across the three phases of recovery: injury onset, rehabilitation, and return to competitive sport. The stages are discussed in relation to the relevant models and concepts that have underpinned the professional practice literature in the psychology of injury rehabilitation. The authors then proceed to provide a number of general guidelines for practitioners in terms of how they can enable injured athletes to facilitate recovery and attain desirable rehabilitation outcomes.

Göran Kenttä and Kate Goodger, in Chapter 6, then proceed to raise awareness of how various issues of burnout impact professional sport psychology practice. The chapter discusses the challenges experienced around defining, measuring and explaining burnout. Specifically, diagnosis, assessment, prevalence, and intervention approaches are examined, together with the presentation of a novel screening tool which practitioners can use in the one-to-one consultancy setting with cases of physically-driven burnout.

Chapter 7, by Natalia Stambulova, provides an evolution of the topic of athletes' career transitions in sport psychology though a meta-review of books and review papers, in which theoretical, empirical and applied aspects of the topic have been thoroughly addressed. Based on this review, a conceptual model for assistance in career transitions (the ACT model) is offered together with a number of challenges for both career transition research and practice.

Chapter 8, by Ronnie Lidor and Gal Ziv, critically reviews the literature focusing on psychological characteristics of young athletes engaged in individual and team sports. The authors then proceed to critically examine the use of psychological interventions in young athletes involved in these sports. A number of methodological concerns and research limitations associated with the existing literature are then discussed, followed by practical implications from the reviewed literature for sport psychology consultants working with athletes in the early phases of talent development.

In the ninth chapter, Daniel Rhind and Sophia Jowett review the theory, research and practice in relation to the quality of the coach–athlete relationship and its maintenance. They focus on the 3+1Cs model of relationship quality and the recent COMPASS model of relationship maintenance. Measurement tools that allow the assessment of the quality of coach–athlete relationships and the strategies used to maintain the effectiveness of these relationships are also discussed, together with a number of case studies to illustrate the ways in which these models can inform sport psychology consultants working with coaches and athletes.

Chapter 10, by Martin Jones, examines the theoretical and applied developments in the life skills training with athletes' literature. Key issues related to the definition of life skills, theoretical foundations, transferability of life skills, and applied strategies are discussed. Models of life skills development from sport psychology and developmental science are reviewed and discussed to provide the reader with an understanding of how the knowledge base has been developed. Research examining how life skills are taught is reviewed, and strategies for teaching life skills to athletes are then described.

In Chapter 11, David Tod and Mark Andersen focus on relationship as the foundation of service delivery, and compare the literature on the relationship in counselling psychology and its application to the relationship in sport psychology. The authors discuss the practitioner as an instrument of service delivery and consider developing relationship-building skills with regard to supervision, client interaction, reflective practice, and counselling-skills reading and courses. The chapter concludes with a comparison of the models of service delivery based on technique with one based on relationships.

In the twelfth and final chapter, Brendan Cropley and Sheldon Hanton review the literature concerning the value of reflective practice for the personal and professional development of applied sport psychology consultants. Specific discussion is provided on how reflective practice may be linked to the development of effective service delivery and the importance of experiential learning in professional training and development. A number of recommendations for future research and the advancement of professional training programmes are then provided.

Sheldon Hanton
Stephen D. Mellalieu

References

Andersen, M. B. (ed.), (2000). *Doing sport psychology.* Champaign, IL: Human Kinetics.

Andersen, M. B. (ed.), (2005). *Sport psychology in practice.* Champaign, IL: Human Kinetics.

Hanton, S. and Mellalieu, S. D. (eds), (2006). *Literature reviews in sport psychology.* Hauppauge, NY: Nova Science.

Mellalieu, S. D. and Hanton, S. (eds), (2009). *Advances in applied sport psychology. A review.* New York, NY: Routledge.

Williams, J. M. (ed.), (2009). *Applied sport psychology: Personal growth to peak performance* (6th edn). London: McGraw-Hill.

1 Models of sport psychology practice and delivery

A review

Mark W. Aoyagi and Artur Poczwardowski

Abstract

Current models of sport psychology practice and delivery are reviewed. Models are categorised in accordance with Poczwardowski *et al.* (2004) into: (a) psychological skills training (PST) models, (b) counselling models, (c) medical models, (d) interdisciplinary sport science models, and (e) supervisory consulting models with integrative approach. The models reviewed are as follows: Consultant's Guide to Excellence (Halliwell *et al.*, 1999), Sport Psychology Service Delivery Heuristic (Poczwardowski, 2001; Poczwardowski *et al.*, 1998), Cognitive-Behavioural Consultation Model (Perna *et al.*, 1995), Youth Sport Consulting Model (Visek *et al.*, 2009), Individual Zones of Optimal Functioning Model (Hanin, 2000, 2007), Pyramid Model of Athletic Excellence (Gould and Damarjian, 1998; Hardy *et al.*, 1996), Resonance Performance Model (Newburg *et al.*, 2002), Wheel of Excellence (Orlick, 2008), Peak Performance Model (Vernacchia, 2003), Integrative Model of Human Performance (Gardner and Moore, 2007), Mental Skills for Athletes and Coaches Model (Vealey, 2007b), Life Development Intervention (Danish *et al.*, 1992, 1995), Periodisation of Mental Training (Blumenstein *et al.*, 2005; Holliday *et al.*, 2008), Educational Model (Weiss, 1995), Organisational Empowerment (Smith and Johnson, 1990), The 5Cs Coaching Efficacy Program (Harwood, 2008), and Multimodel Approach (Gordin and Henschen, 1989). Implications for professional practice are discussed.

Keywords: Sport psychology, models, service delivery, applied practice

Introduction

In order to begin our review of models of sport psychology practice and delivery, we first had to determine what qualified as a model. While this may seem a mundane or perhaps even obvious task, we found it to be a necessary one given the proliferation of literature and the overlapping (and at times contradictory) use of several relevant terms. The key terms relevant to models of practice include: philosophy, frameworks, systems, theory/

theoretical orientation, models, programmes/approaches, strategies/goals, and interventions/techniques/methods. Thus, we will start with an offer of conceptual clarity grounded primarily in the work of Prochaska and Norcross (2010) and Poczwardowski *et al.* (2004).

Perhaps the most useful way to understand the above terms is categorically rather than by strict definitions, due to the divergent usages of the terms. Prochaska and Norcross (2010) present a straightforward classification system based upon the level of abstraction implied within certain terms. Their system includes high (global theories; e.g. psychodynamic, cognitive-behavioural), medium (change processes; e.g. consciousness-raising, catharsis), and low (clinical techniques; e.g. interpretation, two-chair technique) levels of abstraction. While it is likely clear from the examples provided that this classification system was developed purely for psychotherapy, it is nonetheless useful for our purposes. Hence, the key terms relevant to models of practice presented above were intentionally ordered according to their level of abstraction.

Philosophy has been used relatively consistently in the literature in reference to the greatest level of abstraction out of which develops theories, models, goals, and methods (e.g. Poczwardowski *et al.*, 2004; Ravizza, 2002, Vealey, 1988, 2007a). Where the literature lacks consistency in usage of terms is at the level of frameworks, systems, theory/theoretical orientation, models, and approaches. At times these terms are used interchangeably (e.g. Hill, 2001; Vealey, 1988, 2007a), while at others they are differentiated (e.g. Poczwardowski *et al.*, 2004). In the Poczwardowski *et al.* (2004) hierarchical structure of professional philosophy, theoretical paradigms (which would include common usages for the terms frameworks, systems, and theory/theoretical orientation) are differentiated from models of practice (including common usage of the term approach). Combining this structure with the Prochaska and Norcross (2010) level of abstraction analysis, we would have theoretical paradigms in the high abstraction category, and models of practice in the medium abstraction category.

We feel this distinction between theoretical paradigms and models of practice is essential in the sport psychology literature for two reasons. The first is that, while some of the models we describe approach the level of abstraction necessary to fit into the theoretical paradigm category (i.e. higher abstraction), the vast majority do not. Historically, at this level of abstraction the sport psychology literature has relied on adapting theories from psychotherapy rather than developing its own frameworks/systems/theoretical orientations (e.g. Conroy and Benjamin, 2001; Hill, 2001; Strean and Strean, 1998). Thus, there is a clear need in the sport psychology literature for global theories and frameworks developed specifically for sport psychology and performance enhancement (Aoyagi and Poczwardowski, 2011). The second reason for distinguishing between theoretical paradigms and models of practice is that it becomes a delineating point between thinking and doing. While the sport psychology literature may be lacking in original, global ways of conceptualising performance enhancement (i.e. theories of optimal performance), it is replete with excellent resources for applying sport psychology. These models are what we will focus on in this chapter. In addition, a reflection on conceptualisation of sport psychology service delivery (as an art and science; thus, referring to consulting excellence) will be offered to account for the specific contexts (i.e. clients, situations, physical spaces) in which sport psychology consulting takes place. As a final note, reviews of general psychotherapy theories are widely available (e.g. Prochaska and Norcross, 2010), as well as how they can be adapted to sport psychology (e.g. Hill, 2001), and thus this chapter will focus on models developed specifically for sport psychology.

A further distinction must be made between the terms "model" and "programme/approach". As described above, we classify models in the medium level of abstraction and programmes/approaches are at this level of abstraction as well, though slightly lower (closer to the low level of abstraction). The key differentiation is that models are developed with a range of applications in mind, while the terms "programme" and "approach" commonly refer to a specific application, population, and/or goal. Thus, a programme/approach may well become a model, but it first requires investigation with a wider range of applicability, populations, and/or goals (i.e. a higher level of abstraction). We will include a few prototypical examples of programmes/approaches in the interdisciplinary sport science/supervisory consulting with integrative approach section due to the lack of fully developed models in this category. The remaining terms of "strategies/goals" and "interventions/techniques/methods" occur at the lowest level of abstraction, and derive directly from the model of practice being implemented. Most sport psychology books focus on this lowest level (Vealey, 1988, 2007a). See Figure 1.1 for a complete representation of the hierarchical structure.

With the scope of what we will include in our review of models delimited, we return to the Poczwardowski *et al.* (2004) structure in which types of sport psychology service delivery are further parsed into the five most commonly utilised models: (a) psychological skills training (PST) models, (b) counselling models, (c) medical models, (d) interdisciplinary sport science models, and (e) supervisory consulting models with integrative approach. Given the diversity within PST models, we subdivided them into those focusing on practitioners (understanding consulting practices: sport psychology service delivery) and those focused on developing psychological skills in athletes (nurturing athletic excellence). Also, due to the conceptual and philosophical similarities between the interdisciplinary sport science model and the supervisory consulting model with integrative approach, these models were combined into one section (see Table 1.1 for a summary of the models by category).

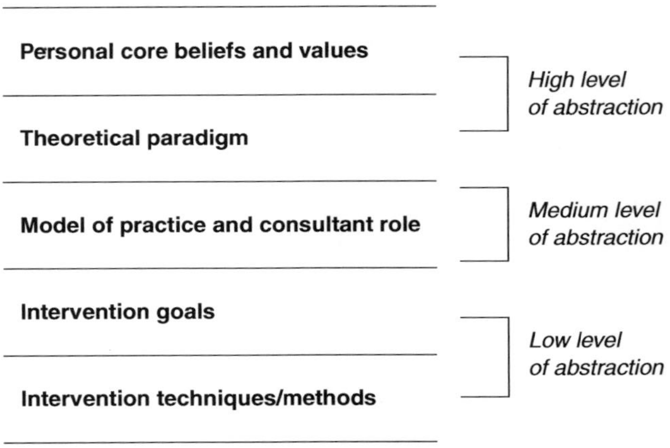

Figure 1.1 Hierarchical categorisation of abstraction levels in sport psychology professional philosophy: combination of conceptualisations by Poczwardowski *et al.* (2004) and Prochaska and Norcross (2010).

Psychological skills training (PST) models

Understanding consulting practices: sport psychology service delivery

Consultant's Guide to Excellence (Halliwell *et al.*, 1999)

Halliwell and colleagues offered their insights into consulting excellence as related to their philosophy of shaping the process of sport and performance enhancement. The main pillars of this conceptualisation were: (a) getting started (e.g. gaining experience, earning trust and respect, readiness); (b) programme delivery (e.g. psychological testing and self-evaluation, consulting moments); (c) making a difference through effective communication, staying focused and in the present, effective listening, athlete or performer commitment, coach commitment, staying fit, staying positive, and a low-profile and confidential approach; and (d) fostering a commitment to the programme (e.g. encouraging daily use of skills, emphasising that only positive action counts). An entire section of quality consulting offered an experientially rich list of guidelines and recommendations (e.g. using a clearly individualised, athlete-centred approach; spending considerable one-on-one time with athletes and coaches; trying to model or "live" the self-regulation skills taught to the clients).

The Consultant's Guide to Excellence went above and beyond the mere meta-aspects of consulting (i.e. process-focused elements or phases), and clearly identified mechanisms behind successful sport psychology practice.

Table 1.1 Summary of models by category

PST: SPSD	*PST: NAE*	*Counselling*	*Medical*	*Interdisciplinary*
Consultant's Guide to Excellence	Individual Zones of Optimal Functioning	Life Development Intervention	None specific to sport psychology	Periodisation of Mental Training
SPSD Heuristic	Pyramid Model of Athletic Excellence			Educational Model
Cognitive-Behavioural Consultation	Resonance Performance			Organisational Empowerment
Youth Sport Consulting	Wheel of Excellence			The 5Cs Coaching Efficacy Programme
	Peak Performance			Multimodel Approach
	Integrative Model of Human Performance			
	Mental Skills for Athletes and Coaches			

The base for these formulations was the collective consulting experiences of the guide's authors that were further supported by past case illustrations and applied anecdotes.

Sport Psychology Service Delivery heuristic (Poczwardowski, 2001; Poczwardowski *et al.*, 1998)

The Sport Psychology Service Delivery (SPSD) heuristic (Poczwardowski *et al.*, 1998) evolved from a number of common themes in sport psychology professional practice as reported by recognised consultants in the field. In this, the model aspired to reflect the common features in the consultant toolbox as applicable to the process of consultation (as opposed to the "content" that reflects known conceptualisations of athletic optimal performance). The SPSD elements included: professional boundaries; professional philosophy; making contact; assessment; conceptualising athletes' concerns and potential interventions; range, types, and organisation of service; programme implementation; managing the self as an intervention instrument; programme and consultant evaluation; conclusions and implications; and leaving the setting.

The SPSD model was reorganised into a more complex structure and was enhanced by additional elements that seem to be critical to successful practice in sport psychology (Poczwardowski, 2001). The revised SPSD model consisted of three fundamental factors: (a) the foundation of service, (b) the process and service, and (c) the working interpersonal alliance. The foundation of service comprised (i) professional philosophy, (ii) professional ethics, and (iii) education, training, and professional experience. The process and service embraced (i) entry and conceptualisation, with three underlying elements – making contact, assessment, and conceptualising athletes' concerns and potential interventions; (ii) implementation, with three underlying elements – range, types, and organisation of service, programme implementation, and managing the self as an intervention instrument; and (iii) conclusion and termination, again with three underlying elements – programme and consultant evaluation, conclusions and implications, and leaving the setting. The working interpersonal alliance was a new category, with three new elements: the consultant–client relationship, the consultant variables, and the client variables.

A qualitative interpretive study with ten accomplished practitioners (Poczwardowski and Sherman, 2011) yielded initial support for both the original (Poczwardowski and Sherman, 2006, 2009) and revised SPSD models (Poczwardowski, 2009) as applied to sport psychology consultation. The meaningfulness and interrelation of all SPSD elements in successful practice was demonstrated. Quantitative designs are needed to further validate the usefulness of the SPSD model in practice, and as a guide to structure graduate curricula.

Cognitive-Behavioural Consultation Model (Perna *et al.*, 1995)

Perna *et al.* (1995) present a cognitive-behavioural consultation model developed by Murphy and Murphy (1992). The model involved eight steps: consultation orientation, sport familiarisation, evaluation and assessment, goal identification, group intervention, individual intervention, outcome evaluation, and reassessment of goals. The authors do not elaborate much on the steps, but rather use a case illustration to demonstrate the model.

A great deal of emphasis is placed on the initial contact with the sport organisation, primarily focused on identifying who the client is and the subsequent ramifications on confidentiality. Sport familiarisation is achieved through observation, and is intended to foster an understanding of the unique culture and characteristics of the client's environment. Evaluation and assessment are done with the BASIC ID approach developed by Lazarus (1981). This involves assessing the client in the areas of behaviour, affect, sensations, imagery, cognition, interpersonal aspects, and drugs/biology. A cognitive-behavioural case conceptualisation is developed from the assessment that addresses the affective, cognitive, and behavioural systems. The case conceptualisation identifies the goals and directs the group and individual interventions. Following the interventions, the outcomes are evaluated and goals are reassessed. No empirical studies were found that tested the model.

Youth Sport Consulting Model (Visek *et al.*, 2009)

Visek and colleagues proposed a six-phase Youth Sport Consulting Model (YSCM) in an effort to account for the process-related specifics of educational consulting work with youth sport teams. The six phases integrated the Poczwardowski *et al.* (1998) SPSD elements (Visek *et al.*, 2009), and included: (a) practitioner considerations, (b) initiating contact, (c) doing sport psychology, (d) termination and continuation, (e) assessing the consulting relationship, and (f) wrapping up the season and consultation.

In the YSCM, developmentally appropriate (e.g. strategy to educate about confidentiality) and context-specific guidelines (e.g. including the dynamics of the coach–athlete–guardian triad) were proposed to guide consultants who focus on youth populations. Although based on sound theoretical underpinnings, empirically based validation of the YSCM as applied to the consulting process with the target populations needs to be undertaken.

Nurturing athletic excellence

Individual Zones of Optimal Functioning Model (Hanin, 2000, 2007)

Originally focused on explaining the relationship between anxiety and performance in elite athletes, the Individual Zones of Optimal Functioning

(IZOF) Model (Hanin, 2000, 2007) has been extended to include an understanding of the range of positive and negative emotions and their effects on performance. As the name indicates, IZOF is an idiographic approach attempting to understand individual differences of subjective emotional experiences. The IZOF model incorporates a multidimensional description of performance affect that includes five aspects: form, intensity, time, context, and content.

Form is the way the emotion is manifested, and is represented by cognitive, affective, motivational, somatic, behavioural, performance, and communicative components. From this perspective, emotion is analysed by the athlete's subjective experiences of it. Intensity is the quantitative aspect of affect, and results in the in–out of the zone concept within IZOF. The model depicts an individualised range for each optimal emotion in which the probability of a successful performance is highest (Hanin, 2000, 2007). Similarly, there is a range for each dysfunctional emotion where the probability of poor performance is greatest (optimal and dysfunctional emotions are defined in the content dimension below). Time describes the dynamics of affect prior to, during, and following the performance. Essentially, the temporal dimension was included because precompetition emotions were not sufficient for predicting performance (Hanin, 2000). Context refers to aspects of the environment (e.g. situational, interpersonal, intra-group) that influence emotional intensity and content. Content is the qualitative aspect of affect, and, due to its importance within the IZOF model, merits a longer discussion.

The IZOF model examines the content of emotions along two dimensions: hedonic tone, and the effect of the emotion on performance. Hedonic tone is determined by the subjective experiencing of the emotion as positive or negative, with each emotion assessed separately on one continuum ranging from high to low in intensity. Considered independently of hedonic tone is the effect of the emotion on performance, which ranges from optimal to dysfunctional. Thus, each emotion can be classified in one of four categories: (1) positive, optimal (P+); (2) negative, optimal (N+); (3) positive, dysfunctional (P–); or (4) negative, dysfunctional (N–).

The IZOF model has generated a great deal of empirical interest, and some of the significant findings will be briefly reviewed here. Not surprisingly, since IZOF originally described the anxiety–performance relationship, research on the anxiety aspect of IZOF is abundant. Hanin (2007) summarised the IZOF anxiety research as supportive of the notion of zones of optimal functioning, affirming of the importance of precompetition anxiety as a predictor of performance, and confirming of the need to examine other emotions in addition to anxiety. The research examining the newer aspects of the IZOF model, specifically the content and intensity dimensions, has similarly been supportive of the predictions of IZOF. Citing numerous studies, Hanin (2007) demonstrated the empirical support for the two-dimensional (i.e. hedonic tone, and effect of emotions on performance) classification of the content of emotions. Further, from available research examining the effects of the content of emotions on performance, Hanin (2007) concluded that positive optimal and negative dysfunctional emotions were the best predictors of performance before and during practices. Finally, reviewing the functional interpretation of emotion–performance relationships, Hanin (2007) argued that the impact of emotion on performance could be better predicted by examining its effects on energy mobilisation and energy utilisation.

Pyramid Model of Athletic Excellence (Gould and Damarjian, 1998; Hardy *et al.*, 1996)

Based on Gould and Damarjian's (1998) extensive review of the literature, Hardy and colleagues (1996) developed one of the most theoretically comprehensive and elaborated psychological skills training models to date: a unifying model of psychological preparation for peak athletic performance. The model consists of: (a) fundamental attributes such as personality, motivational, and philosophical foundation (i.e. trait confidence, goal orientation, individual differences in arousal/activation, trait anxiety [somatic, cognitive, confidence], and attentional style); (b) psychological skills and strategies for peak performance (i.e. process goals, relaxation, goal-setting, mental rehearsal, imagery, self-talk, attributions, mental preparation, performance routines, automaticity, simulation, and association/dissociation); and (c) adversity coping skills which (naturally) comprised most psychological skills for peak performance with the addition of injury coping. Further, all these factors influence the task-specific ideal performance states, such as self-efficacy, arousal, activation, mood, self-determination, burnout, somatic and cognitive anxiety states. Finally, physical, social, psychological, and organisational environments provide the dynamic context for psychological preparation for peak athletic performance.

The unifying model was proposed for both practical considerations and empirical investigations. Hardy *et al.* (1996) conducted a thorough discussion of practical implications, which embraced specific goals for psychological preparation (grounded in reviewed profiles of elite performers) and additional implementation guidelines (e.g. encouraging athlete's taking responsibility for successes and failures [motivational foundation], isolating specific sources of stress and its controllable aspects [coping with adversity]). Additionally, research directions included, for instance, using both quantitative versus qualitative methodology (with increasing rigor in qualitative research); developing systematic lines of research; and grounding research in valid theories and important practical questions to ensure its conceptual meaningfulness and applied importance.

Resonance Performance Model (Newburg *et al.*, 2002)

The Resonance Performance Model (RPM) attempted to combine performance enhancement goals with ones of personal balance and fulfilment, which accounts for the model's unique potential to become a truly holistic tool in sport psychology practice. The experience of resonance is a cyclical (continued) outcome of a fine balance between one's dream (a feeling one wants to experience while pursuing a goal), preparation (as a major source of the lived dream or feeling), obstacles, and revisiting the dream. An elite performer (in athletics or arts) revisits the dream to fully engage in preparation, especially after failures/setbacks (obstacles), to avoid a vicious cycle of ever-expanding work/practice/training. Fulfilment and well-being are natural correlates of resonance. The separation between the dream (feeling that one is doing what one loves and values) and a goal (e.g. a championship) seems essential in teaching the RPM to performers, especially to less elite clients, including youth and children. Helping clients in identifying their dream and understanding and processing obstacles are additional cornerstones in consulting work.

Qualitative data support the RPM's presence in athletic experience and its value in teaching athletes how to "resonate" in sport and life, in both team and individual consulting contexts (Arcand *et al.*, 2007; Callary and Durand-Bush, 2008; Doell *et al.*, 2006). For example, Callary and Durand-Bush (2008), in a constructive case study, demonstrated that the RPM could be successfully used with a female volleyball team (n=16) through group presentations and team discussions, individual follow-ups (e.g. e-mail journalling), and with active involvement of the coach throughout all phases of the intervention and post-intervention follow-ups. Clearly, these findings suggest that the RPM might also be used if a consultant practises from the supervisory consulting with integrative approach model.

Wheel of Excellence (Orlick, 2008)

The Wheel of Excellence was developed by Orlick (2008) to guide individuals toward personal excellence in all domains of sport and performance. The wheel centres on focus, and also includes commitment, mental readiness, positive images, confidence, distraction control, and ongoing learning. Focus is the hub of the wheel, and involves complete absorption in the moment-by-moment process of performance. In order to perform at a consistently high level, it is necessary to have a consistently high-quality focus. Further, the other elements of the Wheel of Excellence grow out of the central element of focus.

Commitment is fostered by discovering a pursuit that incorporates challenge, meaning, and passion. To excel at something, particularly over time, requires a love for the task. It also requires mental readiness to be able to make the transition from thinking about performance excellence to actually pursuing it. Important components of mental readiness include focus, persistence, and a positive mindset. A crucial aspect of a positive mindset is creating positive images of what you want to accomplish. These visions are motivating, and increase the likelihood that what you want to achieve will become a reality. Positive images also help to maintain focus on the possibilities, and this contributes to commitment and persistence. Further, confidence is reinforced through positive images and focusing on the positive during challenging times. Confidence is dependent upon quality preparation and focus, and self-belief. It also shares a reciprocal relationship with excellence, as each allows the other to thrive. The next aspect of the Wheel, distraction control, re-emphasises focus by not allowing distractions to interfere with performance. This is accomplished by developing refocusing plans built around focus points that allow for a reconnection with positive thoughts, feelings, and emotions. Lastly, ongoing learning is an essential aspect of excellence, as it allows for a personalised understanding of the elements that facilitate one's own best performance. Maintaining an open and reflective mind allows for refining the path to excellence and sustaining motivation by learning from setbacks.

The Wheel of Excellence is a naturalistic model developed from the author's own experiences as an elite athlete, coach, and performance enhancement consultant. Emerging, mostly qualitative, support for Orlick's entire model, its parts (e.g. Murphy and Orlick, 2006), or both that was obtained in non-athletic settings (e.g. Talbot-Honeck and Orlick, 1998) is promising and encourages further research in this area. For example, Talbot-Honeck and Orlick found qualitative support for the Wheel of Excellence among top classical musicians, and added important music-specific elements such as creativity, spontaneity, and flexibility.

Peak Performance Model (Vernacchia, 2003)

Vernacchia's (2003) Peak Performance Model (PPM) has strong roots in previous models formulated by Gordin and Reardon (1995) and Moore and Stevenson (1991, 1994) to develop flow and trust, respectively. The PPM presents three personal attributes that are essential for successful performance: passion, attitude, and character. These attributes define the mental environment allowing for the remaining ingredients – quality practice, concentration, confidence, composure, and commitment – to be effective in facilitating peak performance.

Passion is simply defined as "the enduring love of sport" (Vernacchia, 2003, p. 14). The key word is "enduring", as many athletes start with the love of sport, but do not sustain it through challenge and adversity. Peak performance is fuelled by the passion of the athlete. Attitude is the mindset of athletes in practice and competitions, and a successful attitude is consistently engaging in ways of thinking that facilitate performance. In this way, attitude is conceptualised as the precursor of success. Character is manifested not in achievements, but rather in how something is accomplished, also known as sportspersonship. Similar to passion, while some athletes will experience short-term success without it, character is essential for lasting athletic achievement. Within the framework of passion, attitude, and character, the remaining aspects of the PPM – quality practice, concentration, confidence, composure, and commitment – may be nurtured and developed for peak performance.

Quality practice is the foundation for peak performance, as it is essential for effective development of the skills required for successful performance. Vernacchia (2003) presents three principles of quality practice: practice makes permanent, make a concentrated effort, and practise with a purpose. Structuring practices with adequate rest and recovery is an important aspect of practice makes permanent. If athletes are fatigued and practising mistakes, they are creating bad habits. Similarly, athletes should be aware of the larger training goals and cycles so that they can make a concentrated effort on the most important aspects of training with the bigger picture in mind. This way, athletes can understand periodisation and the relationship between practice and performance. Lastly, practising with a purpose means that athletes know what they want to achieve out of practice, and how this contributes to future performances. The guiding principle is a focus on quality as opposed to quantity.

On the foundation of quality practice, Vernacchia (2003) incorporates the 4 Cs of Peak Performance: concentration, confidence, composure, and commitment. In the PPM, concentration centres on Cook's (1996) model of concentration. This approach consists of observing all aspects of the performance environment, and then developing a strategy for successful performance. At this point in the model, all decisions have been made and the goal is to reduce cognitive noise and allow for subconscious execution of the motor programme. This is accomplished by visualising the skill (see it), feeling the body performing the skill (feel it), and then using a cue word to initiate the motor programme (trust it).

Confidence is defined in the PPM as the belief that a particular task can be accomplished. The PPM introduces an "inside-out" approach to building confidence in which athletes are taught to feel good about themselves regardless of their performance outcomes. This is in contrast to an "outside-in" approach in which athletes are not allowed to feel good unless they perform well. The "inside-out" approach facilitates athletes' feelings of competence and maintains their excitement for competition, regardless of the outcome of their previous competition.

Composure consists of managing emotional responses so that an effective mindset can be maintained throughout a performance. Vernacchia (2003) presents a great deal of information regarding pre-, during, and post-competition emotions and composure skills. Some of the prominent themes for exerting personal control during the stresses of performance include revisiting a previously developed philosophy of performance, mastering relaxation training, simulating the stresses of competition in training sessions, incorporating mental and physical routines, and having a strong support group.

Commitment goes beyond completing a task, and is reflected in the quality and effort put forth. It is a pledge that a person dedicates him- or herself to completing, and relies upon follow-through and pride. Vernacchia (2003) conceptualises commitment as a formula: Commitment = Challenge × Pride × Sacrifice × Fortitude. Commitment cannot be measured without significant challenges, and pride results when challenging tasks are mastered. Commitment also necessitates sacrifice, as athletes must prioritise athletic excellence over other aspects of their lives. Lastly, high achievers in all domains are forced to demonstrate fortitude by overcoming significant adversity, hardships, and personal setbacks.

While the PPM was grounded in theory and developed from scientific underpinnings, no studies were found that empirically explored the model as a whole.

Integrative Model of Human Performance (Gardner and Moore, 2007)

The Integrative Model of Human Performance (IMHP; Gardner and Moore, 2007) was developed to illustrate the processes necessary for optimal performance, and includes three phases: pre-performance, performance, and post-performance. The pre-performance phase highlights dispositional characteristics (e.g. personal meaning attached to performance), environmental stimuli (e.g. relationships, injury), and performance demands (e.g. established standards), and the interaction of these variables determines the context of effective behavioural regulation during performance.

In the performance phase, the authors postulate that athletes must attend to personal and environmental cues and adapt their performance accordingly to perform successfully. Central to their conceptualisation, Gardner and Moore (2007) believe the metacognitive processes essential for behavioural self-regulation must remain automatic so that the athlete may be primarily task-focused. Alternatively, when athletes attempt to voluntarily control the metacognitive processes they end up sacrificing task-focus for self-focus. Thus, mindfulness, defined as "paying attention in a particular way: on purpose, in the present moment, and non-judgmentally" (Kabat-Zinn, 1994, p. 4), is viewed as the foundation of optimal performance.

Lastly, the post-performance phase identifies three directions athletes may choose based upon their interpretation of the performance as it relates to their personal values. If there is little or no discrepancy between the performance and the athletes' values, they are likely to remain committed to the sport. On the other hand, if there is a significant discrepancy, athletes may choose to disengage from the activity. With moderate levels of discrepancy, athletes may take some time off before re-engaging with the sport. Of course, the amount of discrepancy experienced is a personal appraisal, and an important tenet of the IMHP is that the wider the range of thoughts, feelings, and emotions athletes are willing to accept, the more effective their performances will ultimately be. In contrast, athletes who avoid certain emotions, feelings, or situations are more likely to experience performance decrements and eventually disengage.

While the IMHP attempts to explain human performance, it does not provide a model of intervention for consultants. To fill this need, the authors promoted Mindfulness–Acceptance–Commitment (MAC; Gardner and Moore, 2007). MAC is an approach to performance enhancement based upon the psychotherapy systems of Acceptance and Commitment Therapy (ACT; Hayes *et al.*, 1999) and Mindfulness-Based Cognitive Therapy (MBCT; Segal *et al.*, 2002). MAC is a renamed adaptation of ACT and MBCT, and thus does not meet our criterion of models designed specifically for sport psychology and will not be reviewed here. The interested reader is referred to Gardner and Moore (2007), as well as the original works of Hayes and colleagues (1999) and Segal and colleagues (2002).

Mental Skills for Athletes and Coaches Model (Vealey, 2007b)

In an extension of a previous model (Vealey, 1988), Vealey (2007b) presented a model of mental skills primarily as a representation of the different types of mental skills influential in both performance and well-being. Hence, the model includes four categories of mental skills: foundation skills, performance skills, personal development skills, and team skills.

Foundation skills are the basic mental skills necessary for success: achievement drive, self-awareness, productive thinking, and self-confidence. Achievement drive includes the desire, effort, and persistence essential to accomplish an important goal. Self-awareness leads to understanding of thoughts, feelings, and behaviours, and is necessary for productive thinking: managing thoughts in a manner facilitating success and well-being. All of these likely influence self-confidence or the belief that one has the skills and abilities to be successful.

Performance skills are specific to the execution of skills during performance, and consist of perceptual-cognitive skill, attentional focus, and energy management. Perceptual-cognitive skill entails the knowledge to strategically organise task-relevant information. Attentional focus is attending to task-relevant cues necessary for performance. Energy management is defined as being able to create the psychoemotional states required to perform optimally.

Personal development skills are mental skills allowing for effective psychological functioning, and include identity achievement and interpersonal competence. Identity achievement is developing a clear sense of one's self through exploration and reflection. Interpersonal competence is achieved by developing the communication skills necessary to interact effectively with others.

Team skills are qualities that are necessary for an effective team environment and success, and consist of team confidence, cohesion, communication, and leadership. Team confidence is trusting that the team has the resources and abilities to achieve success. Cohesion is the ability of the team to pursue its goals in a unified way, and a required skill is effective communication. Leadership involves both coaches and athletes and their ability to influence others toward thoughts and behaviours essential for the team to be successful.

The purpose of Vealey's (2007b) model is to clarify objectives and broaden horizons, and not necessarily as a prescription for implementation. Perhaps for this reason, no empirical studies examining the model were found.

Counselling models

Life Development Intervention (Danish *et al.*, 1992, 1995)

Life Development Intervention (LDI) is a psychoeducational-developmental approach to sport psychology that emphasises continuous growth and change (Danish *et al.*, 1992, 1995). The primary intent of LDI is to cope with critical life events, which are defined as change resulting from life situations. Critical life events may result in decreased functioning, little change, or increased growth, and the LDI framework is designed to view these events as opportunities and attempts to increase the likelihood of a growth-oriented result. Importantly, life events are not discrete events, but rather are processes that begin with a pre-event or anticipatory phase, continue through the event, and conclude at an indeterminate point in the future when the aftermath has been determined and can be assessed. Thus, the timing of intervention is a critical variable to consider.

In terms of timing, interventions implemented prior to an event are called enhancement interventions, interventions that occur during an event are labelled supportive interventions, and interventions following an event are designated counselling interventions. Enhancement interventions are designed to help athletes anticipate normal events, assist in the transfer of skills developed in one area to another (e.g. mental strategies in sport being applied to life challenges), and teach additional coping skills (Danish *et al.*, 1995). As the name implies, the primary goal of supportive interventions is to provide support for the athlete during a critical life event. The LDI specialist may directly provide support and/or assist athletes in locating and forming their own support system. Counselling interventions are focused on helping athletes to grow (rather than stagnate or regress) as a result of life events. This is accomplished by (a) understanding the problem from the person's perspective, (b) assessing coping and support resources, (c) utilising existing resources and teaching new coping skills, (d) helping the person practise new skills and following-up, and (e) planning for future events.

Regardless of the timing of the intervention, there are three major strategies utilised by LDI specialists: counselling skills, goal-setting, and life skills. Counselling skills involve basic helping strategies, primarily listening to and understanding others. Goal-setting is the primary strategy of LDI due to its central role in developing personal competence. Along with goal-setting, the development of interpersonal and intrapersonal (i.e. psychological) skills is important. Lastly, life skills strategies incorporate both teaching new skills and facilitating the transfer of existing skills to new domains. No published studies empirically testing the LDI were found, although references to its data-based effectiveness were made by the authors and their collaborators (Danish *et al.*, 2002).

Medical models

No examples of medical models developed specifically for sport psychology were found. Most likely, this is because there is not an identified need for sport psychology-specific medical models. In other words, athletes are a specific population to whom existing medical models are applicable, and thus there is not a need to develop sport (athlete)-specific medical models (for example, there are no teacher-specific or other domain-specific medical models). However, practitioners desiring to work with athletes utilising a medical model should be aware of the specific needs of this unique population. The interested reader is referred to Hill (2001) for a review of how some of the medical models (i.e. psychodynamic, behavioural, cognitive, humanistic, and neuro-linguistic programming) may be applied within a sport context. Further, Stainback *et al.* (2007) suggest the applicability of the transtheoretical model and motivational interviewing to athlete populations, and more about these models can be found in Prochaska and Norcross (2010) and Miller and Rollnick (2002), respectively.

Interdisciplinary sport science/supervisory consulting with integrative approach models

Periodisation of Mental Training (Blumenstein *et al.*, 2005; Holliday *et al.*, 2008)

Periodisation is a fairly new approach to conceptualising PST in which athletic preparation is utilised as a frame of reference for designing psychological intervention. Namely, a periodised schedule of sport preparation has been parallelled by periodised mental training that uses the same principles in manipulation of the training volume and intensity across the training cycles (i.e. preparatory, competitive, peaking, recovery). Holliday *et al.* (2008) demonstrated theoretical and practical utility of planning mental skills training along the two dimensions of (a) volume (i.e. number of mental training tools, number of targeted mental skills, number of targeted mental plans, number of exercises performed for each skill/tool, and the duration of each exercise), and (b) intensity (i.e. the difficulty, complexity, and specificity of the skills, the complexity of decision-making, and the importance and uncertainty of competitive success). Clearly, this attempt to quantify the two dimensions seems to have potential for developing dose–response data (and eventually, formulas) in the realm of psychological preparation in sports. Further, a volume–intensity cross-over (as volume decreases the intensity increases, and vice versa) was postulated to mimic this essential principle in physical training. A case study with a cross-country skier illustrated the principles of designing and implementing periodised mental training, and also yielded promising preliminary insights into the psychological and performance outcomes of this original approach to sport psychology service delivery.

An important contribution by Blumenstein *et al.* (2005) dealt with the integration of mental training goals with the phases of physical, technical, and tactical preparation for major competition. For example, to account for the high volume of physical and technical training in the preparatory phase, relaxation training was suggested to provide for enhanced recovery and restitution. Similarly, imagery training emphasising tactical solutions against a specific opponent was to be used in competitive and peak phases in the yearly cycle. In addition, the specificity of mental training was reflected in moving mental practice from the office, lab, and homework to the practice and implementation of psychological skills in the actual sport setting (first in physical practice, and ultimately in competition). Case studies with four elite judo players were reported to describe the design and use of the periodisation in mental training, and pre- and post-intervention psychomotor data suggested emerging validity of periodisation as an effective approach to psychological skills training.

The Educational Model (Weiss, 1995)

Weiss's (1995) Educational Model incorporates aspects of both the interdisciplinary sport science model and the supervisory consulting with integrative approach model, as it presents two models: the skill development model and the psychological methods model. It is important to note that the author clearly states "personal development and a healthy lifestyle through positive sport experiences are the primary focus" (Weiss, 1995, p. 42), and thus the context of both models is designed primarily for developmental needs, with performance enhancement a secondary concern. Further, both models are a result of what Weiss (1995) calls an "integrated sport science approach" (p. 42), and fit nicely into what

Poczwardowski *et al.* (2004) call the interdisciplinary sport science model. Lastly, both models emphasise sport psychology consultants providing coach and parent education workshops, with coaches and parents being the ultimate implementers of the models. Thus, the models also fit within the supervisory consulting with integrative approach model.

The skill development model forms a positive feedback loop where increases in competence result in greater self-confidence, which leads to more motivation and consequently to increases in competence. The author's approach emphasises fitting the environment to the child, as opposed to making the child fit into the environment, and thus competence is specified as occurring at optimal levels of challenge. Self-confidence consists of perceived competence and control of movement sensations, and is viewed as a mediator of motivation. Motivation is comprised of task choice, effort, and persistence.

The psychological methods model is also circular, with observation informing teaching behaviours, which leads to personal reflection, then returning to observation. The model encourages coaches and parents to observe for behaviours indicative of the participants' competence, self-confidence, and persistence. Competence refers both to children's skill capabilities and their understanding of the rules and procedures that allow for successful skill execution. Self-confidence is the children's own perceptions of their competence and performance. Persistence is the primary marker of a mastery environment, and may be observed by sustained efforts when the coach is not present, when behaviours continue without immediate rewards (delayed gratification), and when athletes continue to practise despite setbacks.

Following observation comes implementation, and teaching behaviours consist of modifying task difficulty, modelling, feedback and reinforcement, and fostering a mastery-goal orientation. Modifying task difficulty concerns putting children in an optimal environment for skill development and learning, and may be accomplished by providing physical guidance, modifying equipment and/or rules, and providing physical aids. Modelling can be done through adults (i.e. coaches and parents) successfully completing the behaviour, and even more effective are peer-modelling strategies. Feedback and reinforcement provide information to children about their abilities, and should emphasise improvement in personal performance rather than outcome goals. Fostering a mastery-goal environment is accomplished by focusing on the learning and development of skills as opposed to outcomes, and utilising self-referenced markers of competence. Lastly, personal reflection is essential to evaluate the teaching and interventions implemented, and make any necessary refinements or adjustments.

Although all of the individual aspects of the skill development model and psychological methods model are empirically supported, no studies were found that evaluated the models as whole entities.

Organisational Empowerment (Smith and Johnson, 1990)

Smith and Johnson (1990) present a consultation model, called organisational empowerment, in which the consultant trains qualified individual(s) within an organisation to provide sport psychology services. In addition to training, the consultant oversees the programme and provides supervision to the trainees. While their programme was specific to baseball, the authors made it clear that they believed the model could be utilised in other contexts.

Along with finding a qualified consultant, the organisational empowerment model necessitates finding someone within the organisation who is capable of being trained to become competent in implementing the programme. For baseball, the necessary skills were identified as "(a) formal training in counselling, (b) a baseball background, and (c) an interest in being trained to administer the program" (Smith and Johnson, 1990, p. 349). Training involved exposure to applied sport psychology, cognitive-behaviourism, cognitive-affective stress management, and ethics. Training was done both in-person and at a distance, and involved direct instruction, observation, modelling, and supervised practice. Training also included the rest of the baseball staff so that they could understand and support the programme. To increase buy-in, the programme was called mental toughness training.

The organisational empowerment model, while primarily representative of the supervisory consulting with integrative approach model, also included aspects of the interdisciplinary sport science model. Specifically, where indicated and possible, psychological skills training was integrated with physical training and involved both the coach and the player. The primary psychological skills taught were arousal control, concentration, goal-setting, cognitive modification, and mental rehearsal. The programme also involved a formal evaluation process, and data indicate that the programme was highly successful (Smith and Johnson, 1990).

The 5Cs Coaching Efficacy Programme (Harwood, 2008)

Building off Smith and Johnson's (1990) organisational empowerment model, Harwood (2008) developed a programme to help football (soccer) coaches feel confident in designing training sessions to help players develop psychological skills. The programme was called the 5Cs programme, as the five psychological skills taught were commitment, communication, concentration, control, and confidence. The 5Cs programme utilised a supervisory consulting model, with the consultant providing instruction to the coaches, who were the ones implementing the programme in their coaching sessions. The programme is presented within the context of a formal study in which six youth coaches were the participants, with four of them completing the full requirements.

To instruct coaches how to teach the 5Cs, the consultant conducted a 90-minute workshop with the coaches on each of the Cs. The workshops occurred every two weeks, with the coaches expected to implement each new skill during the time between workshops. The ordering of the presented skills was commitment, communication, concentration, control, and confidence (see Harwood, 2008, for a more complete presentation of what was covered in each workshop). Underlying the 5Cs programme were eight behavioural directives which the consultant developed for the coaches: (a) intentionally promote a psychological skill just as with a physical skill, (b) increase awareness of the skill, (c) emphasise the value of the skill, (d) role model the skill, (e) structure sessions to teach the skill, (f) publicly reinforce players who use the skill, (g) incorporate peer reinforcement of the skills, and (h) review the skill throughout the session (Harwood, 2008).

Results indicated that all of the coaches increased their knowledge of how to teach the 5Cs to their players, and at least one coach felt that the programme translated into match results. Overall, the greatest gains appeared to have been made with regard to commitment and communication, and these coaching improvements were associated with increases in players' concentration, self-control, and self-confidence. This study, combined with the work of Smith and Johnson (1990), provides preliminary evidence for the efficacy of the 5Cs programme as well as the organisational empowerment model generally. Of course, more research is needed, with larger sample sizes and different sports and populations, to develop greater empirical support.

The Multimodel Approach (Gordin and Henschen, 1989)

The multimodel approach was developed specifically for the women's artistic programme of the United States Gymnastics Federation, to "systematically prepare young gymnasts mentally for skill development and competition" (Gordin and Henschen, 1989, p. 366). Because it was developed specifically for gymnastics and has not, to our knowledge, been implemented or validated with other populations, the multimodel approach is classified as an approach within our classification system. However, due to the dearth of examples in this section, it will be reviewed here as an early example of the interdisciplinary sport science and supervisory consulting with integrative approach models. The core of the multimodel approach was collecting assessment data, which were then utilised to facilitate rapport-building and develop individualised plans. The results of surveying coaches and athletes indicated assessment would include five areas: self-concept, emotional set, achievement motivation, concentration, and anxiety. Consistent with the interdisciplinary sport science approach, the authors collaborated with other sport scientists in collecting data on exercise physiology, anthropometrics, and orthopaedics, and used this information to further refine the individual development plans of the gymnasts.

While not specifically addressed, it is inferred that Gordin and Henschen (1989) also incorporated aspects of the supervisory consulting with integrative approach. Evidence for this model is seen in the authors' contention that coaches are the real sport psychologists, and in that they made repeated references to working with, training, and educating coaches in addition to the athletes. From this, it is fairly clear that coaches were also implementing aspects of the multimodel approach. As stated earlier, no studies were found investigating the multimodel approach with other populations, and no data were found to support the efficacy of the multimodel approach.

Implications for professional practice and applied research

For practitioners, these models present a variety of different means to achieve a variety of different ends. We believe the distribution of models within the subsections of this chapter is representative of the field of sport psychology; that is, the primary end for which models of sport psychology have been developed is psychological skills training. Next are interdisciplinary sport science/supervisory consulting with integrative approach models, which could also be argued primarily to focus on psychological skills training as their ultimate end. Lastly, counselling and medical models have received less attention in the professional sport psychology literature, perhaps due to a lack of urgency to develop models in these categorisations specifically for sport psychology. In other words, closely related fields to sport psychology may already produce models applicable to counselling and medical model ends that are easily transferable for use within a sport/athletic context. There also seems to be some dispute as to whether the field of sport psychology is truly represented within counselling and medical models, or whether the application of these models to an athlete population is simply doing counselling or therapy with a unique population (Aoyagi and Portenga, 2010).

The models reviewed here provide practitioners with excellent naturalistic insights into how to improve psychological skills, and therefore the belief is that performance will also be positively influenced. While there is emerging empirical evidence for the utility of some of the models in teaching psychological skills, and strong support for psychological skills benefitting performance (e.g. Greenspan and Feltz, 1989; Weinberg and Comar, 1994), testing of sport psychology service delivery models using specific indicators of athletic excellence (i.e. performance data) are lacking. Clearly more empirical studies of this connection are called for, and there have even been direct recommendations for what to study and how to study it (Hardy *et al.*, 1996).

Still, it is also worth noting that 40 years of research on theoretical models in psychology (one of sport psychology's parent disciplines with a much more developed outcome research literature) indicates that model or technique factors account for only 15 per cent of the variance in positive outcomes, regardless of therapists' theoretical orientation (Asay and Lambert, 1999). These specific factors (i.e. factors unique to specific theories/approaches) contribute much less to positive outcomes than what are known as common factors (i.e. factors shared by all approaches). The common factors of client/extratherapeutic and relationship (i.e. therapist/client working alliance) account for 40 per cent and 30 per cent of the contribution to positive outcomes, respectively. The remaining 15 per cent of positive outcomes (the same percentage as specific factors) is attributed to placebo, hope, and expectancy. Based on these results, it was suggested that psychologists adopt a client-directed perspective in which the client is recognised as the engine of change (Duncan *et al.*, 2004). These authors also call for an outcome informed approach (what they label "practice-based evidence") that recognises evaluative feedback as the key factor in consultant efficacy (Duncan *et al.*, 2004). Thus, we recommend that sport psychology practitioners take advantage of this existing body of outcome research and incorporate client-directed perspectives and outcome-informed approaches into models of sport psychology practice, some of which already include these elements but some of which do not.

Finally, the models reviewed here provide guidance on how to achieve certain ends, and what methods and interventions to select to produce these outcomes. However, what is lacking is an explanation for why these models work. Professionals in the field of sport psychology are beginning to call for more abstract, global theories of optimal performance to provide explanations for why what we do works (Aoyagi and Poczwardowski, 2011; Martindale and Collins, 2010). These theories of optimal performance would serve the same function in sport psychology as theories of personality do in the psychotherapy literature: they provide an explanation for why the different systems of psychotherapy work. In psychotherapy, the case conceptualisation, goals, and methods of intervention are all derived based on the personality theory to which the therapist subscribes. This level of integration is lacking in sport psychology, but would be an important addition to our understanding of human performance and our ability to reliably and effectively intervene for the purpose of optimising performance.

Conclusion

This chapter has demonstrated there is no shortage of models of sport psychology practice and service delivery available for use by sport psychology consultants. While this is a positive for the growth of the field, a far less positive spin on the number of available models is that there are as many different models of sport psychology as there are people practising sport psychology. This is clearly an overstatement, but it emphasises the point that, at this stage in its development, the field of sport psychology would do well to consolidate and systematise its models into coherent frameworks and theories of optimal performance. We view this as the next significant developmental milestone in sport psychology, and eagerly anticipate future theories of optimal performance and how they will add to the codification and implementation of the models of sport psychology.

References

Aoyagi, M. W. and Poczwardowski, A. (eds) (2011). *The chronicle of expert approaches to sport and performance psychology: Applied theories of optimal performance.* Morgantown, WV: Fitness Information Technology.

Aoyagi, M. W. and Portenga, S. T. (2010). The role of positive ethics and virtues in the context of sport and performance psychology service delivery. *Professional Psychology: Research and Practice*, 41, 253–259.

Arcand, I., Durand-Bush, N., and Miall, J. (2007). "You have to let go to hold on": A rockclimber's reflective process through resonance. *Reflective Practice*, 8, 17–29.

Asay, T. P. and Lambert, M. J. (1999). The empirical case for the common factors in therapy: Quantitative findings. In M. A. Hubble, B. L. Duncan, and S. D. Miller (eds), *The heart and soul of change: What works in therapy* (pp. 33–56). Washington, DC: American Psychological Association.

Blumenstein, B., Lidor, R., and Tenenbaum, G. (2005). Periodisation and planning of psychological preparation in elite combat sport programs: The case of judo. *International Journal of Sport and Exercise Psychology*, 3, 7–25.

Callary, B. and Durand-Bush, N. (2008). A group resonance intervention with a volleyball team: An exploration of the process between a consultant, coach, and athletes. *The Online Journal of Athletic Insight*, 10. Retrieved 10 May 2009, from www.athleticinsight.com/Vol. 10Iss3/GroupProcess.htm.

Conroy, D. E. and Benjamin, L. S. (2001). Psychodynamics in sport performance enhancement consultation: Application of an interpersonal theory. *The Sport Psychologist*, 15, 103–117.

Cook, D. L. (1996). Creative concentration. In R. A. Vernacchia, R. T. McGuire, and D. L. Cook (eds), *Coaching mental excellence: "It does matter whether you win or lose..."* (pp. 72–80). Portola Valley, CA: Warde.

Danish, S. J., Petitpas, A. J., and Hale, B. D. (1992). A developmental-educational intervention model of sport psychology. *The Sport Psychologist*, 6, 403–415.

Danish, S. J., Petitpas, A. J., and Hale, B. D. (1995). Psychological interventions: A life development model. In S. M. Murphy (ed.), *Sport psychology interventions* (pp. 19–38). Champaign, IL: Human Kinetics.

Danish, S. J., Fazio, R. J., Nellen, V. C., and Owens, S. S. (2002). Teaching life skills through sport: Community-based programs to enhance adolescent development. In J. L. Van Raalte and B. W. Brewer (eds), *Exploring sport and exercise psychology* (pp. 269–288). Washington, DC: American Psychological Association.

Doell, K., Durand-Bush, N., and Newburg, D. (2006). The process of resonance of four track athletes: A resonance-based intervention. *The Online Journal of Athletic Insight*, 8. Retrieved 9 April 2010, from www.athleticinsight.com/Vol. 8Iss2/Process.htm.

Duncan, B. L., Miller, S. D., and Sparks, J. A. (2004). *The heroic client: A revolutionary way to improve effectiveness through client-directed outcome-informed therapy* (Rev. edn). San Francisco, CA: Jossey-Bass.

Gardner, F. L. and Moore, Z. E. (2007). *The psychology of enhancing human performance: The Mindfulness-Acceptance-Commitment (MAC) approach.* New York, NY: Springer.

Gordin, R. D. and Henschen, K. P. (1989). Preparing the USA women's artistic gymnastics team for the 1988 Olympics: A multimodel approach. *The Sport Psychologist,* 3, 366–373.

Gordin, R. and Reardon, J. (1995). Achieving the zone: The study of flow in sport. In K. P. Henschen and W. F. Straub (eds), *Sport psychology: An analysis of athlete behaviour* (3rd edn, pp. 223–230). Longmeadow, MA: Mouvement Publications.

Gould, D. and Damarjian, N. (1998). Mental skills training in sport. In B. Elliot (ed.), *Training in sport: Applying sport science* (pp. 69–116). Chichester, UK: Wiley.

Greenspan, M. J. and Feltz, D. L. (1989). Psychological interventions with athletes in competitive situations: A review. *The Sport Psychologist,* 3, 219–236.

Halliwell, W., Orlick, T., Ravizza, K., and Rotella, B. (1999). *Consultant's guide to excellence.* Chelsea, QC: Orlick Excel.

Hanin, Y. L. (2000). Individual zones of optimal functioning (IZOF) model: Emotion-performance relationships in sport. In Y. L. Hanin (ed.), *Emotion in sport* (pp. 65–89). Champaign, IL: Human Kinetics.

Hanin, Y. L. (2007). Emotions and athletic performance: Individual zones of optimal functioning model. In D. Smith and M. Bar-Eli (eds), *Essential readings in sport and exercise psychology* (pp. 55–73). Champaign, IL: Human Kinetics.

Hardy, L., Jones, G., and Gould, D. (1996). A unifying model of psychological preparation for peak athletic performance. In *Understanding psychological preparation for sport: Theory and practice of elite performers* (pp. 239–248). Chichester, England: Wiley.

Harwood, C. (2008). Developmental consulting in a professional football academy: The 5Cs coaching efficacy program. *The Sport Psychologist,* 22, 109–133.

Hayes, S. C., Strosahl, K., and Wilson, K. G. (1999). *Acceptance and commitment therapy: An experiential approach to behaviour change.* New York, NY: Guilford Press.

Hill, K. L. (2001). *Frameworks for sport psychologists: Enhancing sport performance.* Champaign, IL: Human Kinetics.

Holliday, B., Burton, D., Sun, G., Hammermeister, J., Naylor, S., and Freigang, D. (2008). Building the better mental training mousetrap: Is periodisation a more systematic approach to promoting performance excellence? *Journal of Applied Sport Psychology,* 20, 199–219.

Kabat-Zinn, J. (1994). *Wherever you go there you are.* New York, NY: Hyperion.

Lazarus, A. A. (1981). *The practice of multimodal therapy.* New York, NY: McGraw-Hill.

Martindale, A. and Collins, D. (2010). But *why* does what works work? A response to Fifer, Henschen, Gould, and Ravizza, 2008. *The Sport Psychologist,* 24, 113–116.

Miller, W. R. and Rollnick, S. (2002). *Motivational interviewing: Preparing people for change* (2nd edn). New York, NY: Guilford Press.

Moore, W. E. and Stevenson, J. R. (1991). Understanding trust in the performance of complex automatic sport skills. *The Sport Psychologist,* 5, 281–289.

Moore, W. E. and Stevenson, J. R. (1994). Training for trust in sport skills. *The Sport Psychologist,* 8, 1–12.

Murphy, S. M. and Murphy, A. (1992). *Sport psychology: Performance enhancement for athletes.* Workshop presented at the Annual Meeting of the American Psychological Association, Washington, DC.

Murphy, T. and Orlick, T. (2006). Mental strategies of professional actors. *Journal of Excellence,* 11, 103–125.

Newburg, D., Kimiecik, J., Durand-Bush, N., and Doell, K. (2002). The role of resonance in performance excellence and life engagement. *Journal of Applied Sport Psychology*, 14, 249–267.

Orlick, T. (2008). *In pursuit of excellence: How to win in sport and life through mental training* (4th edn). Champaign, IL: Human Kinetics.

Perna, F., Neyer, M., Murphy, S. M., Ogilvie, B. C., and Murphy, A. (1995). Consultations with sport organisations: A cognitive-behavioural model. In S. M. Murphy (ed.), *Sport psychology interventions* (pp. 235–252). Champaign, IL: Human Kinetics.

Poczwardowski, A. (2001). Sport psychology service delivery model: A heuristic for systematising and optimising consulting practice. In A. Poczwardowski (Chair), *Consultant variables, consultant–client relationship, immersion, and goodness of fit in successful sport psychology service delivery*. Symposium conducted at the 10th World Congress of Sport Psychology, Skiathos, Greece, 31 May 2001.

Poczwardowski, A. (2009). *Revisions to the sport psychology service delivery model: A qualitative exploration*. Association for Applied Sport Psychology 24th Annual Convention, Salt Lake City, USA, 18 September 2009.

Poczwardowski, A. and Sherman, C. P. (2006). Reflecting on professional philosophy in sport psychology service delivery: Results of qualitative investigation. In A. Poczwardowski (Chair), *Professional philosophy in sport psychology service delivery: Advances in reflection and research*. Symposium conducted at the AAASP 21st Annual Convention, Miami, USA, 30 September 2006.

Poczwardowski, A. and Sherman, C. P. (2009). *Best practices in sport psychology service delivery: Results of qualitative, interpretive investigation*. Association for Applied Sport Psychology 24th Annual Convention, Salt Lake City, USA, 17 September 2009.

Poczwardowski, A. and Sherman, C. P. (2011). Revisions to the sport psychology service delivery (SPSD) heuristic: Explorations with experienced consultants. *The Sport Psychologist*, in press.

Poczwardowski, A., Sherman, C. P., and Henschen, K. P. (1998). A sport psychology service delivery heuristic: Building on theory and practice. *The Sport Psychologist*, 12, 191–207.

Poczwardowski, A., Sherman, C. P., and Ravizza, K. (2004). Professional philosophy in the sport psychology service delivery: Building on theory and practice. *The Sport Psychologist*, 18, 445–463.

Prochaska, J. O. and Norcross, J. C. (2010). *Systems of psychotherapy: A transtheoretical analysis* (7th edn). Belmont, CA: Brooks/Cole.

Ravizza, K. H. (2002). A philosophical construct: A framework for performance enhancement. *International Journal of Sport Psychology*, 33, 4–18.

Segal, Z. V., Williams, J. M. G., and Teasdale, J. D. (2002). *Mindfulness-based cognitive therapy for depression*. New York: Guilford Press.

Smith, R. E. and Johnson, J. (1990). An organisational empowerment approach to consultation in professional baseball. *The Sport Psychologist*, 4, 347–357.

Stainback, R. D., Moncier III, J. C., and Taylor, R. E. (2007). Sport psychology: A clinician's perspective. In G. Tenenbaum and R. Eklund (eds), *Handbook of sport psychology* (3rd edn, pp. 310–331). Hoboken, NJ: Wiley.

Strean, W. B. and Strean, H. S. (1998). Applying psychodynamic concepts to sport psychology practice. *The Sport Psychologist*, 12, 208–222.

Talbot-Honeck, C. and Orlick, T. (1998). The essence of excellence: The mental skills of top classical musicians. *Journal of Excellence*, 1, 61–75.

Vealey, R. S. (1988). Future directions in psychological skills training. *The Sport Psychologist*, 2, 318–336.

Vealey, R. S. (2007a). Future directions in psychological skills training. In D. Smith and M. Bar-Eli (eds), *Essential readings in sport and exercise psychology* (pp. 295–304). Champaign, IL: Human Kinetics.

Vealey, R. S. (2007b). Mental skills training in sport. In G. Tenenbaum and R. Eklund (eds), *Handbook of sport psychology* (3rd edn, pp. 287–309). Hoboken, NJ: Wiley.

Vernacchia, R. A. (2003). *Inner strength: The mental dynamics of athletic performance.* Palo Alto, CA: Warde.

Visek, A. J., Harris, B. S., and Blom, L. C. (2009). Doing sport psychology: A youth sport consulting model for practitioners. *The Sport Psychologist*, 23, 271–291.

Weinberg, R. S. and Comar, W. (1994). The effectiveness of psychological interventions in competitive sport. *Sport Medicine*, 18, 406–418.

Weiss, M. R. (1995). Children in sport: An educational model. In S. M. Murphy (ed.), *Sport psychology interventions* (pp. 39–69). Champaign, IL: Human Kinetics.

2 Working with young athletes

Camilla J. Knight and Nicholas L. Holt

Author note

Both authors made an equal contribution to this chapter.

Abstract

The aim of this chapter is to provide a resource for sport psychology consultants interested in working with young athletes. Barriers to and opportunities for providing sport psychology services to young athletes are presented. The chapter then deals with issues related to two main developmental periods; childhood and adolescence. Developmental milestones and sport psychology research associated with each period are discussed, along with implications for sport psychology consultants. Information about delivering sport psychology to young athletes is presented before considering some future directions for the area.

Keywords: Young athletes, developmental milestones, sport psychology consulting, athlete development, parent–child relationships, peer relationships

Introduction

Youth sport is a complex social environment, created and influenced by athletes, peers, coaches, and parents. The interactions of these social agents are largely responsible for the types of experiences young athletes accrue through sport. Sport can provide young athletes with opportunities to deal with challenges they may not experience in other life domains. Competing with others, striving for self-improvement, and performing in a public arena under the scrutiny of peers and adults are some of the unique features of youth sport. If young athletes enthusiastically approach these challenges in a caring and supportive atmosphere, sport participation can help foster psychological, social, and emotional development (Holt, 2008). Sometimes the challenges of sport can exceed young athletes' resources to cope, and they may engage in patterns of negative thinking, have difficulties relating to peers, coaches, and parents, or experience anxiety. Such situations clearly challenge youth development. Sport psychology consultants can play important roles in helping young athletes to thrive in youth sport. Consultants can help further enhance youth athletes' positive experiences *and* help them to deal with any challenges they may face. Indeed, helping young athletes overcome challenges can provide valuable growth experiences that promote youth development.

The importance of sport psychology in youth sport may have increased in recent years. In contemporary society there are numerous types of sporting opportunities available to young athletes. These include instructional camps, recreational leagues, school teams, club teams, representative (e.g. county, state) squads, as well as professional and international teams. Youth sport programmes have become more privatised and subject to adult control, and there has been a trend for imposing a professional sport model onto youth sport (Coakley, 2009). That is, parents, coaches, and administrators observe components of the professional sport system and replicate them in the youth sport domain. The professionalisation of youth sport combined with a greater understanding of the value of psychology for sport performance may account for the growing demand for sport psychology consultations (McCarthy *et al.*, 2010).

The aim of this chapter is to provide a resource for sport psychology consultants interested in working with young athletes. We primarily focus on psychological and social issues, detailing some key developmental milestones associated with childhood and adolescence. We provide implications for consultants who work with young athletes throughout.

Prior to entering this discussion, we believe it is important to establish our philosophical approach to our roles as consultants in youth sport. In fact, we encourage all practitioners to have a clear "picture" of their approach in mind. From our perspective, when working with young athletes our role is to promote healthy psychological, social, and emotional development, no matter what their type or level of sport involvement. Issues such as improving performance, winning, and career development take a back seat. The most important issue is to foster positive youth development through sport.

Sport psychology in youth sport: barriers and opportunities

Within youth sport, as within many adult sports, there continues to be stigma associated with the use of sport psychology consultants (Pain and Harwood, 2004; Martin, 2005). Young athletes may not feel comfortable working with sport psychology consultants for a number of reasons. They may not understand what sport psychology actually entails, how it can be useful, and they may worry about what peers might think of them working with a sport psychology consultant (McCarthy *et al.*, 2010). Concerns regarding confidentiality and the possibility of experiencing distress may prevent young athletes from approaching sport psychology consultants (Blom *et al.*, 2003). Consultants may also encounter resistance from adults who are involved in youth sport (Visek *et al.*, 2009). Parents and coaches may not understand the importance of sport psychology, or they may think they have sufficient knowledge to help athletes deal with any psychological concerns they face (Pain and Harwood, 2004). Consultants can reduce stigma by helping athletes, coaches, and parents understand the value of sport psychology.

Despite the barriers consultants may encounter, they can fulfil important roles in young athletes' development (Harwood, 2008). Researchers have argued that young athletes must learn to manage their emotions and cope with stress, especially during adolescence when the demands of competition often intensify (Crocker *et al.*, 2004). Proactively teaching psychological skills to young athletes gives them time to develop these skills, possibly preventing future internalisation of dysfunctional responses (McCarthy *et al.*, 2010). Perhaps most importantly, consultants can enhance athletes' positive sporting experiences and aid the development of life skills to promote a healthy outlook towards sport, school, and life in general (Harwood, 2008; Harwood *et al.*, 2004).

Key concepts and terms

Although all sport psychology consultations must be adapted to the needs of specific individuals, consultations with young athletes must be both individualised and *developmentally appropriate* (Holland *et al.*, 2010). The effectiveness of interventions may be reduced if they are not appropriate to the developmental stage of the athlete (McCarthy *et al.*, 2010). This chapter deals with two broad developmental periods: childhood and adolescence. In the following section, we detail some key concepts and terms that are used throughout this chapter.

Children

Childhood is a developmental period that occurs in the first decade of life. Although definitions vary and overlap, children can be thought of in terms of being infants (0–12 months), toddlers (1–3 years old), pre-schoolers (3–5 years old), and school-aged (6–10 years old) (Slater *et al.*, 2003). We use the term "children" to refer to school-aged children from approximately 6 to 10 years old.

Adolescents

Adolescence is the developmental period that occurs primarily during the second decade of life. Again, definitions vary between authors, but adolescence may be divided into three general phases: early (11–14 years), middle (15–18 years), and late (19–21 years) (Steinberg, 1993). We used the term "adolescent" to refer to individuals in the second decade of their lives, and, where necessary, differentiate between early, middle, and late adolescence.

Development

Development is regarded as the process of change in functioning that occurs as a consequence of *maturation* and *experience* (Brustad and Partridge, 2002). Maturation refers to "those aspects of development that are primarily under genetic control, and which are relatively uninfluenced by the environment" (Muir and Slater, 2003, p. 5).

Conceptions of age

Developmental and sport psychologists tend to use chronological age as a means of identifying various stages of youth development. However, we must be very careful when using chronological age to discuss development, because increasing age alone contributes nothing to development. Rather, development occurs through a combination of maturation and experience. Young athletes at the same chronological age will not necessarily be at the same developmental stage and, in the context of sport, skill level. An 8-year-old child who has been involved in organised sport since the age of 4 years and who has advanced cognitive and social skills would be at a different developmental stage and skill level than another 8-year-old child who has never played organised sport and has less advanced cognitive and social skills. Chronologically these children are the same age, but they differ developmentally and have different needs. Whereas we refer to chronological age, it is intended only to provide a marker or approximation of developmental milestones that reflect ways in which individuals typically grow and change.

Features of development

Although various developmental milestones can be identified, development is actually highly *individualised*. Development is also *multifaceted*, and developmental trends are manifested in different ways. For example, height and weight advance in a relatively continuous manner, increasing throughout childhood and adolescence. Alternatively, development may occur through a series of stages, whereby each stage is qualitatively different from the preceding and following stages. Some of these developmental functions have been reviewed in more detail (for further reading in sport psychology, see Horn, 2004; Weiss and Williams, 2004). The important point is to remember that development is individualised and multifaceted, and different capabilities manifest themselves in different ways (e.g. continuous versus stage-like advances).

Guiding assumptions for working with young athletes

During the progression through childhood and adolescence the demands associated with school and sport change, as do young athletes' relationships with parents, peers, and coaches. As these changes occur, children and adolescents also develop their psychological, social, and emotional capabilities. Hence, this chapter is based on some fundamental assumptions in terms of the delivery of sport psychology to young athletes: (1) Young athletes are not "mini-adults". Working with young athletes is not the same as working with adult athletes. (2) Sport psychology should be provided in developmentally appropriate ways. (3) Working with young athletes requires practitioners to have a solid grasp of important developmental principles. (4) Young athletes are individuals with unique personal characteristics and preferences. However, by understanding common developmental principles practitioners can gain a better understanding of an individual's uniqueness. That is, through an understanding of common developmental principles, practitioners can partial out or highlight how athletes differ from these norms.

Sport involvement during childhood

Children as young as 3 or 4 years old may be enrolled in various types of sport programmes, but for most children their involvement in organised sport begins between the ages of around 6 and 10 years. Children will often "sample" a range of different sports until they find one that they particularly enjoy (Côté and Hay, 2002). Parents are responsible for initiating sports activities, along with providing logistical and financial support. Emphasis at this time should be on children playing, having fun, and developing a love for different games. Little emphasis should be placed upon competition, and there should be limited to pressure on children to achieve (Bloom, 1985; Côté, 1999).

Psychological considerations during childhood

Although there are competing perspectives, for the purposes of this chapter Piaget's (1950) model of cognitive development serves to illustrate some key psychological issues consultants can consider when working with children. According to Piaget, during the *sensorimotor period* (birth to 2 years old) the child changes from a helpless newborn to a thinking and knowing toddler. The sensorimotor period is characterised by the connection of sensory experiences with motor actions. Infants develop sensory and motor schema, which allow them the carry out physical actions to fulfil sensory needs (e.g. sucking objects, moving objects). During the *preoperational stage* (2–7 years old), children learn to solve concrete problems through the use of means–ends problem-solving, tools, requesting objects, and asking for things to happen. Their communication improves, and they can be presented with ideas through the use of drawings, symbolic play, gestures, and speech. During this period children tend to be egocentric, which limits their thinking because they find it very difficult to see things from another person's point of view.

During the *concrete operations* stage (7–11 years old), children's thinking progresses as they begin to use logic in their thought processes. A classic case is exemplified through one of Piaget's conservation tasks that involves showing children two different glasses containing the same amount of water. One container is tall and thin, the other short and fat. If you ask a typical 4-year-old (preoperational) child and a typical 7-year-old (concrete operational) child to drink the glass with the most water, the younger child will likely select the taller glass and the older child will recognize that the glasses might have the same amount of liquid in them. The preoperational child will normally focus on the length or tallness of the glass and ignore its potential to hold liquid. The concrete operational child will understand that a shorter, fatter glass may hold the same volume of liquid as a taller, thinner glass. This example demonstrates that children at different ages (or, more specifically, different stages of cognitive development) see their worlds in very different ways, and interestingly neither understands the reasoning of the other (Slater *et al.*, 2003). Finally, during the *formal operations* stage (from 11 years old), children learn to reason logically and are introduced into the realm of possibilities. They start to understand that abstract concepts may exist.

A number of adaptations to the consulting process must be made given children's limited ability to process abstract concepts or thoughts (Sherman and Poczwardowski, 2005). The provision of practical/concrete examples and fun activities is necessary to ensure children understand what is required of them and remain interested (Vernon, 2002). Consultants will likely experience little success if they do not match the teaching of psychological skills with a child's cognitive abilities. Consultants must find ways of engaging children's cognitive abilities and imagination. These are difficult tasks and, unfortunately, there has been little research examining best practices for teaching psychological skills to children.

Despite the lack of empirical evidence, some practitioners have provided suggestions for working with children based on their professional experience. Hogg (1997) produced a workbook intended to help teach mental skills to children aged 12 years old and younger. Mental skills training is introduced using cartoon-like animals as characters in a storyline. For example, Eddie Eagle is a champion skier who is described as a leader of the group of animals. Different animals play different sports, and they have particular strengths and weaknesses. Hogg provides examples which require children (with the help of their parents, perhaps) to complete drawings and figures that relate to certain simple psychological skills. For example, to raise awareness of negative thinking the child would write negative self-statements down on a "wall of shame", which is then "demolished" by Bernie

Bulldog with his sledgehammer. This mirrors approaches used in popular children's books and television shows, such as the Franklin the Turtle series. In one Franklin the Turtle storyline, Franklin learns through the narrative of a soccer season that different friends have different types of skills (Moose can head the ball but cannot kick very well, Beaver can "kick" it hard with her tail but cannot run fast). The story essentially reveals that the different animals have different strengths and weaknesses, and that by combining their strengths they can become an effective team. This story helps show children awareness of themselves and others in a more concrete and experiential way than, for example, having them complete a performance profile or perform other (adult-oriented) self-awareness exercises.

Sport psychology consultants can use such examples to introduce mental skills to children. It is incumbent on consultants to develop and use creative teaching tools that are developmentally appropriate for the children with whom they may work. Although there is no specific evidence that shows the activities described above are effective, there are several developmental reasons to suggest why they *may* work. Bringing stories to life through the use of narrative and cartoons allows ideas to be portrayed and presented in a concrete and experiential way. The use of animal characters that display human-like qualities draws on children's capacity for animism, which involves giving lifelike qualities to inanimate objects. Such thinking appears illogical and almost magical, because children lack a logical framework for thought (Muir and Slater, 2003). Rather than thinking about ways to get children to complete tasks designed for adults, the skilled consultant will focus on ways to use the cognitive capabilities children possess.

One of the most difficult issues consultants may confront is children's "readiness for competition". Although the emphasis placed on competition and results should be minimal during early childhood, during latter stages of childhood competition likely takes on greater importance and meaning. Children's understanding of competition and the consequences of winning, losing, effort, and ability are likely to be underdeveloped (Fry and Duda, 1997). Questions exist as to when children are actually ready for competition, because they may not have adequately developed the psychological capacities to understand competition (Passer and Wilson, 2002). Consultants should likely acknowledge that competition exists, but de-emphasise its importance. Rather, the focus should be on the development of children's psychological and social skills, and the importance of trying hard and having fun.

Social considerations during childhood

In addition to enrolling their children in sport and providing logistical and financial support, parents play important roles in terms of providing information about their children's competence, role-modelling behaviours, and interpreting their sporting involvement (Fredricks and Eccles,

2004). Children are likely to be heavily reliant upon their parents for feedback regarding their competence (Weiss and Raedeke, 2004). When working with children, consultants should place substantial emphasis on developing relationships with parents (who are often coaches as well) and ensuring that parents create a positive belief in young athletes about their ability to develop psychological skills (Orlick, 2002; Sherman and Poczwardoski, 2005).

Working alongside parents can also be an important way for consultants to identify parents' reasons for introducing, encouraging, and supporting their children in sport. Some parents introduce children to sport because of a belief that children gain physical, social, and psychological benefits whereas other parents introduce children to sport so they can excel and potentially become elite athletes (Wiersma and Fifer, 2008). The latter perspective may arise from parents who perceive that their children excelling in sport is a reflection of their abilities as parents (Coakley, 2006). Such parents may project their own desires for fulfilment upon their children (Libman, 1998), living vicariously through their children's successes. By working with parents, consultants are likely to identify parents' underlying reasons for their children's involvement in sport more effectively than if they worked with children alone.

Although we have separated psychological and social factors here, in reality they operate together in complex ways. A recent example one of the authors faced highlighted this complexity. The parent of a 9-year-old girl involved in the sport of gymnastics initiated the consultation. Gymnastics is considered an "early specialisation" sport, because athletes reach elite levels of performance during adolescence, so there are often high performance and competition demands placed on young children (see Ryan, 1995). The parent thought her child was struggling because she was not performing well relative to her peers. The child agreed with her parent, reporting that she was not feeling "as confident" as she did in the past. This seemed a fairly clear instance of the parent's feedback and beliefs influencing her child's perceived competence. However, there was a more subtle social context underlying the situation. The parent ultimately was concerned that the child's chance of developing as an elite gymnast was being jeopardised because she was not performing as well as her peers. The parent may have been using her child's experience in sport as a reflection of her own parenting ability or as fulfilment of her own needs, and/or living vicariously through her daughter's sport involvement. While it was important to understand these complex social influences, in fact it seemed that the child's peers were experiencing some rapid strength gains while the child in question was at somewhat of a physical plateau. In other words, she was developing at a different rate than her peers.

In this case, the consultant's approach was to have the parent consider her own goals for her child and reflect upon how they may differ from her child's goals. It was also important to explain some developmental principles, focusing on the different rates and ways in which children experience developmental growth (i.e. development is individualised and multifaceted). The child was asked to identify the most enjoyable aspects of her sport, and ways in which she could enjoy improving rather than winning. The mother was asked to positively reinforce her child's level of effort and personal improvements, and avoid making any comments on performance outcomes. This example highlights the importance of understanding the context of the particular sport, how social agents can influence a child's psychological development, and the need to appreciate that development is individualised and multifaceted.

Sport involvement during adolescence

During adolescence, individuals must negotiate multiple transitions based on the attainment of a variety of developmental tasks. These tasks continue over the lifespan, but are particularly significant during adolescence, when there is a search for new orientations to the world (Brettschneider and Heim, 1997). In terms of sport involvement, adolescence is the period when athletes typically make a commitment to one or two sports and seek to develop their skills though intensive training (Côté, 1999; Côté *et al.*, 2007). This increase in training is matched with an increase in competition, and with it the potential to experience more pressure to succeed (Côté and Hay, 2002). Simultaneously, adolescents are experiencing numerous developmental transitions which influence their sport involvement and lives beyond sport (Wylleman and Lavallee, 2004).

Although adolescents are in the process of transitioning to adulthood and at times may display adult-like qualities, it is important that consultants do not fall into the trap of treating adolescents like adults (Visek *et al.*, 2009). Just as when working with children, consultants who work with adolescents need to understand key developmental milestones (Harwood, 2008; Holland *et al.*, 2010). By understanding these developmental milestones, consultants can provide individualised and effective services to adolescent athletes.

Psychological considerations during adolescence

The terms "storm" and "stress" (Hall, 1904) have traditionally been used to symbolise adolescence as a period of chronic turbulence. Hall argued it was characteristic of adolescents to vacillate between extremes of sorrow and exuberance, and to shift unexpectedly between friendly altruism and selfish hoarding. However, it has been claimed that viewing adolescence as a period of storm and stress has been exaggerated by studying individuals already in turmoil (Offer, 1969). The extent to which individuals experience storm and stress may be based on the personal resources they possess.

Certain individuals may have heightened sensitivity to change during adolescence, whereas others may have sufficient personal resources to cope with the range of transitions they experience (Coleman and Roker, 1998; Graber and Brooks-Gunn, 1997).

Psychological transitions during adolescence include the development of more advanced cognitive reasoning abilities and the capacity for abstract thought. Piaget (1950) argued that the growth of formal-operational thinking is the prominent feature of adolescent thinking that differentiates it from the type of thinking employed by children. Formal-operational thinking is displayed through adolescents' increasing ability to consider abstract concepts, to reason logically, and to gather information from a range of sources available to them. Through formal-operational thinking adolescents have an increasing capacity to learn through trial and error, often developing hypotheses which they then test through their actions and behaviours.

The development of formal thinking is proposed to take place in two stages. In the first stage, adolescents demonstrate formal thinking intermittently. By the second stage, formal thinking becomes more integrated into the individual's general approach to reasoning. If levels of environmental stimulation are sufficient, formal-operational abilities are consolidated sometime during middle or late adolescence. Contemporary research suggests that advanced reasoning capacities develop gradually and continuously from childhood through adolescence and beyond, probably in more fluid, less uniform manner than originally proposed by Piaget's stage model (Steinberg, 1993).

Understanding adolescents' advancing cognitive abilities may have important consequences for sport psychology consultants. First, it is important to remember that development is individualised, multifaceted, and not a function of chronological age. It is also important to realise that the adolescent period is often associated with rapid developmental changes. Within the space of a couple of months, adolescents can experience immense psychological growth. Therefore, during initial meetings with adolescent athletes, consultants should strive to understand where the individual is "at" developmentally and, as work progresses over time, recognise that the athlete's capabilities are in a state of developmental change.

As they progress through adolescence, athletes' abilities to think abstractly and process and retrieve information improve compared to when they were younger (Sherman and Poczwardowski, 2005). However, early and middle adolescents may still be unable to fully link feelings to events, and they are unlikely to be able to fully consider all the alternatives in different situations (Vernon, 2002). Thus, sport psychology consultants are still cautioned to adapt their programmes within this developmental stage. Early- and middle-adolescent athletes may require "scaffolding" to help advance their thinking.

Scaffolding is a concept commonly used in teaching, whereby an individual with more knowledge (in this instance a sport psychology consultant) supports a less knowledgeable individual's (the athlete's) development by helping them to build on information they currently have (Raymond, 2000). Through scaffolding, a sport psychology consultant can provide support for the learning of small chunks of information which build on previous knowledge. The sport psychology consultant can guide athletes through skills and enhance understanding by making links between new information and previously learnt information. As the athlete progresses, the sport psychology consultant's support can be gradually withdrawn and athletes can develop links between new and prior knowledge themselves. Consider the example of working with early-adolescent athletes to develop a conception of the characteristics of a successful team. A consultant could expect these athletes to be able to think about the characteristics of a successful team in a very concrete manner (e.g. in terms of issues like goals, points, win/loss record). However, the athletes may require help to understand that relationships between team members can influence team development and functioning – concepts which represent a higher level of abstraction. The role of the consultant in this instance may be to reinforce athletes' knowledge of what success is, and then guide them to understand how success develops within a team. From here, the consultant may encourage athletes to understand the role of teamwork in developing success within a team and then illustrate how individual roles and the relationships between individuals underpin the teamwork athletes require to be successful. By establishing concrete ideas initially and then moving to higher levels of abstraction, the consultant is likely to aid adolescents' understanding of complex constructs.

Adolescents' mental functions also improve with repeated exposure to problem-solving situations (Sherman and Poczwardowski, 2005). Providing athletes with opportunities to repeat tasks is likely to enhance their success. As adolescents are able to focus for longer periods of time than children and select information that is most applicable to the task at hand, they can be given cognitively demanding tasks to help develop their psychological abilities (Passer and Wilson, 2002). Nonetheless, consultants need to remember that adolescents may require more repeated and sustained instructions in terms of learning particular skills than adult athletes.

Through the adolescent period, athletes develop a capacity to clearly differentiate between effort and ability. Unlike children, adolescents realise that differences in ability between themselves and their peers are not simply consequences of effort (Fry and Duda, 1997). The differentiation of effort from ability can cause problems for athletes if they remain focused on normative comparisons of ability. If athletes are primarily focused on comparing their ability to others (i.e. ego-oriented) and are continually unsuccessful, it may result in a withdrawal of effort or interest in sport (Harwood *et al.*, 2008). Furthermore, through the increasing intensity of competition, adolescent athletes frequently test their abilities against their peers. Perceptions of sporting competence can actually decrease during adolescence – possibly as they become more realistic (Weiss and Raedeke, 2004). A practical implication here is that consultants should help adolescent athletes realise that although their perceptions of competence may be low, they may well be improving their skills. The key is to highlight the importance of athletes making self-referenced judgements about their abilities to help demonstrate that they are improving personally, rather than rely on comparisons with others.

Social considerations during adolescence

Social transitions reflect the beginning of training for adult roles in early adolescence, to the attainment of full adult status and privileges by the end of adolescence. In general terms, as the individual enters middle adolescence the influence of the family tends to diminish and the peer group becomes an increasingly important social force (Payne and Isaacs, 1999). Peer groups play a vital and needed role in the socialisation of adolescents for adulthood, providing a set of equal relationships and friendships that could not be achieved in the family. The peer group is transitory, but it has the capability of shaping adolescents' dress, speech, or actions (Brown, 1990). Through involvement in peer groups and a decreasing reliance on the family, adolescents prepare themselves for the adoption of more adult roles in society.

Understanding peer-group interactions during adolescence may be useful for consultants. A recent study of peer interactions among early-adolescent females (Holt *et al.*, 2008a) distinguished peer groups on a soccer team by various levels of social complexity. At the *interaction* level, players integrated new members into the team and learned to interact with different types of people. At the *relationship* level, players learned about managing peer conflict. At the *group* level, a structure of leadership emerged and players learned to work together. A practical implication from this study is that consultants can use the levels of social complexity as a framework for identifying and analysing the types of peer relationships that occur on a team. Additionally, the study showed the importance of early-adolescent athletes attempting to deal with, rather than avoid, any peer conflicts that may arise.

Although adolescent athletes experience shifting social relationships, those who are highly committed to sport may have relationships with adults that differ from the general trend toward independence. For example, athletes remain reliant upon their parents for logistical and financial support (Wylleman and Lavallee, 2004), and coaches are also increasingly important as more time is spent in training (Côté and Hay, 2002). Hence, adolescent athletes often find themselves in a complex and almost paradoxical situation where on the one hand they are gaining increasing independence from parents and peer relationships are becoming more important, while on the other hand parents and coaches continue to fulfil important roles in sport. Adding to this complexity, adolescent athletes are also trying to understand and explore their identities. As such, these athletes may encounter a number of competing influences or tensions that could alter their perceptions of competence, ability, enjoyment, and success. Consultants must account for and work within the complex social world that adolescents are in the process of negotiating.

Adolescent athletes' relationships with their parents often present important issues for consultants. In addition to the paradox of adolescents striving for independence from their parents but still depending on them to fulfil certain requirements in their sporting lives, parents must also acknowledge and adjust to changing roles as athletes progress through adolescence. Parents slowly transition from primary providers and supporters of sport during early adolescence to fulfilling more peripheral roles as middle- and late-adolescent athletes place more emphasis on their relationships with peers and coaches (Côté and Hay, 2002). This transition can be difficult for parents, and there is potential for conflict to arise between parents and their children. Adolescents who perceive excessive pressure from their parents have reported heightened anxiety, lower self-esteem, and lower self-confidence than athletes who perceive their parents to be supportive (Gould *et al.*, 1996; Leff and Hoyle, 1995). One reason for this is that adolescents are often acutely self-conscious, and likely to be particularly sensitive to feedback or criticism (Vernon, 2002).

It may be necessary to work with parents to help improve the quality of adolescents' sport experiences. A recent study of parental behaviors during early-adolescents' soccer games showed that parents' verbal reactions to their children's sport performance could be classified on a continuum from more supportive to more controlling comments (Holt *et al.*, 2008b). These comments were categorised as praise/encouragement, performance-contingent feedback, instruction, striking a balance, negative comments, and derogatory comments. Although the minority of recorded comments were negative or derogatory, the study showed that parents experienced empathy, as they perceived sharing the emotions their children felt in sport. Parents' emotions appeared to change in relation to game dynamics and contextual circumstances, and they appeared more likely to make negative comments when they were emotionally involved in a game. Practically, this highlights the importance of making parents aware of how their comments may change as they become more emotionally involved. It is also important to recognise that parents themselves experience stress while watching games, and consultants may be required to teach parents coping skills (Harwood and Knight, 2009).

The complex social transitions experienced during adolescence have emotional consequences related to the detachment from parents and attainment of a separate, unique, and worthwhile sense of identity (Steinberg, 1993). Erikson (1968) and Marcia (1966), pioneers of identity research, suggested that the establishment of a coherent sense of identity is the chief "psychosocial crisis" that must be managed during adolescence. Adolescents must develop a sense of individuation-separation, whereby they learn to take personal responsibility for their choices and actions instead of looking toward their parents to do it for them (Blos, 1967).

It is plausible that, through their involvement and success in sport, adolescent athletes become valued and recognised as individuals outside their home, which contributes to the development of an athletic identity (Tiihonen, 1994). Athletic identity represents the degree to which athletes define their self-worth in terms of their participation and achievement in sport (Taylor and Ogilvie, 2001). However, when athletes commit heavily to sport, their opportunities to engage in exploratory behaviour in other areas may be curtailed (Chartrand and Lent, 1987). Research shows that individuals with a strong, exclusive, and early commitment to the athlete role are less prepared for post-sport careers than individuals who have invested less in the athlete role (Pearson and Petitpas, 1990). Although involvement in sport may provide adolescents with a pathway to the development of a coherent identity, early and exclusive commitment to an athletic role can be problematic when that role is terminated by injury or retirement. From a consulting perspective, it can be useful to help adolescent athletes explore other aspects of their life and identity, such as developing relationships with peers and other adults outside sport, and pursuing other types of extracurricular activities.

Sometimes, convincing athletes to explore other areas of their lives in order to develop a more balanced sense of identity can be a challenging task. One of the authors recently worked with a 19-year-old university-level basketball player. She had a classic case of identity foreclosure, having made a premature and exclusive commitment to athletic identity. She was struggling to cope with an injury, and unable to compete to her satisfaction. As a consequence, she began to question her entire sense of self, both in basketball and in her life in general. The consulting work involved helping the athlete to explore other roles she fulfilled in addition to being a basketball player. She was encouraged to spend more time with her parents, her boyfriend, and her nieces and nephews – activities she had previously curtailed for fear they would interfere with her basketball. She was also encouraged to take time "for herself" and to engage in activities she enjoyed – it could be as simple as going to a movie with (non-basketball) friends. After several months of careful consideration, the athlete decided to play for one more season and then retire even though she had years of eligibility remaining. The situation was explained to her coach, who was understanding and supportive. The player left the sport as planned, and pursued other areas of her life. As a consultant this was a difficult experience, because the ultimate outcome was that the athlete retired from sport; however, the athlete in question became a happier, more balanced individual. She enjoyed her final year of basketball, was content with her decision, and enthusiastically looked forward to a healthy life. Although troubling in some respects, this example fits with our philosophy of prioritising personal development over sport performance. It also reflects how sport psychology consultants must be particularly attuned to the non-sport related concerns or changes that are occurring within adolescent athletes' lives.

Practical considerations for providing sport psychology to young athletes

Many potential differences exist in any consulting situation, as consultants often have their own particular style and different athletes have their own unique needs (Taylor, 1995). Thus, it is not possible to prescribe "cookie-cutter" instructions regarding what works with young athletes across all situations. Providing prescriptive information is further complicated by the lack of literature considering the specific details (e.g. how, where, when) associated with developing and implementing psychological skills in youth sport programmes (Harwood, 2008). Nevertheless, by drawing on several consulting principles, the developmental considerations previously discussed, and some recent models of applied youth sport psychology, it is possible to provide a general idea of factors consultants should be aware of when working with young athletes.

Consultants may provide their services through sessions with teams or groups, or alternatively by working with individual athletes one-on-one (for examples, see Efran *et al.*, 1994; Hellstedt, 1987; Mamassis and Doganis, 2004). Compared with group sessions, when working on an individual level a consultant may have more opportunities to address broader aspects of the athlete's life (e.g. issues with school work, family concerns, etc.) in addition to mental skills (Taylor, 2008). Several models for guiding consultations with young athletes have been presented in the literature. For example, Sherman and Poczwardowski (2005) discussed an integrative programme where psychological skills are taught in conjunction with physical skills. Visek and colleagues (2009) presented a model focused on developing and implementing mental skills programmes as separate sessions. A third approach to working with young athletes is by teaching coaches to implement psychological skills and practices within their coaching (e.g. Harwood, 2008; Smith and Smoll, 1997). Drawing broadly from these models and other related literature, we discuss three practical issues related to the provision of sport psychology services to young athletes: gaining entry and developing relationships; conducting sessions; and evaluating and terminating relationships.

Gaining entry and developing relationships

Regardless of the approach a consultant selects, the first steps in the consulting process are gaining entry and developing relationships. In terms of gaining entry, it is likely that the first point of contact is a parent or a coach (Visek *et al.*, 2009). After all, these are the people who typically pay for the consultant's services. Ensuring that a strong relationship is developed with parents and coaches is critical to ensuring the continuity of a consultant's services with an athlete (Conroy and Coatsworth, 2006; Petitipas *et al.*, 1999). Orlick and McCaffery (1991) suggested that if parents' and coaches' recommend and value sport psychology services, athletes are likely to be more open to adopting them and implementing them in their life. Consultants must make time to talk to parents and coaches, explain what can be expected from the consultations, and discuss how they may help the process (Fifer *et al.*, 2008).

Effective consulting relationships are characterised by trust, openness, and honesty (Anderson *et al.*, 2002). Consultants should display respect for athletes, have good communication skills, and show that they care (Dunn and Holt, 2003; Fifer *et al.*, 2008). In addition to these characteristics, consultants may have to spend additional time setting ground rules at the beginning of the relationship with young athletes (LaRose, 1988). This is particularly important when working with young athletes due to the involvement of parents and coaches in athletes' lives (Visek *et al.*, 2009).

A trusting consultant–athlete relationship is a hallmark of effective sport psychology work. A strong foundation for the development of relationships can be established by explaining to athletes that the information they share is confidential (Andersen, 2000). However, given the extent of parents' and coaches' involvement within an athlete's life, the consultant may encounter issues regarding the amount of information that is provided to parents and coaches (Pain and Harwood, 2004). Parents and coaches may feel that they have a right to know what is happening (Visek *et al.*, 2009), but revealing information about an athlete may breach confidentiality and reduce trust. Explaining the importance of confidentiality to the consulting process and being upfront about the amount of information that will be shared with parents and coaches is necessary at the outset of the relationship. One approach could be to indicate to all parties that information about the consultation will only be discussed with the athlete's permission. This can help parents and coaches understand what information they may receive, but also help the athletes feel reassured that the information they share will remain private (Martin, 2005). As with all sport psychology consultations, once rules regarding confidentiality have been established, they must be consistently implemented.

At times, athletes may experience issues or problems that stem directly from the behaviours of a parent or a coach. With the athletes' permission, it may be possible to present concerns to parents and coaches. For example, Taylor (2008) uses a process he calls "sport family engineering" whereby he works with parents to help them understand the positive or negative effect they may have upon their child, and how they can help ensure healthy development. Ensuring the creation of supportive and trusting relationships with athletes, parents, and coaches at the beginning of the process will enhance the success of these interactions at a later date.

Conducting sessions

The initial step in producing a programme is identifying what the athletes actually need (Taylor, 1995). Very little research has considered the actual psychological needs of youth athletes. An exception is a recent study by Holland *et al.* (2010) which sought to identify what mental qualities middle-adolescent rugby players perceived were important for success in rugby, and what psychological techniques they used to develop these qualities. Athletes specified that enjoyment, responsibility for self, adaptability, squad spirit, self-awareness, determination, confidence, game sense, appropriate attentional focus, and mental toughness were the main mental qualities required for rugby success. Although qualities such as determination and self-awareness are similar to the skills adult athletes may require (see, for example, Ravizza, 2001), issues such as adaptability and responsibility for self may be unique to adolescents. Consultants need to take additional care in identifying the needs of youth athletes, and not assume they are the same as for adult athletes.

Common ways for consultants to identify the needs of individual athletes are through the use of psychological assessment tools, intake interviews, and/or observations (Fifer *et al.*, 2008). Consultants may encounter issues if they attempt to use psychological assessment tools that are not developmentally appropriate for youth athletes (Visek *et al.*, 2009). There is also the potential that athletes may not be forthcoming with information during intake interviews before an adequate level of trust has been developed (Andersen, 2000). Observations may be useful because they provide insights into the interactions that occur between athletes and support staff (Visek *et al.*, 2009). The point here is that consultants may wish to utilise multiple methods of gaining information to identify young athletes' needs.

Studies have illustrated that mental skills programmes can enhance young athletes' performance and psychological development. The benefits of mental training programmes with adolescent athletes have been seen from brief contact interventions of just a few minutes prior to a competition (e.g. Miller and Donohue, 2003), to programmes of several weeks (e.g. Sheard and Golby, 2006), or months (e.g. Fournier *et al.*, 2005). Further, programmes have been successful in teaching one technique to enhance a certain mental skill (e.g. Johnson *et al.*, 2004), or multiple psychological techniques and skills to enhance a range of performance and psychological indicators (e.g. Fournier *et al.*, 2005; Gucciardi *et al.*,

2009a, 2009b; Mamassis and Doganis, 2004; Sheard and Golby, 2006). These studies suggest that consultants can use a range of approaches to conduct sessions, and it may be necessary to tailor the approach to the circumstances and needs of the young athletes.

Whatever method or approach is adopted, the language used by consultants should be appropriate to the sport and the experiences of the athletes (Pain and Harwood, 2004). Keeping the programme fun and appropriate will help athletes to perceive some value to it (Orlick, 2002). Ensuring athletes are praised for their effort and improvements will help to keep them motivated to work on the skills (Visek *et al.*, 2009). Using other athletes as role models may provide another avenue through which skills can be taught and the value of the programme illustrated (Orlick, 2002). Finally, using a creative and flexible approach can ensure successful consultations (Visek *et al.*, 2009).

Evaluating and terminating relationships

The emphasis on evaluation has significantly increased within the area of sport psychology, as there is an increasing requirement for accountability and professionalism (Anderson *et al.*, 2002). Evaluating consultants' effectiveness provides important information regarding the knowledge, delivery style, and characteristics of the consultant. This information can then be used by consultants to identify what did and did not work with athletes, and, if necessary, lead to changes in consulting style (Anderson *et al.*, 2004). In youth sport settings, it may be necessary to obtain evaluative feedback not only from athletes but also from parents and coaches (Visek *et al.*, 2009).

When working with children and adolescents, additional care may need to be taken when ending relationships – especially if it is a relationship that has built up over a long time (Vernon, 2004). It is important, where possible, for consultants to inform youth athletes that they are approaching the end of the relationship, so that athletes can begin to process the idea and prepare themselves for this change (Visek *et al.*, 2009). Our suggestion would be to continually engage in dialogue with the athlete (and their parents or coach, if deemed necessary) regarding how the programme is progressing, and how and when it may come to an end.

Future of the subdiscipline

Although there has been an increase in the number of sport psychology consultants working with youth athletes, there is huge potential for more work to be conducted with this population (Harwood, 2008). Researchers and practitioners are increasing their understanding of the developmental aspects associated with working with young athletes, allowing the construction of more developmentally appropriate sport psychology programmes (e.g. Sherman and Poczwardowski, 2005; Visek *et al.*, 2009). Although there is a growing evidence base, more applied research is required to help establish the most effective ways of providing sport psychology programmes to young athletes. Research is needed to examine ways in which mental skills may be taught to children. Although programmes and frameworks for working with adolescents have been provided, research is required to evaluate the effectiveness of different approaches. There is also a need to develop knowledge of the psychological needs of young athletes at different developmental stages (Holland *et al.*, 2010). Another line of research that may expand in the future comprises accounts of consultants' experiences of working with young athletes. Such experiential accounts have been provided by experienced consultants who have worked with elite adult athletes (e.g. Fifer *et al.*, 2008) and neophyte consultants "learning their trade" (e.g. Holt and Strean, 2001), and they can provide important insights into professional practice.

Conclusion

This chapter has revealed some of the complexities of providing sport psychology services to young athletes. Parents and coaches are often closely involved in young athletes' lives, and the provision of services is further complicated by the need to understand key developmental principles. Although barriers may remain, sport psychology appears to be becoming increasingly important in youth sport. To help ensure success, sport psychology services must be developmentally appropriate. Understanding developmental trends can help consultants understand athletes' needs and create individualised approaches.

Many consultants start their careers volunteering their services or working with young athletes as a stepping stone to working with adult or professional athletes. Taylor (2008) advised new sport psychology consultants that they should work their way up "the ladder" of sport performance. He suggested that this "means working with young, low-level athletes as a means of gaining knowledge, experience, and expertise before you consult with higher-level athletes who are more discriminating and more demanding" (p. 174). We could not disagree more with this statement! Rather, we agree with Harwood (2008) that there is great value in working with young athletes for its own means, and successful consultations with young athletes require a specialised skill set and understanding of key developmental principles. Working with young athletes provides consultants with opportunities to help young people thrive. There are few more important tasks in life.

References

Andersen, M. B. (ed.), (2000). *Doing sport psychology*. Champaign, IL: Human Kinetics.

Anderson, A., Miles, A., Mahoney, C., and Robinson, P. (2002). Evaluating the effectiveness of applied sport psychology practice: Making the case for a case study approach. *The Sport Psychologist*, 16, 432–453.

Anderson, A, Miles, A, Robinson, P., and Mahoney, C. (2004). Evaluating the athlete's perception of the sport psychologist's effectiveness: What should we be assessing? *Psychology of Sport and Exercise*, 5, 255–277.

Blom, L. C., Hardy, C. J., Burke, K. L., and Joyner, A. B. (2003). High school athletes' perceptions about sport psychology and preferences for service. *International Sports Journal*, 7, 18–24.

Bloom, B. (1985). *Developing talent in young people.* New York, NY: Ballantine Books.

Blos, P. (1967). The second individuation process of adolescence. *Psychoanalytic Study of the Child*, 22, 162–186.

Brettschneider, W. D. and Heim, R. (1997). Identity, sport, and youth development. In K. R. Fox (ed.), *The physical self: Motivation to well-being* (pp. 205–227). Lewes, UK: Falmer Press.

Brown, B. B. (1990). Peer groups and peer cultures. In S. S. Feldman and G. R. Elliott (eds), *At the threshold: The developing adolescent* (pp. 171–196). Cambridge, MA: Harvard University Press.

Brustad, R. J. and Partridge, J. A. (2002). Parental and peer influence on children's psychosocial development through sport. In F. L. Smoll and R. E. Smith (eds), *Children and youth in sport: A biopsychosocial perspective* (pp. 187–210). Dubuque, IA: Kendall/Hunt.

Chartrand, J. M. and Lent, R. W. (1987). Sports counselling: Enhancing the development of the student athletes. *Journal of Counselling and Development*, 66, 164–167.

Coakley, J. (2006). The good father: Parental expectations and youth sports. *Leisure Studies*, 25, 153–163.

Coakley, J. (2009). *Sports in society: Issues and controversies* (10th edn). New York, NY: McGraw Hill.

Coleman, J. and Roker, D. (1998). Adolescence. *The Psychologist*, 11, 593–596.

Conroy, D. E. and Coatsworth, J. D., (2006). Coach training as a strategy for promoting youth social development. *The Sport Psychologist*, 20, 128–144.

Côté, J. (1999). The influence of the family in the development of talent in sport. *The Sport Psychologist*, 13, 395–417.

Côtè, J. and Hay, J. (2002). Children's involvement in sport: A developmental perspective. In J. M. Silva and D. E. Stevens (eds), *Psychological foundations of sport* (pp. 484–502). Boston, MA: Allyn and Bacon.

Côté, J., Baker, J., and Abernethy, B. (2007). Practice and play in the development of sport expertise. In G. Tenenbaum and R. C. Eklund (eds), *Handbook of sport psychology*, (3rd edn, pp. 184–202). Hoboken, NJ: Wiley.

Crocker, P. R. E., Hoar, S. D., McDonough, M. H., Kowalski, K. C., and Niefer, C. (2004). Emotional experience in youth sport. In M. R. Weiss (ed.), *Developmental sport and exercise psychology: A lifespan perspective* (pp. 197–222). Morgantown, WV: Fitness Information Technology.

Dunn, J. G. H. and Holt, N. L. (2003). Collegiate ice hockey players' perceptions of the delivery of an applied sport psychology program. *The Sport Psychologist*, 17, 351–368.

Efran, J. S., Lesser, G. S., and Spiller, M. J. (1994). Enhancing tennis coaching with youths using a metaphor method. *The Sport Psychologist, 8*, 349–359.

Erikson, E. H. (1968). *Identity: Youth and crisis.* New York, NY: Norton.

Fifer, A. M., Henschen, K., Gould, D., and Ravizza, K. (2008). What works when working with athletes. *The Sport Psychologist*, 22, 356–377.

Fournier, J. F., Camels, C., Durand-Bush., N., and Salmela, J. H. (2005). Effects of a season-long PST program on gymnastic performance and on psychological skill development. *International Journal of Sport and Exercise Psychology*, 3, 59–77.
Fredricks, J. A. and Eccles, J. S. (2004). Parental influences on youth involvement in sports. In M. R. Weiss (ed.), *Developmental sport and exercise psychology: A lifespan perspective* (pp. 145–164). Morgantown, WV: Fitness Information Technology.
Fry, M. D. and Duda, J. L (1997). Children's understanding of effort and ability in the physical and academic domains. *Research Quarterly for Exercise and Sport*, 68, 1–14.
Gould, D., Tuffey, S., Udry, E., and Loehr, J. (1996). Burnout in competitive junior tennis players: II. Qualitative analysis. *The Sport Psychologist*, 10, 341–366.
Graber, J. A. and Brooks-Gunn, J. (1997). Transitions and turning points: Navigating the passage from childhood through adolescence. *Developmental Psychology*, 32, 768–776.
Gucciardi, D. F., Gordon, S., and Dimmock, J. A. (2009a). Evaluation of a mental toughness training program for youth-aged Australian Footballers: I. A quantitative analysis. *Journal of Applied Sport Psychology*, 21, 307–323.
Gucciardi, D. F., Gordon, S., and Dimmock, J. A (2009b). Evaluation of a mental toughness training program for youth-aged Australian Footballers: II. A qualitative analysis. *Journal of Applied Sport Psychology*, 21, 324–339.
Hall, G. S. (1904). *Adolescence: Its psychology and its relations to physiology, anthropology, sociology, sex, crime, religion and education.* New York, NY: Appleton and Company.
Harwood, C. (2008). Developmental consulting in a professional football academy: The 5Cs coaching efficacy program. *The Sport Psychologist*, 22, 109–133.
Harwood, C. and Knight, C. (2009). Stress in youth sport: A developmental investigation of tennis parents. *Psychology of Sport and Exercise*, 10, 447–456.
Harwood, C., Cumming, J., and Fletcher, D. (2004). Motivational profiles and psychological skill use within elite youth sport. *Journal of Applied Sport Psychology*, 16, 318–332.
Harwood, C., Spray, C. M., and Keegan, R. (2008). Achievement goal theories in sport. In T. S. Horn (ed.), *Advances in sport psychology* (3rd edn, pp. 157–186). Champaign, IL: Human Kinetics.
Hellstedt, J. C. (1987). Sport psychology at a ski academy: Teaching mental skills to young athletes. *The Sport Psychologist*, 1, 56–68.
Hogg, J. (1997). *Mental skills for young athletes.* Edmonton, AB: Sports Excel.
Holland, M. J. G., Woodcock, C., Cumming, J., and Duda, J. L. (2010). Mental qualities and employed mental techniques of young elite team sport athletes. *Journal of Clinical Sport Psychology*, 4, 19–38.
Holt, N. L. (2008). *Positive youth development through sport.* London, UK: Routledge.
Holt, N. L. and Strean, W. B. (2001). Reflecting on the initial intake meeting in sport psychology: A self-narrative of neophyte practice. *The Sport Psychologist*, 15, 188–204.
Holt, N. L., Black, D. E., Tamminen, K. A., Fox, K. R., and Mandigo, J. L. (2008a). Levels of social complexity and dimensions of peer experiences in youth sport. *Journal of Sport and Exercise Psychology*, 30, 411–31.
Holt, N. L., Tamminen, K. A., Black, D. E., Sehn, Z. L., and Wall, M. P. (2008b). Parental involvement in competitive youth sport settings. *Psychology of Sport and Exercise*, 9, 663–685.

Horn, T. S. (2004). Lifespan development in sport and exercise psychology: Theoretical perspectives. In M. R. Weiss (ed.), *Developmental sport and exercise psychology: A lifespan perspective* (pp. 27–72). Morgantown, WV: Fitness Information Technology.

Johnson, J. J. M., Hrycaiko, D. W., Johnson, G. V., and Halas, J. M. (2004). Self-talk and female youth soccer performance. *The Sport Psychologist*, 18, 44–59.

LaRose, B. (1988). What can the sport psychology consultant learn from the educational consultant? *The Sport Psychologist*, 2, 141–153.

Leff, S. S. and Hoyle, R. H. (1995). Young athletes' perceptions of parental support and pressure. *Journal of Youth and Adolescence*, 24, 187–203.

Libman, S. (1998). Adult participation in youth sports: A developmental perspective. *Child and Adolescent Psychiatric Clinics of North America*, 7, 725–744.

Mamassis, G. and Doganis, G. (2004). The effects of a mental training program on juniors' pre-competitive anxiety, self-confidence, and tennis performance. *Journal of Applied Sport Psychology*, 16, 118–137.

Marcia, J. E. (1966). Development and validation of ego-identity status. *Journal of Personality and Social Psychology*, 3, 551–558.

Martin, S. B. (2005). High school and college athletes' attitudes toward sport psychology consulting. *Journal of Applied Sport Psychology*, 17, 127–139.

McCarthy, P. J., Jones, M. V., Harwood, C. G., and Olivier, S. (2010). What do young athletes implicitly understand about psychological skills? *Journal of Clinical Sport Psychology*, 4, 158–172.

Miller, A. and Donohue, B. (2003). The development and controlled evaluation of athletic mental preparation strategies in high school distance runners. *Journal of Applied Sport Psychology*, 15, 321–334.

Muir, D. and Slater, A. (2003). The scope and methods of developmental psychology. In A. Slater and G. Bremner (eds), *An introduction to developmental psychology* (pp. 3–34). Oxford, UK: Blackwell.

Offer, D. (1969). *The psychological world of the teenager*. New York, NY: Basic.

Orlick, T. (2002). Enhancing children's sport and life experiences. In F. L. Smoll and R. E. Smith (eds), *Children and youth in sport: A biopsychosocial perspective* (2nd edn, pp. 465–474). Dubuque, IA: Kendall/Hunt.

Orlick, T. and McCaffrey, N. (1991). Mental training with children for sport and life. *The Sport Psychologist*, 5, 322–334.

Pain, M. A. and Harwood, C. (2004). Knowledge and perceptions of sport psychology within English soccer. *Journal of Sports Sciences*, 22, 813–826.

Passer, M. W. and Wilson, B. J. (2002). Motivational, emotional, and cognitive determinants of children's age-readiness for competition. In F. L. Smoll and R. E. Smith (eds), *Children and youth in sport: A biopsychosocial perspective* (2nd edn, pp. 83–104). Duqbuque, IA: Kendall/Hunt.

Payne, V. G. and Isaacs, L. D. (1999). *Human motor development: A lifespan approach* (4th edn). Mountain View, CA: Mayfield.

Pearson, R. E. and Petitpas, A. J. (1990). Transitions of athletes: Developmental and preventive perspectives. *Journal of Counselling and Development*, 69, 7–10.

Petitipas, A. J., Giges, B., and Danish, S. J. (1999). The sport psychologist–athlete relationship: Implications for training. *The Sport Psychologist*, 13, 344–357.

Piaget, J. (1950). *Psychology of intelligence*. London, UK: Kegan Paul.

Ravizza, K. (2001). Increasing awareness for sport performance. In J. M. Williams (ed.), *Applied sport psychology: Personal growth to peak performance* (4th edn, pp. 179–189). Mountain View, CA: Mayfield.

Raymond, E. (2000). Cognitive characteristics. *Learners with mild disabilities.* Needham Heights, MA: Allyn and Bacon.

Ryan, J. (1995). *Pretty girls in little boxes: The making and breaking of elite gymnasts and figure skaters.* New York, NY: Doubleday.

Sheard, M. and Golby, J. (2006). Effect of a psychological skills training program on swimming performance and positive psychological development. *International Journal of Sport and Exercise Psychology*, 4, 149–169.

Sherman, C. P. and Poczwardowski, A. (2005). Integrating mind and body: Presenting mental skills to young teams. In M. B. Andersen (ed.), *Sport psychology in practice* (pp. 17–43). Champaign, IL: Human Kinetics.

Slater, A., Hocking, I., and Loose, J. (2003). Theories and issues in child development. In A Slater and G. Bremner (eds), *An introduction to developmental psychology* (pp. 34–63). Oxford, UK: Blackwell.

Smith, R. E. and Smoll, F. L. (1997). Coach-mediated team building in youth sports. *Journal of Applied Sport Psychology*, 9, 114–132.

Steinberg, L. D. (1993). *Adolescence* (3rd edn). New York, NY: McGraw-Hill.

Taylor, J. (1995). A conceptual model for integrating athletes' needs and sport demands in the development of competitive mental preparation strategies. *The Sport Psychologist*, 2, 318–336.

Taylor, J. (2008). Prepare to succeed: Private consulting in applied sport psychology. *Journal of Clinical Sport Psychology*, 2, 160–177.

Taylor, J. and Ogilvie, B. C. (2001). Career termination among athletes. In R. N. Singer, H. A. Hausenblas, and C. M. Janelle (eds), *Handbook of sport psychology* (2nd edn, pp. 672–691). New York, NY: Wiley.

Tiihonen, A. (1994). Asthma: The construction of the masculine body. *International Review for Sociology of Sport*, 29, 50–62.

Vernon, A. (2002). *What works when working with children and adolescents: A handbook of individual counselling techniques.* Champaign, IL: Research Press.

Vernon, A. (2004). Working with children, adolescents, and their parents: Practical application of developmental theory. In A. Vernon (ed.), *Counselling children and adolescents* (pp. 1–34). Denver, CO: Love publishing company.

Visek, A. J., Harris, B. S., and Blom, L. C. (2009). Doing sport psychology: A youth sport consulting model for practitioners. *The Sport Psychologist*, 23, 271–291.

Weiss, M. R. and Raedeke, T. D. (2004). Developmental sport and exercise psychology: Research status on youth and directions toward a lifespan perspective. In M. R. Weiss (ed.), *Developmental sport and exercise psychology: A lifespan* perspective (pp. 1–26). Morgantown, WV: Fitness Information Technology.

Weiss, M. R. and Williams, L. (2004). The why of youth sport involvement: A developmental perspective on motivational processes. In M. R. Weiss (ed.), *Developmental sport and exercise psychology: A lifespan perspective* (pp. 223–268). Morgantown, WV: Fitness Information Technology.

Wiersma, L. D. and Fifer, A. M. (2008). "The schedule has been tough but we think it's worth it": The joys, challenges, and recommendations of youth sport parents. *Journal of Leisure Research*, 40, 505–530.

Wylleman, P. and Lavallee, D. (2004). A developmental perspective on transitions faced by athletes. In M. R. Weiss (ed.), *Developmental sport and exercise psychology: A lifespan perspective* (pp. 503–524). Morgantown, WV: Fitness Information Technology.

3 Psychological perspectives on athletes with physical disabilities

Jeffrey J. Martin

Abstract

In recent years a quickly developing body of knowledge in disability sport psychology has been established (e.g. Hanrahan, 2005; Martin, 2006). The present chapter reviews the research related to performance enhancement for athletes with physical disabilities in the following fashion. I first provide a brief non-sport-specific "disability primer", as it is important for sport psychologists to understand important disability issues. Second, research on the psychological factors associated with superior performance or other favourable psychological states is then reviewed. Next, psychological skill use among athletes with disabilities is discussed, and intervention research involving athletes with disabilities is examined. Fourth, a perusal of disability sport-specific challenges that athletes with disabilities encounter is proffered. At the end of each section, as well as throughout the chapter where appropriate, I weave in professional practice considerations for sport psychologists working with athletes with disabilities. Finally, the guiding framework for this chapter is a holistic human development model of professional practice (Martin, 1999a, 2005).

Keywords: disability, sport psychology, Paralympics, wheelchair sports

Introduction

Although the discipline and profession of sport psychology can be dated back to the early 1900s, its most significant growth has occurred in the past 50 years (Gill, 1997). During this time, the number of journals and textbooks devoted to sport psychology has increased tremendously. Unfortunately, with a few exceptions (e.g. Hanrahan, 1995a), a perusal of virtually all textbooks devoted to sport psychology prior to 2000 reveals an almost complete absence of any research referring to athletes with any disabilities. Fortunately, sport psychology scholars in the twenty-first century have started to examine common sport psychology theories and research questions with athletes with disabilities. As a result a small but quickly growing body of knowledge has been developed, and editors of exercise and sport psychology textbooks are recognising this by including chapters on exercisers and athletes with disabilities (e.g. Hanrahan, 2005; Martin, 2000, 2006, 2010, 2011a, 2011b, 2011e; Martin and McCaughtry, 2004; Martin and Wheeler, 2011).

Hence, in furtherance of this trend, the purpose of this chapter is to review the quickly expanding body of research on the psychology of disability sport. It should be noted that that research reviewed is based on athletes with physical disabilities, and I do not cover the literature examining athletes with cognitive disabilities (e.g. Special Olympics). The current chapter is organised in five sections. First, the reader is provided with a brief non-sport-specific "disability primer". Just as sport psychologists are expected to have competencies in psychology and the sport sciences (Association for Applied Sport Psychology; AASP, 2009), it is helpful for sport psychologists to have an understanding of important disability issues. Second, research examining psychological factors associated with superior performance or other favourable psychological states is reviewed. Third, psychological skill use among athletes with disabilities is discussed. Fourth, a review of disability sport-specific challenges that athletes face is offered. Throughout the chapter, I weave in professional practice considerations for sport psychologists working with athletes with disabilities. The guiding framework for this chapter is a holistic human development model of professional practice (see Martin, 1999a, 2005).

The disability world

Although people with and without disabilities share much in common, people with disabilities move through a world that is different from the able-bodied world. Furthermore, their life experiences directly and indirectly influence their athletic goals. The influence of a disability is ubiquitous, and includes body image, self-concept, employment, education, travel, friendships, and health. Individuals with disabilities, for example, often receive negative body-image judgements from others, making it difficult to develop positive body images (Martin, 2011a).

People with disabilities have lower levels of income and live in homes with less income compared to people with no disabilities. Similarly, a greater percentage of individuals with disabilities in the USA live in poverty and live alone, compared to people with no disabilities. Far less people with disabilities, relative to those without disabilities, graduate from high school and college. People with disabilities are also more likely to be crime victims. Women with disabilities, for example, have a 40 per cent greater chance of being physically or sexually assaulted compared to women without disabilities. Even simple tasks such as hailing a taxi can be problematic, because some taxi drivers do not want to deal with storing a wheelchair in the trunk. In brief, an athlete with a disability lives in a world that can be, at times, profoundly different from the one in which an able-bodied person lives. Sport psychologists who are aware of this social-cultural milieu will have a deeper understanding of the non-sport challenges that could influence sport training and competition.

Adapting to a disability

About 15 per cent of athletes with disabilities have a congenital disability (i.e. since birth), and have not experienced life without a disability. However, most athletes with disabilities (i.e. 85 per cent) have had to manage a progressive disease over time, or have had a serious traumatic injury (i.e. an acquired disability). A major ramification of experiencing a sudden and permanent injury is a serious disruption of psychological equilibrium.

Significant psychological and physical adjustment demands are placed on individuals when they go from walking and running in one moment to being unable to move their arms or legs a day later. Perhaps indicating how severe such a feeling can be is captured by the words of a former rugby union player who reported, "Now I am nothing. Life moves on, without me. That is how it is. How it will always be. I just survive. No ambitions. Nothing ... Sometimes I don't think I can go on." (Smith and Sparkes, 2005, p. 1101).

Many people eventually adjust to an acquired disability, but the previous quote illustrates that some people consider suicide due to the life-changing nature of their injury. A loss of function is an obvious and far-reaching ramification of acquiring a disability, and often becomes the most dominating feature of the disability experience. In brief, a primary characteristic of experiencing a significant and permanent injury is a loss of function, and people often become defined as, and by, their disabilities.

A second major area of disruption involves relationships, as exemplified by a 43-year-old woman with a spinal cord injury (SCI) who stated, "Your friendships are greatly affected by your disability. I don't have any friends except maybe two from the pre-disability days" (Lyons *et al.*, 1995, p. 38). Lyons and colleagues found that people with disabilities see their former friends less, have difficulty relating to old friends, and often experience rejection by old friends. For married couples the marital union is often disrupted, and disability is a risk factor for divorce.

Parent–child relationships are also affected. For example, Donald, a father with a disability, noted, "another thing that makes it hard is the fact that I can't run with [my children]" (Kleiber *et al.*, 1995, p. 293). Young children's inability to understand exacerbates the stress parents experience in managing the change in the parent–child relationship. For example, Donald reflected on his daughter and reported that, "She's not accepting the fact, I don't think, that I can't walk, she'll tell me to put on my shoes, and I can walk. So, see, that makes it hard on me." (p. 293).

Sparkes and Smith (2002) and Smith and Sparkes (2005) described men's SCI-related athletic experiences. For able-bodied male athletes who had strong masculine athletic identities and who derived substantial self-esteem from sport, both of these critical aspects of their self-concepts were severely damaged when they became disabled. One participant indicated, "Your masculinity is gone, broken, you just struggle to live up to [being a man]" (Sparkes and Smith, 2002, p. 269). Some athletes may completely disregard disability sport as a choice. One man, for example, stated, "How can you play sports like that? I mean I can understand people using sport for rehabilitation and everything. For me though, they aren't real sports, not really" (Sparkes and Smith, 2002, p. 270). A related sentiment was expressed by a former able-bodied basketball player who noted, "No way would I settle for less with a sport I had excelled in on my feet. So in the hospital I set my mind on the triathlon" (Hutchinson and Kleiber, 2000, p. 50).

Experiencing an acquired disability is world-changing. Athletes heavily invested in sports and struggling with disruptions to their self-schema may face particularly difficult times. The above information is particularly pertinent for athletes who start sport shortly after their acquired injuries and then have short careers (e.g. less than two years). Adjusting to a major trauma may take as long as two years, and adjusting one's self-concept may take as long as four years (Trieschmann, 1988). Athletes may have to adjust to significant trauma, get ready for a major competition, manage a secondary disability such as a chronic injury, and deal with possibly leaving high-level disability sport in the near future (Martin, 1996, 1999b). Clearly, from a professional practice perspective, sport psychologists who understand the above temporal sequence of challenges are more apt to be helpful.

Psychological factors

Efficacy and confidence

Similar to able-bodied sport psychology research, the role of self-confidence and self-efficacy has also assumed a prominent position in disability sport psychology research. For instance, Lowther and colleagues examined self-efficacy, psychological skills, and performance for 15 elite amputee male soccer players over a six-game Amputee World Cup tournament (Lowther *et al.*, 2005). Athletes with the strongest self-efficacy performed better relative to soccer players with weaker efficacy. Higher self-efficacy was also associated with stronger psychological skills, such as self-talk, emotional control, and imagery. In a study of Greek athletes participating in the National Wheelchair Basketball Championships, self-efficacy predicted, along with past performance, passing performance (Katartzi *et al.*, 2007). Schliermann and Stoll (2007) also examined self-efficacy with 45 elite female German basketball players with physical disabilities. Contrary to their expectations, basketball self-efficacy was unrelated to somatic anxiety, worry, and concentration disruption. In their study they employed a sport (but non-basketball)-specific measure of anxiety and a basketball-specific measure of self-efficacy. The lack of congruence between the measures may have been substantial enough, combined with a small sample, to result in the non-significant findings (Schliermann and Stoll, 2007).

Training self-efficacy, performance self-efficacy, efficacy for overcoming barriers to successful racing, and positive affect were all shown to be positively linked with wheelchair road-racing performance (Martin, 2002). Athletes with stronger multidimensional efficacy and positive affect raced faster compared to wheelers who were less efficacious and reported lower positive affect. In a similar study with wheelchair basketball players, Martin (2008) also found positive relationships among training efficacy, performance self-efficacy, thought control self-efficacy, and resiliency self-efficacy. Basketball players who could control distressing thoughts and maintain an upbeat attitude also had greater efficacy in their ability to play basketball and train well despite barriers, relative to players who expressed weaker efficacy in their ability to manage their negative thoughts.

Swimmers with disabilities who had strong training self-efficacy also reported receiving high levels of emotional and technical challenge support from their coaches and parents. This finding affirms the value of a strong support system (Martin and Mushett-Adams, 1996). In a study of 42 national- and international-level athletes with disabilities, Ferreira and colleagues reported on their confidence leading up to competition (Ferreira *et al.*, 2007). They found that the athletes' confidence decreased just prior to competition. Although effect sizes were not reported in absolute terms (i.e. means), the decrease from two hours prior to 20 minutes before (27.7 to 27.3 and 28.7 to 28.4 for national- and international-level athletes, respectively) seems insubstantial.

As might be expected, quad rugby athletes had much stronger quad rugby skill self-efficacy (e.g. sprint right, cut left, catch ball from feeder) compared to non-quad rugby players (Adnan *et al.*, 2001). Additionally, athletes' sport self-efficacy likely transferred to feelings of efficacy for activities of daily living (ADL). In particular, athletes expressed much stronger self-efficacy for transferring from wheelchair to bed and seat and back to their wheelchair, compared to non-athletes. Adnan and colleagues' findings supported earlier research on wheelchair tennis players (Greenwood *et al.*, 1990). Greenwood and colleagues (1990) found that wheelchair tennis self-efficacy was positively correlated with wheelchair mobility self-efficacy. They suggested that participation in wheelchair tennis led to enhanced efficacy for non-sport efficacy, such as wheeling up ramps and going down curbs (Greenwood *et al.*, 1990).

Cumulatively, the above findings support the relevance and important role of efficacy and confidence in sport performance and in ADL for athletes with disabilities. The implications from a professional practice perspective are three-fold. First, sport psychologists should strive to help their clients build sport self-efficacy. Second, understanding the determinants of self-efficacy (i.e. mastery experiences, modelling, persuasion, and affective states) will give athletes and sport psychologists a road map to follow. For instance, self-modelling (e.g. a personalised DVD presentation of effective performance) can simultaneously be motivating and efficacy-building as well as strategically and technically edifying (Ram and McCullagh, 2003). Third, building sport self-efficacy can also generalise to other areas of day-to-day life (e.g. ADL) and mental health (e.g. self-esteem), making it a multibeneficial approach.

Coping, stress and anxiety

Scholarly inquiries into stress and coping have been prominent in disability sport. Campbell and Jones (1994, 1997, 2002a, 2002b) examined stress and anxiety in elite wheelchair athletes across a series of four studies. In their 1997 study, they found that somatic anxiety increased as competition approached. Somatic anxiety was high compared to relevant norms, and intensity varied greatly among the athletes, suggesting heightened individual variability. Campbell and Jones (1997) anticipated finding relatively low levels of somatic anxiety because of athletes' SCI. They speculated that athletes may have simulated physiological "arousal" via imagery to prepare for competition.

Campbell and Jones (2002a) also examined sources of stress in elite male wheelchair basketball players. Athletes stressors were as follows: pre-competition issues (e.g. not making the team), negative competition readiness (e.g. concern about equipment), performance worries (e.g. lack of playing time), post-match performance concerns (e.g. playing poorly), negative ramifications of a major event (e.g. being away from home), poor group cohesiveness (e.g. conflict with team members), negative coaching (e.g. limited positive reinforcement), relationship issues (e.g. worried about partner being alone), demands of sport (e.g. lack of money for equipment), and lack of disability awareness (e.g. inaccessible toilets). Wheelchair basketball players dealt with unique sport stressors (e.g. equipment concerns), disability-related stress (e.g. concern about pressure sores), and common sport worries (e.g. a lack of fitness).

In their follow-up study with the same athletes, Campbell and Jones (2002b) asked participants to cognitively appraise the previous ten sources of stress. Athletes who perceived stressors as challenging also viewed the same stressors as controllable ($r=0.71$). This finding affirmed the value of framing stressful events as challenges to overcome, instead of unmanageable difficulties. Athletes who viewed stressors as severe were also likely to rate them as threatening ($r=0.71$) and harmful ($r=0.66$). Negative coaching behaviours, relationship issues, and the costs of wheelchair basketball were the most severe stressors, and were negatively appraised. The demands of wheelchair basketball were the most frequent stressors.

Although not mentioned by the athletes in the Campbell and Jones (2002a) study, wheelchair rugby athletes in Lindemann's (2010) qualitative study suggested that worrying about urinating while playing may interfere with performing. Because of their SCI, wheelchair rugby players use catheters and urine bags to drain the bladder. The fast nature of wheelchair rugby and the high level of competition can often preclude a bathroom break. The physical element of the game may also result in equipment troubles. As a result, urine spills are not uncommon. Although experienced players may take such occurrences in their stride, novices may find it embarrassing (Lindemann, 2010).

Perreault and Marisi (1997) found that wheelchair basketball players had low to moderate levels of anxiety prior to competition. Ferreira and colleagues also examined the temporal pattern of anxiety for 42 athletes with disabilities (Ferreira *et al.*, 2007). Over the week leading up to competition, athletes reported an increase in anxiety; a common finding with non-disabled athletes. Cognitive anxiety remained relatively stable over a one-week period. Although the pattern of somatic anxiety was similar for all athletes, international-level athletes and more experienced athletes reported lower somatic and cognitive anxiety, compared to national-level athletes and less experienced athletes, respectively. The Schliermann and Stoll (2007) study found that worry was positively correlated with both somatic anxiety and concentration disruption, as hypothesised. Furthermore, mean scores for somatic anxiety, worry, and concentration disruption all indicated that the elite female wheelchair athletes scored slightly lower on all three measures compared to a sample ($n \approx 1{,}000$) of German able-bodied female athletes.

Pensgaard *et al.* (1999) examined Norwegian Paralympians and found they reported moderate use of functional coping skills, such as planning and redefining stress, as an opportunity for growth. Scores for more ineffective coping skills, such as behavioural disengagement and denying stress, were substantially lower. In general, Paralympians and Olympians reported similar levels of coping.

Overton *et al.* (1995) examined 197 adult athletes, most with cerebral palsy (CP), to assess whether they used sport to cope with their disability and whether their coping skills were adequate. Social competence and life quality were proxies for coping skills. Athletes reported being moderately high on coping ability for successfully managing social interactions, and they enjoyed a satisfying quality of life. Overton and colleagues also found differences between athletes planning to continue sport (i.e. persisters) and those who had no intention to continue (i.e. non-persisters). First, persisters tended to find positive aspects in stressful situations, whereas non-persisters were more likely to deny or avoid stress. Second, persisters were more likely to focus on how to manage their stress. Third, non-persisters were more likely to respond to stress with anger. Overton and colleagues concluded that sport helped athletes to cope with their disability and promoted coping skills, and that these skills transferred to other life domains.

In short, athletes with disabilities experience both sport-specific and disability-specific anxiety. In addition, limited evidence suggests that elite-level athletes with disabilities develop skills for effectively coping with sport stress. Sport may contribute to the development of coping skills, particularly in committed athletes, that can extend to stressful non-sport situations. Sport psychologists can best help athletes with disabilities by helping them anticipate potential stressors and planning effective coping strategies. For instance, visually impaired athletes who managed to stay involved in soccer learned how to navigate a myriad of subway routes to competition locations that often took all day to travel (Macbeth, 2009). Less experienced and younger athletes may need some initial help in managing such travel-related stress so that they arrive at their match rested and ready to perform well.

Mood and emotion

Mood states have commonly been researched using the Profile of Mood States (POMS; McNair *et al.*, 1971). The goal of most researchers has been to determine whether athletes report an "iceberg profile" indicative of positive mental health. The iceberg profile is characterised by scores above the norm for vigour, and below the norm for anger, confusion, depression, fatigue, and tension.

Campbell and Jones (1994) determined that wheelchair sport participants reported lower anger, confusion, depression, and tension scores and higher vigour scores compared to wheelchair users who were inactive. Additionally, athletes exhibited iceberg profiles indicative of mental health. The most accomplished athletes reported the strongest feelings of vigour. Very similar findings were also found with wheelchair tennis players and non-tennis players with disabilities (Greenwood *et al.*, 1990). Tennis participants reported higher than the norm on vigour scores, and lower than the norm on tension, anger, confusion, fatigue, and depression, indicative of the iceberg profile of mental health. Tennis players also scored higher on vigour and lower on the negative states compared to non-tennis players (Greenwood *et al.*, 1990). Fung and Fu (1995) compared 150 Chinese wheelchair athletes who were finalists in the National Games to 150 non-finalists, and found that, collectively, mood scores for vigour, confusion, tension, and sport commitment distinguished finalists from non-finalists in 78 per cent of the cases. Finalists reported feeling less tense and confused, and had greater vigour and commitment, than did non-finalists.

Jacobs *et al.* (1990) compared wheelchair athletes and non-athletes to able-bodied athletes. Both groups of athletes reported greater feelings of vigour, whereas non-athletes reported higher scores for depressed mood. Jacobs and colleagues speculated that sport participation provides physiological benefits leading to increased feelings of vigour. Horvat *et al.* (1989) compared able-bodied athletes with athletes with disabilities who were similar in training habits and experience. Again, athletes with disabilities exhibited iceberg profiles, and the authors concluded that sport helps athletes with disabilities learn to cope with their disability. Henschen *et al.* (1992) examined the mood states of 24 athletes invited to try out for the USA Paralympic basketball team, and all the athletes reported a positive mental health profile. However, the nine athletes selected for the team reported less tension and anger compared to the 15 athletes who did not make the team.

Campbell (1995) compared mood states among wheelchair athletes with congenital versus acquired disabilities. Both groups reported iceberg profiles, but athletes with acquired disabilities reported lower scores for anger, confusion, fatigue, and depressed mood, and higher scores for vigour, compared to those with congenital disabilities. Athletes did not differ on tension. Campbell suggested that athletes with an acquired disability, relative to athletes with congenital disabilities, may learn better coping skills in order to manage their affect.

Although many researchers have focused on basketball wheelchair athletes, Mastro *et al.* (1987) examined 49 visually impaired, national-level athletes and found that male athletes reported iceberg profiles whereas female athletes tended to report profiles similar to those of non-athletic populations. Also, Masters *et al.* (1995) examined mood responses among elite athletes with CP, or comparable levels of brain trauma. Athletes reported reduced tension and anger from the beginning to the end of the six-day camp, followed by an increase in tension and anger one month later at the Paralympic trials. Further, Mastro *et al.* (1988) compared 75 male visually impaired and 46 sighted beep-baseball players competing in the World Series of beep baseball. Unsighted athletes were higher in depressed mood and tension. Visually impaired athletes may have experienced more tension because of limited time to adjust to an unfamiliar competition site. In brief, athletes with disabilities have typically reported iceberg mood profiles, suggesting that athletic participation might be associated with positive moods and buffer against negative mood states.

Similar to the sections on efficacy and confidence, and coping, stress and anxiety, the body of knowledge in this area suggests that sport psychologists can be of value by helping athletes learn how to manage their mood states. In particular, sport psychologists can aid athletes in monitoring their mood states and training in order to avoid fatigue and overtraining. Having the confidence to taper and reduce hard training can sometimes be difficult. It might be especially difficult for some athletes who devote substantial parts of their day to training, and rely on daily mastery experiences for enhancing self-efficacy, to reduce their training load. Substituting increased mental training for physical training is one way to circumvent any reluctance by athletes to reduce how much physical effort they expend.

Psychological skills

Research on psychological skill use and psychological skill training with athletes with disabilities is scare. However, recent evidence suggests that this is a fertile area for research and practice. For instance, Perreault and Vallerand (2007) have reported that many athletes with disabilities use psychological skills. Kirby (1995) and Clark and Sachs (1991) both found that athletes with disabilities want to learn more about psychological skills, while Page and colleagues found that athletes with disabilities have positive views towards sport psychologists (Page *et al.*, 2001). More specifically, athletes reported a need for sport psychology services, openness towards working with a sport psychologist, and variation in "stigma tolerance". This latter result suggests that some athletes perceive that working with a sport psychologist might be viewed negatively by their coaches and teammates (Page *et al.*, 2001). In the following sections, research on multiple psychological skills (e.g. arousal management, imagery, etc.) is examined first, followed by research focused on single specific psychological skill such as self-talk.

General psychological skill use

Watanabe and colleagues examined 42 athletes with various disabilities participating in a variety of sports at a National Wheelchair Athletic Association elite and developmental camp (Watanabe *et al.*, 1992). They found that 82 per cent of the athletes reported using mental preparation. Unfortunately, the precise nature (e.g. imagery versus self-talk) of the mental preparation was not determined. Clark and Sachs (1991) had 26 deaf athletes of various levels (ranging from deaf Olympians to recreational athletes) complete Mahoney's (1987) Psychological Skills Inventory for Sports (PSIS). With one exception, they found no differences in anxiety, concentration, confidence, mental preparation, motivation, or teamwork among the various levels of athletes.

Cox and Davis (1992) also used the PSIS to examine the psychological skills of elite wheelchair athletes and to compare their psychological skills to those of able-bodied athletes. A common perspective regarding athletes with disabilities is that they have well-developed coping skills established since birth for athletes with congenital disabilities (i.e. cerebral palsy), or since a traumatic injury (e.g. car accident) resulting in an acquired disability. The coping skills developed to manage life with a disability are then thought to be transferable to sport settings. In the Cox and Davis (1992) study, the elite wheelchair athletes scored higher in confidence, anxiety, and motivation compared to an able-bodied athlete comparison group. Unfortunately, the comparison group of college athletes was not competing at the same elite level as the wheelchair athletes, making attributing the differences to disability versus skill- and experience-level problematic.

The Test of Performance Strategies (TOPS; Thomas *et al.* 1999) has been utilised by researchers in three separate studies to examine psychological skills used by athletes with disabilities. First, Dummer and colleagues examined two world-record setting American Paralympic swimmers using the Test of Performance Strategies (Dummer *et al.*, 2000). The TOPS assesses eight common psychological skills, including activation, relaxation, imagery, goal-setting, self-talk, automaticity, and emotional control for both practice and competition. Attention is scored for practice only, and negative thinking for competition only. Scores can range from a low of 4 to a high of 20, which is indicative of extensive use of that skill. With few exceptions, both swimmers used all the mental skills, with most scores ranging from 12 to 20. Based on combined means for both athletes across competition and practice, the most used skills were imagery (M=17.5), goal-setting (M=17.5), and emotional control (M=16.5). The least-used skills were automaticity (M=12.0) and activation (M=14.5). In terms of mental skill use, these two swimmers reported much stronger mental skill used compared to 39 swimmers with disabilities who participated in a training camp at the United States Training Centre (Fitzpatrick *et al.*, 1996). Dummer *et al.* (2000) concluded that the less-accomplished group of 39 swimmers would benefit from greater use of mental skills.

The TOPS was also used by Lowther *et al.* (2002) to examine the psychological skills of 15 male amputee soccer players competing in the World Cup. Most scores hovered just above the midpoint ($M \approx$ 12.0–13.0), with the strongest scores reported for competition goal-setting (M=15.6) and activation (M=14.5) and the lowest scores for training relaxation (M=8.0) and competition emotional control (M=9.5). In general, the pattern of scores suggests much room for improvement.

Third, Goudas *et al.* (2006) used the TOPS in a study of 50 Greek athletes with disabilities. Although the primary purpose of their study was to examine the psychometric properties of the TOPS, they also obtained descriptive and correlational information. Contrary to results (Thomas *et al.*, 1999) found in the development of the TOPS, there were only two of seven significant relationships between specific psychological skills (e.g. goal-setting) used in practice and in competition. Mean values indicated that athletes tended to use some specific psychological skills slightly more often (four of seven) in competition than practice. Absolute values were often high (e.g. $M \approx 4$) in both practice and competition based on the five-point scale, and suggested that athletes use psychological skills. The athletes were competing in the Greek National championships and had six years of athletic experience, indicating that they were performing at a level that would certainly be above the recreational category.

A precursor to the TOPS, the Sports Inventory of Mental Skills (SIMS; United States Olympic Center, 1993), was employed by Martin and Mushett (1997) to understand the psychological skill use of 19 elite USA athletes with CP. In general, goal-setting and self-talk were used more often in practice and competition relative to automaticity and activation. The lower use of automaticity and activation is consistent with Dummer and colleagues' (2000) findings with two elite swimmers. Speculating on their findings, Martin and Mushett suggested that athletes with CP can more easily use cognitive skills such as goal-setting and self-talk. In contrast, muscle spasticity may interfere with experiencing automaticity, and getting psyched up (i.e. activation) may increase spasticity.

Researchers have also used the Athletic Coping Skills Inventory-28 (ACSI-28; Smith *et al.*, 1995) to assess a range of sport psychological skills. For instance, Perreault and Vallerand (2007) examined 72 wheelchair basketball players who were able bodied and had disabilities. One of their purposes was to determine if athletes' psychological skills were related to motivation using self-determination theory (Deci and Ryan, 1985). In general, their results indicated that athletes with stronger sport psychological skills possessed more intrinsic types of motivation compared to athletes with weaker psychological skills. Stated differently, athletes with strong psychological skills participated in sport because they were motivated by the pleasure they experienced when learning new things about disability sport, the sensations they felt when playing wheelchair sport and accomplishing goals in sport. Given the correlational nature of their study, it is not clear whether self-determined motivation promotes psychological skills or whether psychological skills lead to self-determination. It is plausible that reciprocal influences exist such that highly intrinsically motivated athletes put in time learning and practising psychological skills. Conversely, sport psychologists often present the psychological skill of goal-setting as a tool to enhance motivation. In a study of 27 Japanese male wheelchair athletes, those who were motivated by competition (versus health promotion) had stronger mental skills, particularly in the areas of confidence, cooperation, and volition (Wakaki *et al.*, 2007).

Specific psychological skill use

Relaxation and self-talk

Athletes with disabilities have used relaxation techniques to reduce muscle spasticity, but at the same time muscle spasticity may make some relaxation exercises difficult. Page and Wayda (2001) noted that spasticity (i.e. muscle contractures), athetosis (i.e. uncoordinated muscle movement), and ataxia (i.e. low muscle tone) all made it difficult for CP athletes to learn traditional progressive muscle relaxation.

Because athletes with disabilities may have more control over their thoughts than their physiology, self-talk for relaxation purposes might be a method of choice, although no research can substantiate this perspective. However, researchers have found that self-talk (e.g. eye on the ball), has been used for improving technique in sports such as wheelchair basketball and tennis. In a recent study of wheelchair basketball players, the impact of self-talk on passing and dribbling performance was examined (Harbalis *et al.*, 2008). The self-talk group increased in both skills relative to the control group, providing support for the value of teaching self-talk skills. Self-talk has also been used for correct technique in goal-ball athletes. Stamou and colleagues showed that goal-ball athletes prefer to use instructional self-talk rather than motivational self-talk (Stamou *et al.*, 2007). Finally, Henschen *et al.* (1992) showed how a four-month programme of psychological skills training helped nine Paralympic wheelchair basketballers engage in less critical self-talk.

Martin (2008) found that wheelchair basketball players confident in their ability to remain positive during times of difficulty experienced more positive affect and less negative affect compared to less confident athletes. Martin's findings suggest that athletes who manage their self-talk can enhance their quality of life (e.g. enjoy more positive affect and less affect).

Psychological skills training intervention research

A few sport psychologists have helped athletes with disabilities develop their psychological skills, and have documented their findings. Hanrahan (1995b) worked with six amputee and wheelchair athletes over a three-month period that included eight group sessions. After an introductory session, subsequent workshops targeted goal-setting, arousal control, concentration, imagery, self-talk, confidence-building, and competition preparation. Pre- and post-test assessment focused on knowledge, use, and importance of psychological skills. The quantitative results indicated minimal changes, partly the result of a small sample size and some ceiling effects, on the pre- to post-test scores. Athletes, however, reported an increase in knowledge of imagery, greater use of positive self-talk, and no change in knowledge or use of the other skills or in the importance of psychological skills. Given that the small sample size contraindicated the use of quantitative analyses, Hanrahan (1995b) also obtained qualitative information, and in general the qualitative data supported the value of the training programme. Hanrahan (1995b) concluded that psychological skills training helped the athletes, and suggested more athletes with disabilities would benefit from such programmes.

A second intervention study by Hanrahan and colleagues involved six blind Australian athletes who learned psychological skills such as arousal control, regulation of motivation, competition preparation, and coping skills (Hanrahan *et al.*, 1990). After a five-week training programme involving weekly meetings, the athletes unanimously agreed that learning relaxation was of value. Goal-setting and creating a music tape for motivational purposes were also highly thought of.

Mixed results were found for the effectiveness of a four-week imagery intervention with members of the British Paralympic men's wheelchair basketball team (Shearer *et al.*, 2009). Using a three-group multiple baseline design, Shearer and colleagues sought to determine whether their video-based imagery intervention enhanced collective efficacy. Using visual inspection analyses of three groups' scores on a collective efficacy measure, they concluded that some athletes perceived increases in collective team efficacy. A social validation measure indicated that most players believed that the imagery programme was of value (Shearer *et al.*, 2009). Finally, a 21-month mental skills training intervention with a single male wheelchair athlete indicated that gradual implementation of the programme produced performance and mental skill enhancement benefits). Qualitative results also indicated that the athlete perceived the mental training positively (Uchida *et al.*, 2007).

In summary, the cross-sectional data and limited intervention research conducted suggests that athletes with disabilities can benefit from learning mental skills, and are open-minded to learning mental skills. At the risk of over-simplification, the professional practice implications are straightforward: sport psychologists should teach psychological skill development. The one caveat to this message is that they should always be cognisant of how an athlete's specific disability might dictate an alteration to a specific psychological method or skill.

Disability sport-specific considerations

The purpose of this section is to provide disability sport-specific information that sport psychologists can use to inform and guide their work in subtle as well as in more obvious and straightforward ways. For instance, it is important to avoid using language that glorifies or minimises athletes with disabilities. Furthermore, there are unique aspects (e.g. classification) to disability sport that sport psychologists should be aware of.

Athletes, Supercrips, or pseudo-athletes?

Research on athletic identity has demonstrated that although many athletes with disabilities view themselves as committed and serious athletes, they typically feel that the public does not view them as legitimate athletes (Martin *et al.*, 1994, 1995). One reason for this is that individuals with disabilities are often equated with their disabilities, and their capabilities go unrecognised. Being an athlete is thought to counteract the stereotype of a helpless disabled person (Hardin and Hardin, 2003; White *et al.*,

2006), and as a result make them somewhat immune from negative attitudes and prejudice (Hardin and Hardin, 2003). Unfortunately, researchers have shown that even athletes with disabilities face strong negative biases when "implicit" attitude measures are used (White *et al.*, 2006).

Contrary to the above view is the "Supercrip" stereotype, whereby athletes with disabilities are viewed as heroes simply because they play a sport. However, most athletes with disabilities do not view themselves as heroes, or that their achievements represent a personal victory over their disabilities. Athletes perceive the "Supercrip" and hero labels as inaccurate because they view their sport successes as normal athletic achievements (Hardin and Hardin, 2004).

In brief, most elite-level athletes with disabilities do not want to be reduced to a "Supercrip" stereotype or be viewed as pseudo-athlete. They simply want their legitimate athletic accomplishments to be recognised as such (Berger, 2008). Sport psychologists should recognise that even elite athletes with disabilities, who may have medalled at the Paralympics, may face a public that diminishes their accomplishments. Second, sport psychologists should interact with athletes with disabilities as individuals who play sport, and focus on their athletic goals and not their disabilities. At the same time, as elucidated next, sport psychologists should not act as if athletes' disabilities do not exist or matter.

Training

Social support

Many athletes with disabilities have to train by themselves or train with lesser-skilled athletes. This can be particular problematic for team sport athletes, where the ability to practise together is critical. For instance, the 2009 USA National Wheelchair Rugby Team came from 11 different states and could only work together at national training camps. Many researchers have found that athletes receive social support as a result of team sport involvement. Clearly, the sport-related support obtained from training partners and teammates can be important in helping athletes adhere to demanding training schedules. Martin (2002, 2008) speculated that one reason athletes' training self-efficacy for overcoming common training barriers was not optimal was because they faced many social (e.g. lack of training partners) and environmental (e.g. inaccessible exercise facilities) barriers to training.

Training facilities

Rimmer and colleagues' line of research examining fitness and health clubs suggests that athletes who wish to make use of a commercial fitness facility for training purposes would have a difficult time doing so (Rimmer *et al.*, 2004, 2005). Rimmer *et al.* (2005) examined 35 health clubs across the USA in urban and suburban settings in the areas of the built environment, equipment, information, policies, professional behaviour, and the swimming pool. Most facilities were likely (>50 per cent) to have helpful assistive devices, such as shower grab bars. In contrast, most facilities were not likely (<50 per cent) to have curb cuts for easy access or paths to lockers that were not blocked.

Many facilities did not allow adequate room for wheelchair-to-exercise equipment transfers, although they had adequate access to the exercise area in general. Many of the exercise facility shortcomings had no adaptive exercise equipment. Rimmer *et al.* (2005) concluded that people with mobility disabilities and visual impairments would "have difficulty accessing various areas of fitness facilities and health clubs" (p. 2022). This conclusion can clearly be extended to include athletes with disabilities.

Neighbourhood

While able-bodied athletes, for example, might easily venture out into the surrounding urban area or local park to run, such taken-for-granted behaviour is difficult for athletes with disabilities. Even outdoor areas often designed to facilitate and support play and sport can inadvertently present barriers to individuals with disabilities. For example, poorly lit walking paths or wooded walking trails with rocks or fallen branches can be barriers to individuals with vision loss (Rimmer, 2006). A lack of audible signals at traffic lights and curb cuts that do not have high-colour contrast markings to make them distinctly visible are also barriers for individuals with vision loss (Rimmer, 2006).

Spivock *et al.* (2007) surveyed 112 neighbourhoods in Montreal, Canada, to determine whether the environment made it easy or difficult for people with disabilities to be active. They assessed walking surfaces (e.g. paths wide enough for a wheelchair), signage (e.g. auditory signals on the crosswalks), and surroundings (e.g. access ramps, parking for people with disabilities). Mean scores were low in absolute terms (i.e. under the midpoint of the scale). In relative terms, there were significantly lower than reference items for non-disabled individuals.

Even if wheelchair athletes living in northern climates got creative and attempted to avoid inclement outside winter weather by using shopping malls to train/wheel in, they would likely be frustrated. McClain (2000), for example, studied three large shopping malls by examining various features such as the parking lots, elevators, ramps, and restrooms to see if they met American with Disabilities Act (ADA) requirements. She obtained mixed results in finding that although the malls had wheelchair ramps, two of the three malls had too steep ramp slopes. Finally, even when athletes are members of disabled sport teams and can train in sport facilities, they still rate difficulties with accessing and using toilet and changing facilities as their number one complaint. Few ramps and lack of room to accommodate a wheelchair were also common barriers in sport facilities (French and Hainsworth, 2001).

Pain

Athletes with and without disabilities will at times have to deal with pain in training and competition. For instance, pain may interfere with training for people with SCI, as up to 94 per cent of them indicate that they have pain (Martin Ginis *et al.*, 2002, 2003). Other researchers have reported that pain limits physical activity (PA) (Henderson and Bedini, 1995), and in some cases individuals have indicated that their pain is more limiting of their PA than is their disability (Goodwin and Compton, 2004). Even sport and PA itself can be painful (Rollins and Nichols, 1994). Athletes with disabilities report more sport-related muscle pain (SRMP) as their training volume increases (Bernardi *et al.*, 2003). Furthermore, 18 per cent reported that SRMP interrupted their training from one to four weeks.

Injury and illness

Training is also disrupted by injury and illness. Relative to their able-bodied counterparts, athletes with disabilities lose more training time due to injury (Davis and Ferrara, 1995). Researchers examining athletes at the 1996 Paralympic Games found that visually impaired runners experienced lower leg overuse injuries that were similar in nature to those of non-visually impaired athletes (Nyland *et al.*, 2000). Athletes with unilateral amputations (i.e. one leg) suffered more injuries in the ankle area of the non-amputated foot/leg. For other athletes, their disability, sport-specific stressors, and adaptive or guidance aids (e.g. prosthetic device) often interact, leading to the development of an injury. Nyland and colleagues found that shoulder injuries were the most common injury among wheelchair athletes. Bernardi *et al.* (2003) speculated that the everyday demands of wheeling, combined with wheeling for sport, did not allow enough time for rest and adaptation to occur. Athletes with disabilities may also be at risk of upper respiratory tract infections (URTI). For instance, wheelchair marathon racers experienced more (19 per cent) URTIs than did the able-bodied control subjects (15.4 per cent) in the two weeks after a race. Wheelers who trained hard post-marathon also experienced more URTI episodes compared to marathoners training less, suggesting that they were overtraining when they should be recovering (Furusawa *et al.*, 2007). Finally, it is important to understand the increased risk of heat exhaustion and related outcomes (e.g. heat stroke) for athletes with SCI because they have difficulty regulating body temperature, particularly when competing in high temperatures (Filho *et al.*, 2006).

Coaching

Some high-level (e.g. Paralympian) athletes from wealthy countries (e.g. the USA, UK, and Canada) benefit from excellent coaching. For instance, Canadian Paralympic swimmers have access to the same high-level coaches as non-disabled swimmers (Cregan *et al.*, 2007). However, most athletes with disabilities do not have a coach, or their coaches do not have the appropriate sport science education. Even elite athletes (e.g. Kenyans competing in the Paralympic Games) from poorer countries may have no coaches (Crawford and Stodolska, 2008), and being from a wealthy country (e.g. the USA) is no guarantee of adequate coaching. For example, as of 1996 only 58 per cent of 319 elite adult athletes from the USA (Ferrara and Buckley, 1996) and 33 per cent of a diverse group of international athletes (e.g. Australian, Dutch, Japanese; Liow and Hopkins, 1996) reported having coaches. Britain, a country with a proud history of supporting disability sport, has athletes who report having limited access to coaches.

Many athletes overtrain, train inconsistently, in non-sport-specific ways, fail to taper for major competitions, and fail to rest after major performance efforts (Filho *et al.*, 2006; Liow and Hopkins, 1996). For athletes who self-coach, appropriate disability sport-specific information is often hard to find. Clearly, ill-advised physical training can undermine superior psychological skill development. Hence, sport psychologists might consider helping athletes find quality coaching.

Classification

Most able-bodied athletes who are classified (e.g. by weight) usually know their classifications, and thus can reasonably predict their classification. However, athletes with disabilities are functionally classified, which means they are graded based on their abilities to perform physical tests. For example, in wheelchair rugby high-functioning athletes might be graded 3.5 (a high pointer) whereas low-functioning athletes might be classified 0.5 (a low pointer). Athletes with different disabilities may also compete against each other. Hence, a swimmer with cerebral palsy may race against a swimmer missing a limb. Being classified, which occurs prior to competition, can be stressful for a number of reasons. First, the process can be stressful if athletes fear being reclassified at a different level than they have normally been rated at. Second, if athletes are reclassified at a more functional level, they end up competing against athletes who can perform better than their previous competitors who were at a lower level. It is certainly plausible that competing against more functional athletes may reduce confidence and increase anxiety at a critical time (e.g. 48 hours before competition). Functional classification is clearly a potential stressor. Sport psychologists should consider helping their athletes prepare for any anxiety about the classification process through common psychological methods such as relaxation, deep breathing, and self-talk.

Wheelchair rugby players also face ethical issues related to classification. Wheelchair rugby teams are composed of four players, and the total number of points allowed on the floor is eight. Thus, a team could have two high-functioning athletes at 3.5 and two low-functioning athletes at 0.5. According to Lindeman's (2008) study of USA quad rugby players, their families, friends and referees, it was not uncommon for players to engage in "sandbagging" or attempting to get classified at a level that was lower (less functional) than their true functional ability. Athletes were even advised by sport personnel (e.g. physical therapist) to not give their absolute best during the classification procedure in order to avoid being classified too high. According to Lindemann (2008), "...sandbagging seems to be accepted as a common practice in the sport" (p. 107). Sport psychologists should be prepared for ethical conversations similar to the above scenario.

Summary

In summary, all athletes are affected by the events and conditions of the sport world. However, athletes with disabilities face unique challenges in the areas of identity, training, pain, illness, injury, coaching, and classification. Although able-bodied athletes also deal with some of these challenges, they often do not experience them in the same way, encounter less of them, or manage them in different ways. These unique conditions and challenges ultimately pose barriers to superior sport performance.

Sport psychologists working with able-bodied athletes need to know the sport sciences and sport psychology as well as the world of competitive sport. For professionals working with athletes with disabilities, the additional challenge of understanding disability is important. Knowledge of coping with a disability, disability stereotypes, and disability culture are just a few salient considerations of value. Researchers investigating confidence and efficacy, coping, stress and anxiety, and mood states have reported results that mostly parallel research with able-bodied athletes. A few findings specific to the disability sport or disability condition illuminate the subtle differences between disability and non-disability sport. Athletes with disabilities use psychological skills, and can improve their psychological skills with training. However, increased opportunities and access to sport psychologists would clearly help athletes refine and optimise their psychological skills.

References

Adnan, Y., McKenzie, A., and Miyahara, M. (2001). Self-efficacy for quad rugby skills and activities of daily living. *Adapted Physical Activity Quarterly*, 18, 90–101.

Association of Applied Sport Psychology (2009). *Becoming a certified consultant.* Retrieved 1 September 2009, from http://appliedsportpsych.org/consultants/become-certified.

Berger, R. J. (2008). Disability and the dedicated wheelchair athlete: Beyond the "Supercrip" critique. *Journal of Contemporary Ethnography*, 37, 647–678.

Bernardi, M., Castellano, V., Ferrara, M. S., Sbriccoli, P., Sera, F., and Marchetti, M. (2003). Muscle pain in athletes with locomotor disability. *Medicine and Science in Sports and Exercise*, 35, 199–206.

Campbell, E. (1995). Psychological well-being of participants in wheelchair sports: Comparison of individuals with congenital and acquired disabilities. *Perceptual and Motor Skills*, 81, 563–568.

Campbell, E. and Jones, G. (1994). Psychological well-being in wheelchair sport participants and nonparticipants. *Adapted Physical Activity Quarterly*, 11, 404–415.

Campbell, E. and Jones, G. (1997). Precompetition anxiety and self-confidence in wheelchair sport participants. *Adapted Physical Activity Quarterly*, 14, 95–107.

Campbell, E. and Jones, G. (2002a). Sources of stress experienced by elite male wheelchair basketball players. *Adapted Physical Activity Quarterly*, 19, 82–99.

Campbell, E. and Jones, G. (2002b). Cognitive appraisal of sources of stress experienced by elite male wheelchair basketball players. *Adapted Physical Activity Quarterly*, 19, 100–108.

Clark, R. A. and Sachs, M. L. (1991). Challenges and opportunities in psychological skills training in deaf athletes. *The Sport Psychologist*, 5, 392–398.

Cox, R. and Davis, R. (1992). Psychological skills of elite wheelchair athletes. *Palaestra*, 8, 16–21.

Crawford, J. L. and Stodolska, M. (2008). Constraints experienced by elite athletes with disabilities in Kenya, with implications for the developmental of a new hierarchical model of constraints at the societal level. *Journal of Leisure Research*, 25, 128–155.

Cregan, K., Bloom, G. A., and Reid, G. (2007). Career evolution and knowledge of elite coaches of swimmers with a physical disability. *Research Quarterly for Exercise and Sport*, 78, 339–350.

Davis, R. W. and Ferrara, M. S. (1995). Sports medicine and athletes with disabilities. In K. P. DePauw and S. J. Gavron (eds), *Disability and sport* (pp. 133–149). Champaign, IL: Human Kinetics.

Deci, E. L. and Ryan, R. M. (1985). *Intrinsic motivation and self-determination in a human behaviour.* New York, NY: Plenum.

Dummer, G., Battista, R., Tuffey, S., Riewald, S., and Sokolovas, G. (2000). Performance capabilities of swimmers with disabilities. Retrieved 21 August 2009, from http://whybedry.org/USASWeb/_Rainbow/Documents/8c79763c-42a0–48c2–964a-5c5a4d48bdeb/dummerbattistaetal.pdf

Ferrara, M. S. and Buckley, W. E. (1996). Athletes with disabilities injury registry. *Adapted Physical Activity Quarterly*, 13, 50–60.

Ferreira, J. P. L., Chatzisarantis, N., Gaspar, P. M., and Campos, M. J. (2007). Precompetitive anxiety and self-confidence in athletes with disability. *Perceptual and Motor Skills*, 105, 339–346.

Filho, J. A. O., Salvetti, X. M., de Mello, M. T., da Silva, A. C., and Filho, B. L. (2006). Coronary risk in a cohort of Paralympic athletes. *British Journal of Sports Medicine*, 40, 918–922.

Fitzpatrick, J. M., Dummer, G. M., Ewing, M. E., and Colon, G. (1996). Use of sport psychology techniques by elite swimmers with disabilities. Paper presented at the North American Federation of Adapted Physical Activity, Banff, Alberta, Canada.

French, D. and Hainsworth, J. (2001). "There aren't any buses and the swimming pool is always cold!" Obstacles and opportunities in the provision of sport for disabled people. *Managing Leisure*, 6, 35–49.

Fung, L. and Fu, F. H. (1995). Psychological determinants between wheelchair sport finalists and non-finalists. *International Journal of Sport Psychology*, 26, 568–579.

Furusawa, K., Tajima, F., Okawa, H., Takahashi, M., and Ogata, H. (2007). The incident of post-race symptoms of upper respiratory tract infection in wheelchair marathon racers. *Spinal Cord*, 45, 513–517.

Gill, D. (1997). Sport and exercise psychology: In J. D. Massengale and R. A. Swanson (eds), *The history of exercise and sport science* (pp. 293–320). Champaign, IL: Human Kinetics.

Goodwin, D. L. and Compton, S. G. (2004). Physical activity experiences of women aging with disabilities. *Adapted Physical Activity Quarterly*, 21, 122–138.

Goudas, M., Kontou, M. G., and Theodorakis, Y. (2006). Validity and reliability of the Greek version of the Test of Performance Strategies (TOPS) for athletes with disabilities. *Japanese Journal of Adapted Sport Science*, 4, 29–36.

Greenwood, C. M., Dzewaltowski, D. A., and French, R. (1990). Self-efficacy and psychological well-being of wheelchair tennis participants and wheelchair non-tennis participants. *Adapted Physical Activity Quarterly*, 7, 12–21.

Hanrahan, S. J. (1995a). Sport psychology for athletes with disabilities. In T. Morris and J. Summers (eds), *Sport psychology: Theory, applications and issues* (pp. 502–513). New York: Wiley.

Hanrahan, S. J. (1995b). Psychological skills training for competitive wheelchair and amputee athletes. *Australian Psychologist*, 30, 96–101.

Hanrahan, S. J. (2005). Able athletes with disabilities: Issues and group work: In M. B. Andersen (ed.), *Sport psychology in practice* (pp. 223–248). Champaign, IL: Human Kinetics.

Hanrahan, S. J., Grove, J. R., and Lockwood, R. J. (1990). Psychological skills training for the blind athlete: A pilot program. *Adapted Physical Activity Quarterly*, 7, 143–155.

Harbalis, T., Hatzigeorgiadis, A., and Theodorakis, Y. (2008). Self-talk in wheelchair basketball: The effects of an intervention program on dribbling and passing performance. *International Journal of Special Education*, 23, 62–69.

Hardin, B. and Hardin, M. (2003). Conformity and conflict: Wheelchair athletes discuss sport media. *Adapted Physical Activity Quarterly*, 20, 246–259.

Hardin, M. and Hardin, B. (2004). The "Supercrip" in the sport media: Wheelchair athletes discuss hegemony's disabled hero. *Sociology of Sport Online*, 7, 1–10.

Henderson, K. A. and Bedini, L. A. (1995). "I have a soul that dances like Tina Turner but my body can't": Physical activity and women with mobility impairments. *Research Quarterly for Exercise and Sport*, 66, 151–161.

Henschen, K. Horvat, M., and Roswal, G. (1992). Psychological profiles of the United States wheelchair basketball team. *International Journal of Sport Psychology*, 23, 128–137.

Horvat, M., Roswal, G., Jacobs, D., and Gaunt, S. (1989). Selected psychological comparisons of able-bodied and disabled athletes. *Physical Educator*, 5, 202–207.

Hutchinson, S. L. and Kleiber, D. A. (2000). Heroic masculinity following spinal cord injury: Implications for therapeutic recreation practice and research. *Therapeutic Recreation Journal*, 34, 42–54.

Jacobs, D. P., Roswal, G. M., Horvat, M. A., and Gorman, D. R. (1990). A comparison between the psychological profiles of wheelchair athletes, wheelchair non-athletes, and able bodied athletes. In G. Doll-Tepper, C. Dahms, B. Doll, and H. von Selzam (eds), *Adapted physical activity: An interdisciplinary approach* (pp. 75–79). New York: Springer-Verlag.

Katartzi, E., Theodorakis, Y., Tzetzis, G., and Vlachopoulos, S. P. (2007). Effects of goal setting and self-efficacy on wheelchair basketball performance. *Japanese Journal of Adapted Sport Science*, 5, 50–62.

Kirkby, R. J. (1995). Wheelchair netball: Motives and attitudes of competitors with and without disabilities. *Australian Psychologist*, 30, 109–112.

Kleiber, D., Brock, S., Lee, Y., Dattilo, J., and Caldwell, L. (1995). The relevance of leisure in an illness experience: Realities of spinal cord injury. *Journal of Leisure Research*, 27, 283–299.

Lindemann, K. (2008). "I can't be standing up out there": Communicative performances of (Dis)Ability in wheelchair rugby. *Text and Performance Quarterly*, 28, 98–115.

Lindemann, K. (2010). Cleaning up my (Father's) mess: Narrative containments of "leaky" masculinities. *Qualitative Inquiry*, 16, 29–38.

Liow, D. K. and Hopkins, W. B. (1996). Training practices of athletes with disabilities. *Adapted Physical Activity Quarterly*, 13, 372–381.

Lowther, J., Lane, A., and Lane, H. (2002). Self-efficacy and psychological skills during the amputee soccer world cup. *Athletic Insight: The Online Journal of Sport Psychology*, 4, 23–34. Retrieved 1 May 2008, from www.athleticinsight.com/Vol.4Iss2/SoccerSelfEfficacy.htm.

Lyons, R. F., Ritvo, P. G., and Sullivan, M. J. L. (1995). *Relationships in chronic illness and disability*. Thousand Oaks, CA: Sage.

Macbeth, J. L. (2009). Restrictions of activity in partially sighted football: Experiences of grassroots players. *Leisure Studies*, 28, 455–467.

Mahoney, M. J. (1987). *Psychological skills inventory for sport*. Unpublished manuscript.

Martin, J. J. (1996). Transitions out of competitive sport for athletes with disabilities. *Therapeutic Recreation Journal*, 30, 128–136.

Martin, J. J. (1999a). A personal development model of sport psychology for athletes with disabilities. *Journal of Applied Sport Psychology*, 11, 181–193.

Martin, J. J. (1999b). Loss experiences in disability in sport. *Journal of Loss and Interpersonal Loss*, 4, 225–230.

Martin, J. J. (2000). Sport transitions among athletes with disabilities. In D. Lavallee and P. Wylleman (eds), *Career transitions in sport: International perspectives* (pp. 161–168). Morgantown, WV: Fitness Information Technology.

Martin, J. J. (2002). Training and performance self-efficacy, affect, and performance in wheelchair road racers. *The Sport Psychologist*, 16, 384–395.

Martin, J. J. (2005). Sport psychology consulting with athletes with disabilities. *Sport and Exercise Psychology Review*, 1, 33–39.

Martin, J. J. (2006). The self in disability sport and physical activity. In F. Columbus (ed.), *The concept of self in education, family and sports* (pp. 75–90). Hauppage, NY: Nova Science.

Martin, J. J. (2008). Multidimensional self-efficacy and affect in wheelchair basketball players. *Adapted Physical Activity Quarterly*, 25, 1–15.

Martin, J. J. (2010). Athletes with physical disabilities. In S. J. Hanrahan and M. B. Andersen (eds), *Handbook of applied sport psychology* (432–440). New York, NY: Routledge.

Martin, J. J. (2011a). Social physique anxiety, body image, disability, and physical activity. In F. Columbus (ed.), *Social anxiety: Symptoms, causes, and techniques* (p. 29–46). Hauppage, NY: Nova Science.

Martin, J. J. (2011b). Psychosocial aspects of youth disability sport. *Sport Science Review*, 19, 49–69.

Martin, J. J. (2011c). Coping and emotion in disability sport. In D. Lavallee, J. Thatcher, and M. Jones (eds), *Coping and emotion in sport* (2nd edn) (in press). London: Routledge.

Martin, J. J. (2011d). Exercise psychology for people with disabilities. In E. Acevedo (ed.), *Oxford handbook of exercise psychology* (in press). New York, NY: Oxford University Press.

Martin, J. J. (2011e). Disability and sport psychology. In T. Morris and P. Terry (eds), *Sport and exercise psychology: The cutting edge* (in press). Morgantown, WV: Fitness Information Technology.

Martin, J. J. and McCaughtry, N. (2004). Coping and emotion in disability sport. In D. Lavallee, J. Thatcher and M. Jones (eds), *Coping and emotion in sport* (pp. 225–238). Hauppage, NY: Nova Science.

Martin, J. J. and Mushett, C. A. (1997). Mental skills of athletes with cerebral palsy. In R. Lidor and M. Bar-Eli. (eds), *Proceedings of the International Society of Sport Psychology (ISSP) IX World Congress of Sport Psychology*. Israel.

Martin, J. J. and Mushett-Adams, C. (1996). Social support mechanisms among athletes with disabilities. *Adapted Physical Activity Quarterly*, 13, 74–83.

Martin, J. J. and Wheeler, G. (2011). Sport psychology. In Y. Vanlandewijck and W. Thompson (eds), *The paralympic athlete*. London: International Olympic Committee.

Martin, J. J., Mushett, C. A., and Eklund, R. C. (1994). Factor structure of the Athletic Identity Measurement Scale with adolescent swimmers with disabilities. *Brazilian International Journal of Adapted Physical Education Research*, 1, 87–99.

Martin, J. J., Mushett, C. A., and Smith, K. L. (1995). Athletic identity and sport orientation of adolescent swimmers with disabilities. *Adapted Physical Activity Quarterly*, 12, 113–123.

Martin Ginis, K. A., Latimer, A. E., Francoeur, C., Hanley, H., and Watson, K. (2002). Sustaining exercise motivation and participation among people with spinal cord injuries: Lessons learned from a 9-month intervention. *Palaestra*, 18, 38–50, 51.

Martin Ginis, K. A., Latimer, A. E., McKenzie, K., Ditor, D. S., McCartney, Hicks, A. L., Bugaresti, J., and Craven, B. C. (2003). Using exercise to enhance subjective well being among people with spinal cord injury: The mediating influences of stress and pain. *Rehabilitation Psychology*, 48, 157–164.

Masters, K. S., Wittig, A. F., Cox, R. H., Scallen, S. F., and Schurr, K. T. (1995). Effects of training and competition on mood state and anxiety among elite athletes with cerebral palsy. *Palaestra*, 11, 47–52.

Mastro, J. V., Sherrill, C., Gench, B., and French, R. (1987). Psychological characteristics of elite visually impaired athletes: The iceberg profile. *Journal of Sport Behaviour*, 10, 39–46.

Mastro, J. V., Canabal, M. Y., and French, R. (1988) Psychological mood profiles of sighted and unsighted beep baseball players. *Research Quarterly for Exercise and Sport*, 59, 262–264.

McClain, L. (2000). Shopping centre wheelchair accessibility: Ongoing advocacy to implement the Americans with Disabilities Act of 1990. *Public Health Nursing*, 17, 178–186.

McNair, D. M., Lorr, M., and Droppleman, L. F. (1971). *Profile of Mood States manual.* San Diego, CA: Education and Industrial Testing Services.

Nyland, J., Snouse, S. L., Anderson, M., Kelly, T., and Sterling, J. C. (2000). Soft tissue injuries to USA Paralympians at the 1996 summer games. *Archives of Physical Medicine and Rehabilitation*, 81, 368–373.

Overton, S., Habeck, R., Ewing, M., and Dummer, G. (1995). Sports, disability, and coping. In F. M. Robinson, D. West, and D. Woodworth (eds), *Coping plus: Dimensions of disability* (pp. 219–223). Westport, CT: Praeger Publishers.

Page, S. J. and Wayda, V. K. (2001). Modifying sport psychology services for athletes with cerebral palsy. *Palaestra*, 17, 10–14.

Page, S. J., Martin, S. B., and Wayda, V. K. (2001). Attitudes toward seeking sport psychology consultation among wheelchair basketball athletes. *Adapted Physical Activity Quarterly*, 18, 183–192.

Pensgaard, A. M., Roberts, C. G., and Ursin, H. (1999). Motivational factors and coping strategies of Norwegian Paralympic and Olympic winter sport athletes. *Adapted Physical Activity Quarterly*, 16, 238–250.

Perreault, S. and Marisi, D. Q. (1997). A test of multidimensional anxiety theory with male wheelchair basketball players. *Adapted Physical Activity Quarterly*, 14, 108–118.

Perreault, S. and Vallerand, R. J. (2007). A test of self-determination theory with wheelchair basketball players with and without disability. *Adapted Physical Activity Quarterly*, 24, 305–316.

Ram, N. and McCullagh, P. (2003). Self-modelling: Influence on psychological responses and physical performance. *The Sport Psychologist*, 17, 220–241.

Rimmer, J. H. (2006). Building inclusive physical activity communities for people with vision loss. *Journal of Visual Impairment and Blindness*, 100, 863–865.

Rimmer, J. H., Riley, B., Wang, E., and Rauworth, A. (2004). Development and validation of AIMFREE: Accessibility instruments measuring fitness and recreation environments. *Disability and Rehabilitation*, 26, 1087–1095.

Rimmer, J. H., Riley, B., Wang, E., and Rauworth, A. (2005). Accessibility of health clubs for people with mobility disabilities and visual impairments. *American Journal of Public Health*, 95, 2022–2028.

Rollins, R. and Nichols, D. (1994). Leisure constraints, attitudes and behaviour of people with activity restricting physical disabilities. In I. Henry (ed.), *Leisure: Modernity, postmodernity and lifestyles* (pp. 277–290). London: Leisure Studies Association.

Schliermann, R. and Stoll, O. (2007). Self-efficacy and sport anxiety in German elite female wheelchair basketball players. *Journal of the Brazilian Society of Adapted Motor Activity*, 12, 135–139.

Shearer, D., Mellalieu, S. D., Shearer, C., and Roderique-Davies, G. (2009). The effects of a video-aided imagery intervention upon collective efficacy in an international Paralympic wheelchair basketball team *Journal of Imagery Research in Sport and Physical Activity*, 4, 1–25.

Smith, R. E., Schutz, R. W., Smoll, F. L., and Ptacek, J. T. (1995). Development and validation of a multidimensional measure of sport-specific psychological skills: The Athletic Coping Skills Inventory-28. *Journal of Sport and Exercise Psychology*, 17, 379–398.

Smith, B. and Sparkes, A. C. (2005). Men, sport, spinal cord injury, and narratives of hope. *Social Science and Medicine*, 61, 1095–1105.

Sparkes, A. C. and Smith, B. (2002). Sport, spinal cord injury, embodied masculinities, and the dilemmas of narrative identity. *Men and Masculinities*, 4, 258–285.

Spivock, M., Gauvin, L., and Brodeur, J. J. (2007). Neighbourhood-level active living buoys for individuals with physical disabilities. *American Journal of Preventive Medicine*, 32, 224–230.

Stamou, E., Theodorakis, Y., Kokaridas, D., Perkos, S., and Kessanopoulou, M. (2007). The effect of self-talk on the penalty execution in goalball. *The British Journal of Visual Impairment*, 25, 233–247.

Thomas, P. R., Murphy, S. M., and Hardy, L. (1999). Test of Performance Strategies: Development and preliminary validation of a comprehensive measure of athletes' psychological skills. *Journal of Sports Sciences*, 17, 697–711.

Trieschmann, R. B. (1988). *Spinal cord injuries: Psychological, social and vocational rehabilitation* (2nd edn). New York, NY: Demos.

Uchida, W., Hiraki, T., Hashimoto, K., Tokunaga, M., and Yamazaki, M. (2007). A study on the effect of mental training in enhancing the psychological competitive ability of a wheelchair athlete. *Japanese Journal of Adapted Sport Science*, 5, 41–49.

United States Olympic Centre (1993). *Sports inventory for mental skills*, unpublished manuscript. Colorado Springs, CO.

Wakaki, U., Kimio, H., Koji, T., Hirokazu, A., and Koichiro, O. (2007). The correlates with psychological-competitive ability for male wheelchair athletes. *Japanese Journal of Adapted Sport Science*, 5, 49–56.

Watanabe, K. T., Cooper, R. A., Vosse, A. J., Baldini, F. D., and Robertson, R. N. (1992). Training practices of athletes who participated in the National Wheelchair Athletic Association training camps. *Adapted Physical Activity Quarterly*, 9, 249–260.

White, M. J., Gordon, P., and Jackson, V. (2006). Implicit and explicit attitudes towards athletes with disabilities. *Journal of Rehabilitation*, 72, 33–40.

4 Professional practice issues when working with team sports

Chris Harwood and Richard Anderson

Abstract

The purpose of this chapter is to appraise the professional literature that has focused on psychological service provision within team settings. Drawing from senior and neophyte practitioner reflections, case studies, and consulting service reviews, attention to professional practice issues is presented in four distinct sections. First, the major pre-consultancy factors and early-stage initiatives underpinning trust building with a team are discussed. Second, methods of team-based psychological assessment will be appraised. Third, consideration is given to the range of services and popular strategies noted by consultants in their intervention work. Finally, methods of evaluating consulting effectiveness that have been documented by consultants will be examined. In addition, the first author's own personal insights and experiences from working with elite-level and professional teams will supplement this knowledge in order to reinforce the framework of critical considerations for team sport consultants.

Keywords: team sport, professional practice, sport psychology consultant

Introduction

> So when the sport psychologist left, the word "psychology" in this place was taboo. The manager felt that these people don't have any skills and all they do is put pieces of paper on walls with positive thinking ideas. Calls them "interior decorators"! But he doesn't realise how good a psychologist he is, despite him holding no qualifications.
>
> (Pain and Harwood, 2004, p. 818)

The above quote from a coach of a UK professional soccer club represents a single example of the knowledge and perceptions of sport psychology that existed at that moment in time within a team sport context. Equipped with this insight, imagine for a moment that you were the next sport psychologist keen to offer your services to this professional team and its coaching staff. In order to *gain entry* and ultimately *provide an effective service*, who do you need to consider? What are you going to do? How are you going to do it? When are you going to do it, and where?! Such simple questions upon which to reflect do not promise easy answers. Yet, done well, these reflections form the basis of a roadmap for one's services within the complexity of a team sport environment (Gardner, 1995).

In actuality, when one dissects the above coach's statement, professional themes and implications begin to emerge that have entertained and challenged sport psychology consultants (SPCs) in team settings for over 20 years. These include: the damage left by prior SPCs in the beliefs of team members about sport psychology; the subsequent difficulties in gaining entry and establishing credibility and trust; the precise scope of psychological services and the communication of these to the manager/head coach and players; the education of stakeholders on credentialing in sport psychology and clarifying how "qualified" practitioners are appropriately trained; and the importance of the quality of "relationship" and interpersonal rapport with a player, in spite of any use of, or strengths and weaknesses in, technical strategies (e.g. interior decorating with inspirational phrases!).

It is clear that professional practice issues when working with teams represent far more than simply the strategic content of services. Renowned SPCs have been generous in sharing their knowledge and experience of philosophical, logistical, methodological, ethical, and organisational issues and challenges when consulting with teams (e.g. Botterill, 1990; Bull, 1995; Fifer *et al.*, 2008; Gardner, 1995; Gilbourne and Richardson, 2006; Gordon, 1990; Hardy and Parfitt, 1994; Lidor *et al.*, 2007; Ravizza, 1988, 1990; Shambrook, 2009; Smith and Johnson, 1990). The result is a substantial body of literature on team-related professional practice, and it is the aim of this chapter to coherently synthesise the main issues, services, and messages from this rich volume of knowledge in order to inform the future practice of SPCs in team sports.

Given the focus of this chapter on *professional practice* experiences (as opposed to *applied research* in teams; see Eccles and Johnson, 2008; Mellalieu and Hanton, 2008), the major sources of literature have encompassed senior and neophyte practitioner reflections, case studies, and consulting service or programme reviews within key journals and selective book chapters. These journals include *The Sport Psychologist* (professional practice section), *Journal of Applied Sport Psychology*, *Psychology of Sport and Exercise*, *Journal of Sport Sciences*, and the *International Journal of Sport and Exercise Psychology*. In addition, the first author's own personal insights and experiences from working with elite-level and professional teams will supplement this knowledge in order to reinforce the map of critical considerations for team sport consultants.

The chapter is divided into four main sections. The first section reviews the major pre-consultancy factors and early-stage processes that are believed to underpin the team or organisation's decision to work with the SPC, the SPC's decision to work with the team, and the subsequent acceptance and trust of the SPC by team members and staff. The second section focuses on practitioners' appraisals of the various methods of team-based psychological assessment that have been employed, drawing out the advantages and disadvantages of particular techniques. The third section considers the range of services, contexts, and focus of interventions that have been presented by SPCs within the scope of their team-based consulting. This section also integrates examples of the more specific or popular strategies used by consultants in their intervention work. Finally, the fourth section concludes the chapter by presenting methods of evaluating effectiveness that have been documented by consultants, as well as examples from personal experience.

Pre-consultancy factors and first-stage initiatives

In his seminal paper on "gaining entry" for long-term consulting with athletic personnel (e.g. athletes, teams, coaches, support staff), Ken Ravizza noted:

> Unfortunately, little attention has been paid to the importance of gaining entry to athletic teams and personnel in the professional applied sport psychology literature. Indeed, writers in the field have focused exclusively on intervention methods and techniques, without stopping to consider whether athletes and coaches will readily accept the consultant in their environment.
>
> (Ravizza, 1988, p. 244)

In echoing Ravizza's sentiments, some of the most important process outcomes cited by practitioners (Fifer *et al.*, 2008; Gardner, 1995; Gilbourne and Richardson, 2006; Orlick, 1990; Petitpas *et al.*, 1999) are the perceptions of acceptance, trust, receptivity, credibility, and respect that they gain from team members and staff. However, achieving these outcomes is a challenging task involving a wide range of considerations even before initiating services with a team. Rarely does a full complement of players, coaches, and support staff greet the arrival of a sport psychologist with open arms (Ravizza, 1988). Whether or not the SPC has been directly approached by an organisation or team, or is proactively soliciting their services to a manager or coach, it is important to remain cognisant of the barriers and obstacles that may exist to their work. Pain and Harwood's (2004) investigation of the knowledge and perceptions of sport psychology within UK soccer clubs offered a valuable summative view of the key internal and external barriers that many practitioners may face in the team context (Figure 4.1). Beyond financial concerns, a lack of knowledge of sport psychology within staff and perceived poor role and service clarity by SPCs were cited as the most significant barriers. In addition, coach interview data also revealed negative perceptions of "psychology" by coaches and players, a consultant's lack of sport-specific knowledge, and a concern over a psychologist's ability to "fit" into the team subculture (i.e. integration and acceptance).

In signposting and dealing with these potential barriers, the professional practice literature is virtually unanimous on the consultant characteristics, stages, and processes that should determine the adoption of consultancy and facilitate consultant effectiveness in the early periods of work. The following six points should be on the radar of the SPC, in part as a self-referenced checklist and when initiating discussions with a team.

Knowledge of the sport demands

A clear understanding of the performance demands of the sport alongside knowledge of idiosyncratic jargon and terminology is a key consultancy requirement (Balague, 1999; Fifer *et al.*, 2008; Ravizza, 1988, 1990). In reflecting on his services within baseball, Dorfman (1990) beautifully articulates the issue of credibility and the need for the SPC to know the specific elements of the game and the nature of specific situations in order to understand player responses and specific performance needs. One's credibility is tested "when a hitter asks why he tensed up when the count was two balls and no strikes, or three balls and one strike, but 'smoked the

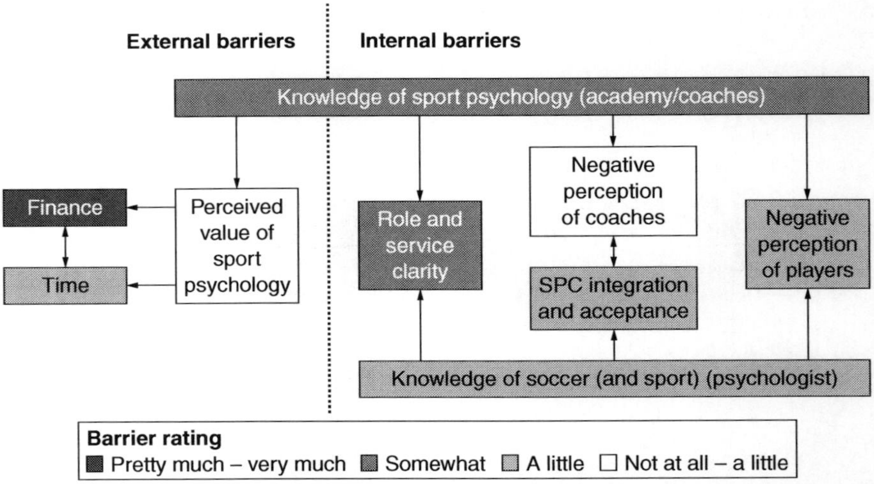

Figure 4.1 Perceived barriers to sport psychology consulting in professional football. Reproduced from Pain and Harwood (2004), with permission.

ball' on 0–2 counts or on hit-and-run plays" (Dorfman, 1990, p. 345). Whether through playing the sport, observation, "hanging around" practice and competition, reading books or watching DVDs (Fifer *et al.*, 2008), one's credibility and respect is highly dependent on understanding sport-specific demands. It is also critical for the SPC to understand the organisational dynamics or culture of the team, and be fully aware of the roles and interactions of the upper management, coaching staff, sports medicine team, and communication/media personnel (Gardner, 1995).

High-quality intrapersonal and interpersonal skills

Given the expectation that members of elite teams possess excellent intrapersonal qualities (e.g. motivation, self-control, adaptability) and interpersonal skills (e.g. communication, respect), there is a reciprocal expectation that SPCs model similar qualities. Hardy and Parfitt (1994), in a very honest and critical review of consulting work with gymnastic teams, noted the importance of visiting gymnasts in their home clubs and attending a wide variety of trials and competitions in order to maximise what McCann (2008) effectively refers to as "face time" with clients. This also means being prepared to adopt multiple roles and doing "odd jobs" (e.g. getting water, videotaping practices, driving a minibus) during early morning practices or inclement weather (Fifer *et al.*, 2008; Hardy and Parfitt, 1994; Tonn and Harmison, 2004). These additional activities and roles demonstrate an "immersed" commitment to the team that serves to build a sense of trust, rapport, and a working alliance amongst its members (Bull, 1995; Dunn and Holt, 2003). Kirschenbaum *et al.* (1993) noted that consultants rated most favourably demonstrated professionalism within a practical and flexible approach, a finding echoed by Gardner (1995) and Neff (1990). However, it is May, reflecting upon work with the US Olympic Ski Team, who perhaps articulates this process most clearly:

> My presence on the ski hill each day reminded the athletes of their psychological programs and of what they could do to reach their potential. Because of my visibility, there was continual favourable feedback on my availability of psychological services. The athletes seemed to value my willingness to be out on a snowy, windy, freezing hill riding chairlifts with them in addition to the traditional office visits. This relationship made the program more practical and realistic for the athletes and coaches. It solidified my position as a fellow staff member willing to assist in the tasks of carrying poles, helping with course preparation, observing training runs, timing, videotaping and so forth.
>
> (May and Brown, 1989, p. 325)

A sense of trust and respect also stems from SPCs who demonstrate effective counselling skills, confidentiality, and professional integrity (Dorfman,

1990; Halliwell, 1990). Petitpas *et al.* (1999) refer to the importance of congruence, empathy, and unconditional positive regard as key Rogerian, client-centred counselling characteristics within an effective, trusting SPC–athlete team-member relationship. Gilbourne and Richardson (2006), in their reflection on psychological support in professional soccer, reinforce this by stating that thriving and surviving as a SPC in such a challenging culture is associated with more than just knowledge of psychological skills training strategies. They argue for the importance of "caring qualities", and that SPCs subtly demonstrate empathy, compassion, and altruism as part of their daily practice with players.

In sum, Fifer *et al.* (2008) note the value of being flexible, accessible, positive, and supportive, and where just "hanging around", helping out and showing that you care is sufficient behaviour in building respect and integrating into the team (Andersen, 2000). The challenge for the SPC working with a team relates significantly to the nature of their contract and contact with a team, and their willingness both to adopt multiple roles (whilst remaining professional and establishing their psychological service role) and to work potentially unsociable and voluntary (i.e. unpaid) hours. Many authors cite the salience of "apprenticeship", and the requirement for young consultants to work more hours than they are paid and to take the opportunity to work with a team as a key educational opportunity.

Confidence and assuredness in the model of practice

Whilst neophyte practitioners may be "working out" and refining their philosophy and models of practice with a team, more senior practitioners refer to working with teams with a confident vision and assured model of practice before they commence work (Balague, 1999; Bull, 1995; Dorfman, 1990; Gipson *et al.*, 1989; Gordon, 1990; Harwood, 2008; Lidor *et al.*, 2007; Neff, 1990; Orlick, 1989; Ravizza, 1990; Smith and Johnson, 1990). The vast majority of consultants extolled the value of educational and developmental approaches that included traditional psychological skills training (PST) within a cognitive-behavioural paradigm (e.g. Bull, 1995; Gipson *et al.*, 1989). However, few practitioners advocated a pre-packaged PST approach with a team. Instead, individual athlete-centred work focusing on both direct performance-related concerns and more personal, non-performance issues with each team member was highly valued alongside group education where appropriate.

A clinical referral system for serious non-performance and pathological issues beyond their competency was assumed by these senior consultants (Gardner, 1995, Ravizza, 1990). In addition, a humanistic and holistic approach to the performance, personal development, and well-being of team members was evident in the most established consultants (see Balague, 1999; Dorfman, 1990; Gilbourne and Richardson, 2006; Gordon, 1990; Orlick, 1990). Gordon's model of elite cricketer development (see

Figure 4.2) is an excellent early example of a holistic integrated skills approach where the vision is to foster personal growth of the players through sport as well as performance enhancement. Likewise, Dorfman's reflections on the clinical and educational services within the Oakland Athletics baseball organisation over 20 years ago illustrate the dual objectives of performance enhancement and personal care/psychological health of its team members.

One notable outlier as a model of practice in teams is Smith and Johnson's (1990) organisational empowerment model. The premise here is to supervise and train an appropriate service provider from "within" the organisation and sport who will have an easier time establishing credibility and coordinating psychological work because of their deeper knowledge of the game and general life associated with the sport. The nature of the programme is predominantly PST-, leadership- and communication skills-focused, and it is delivered by the inside specialist (through training and supervision) throughout the baseball organisation (i.e. both major and minor league teams). This approach thus empowers a club, organisation,

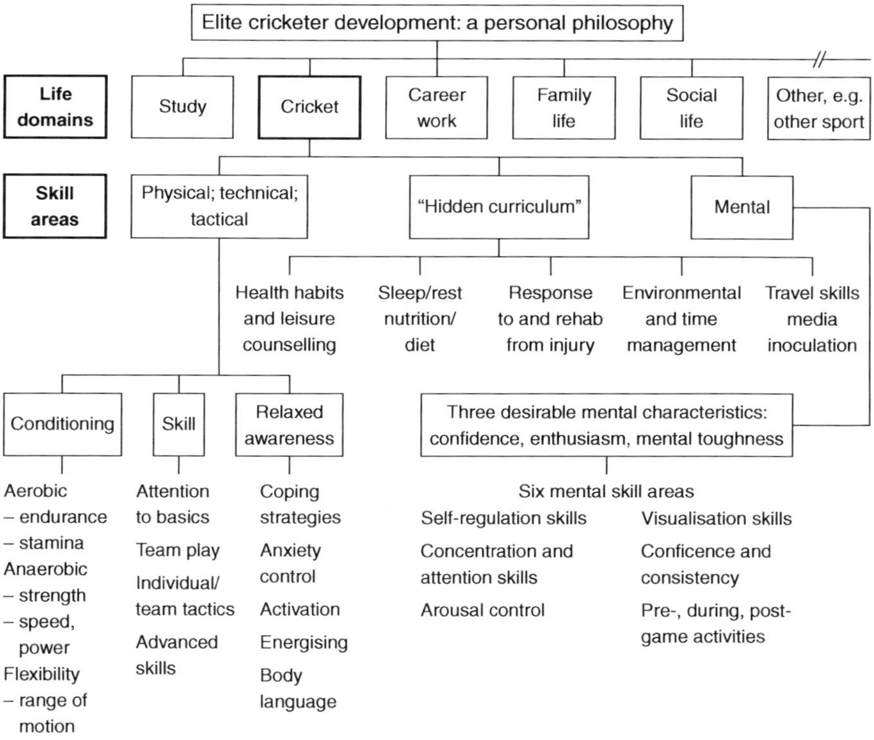

Figure 4.2 A holistic and integrated approach to elite cricketer development. Reproduced from Gordon (1990), with permission.

or team to provide its own sport psychology services under the guidance of a consultant. Harwood (2008) most recently adopted elements of this approach when training and supervising soccer coaches in a professional club academy to integrate the 5C skills and strategies (commitment, communication, control, concentration, confidence) within their squad training sessions over the course of a season. Congruent work with the academy parents as part of this developmental consulting approach aimed to instil a stronger mental skills culture within the club that was reproduced by these ongoing coaching and parental activities.

Clarifying services, competencies, ethics, and ways of working

With one's vision, model, and philosophy in mind, it is important as an SPC to help stakeholders (team manager, coaches, and players) understand exactly the type of SPC that they are employing. As alluded to earlier, many coaches and managers may not have a clear understanding of the range of psychological services that are possible, nor may they appreciate that consultants with different training backgrounds or philosophies will possess different competencies and ways of working. Gardner (1995), in an excellent presentation of the consulting issues in a team-organisational context, stresses that team personnel (e.g. coaching staff, trainers) often do not distinguish between educational and clinically-trained sport psychologists. Hence, there is an expectation that a "sport psychologist" has a panoramic range of competencies, and therefore services. Ravizza (1988) reinforces the significance of discussing one's competencies, establishing one's ethical positions (e.g. confidentiality and its limits, integrity, referral processes), and the need for open and honest communication with coaches where appropriate. Explaining your ethical code of practice and what the application of these principles mean for your working practice is simply vital. Do not assume that all coaches will understand the principle of confidentiality and informed consent. Clarifying "who is the client?" (Marchant and Gibbs, 2004) is an important step in the negotiation/discussion process, and it is worth carefully establishing the ethical responsibilities that you have to your employer (i.e. the organisation) compared to the ethical responsibilities that you need to maintain for the team member. Failure to deal with the murky waters of ethics effectively at the beginning will present problems for your relationships with players and staff at some point in due course.

Additionally, whilst some of the aforementioned processes may take place at management or board level, it is also a valuable step to present to coaches and athletes "on the ground", in order to gain their interest and support. It is important to keep these sessions relatively short, but with specific examples that demonstrate critical values and skills around performance and personal development, and that illustrate your in-depth knowledge of the sport (Fifer *et al.*, 2008; Ravizza, 1988). Prior to working for a team, it is imperative that an SPC is able to present who they are, what they stand for, and what expectations they have of themselves (and of coaches/manager). From this vantage point, the SPC can then address the issues of "Will I fit in? Will this work?" and the team can determine whether they have the right person for the job.

Assessing receptivity, awareness, and support for your work

Consultant–environment fit (Gardner, 1995; Meyers, 1997; Neff, 1990) is a salient point in the literature, and one's assessment of this essentially begins during the above stage of service clarification and presentation to team members. Specifically, the SPC is appraising whether their role as a consultant is going to be viable through an assessment of a team's receptivity and the coaching staff's support for your work (Fifer *et al.*, 2008; Ravizza, 1988). The amount of time and team access that the SPC gains for their work, and the timing of this access (e.g. before and around training), sends a message to the team as to whether sport psychology is important. The accessibility for the SPC to work with coaches to integrate psychological strategies within typical practice time, and for coaches to reinforce these principles in their coaching, are further indicators that staff take psychology seriously. It is important not to underestimate the importance of establishing a sense of receptivity *prior* to initiating work with a team. This was a personal error that I (Harwood) made within professional soccer in the process of failing to establish whether my model of practice and range of services were acceptable to all concerned (Harwood, 2003). It transpired that the coaching staff and management were focused on my direct role with the players and team. I had mistakenly assumed that coaches would be open to education and development as part of facilitating my performance enhancement work with the team. However, in the early stages of my contract it became clear that coaches were not willing recipients of work on their own coaching behaviours. Such a focus on improving their skills would have assisted my interventions with specific players and the team as a collective. However, be aware that some coaches in some cultures will rarely see themselves as individuals who might benefit from psychological support and education. The lesson for me (following this experience) is that I will never accept a contract or consulting opportunity with a team without first negotiating clearly that my roles and responsibilities lie as much with the coaching staff as they do with team members (within my personal philosophy/model of practice). If this is unacceptable to a coach/manager, or you feel that your programme would have little chance of success given coach or team-member attitudes or behaviour, then the solution (at least for me) is to opt out (Ravizza, 1988). In recent years, there has been greater momentum focused on SPCs providing services specifically to the coach, and through the coach to teams (Gardner, 1995; Giges *et al.*, 2004; Harwood, 2008). The recognition here is that coaching is a performance industry with excessive pressure, distraction, heightened expectation, and emotional labour. SPCs are a valuable resource for coaches in helping them to communicate effectively with a particular athlete and fostering appropriate leadership behaviours for specific situations. However, they are equally valuable in providing social support for coaches who may neglect themselves (and, more specifically, their well-being) whilst being immersed in such a pressurised fishbowl (Giges *et al.*, 2004).

Establishing credibility and acceptance of support staff

A final challenge to consider when starting with a new team is to gain the acceptance and buy-in from key support staff that may have informal but influential team roles. This could include anyone – the physiotherapy or massage staff, the strength and conditioning coach/trainer, the nutritionist, the team doctor, even the equipment/kitman! Some of these individuals may have occupied the role of counsellor or pseudo-psychologist before you arrive, and may feel that you are invading their space and threatening their prior role. Likewise, these individuals may be the staff in whom team members currently confide, and an opportunity exists for the SPC to involve and educate these individuals so that they have a valued role to play in supporting your work. In my experience of professional soccer, the physiotherapists or athletic trainers tended to be privileged with the most valuable information from players, who played a support role for them. Gardner (1995) speaks of the importance of being an integrated and accepted member of the sports medicine team, as well as servicing more performance-related roles under the management of the head coach. When it comes to acceptance from support staff, Ravizza (1988) astutely points out that without ample sensitivity to issues such as this, one's entire programme can be sabotaged by those who feel that they have been alienated. In sum, there are a number of processes and considerations that represent professional practice with a team as part of negotiating and establishing the nature of consultancy, and of subsequently developing a strong, trusted working alliance with team members and staff.

Psychological assessment and team-needs analysis

When commencing work with a team, the SPC's model and philosophy of practice tends to govern the methods by which they assess the needs of the team and individual team members. However, consultants may be constrained by the amount of contact time that they have with the team and its team members and staff in order to do their consulting philosophy justice. At present, the professional practice literature tends to comprise two types of team-based consulting experience. The first is the specific, or one-off, intervention project, whereby the SPC may be brought in to deal with a specific issue or prepare the team for a specific event (e.g. Holt and Dunn, 2006; Pain and Harwood, 2009; Thelwell, 2009), perhaps in the context of having a limited contract with the team. The second is a more substantive approach, where the SPC reflects upon developing their practice within a team and organisation in a more immersed manner (e.g. Botterill, 1990; Bull, 1995; Dorfman, 1990; Dunn and Holt, 2003; Gardner, 1995; Gordon, 1990; Ravizza, 1990; Shambrook, 2009).

The former type of consulting project tends to encourage direct work with the team as a whole, and, whilst the assessment/needs analysis process might benefit from observations, one-to-one interviews, and a triangulation of perspectives, a common assessment technique is the use of team performance profiling (Butler and Hardy, 1992). Thelwell's (2009) work with a First Division soccer team exemplifies the technique of team members brainstorming and agreeing the ideal qualities of a "promotion winning" team, and then individual members rating the team as a collective on each quality at that point in the pre-season phase. In Thelwell's work, the aggregate scores provided a baseline of team-agreed strengths and target areas for development that subsequently informed a season-long goal-setting intervention and educational team workshops. The performance profile can then be revisited and used as a mid-term monitoring, review, and team discussion tool (Halliwell, 1990). Pain and Harwood (2009) took a more intensive approach to assessment and monitoring during a season-long intervention with a university soccer team. Based on prior research findings (Pain and Harwood, 2007, 2008) the authors developed the Performance Environment Survey (PES), whereby players were asked to rate the quality of psychological, physical, social, and coaching processes and characteristics that represented key team performance-related factors. Players completed the PES after every game for six games in order to create baseline data on the team's collective aggregate perceptions. These collective perceptions of the team's "performance environment" were then presented as feedback in a team meeting, and used as a stimulus tool for discussion within its members. The open discussion of team functioning through quantitative feedback led to action points and strategies for each upcoming match. The PES scores were then reviewed by the team on a match-by-match basis, leading to improvements in reported communication, trust, and cohesion over the course of the season. In sum, a profiling approach (with coaches, players, or both) has served as a popular needs analysis and monitoring tool for practitioners. Its merits lie in enhancing team awareness from within, and facilitating its focus on desirable preparation and performance processes that can ultimately improve team functioning and collective efficacy.

In terms of the more substantive and integrated consulting work, it is clear that SPCs do not always follow such a linear model of practice (e.g. Thomas, 1990) whereby formal psychological evaluations or assessments lead to specific intervention plans. Shambrook (2009), in reflecting upon his 12-year delivery to the Olympic rowing team, explains the "nonlinear consulting reality" within which he operates:

> A needs analysis of a formal nature might most typically be carried out for a one-off project or when a psychologist is called in to solve a problem. Immersion into the sport for an extended period of time results in a constant process of responding to specific needs, but more importantly, shaping a view of activities to carry out that will proactively allow athletes and coaches to systematically improve their psychological performance.
>
> (Shambrook (2009, p. 113))

Working within a team context is more than simply working on the performance psychology of the team itself, and on the psychological needs of its individual members. There is a requirement, where possible and manageable, to spend an initial period observing behaviour in training and competition, interviewing athletes and coaches, and navigating one's way around the environment. This helps the SPC to gain a more grounded understanding of the cultural norms, processes, hierarchies, and organisational structures that (currently) influence team functioning from internal and external perspectives. Gardner (1995) reminds us of the importance of not doing "too much, too soon", and that the development of a programme of services to a team is an evolutionary process as opposed to a revolutionary event.

In this respect, it is important to be able to "walk a mile in the world" of the team and the team member. In doing so, the SPC will be able to more accurately pinpoint those factors that are potentially impacting on the psychological functioning of the player. They will be in a position to understand the "individual" psychological strengths and areas of development that exist (i.e. PST awareness/education), as well as any social-organisational influences (e.g. coaching style, group structure, leadership behaviour, coach/player dyadic bonds, "peer" relationships with teammates; Fletcher *et al.*, 2006; Woodman and Hardy, 2001) and mediators (e.g. role clarity, role acceptance, contractual status). Both qualitative and quantitative forms of assessment have been cited by SPCs when developing their range of services in this manner.

Shambrook (2009) refers to the importance of ongoing information-gathering through the chief coach's perceptions of needs, observations of athletes and crews, discussions with sport science staff, and one-on-one intake interviews with athletes. He refers to an ongoing appraisal of opportunities to take action, followed by taking action and appraising the results in an action-learning oriented manner. In his case, ongoing assessment led to the use of the Myers-Briggs Type Indicator (MBTI; Myers, 1962) as a method of developing self-awareness, self-management, awareness of others, and management of others within the crew. Raising awareness of personality dynamics in a team and moving the team beyond a simple psychological skills training approach has garnered popularity in recent years. In this case, the MBTI was used as a tool for increased understanding, communication, and emotional intelligence in order to exploit crew strengths, as opposed to an assessment tool *per se*.

Gipson and colleagues (1989) employed a far more behavioural approach to their assessment and subsequent interventions with the US Volleyball team. There was a keen focus on the measurement of coach and player behaviour in practice and competition through video and observation. In addition, self-report measures of the players' use of mental preparation procedures, and their satisfaction with coaches and coach behaviours, roommates, travel schedules, and practice content represented a more open-ended needs analysis. All of this information fed into subsequent educational and behavioural interventions with the team.

A variety of team consultants have cited the use of more traditional self-report measures of psychological skills and their use (Gordon, 1990; Hardy and Parfitt, 1994; Neff, 1990), but only in the context of informing an educational baseline from which to develop one-to-one work with that team member. Bull (1995) found the use of psychometric tests to be particularly ineffective in women's cricket, but did employ the Group Environment Questionnaire (GEQ; Widmeyer *et al.*, 1985) as an effective means of assessing team cohesion and using the scores as stimuli for discussion amongst the team members. Interestingly, he used these figures to illustrate that players did not all feel the same way regarding team cohesion, and that tolerance of individual differences was necessary.

It is clear from the literature that some SPCs are philosophically and logistically against any type of "quantitative" psychometric inventory on a basis of validity, cost, inconvenience, and athlete resistance (Dorfman, 1990; Halliwell, 1990; Orlick, 1989; Ravizza, 1990). Personal experience would also caution against the use of self-report inventories for "diagnostic purposes" if they add little to what might be gained from thorough, sensitive, and skilful intake interviews with team members and staff. However, the development of a sport-specific survey or instrument to garner perceptions of a particular contextual issue can be highly valuable (e.g. players' perceptions of coaching behaviour; quality of intra-team communication; assessments of role clarity and role acceptance; use of psychological strategies in training situations; shared perceptions of in-event situations). In professional soccer, I (Harwood) employed the simple exercise of asking each player to rate their physical effort and mental effort (e.g. task concentration, communication) for the three separate stages of a training session – warm-up, game conditioning exercises/drills with the ball, and open play. I presented all of the anonymous raw data scores and squad averages for each stage as a way of showing the level of individual differences that existed in the squad, and used this as stimulus for discussion about shared mental and physical outputs across all components of training. This simple quantitative assessment served to make a point about collective physical and psychological effort, and a reinforcement of what standards were possible if all players gave a little extra together. It also paved the way for players to understand the purpose and role of goal-setting when excited by the prospect of the team collectively aiming for higher subjective ratings.

Further, for the knowledgeable and inquisitive team member who enjoys the journey of self-awareness, the use of a psychometrically validated self-report tool (beyond interviews and observations alone) may greatly assist in their psychological skill and personal development process. Much therefore depends on judging your audience, and evaluating the most effective ways of gathering ecologically valid information that may then be used as an evidence base for intervention at a team or individual level. Gardner (1995) offers some excellent summative insights and a rational perspective about the functions of psychological testing for problem identification and intervention planning. He notes that:

> Psychological testing used in conjunction with interview and behavioural observations can provide useful information for the team psychologist in developing a full understanding of interpersonal dynamics, individual personality structure and mental skills development of player personnel. The information obtained from psychometric instruments can also be used in helping athletes more completely understand the rationale for various intervention efforts.... The instruments used in a psychologist's assessment often receive a great deal of criticism, whereas the fact that professionals often misuse the instruments typically receives very little.... If the psychologist has strong skills in administration and interpretation and fully understands the numerous issues surrounding test interpretation, then psychometric instruments are likely to be reliable and valid predictors of human behavioural characteristics.
>
> (Gardner, 1995, pp. 161–162))

Gardner's experience of team sport consulting proffers that athletes and coaches are both inquisitive and open to psychological testing when its value in increasing awareness, understanding, and behaviour is closely linked with performer and team development. It is the skill of the SPC in administering, interpreting, and explaining the results of an inventory through the use of empowering feedback that is also critical.

In summary, what appears important to reinforce from the literature is that consulting in a team sport context revolves around methods of assessment and interventions that are somewhat focused on the individual team member as opposed to the team as a collective (see Gardner, 1995; Gordon, 1990; Lidor *et al.*, 2007). Most consultants refer to the frequency of individual consultations or work with a coach for the purposes of player and team development, compared to team-based sessions. Although few authors refer to Steiner's (1972) model of group productivity in their consulting models, I (Harwood) found it personally useful (through qualitative and quantitative means) to better understand the degree to which motivation- and coordination-related "process losses" characterised a team at any point in time. In my experience, players and coaches understand that team performance is heavily dependent on a highly motivated and coordinated use of resources – these resources being the team itself. Where low effort, complacency, boredom/lack of challenge, and a perception of being undervalued threatens a team (motivation losses), and when team members fail to communicate and listen effectively, to focus in sync on the same drill, to anticipate each other's moves, or to think on the same page (coordination losses), then team performance suffers. This is an equation that most team members and coaches understand and sense even if there is not necessarily the expertise to work out what is really going on. Therefore, an assessment of where the "process gains" lie is always a valid one for the SPC, and this means being acutely switched on to appraising the social psychology of the team (Carron *et al.*, 2005) and understanding how its resources can be maximised.

Range of service provision

Closely aligned with a SPC's approach towards psychological assessment, their overall philosophy of practice, and breadth of competencies is the range of services and strategies that they employ within a team sport context. Gardner (1995) conceptualises the team psychologist as a fully integrated "internal consultant" whose knowledge is available to all and who is seen as the primary resource regarding human behaviour related to but not limited to sport. Within the consulting literature, the focus of an SPC's services has applied to several different stakeholders. First, these include interventions that involve the team as a collective; second, they involve interventions with individuals in the team; and third, they incorporate services for coaches, other support staff members, and families. This section will review the range of strategies that have been utilised by SPCs when their focus has been within these three client domains.

Team-based services and strategies

When working at a team level and addressing the team as a collective, the SPC's services are essentially captured within five related objectives. First, there is a focus on education and awareness of key psychological skills in order for team members to have a common understanding of the strategies and qualities that underpin a mentally tough team (Bull, 1995; Halliwell, 1990; Neff, 1990). Fifer *et al.* (2008) refer to group sessions focused on creating a team vision, goal-setting, and what it takes to move from good to great. Bull refers further to sessions within cricket on relaxation, imagery, concentration, positive thinking, and pre-competition planning. Gilbourne and Richardson (2006) refer to the importance of education around personal and shared responsibility, as well as communication (Sullivan, 1993). However, many of these consultants share the important caveat of achieving this "educational" objective by ensuring short-duration sessions, with interactive exercises that engage players, and the inclusion of a secondary objective – that of "modelling".

Examples of role-model teams or players (e.g. a senior player) who demonstrate a particular quality through the use of video or taped interviews represent a vicarious method of establishing a player's belief in the value of the skill. It is important for practitioners to illustrate some of the positive consequences of a team and its members possessing a particular attribute contrasted with some of the negative outcomes and inefficiencies when a team lack such qualities (e.g. a player "red carded" for petulant lack of emotional control resulting in a loss of team focus, inability to adapt quickly, elevated confidence and momentum in the opposition, and a resultant goal being conceded). Additionally, many consultants refer to the use of sports movies to illustrate a particular model or theme in action (Dunn and Holt, 2003; Fifer *et al.*, 2008). Such films as *The Legend of Bagger Vance* (imagery), *Remember the Titans, Gladiator, Braveheart,* and *The Replacements* (communication, leadership, coordination, collective efficacy, shared understanding), *For Love of the Game* (concentration, relaxation, imagery; "clear the mechanism"), *Touching the Void,* and *Any Given Sunday* (goal-setting, motivation, resilience) are among many examples that can inspire a "can do" attitude towards teamwork, mental preparation, resilience, personal accountability, and communication.

A third objective, aided by these latter two, is the use of open discussion, communication, and bonding sessions whereby players (and coaching staff, where appropriate) are encouraged to openly share their goals or opinion on a particular issue and, equally importantly, to engage in effective listening and attending skills while teammates communicate their thoughts (Lidor *et al.*, 2007; see Sullivan, 1993, for interactive team communication exercises). Tonn and Harmison (2004) refer to the popular strategy of using small groups to brainstorm and agree a set number of challenging outcome goals, followed by the establishment of the specific behaviours and characteristics required of team members to attain these goals. Bull (1995) expresses a similar strategy of open communication in filtering towards specific, agreed behaviour codes for training, pre-match, match, and post-match situations that would optimise team functioning at a World Cup tournament. Hardy and Crace (1997) present a more detailed variation of this strategy within a special issue on Team Building in the *Journal of Applied Sport Psychology*. Their approach focuses on a team identifying and building its core values, and then developing agreed team behaviours that align with such values.

Such team sessions may also be about specific past performances or upcoming matches (see Dunn and Holt, 2003; Higham *et al.*, 2005; Lidor *et al.*, 2007; Pain and Harwood, 2009) in order to facilitate collective preparation and share perceptions of where momentum was won or lost, and what particular needs a team member has in terms of both individual and team performance. However, it can also be focused more specifically on building team spirit and cohesion (Bull, 1995; Sullivan, 1993). An excellent more recent example of this is work by Dunn and Holt (2004) and Holt and Dunn (2006), who presented their process of personal-disclosure mutual sharing among group members. This activity involved each team member disclosing a personal story about themselves, a story reflective of qualities that they wanted team members to recognise that they had and that promoted the perception that they could rely on them in times of adversity. This type of intervention was found to be effective in enhancing group cohesion, efficacy in teammates, and their understanding of self and others (Holt and Dunn, 2006).

A fourth objective of team-based services is to employ team meetings for the specific purposes of performance review and positive reinforcement. As noted above, a team-profiling and goal-setting strategy may have enabled the SPC and team to have targeted the key strengths of the team and to have developed an agreed list of behaviours and responses (e.g. process goals) to reproduce within matches (e.g. Bull, 1995; Tonn and Harmison, 2004). The review of these behaviours may be aided by a "player-on-team report" rating (to give a collective score/team average) or in a discursive manner by the team. However, the subsequent use of video is excellent as a feedback/monitoring tool for performance analysis (Gipson *et al.*, 1989) and as a motivation/confidence building tool when demonstrations of specific model behaviours and strengths are highlighted and reinforced. Video-based team meetings can subsequently enable the open communication and discussion of objectives (in view of improving performance further, or discussing training needs) after the use of video or collective ratings has reinforced where the team is currently at (Pain and Harwood, 2009).

A final objective of team-based sessions revolves around preparation and rehearsal for specific events or matches (Gardner, 1995). Beyond introductory education about skills and strategies (and perhaps the development of a psychological performance review system for matches), a specific opponent, situation, time in the season, or competition may necessitate a more bespoke level of planning and rehearsal. For example, Shambrook (2009) refers to his application of the "Johari Window" (Luft and Ingham, 1955) in helping a rowing team to uncover their collective strengths and areas for development against a template of what is known or hidden with respect to knowledge about themselves and a specific rival European team. He referred to this as a Competitive Knowledge Window.

In professional soccer, a popular strategy that I (Harwood) used with players was to write a pre-match "primer" the day/night before a game that included a narrative of what the local newspaper report might say the day "after" the match (i.e. a "back to the future" exercise). Within this positive projection, I was able to reinforce some specific mental qualities of the defensive, midfield and attacking units in the context of the opposition and the directives that players had been given by coaches. This served as a mental rehearsal technique that incorporated a priming of the same fundamental strengths that had been identified in past meetings, but written within the context of the specific match situation, venue, opponent, and unit goals.

A caveat to the above strategies is offered by Fifer *et al.* (2008), who caution over-analysis and over-planning of the "Big Game" situation. They note that nothing really changes during "Big Games" except the athlete's perception of the challenge. Therefore, it is important for the SPC to maintain an environment of "normal service" as much as possible. However, it may be prudent, as appears to be the case in the literature, that SPCs preface this "normal service" with a collaborative team meeting and discussion focused on reinforcing "doing what you do, and not changing anything".

As the reader may have gathered, a clear emphasis of professional services at a team level is on the collective education and reinforcement of attributes and strategies that depict successful teams. Winning attitudes, commitment, courage, effective pre-game/preparation routines, positive affirmations, social support, responsibility, discipline, resilience, collective role clarity, and accountability are all part of the educational and philosophical nomenclature (Dorfman, 1990; Dunn and Holt, 2003; Holt and Dunn, 2004). However, non-performance services and strategies are also presented in the literature, and the most distinct of these, at a team level, relates to crisis or "critical incident" management.

Vernacchia *et al.* (1997) present a case study of sudden death in sport involving a university male basketball player who died of a heart attack in his sleep. As noted by the authors, distinct stages were displayed by team members who experienced this sudden death incident: (a) shock, confusion, and denial; (b) performance resolve; (c) realisation of loss; (d) glorification and memorialisation; (e) closure and relief; (f) avoidance and debriefing; and (g) re-entry and acceptance. The sport psychologist sought advice from a clinical psychologist who specialised in critical-incident stress debriefing. The authors note that critical-incident stress debriefings are structured group meetings that emphasise ventilation of emotions and other reactions to the event, as well as emphasising educational and informational elements that help participants to understand and deal with the event and sense of loss associated with it. Space precludes a full discussion here of the seven phases of the debriefing process, but readers are encouraged to access this particular study (Vernacchia *et al.*, 1997). In addition, a paper by

Buchko (2005) presents the case of suicide in sport and the subsequent processes and experiences that followed with the team members and staff. The author describes four phases of intervention – (a) remembering, (b) recalling, (c) re-organising, and (d) restoring – alongside the therapeutic roles that the sport psychologist appeared to take on board. These examples remind the SPC to have an appropriate referral system in place and to have considered their response and role within a crisis management scenario.

Team-member based services and strategies

As alluded to earlier, the strategies that one would expect an SPC to employ with athletes in individual sports apply equally to individual members of a team. Service provision is characterised (to a greater or lesser extent) by a dual focus on individual performance enhancement and on psychological well-being and personal development (Gilbourne and Richardson, 2006; Gordon, 1990). However, beyond their role across an organisation of players, coaching staff, and sports medicine personnel (Gardner, 1995), there are at least two additional competencies required of the SPC in a team context. The first is to have an acute appreciation of the interpersonal, interdependent, and relational qualities demanded of successful teams. The second is to understand and empathise with the motivational implications of team selection and non-selection. With the former point in mind, the service implication relates to working with individual members in ways that help that individual coordinate and communicate effectively with others (e.g. strategies to facilitate coach–player relationships; on-pitch teammate–player communication work). In view of the latter point, the service implication often relates to benchwarmer counselling and working with these substitutes and "fringe" players, who are often not selected, in order to maintain their motivation, and for them to have a clear development and goal-setting plan (see Botterill, 1990; Bull, 1995; Woods and Thatcher, 2009). In addition, it is also important to focus on the regular starters and provide support that challenges them to keep "growing" and improving from a motivational perspective. In many professional sports these players are paid large amounts of money to play (regardless of whether they underperform or not), and, unlike, individual professional sports (e.g. tennis), they are still paid even if they don't play.

Within his integrative model, Gordon (1990) presents a detailed workbook approach to educate team members outside of traditional team sessions. Six key psychological skill areas – self-regulation, concentration/attention, arousal control, visualisation, confidence/consistency, and pre-, during and post-game activities – are presented within a comprehensive manual in order to foster autonomy and independence with respect to personal skill development. Gordon is honest in his disclosure that only 40–50 per cent of players reported using the manual regularly, but those that did found it to be very beneficial.

Whilst there are a number of resources that offer detailed examples of how individual team members can work on their own mental preparation and performance routines within a team context (see Higham *et al.*, 2005; Ravizza and Hanson, 1995), individual support and attention from a SPC is most probably critical in optimising the adherence of players. Lidor *et al.* (2007) present a systematic, periodised approach in elite European basketball that incorporates specific one-to-one work with players, compulsory laboratory-type mental training with biofeedback exercises, alongside the traditional group session and performance review processes. My own experience in soccer (Harwood) has also reinforced the value of individualised video- and audio-based interventions through the use of personal highlight DVDs or motivational/confidence-building MP3 files. In the latter case, the ability to reinforce the importance of communication and support to teammates was achieved by inclusion of relevant response propositions on an audio-recorded imagery script.

A further service for individuals in a team setting is psychological support for injury, and a number of authors articulate the importance of having a system in place when injury occurs (Fifer *et al.*, 2008; Gutkind, 2004; Hardy and Parfitt, 1994). Gutkind presents a counselling-based approach to working with the injured athlete, and notes the importance of positive self-talk, goal-setting and directedness, imagery, relaxation, positive attitude and outlook (through cognitive restructuring), self-motivation, and a desire to heal. Understanding what the injury means to the athlete, and the impact of the injury on their life and self-identity, is a key assessment goal for the SPC. In addition, social support from the athlete's primary social network is viewed as significantly important as part of the coping process. Educating coaches, family members, and close friends on support roles for the athlete is an important function for the SPC. Keeping the athlete involved in sport situations and around the team (when appropriate) is valuable in order to avoid the feelings of isolation that can occur. The "inclusive" attitude and care of the coach here is fundamental, and Fifer and colleagues also suggest the effectiveness of using a recovered injured athlete or a veteran athlete to emotionally mentor the injured athlete through rehab, and to share their experiences. Cecil *et al.* (2009) have recently presented a detailed case study of a multidisciplinary support programme for an injured rugby player that was led by the sport psychology consultant.

A final team-member service noted by SPCs is the brief contact intervention (BCI). As explained by Giges and Petitpas (2000), BCIs are short-duration, often unplanned, interactions that take place between the SPC and athlete. Consulting interventions in sport psychology can take place in a variety of locations because practitioners do not always operate within the confines of an office or consulting room. Many informal five- to ten-minute encounters will occur with athletes if the SPC travels with the team, and these encounters in themselves offer an opportunity for rapport-building, listening, reinforcement, and cognitive restructuring (Gardner, 1995). The BCI is in many respects as much a fundamental, staple service provided by the SPC as the lengthier one-on-one consultation or team meeting. Whether in a hotel lobby, on a bus, walking to training, in the training room, or at a meal (Fifer *et al.*, 2008), BCIs involve "teachable moments" that are action-oriented and present-focused. By focusing on the athlete's problem or issue, and using their strengths and options, their purpose is to help an athlete gain a new perspective on a situation. Changes in perceptions away from a less productive pattern of thinking or behaviour may lead to solutions in the form of even a small positive change in behaviour (Giges and Petitpas, 2000).

Services to coaches, support staff, and families

Few articles within the team sport professional practice literature talk in terms of interventions solely with coaches as opposed to players (i.e. consultant–coach services). However, alongside insights by Gardner (1995), Giges *et al.* (2004) are a notable exception in viewing the coach as a performer with many of the same psychological issues (and exposure to a variety of stressors) as athletes. When one considers the importance of factors such as leadership style, coach expectancy effects, quality of coach–athlete relationship and communication, perceived motivational climate, and that coaches spend far more time with players than the consultant ever will, it pays for SPCs to have more than one eye on coaching behaviour and the coach's psychological well-being.

Many of the articles presented in this chapter offer insights from SPCs about working relationships and strategies with coaching staff. Indeed, Gipson *et al.* (1989), in women's volleyball, seem to combine as much work with coaches or "on coaches" (e.g. coaching behaviour assessments) as they do with players and team, giving a sense that the programme has a "We're in this together" type of philosophy. However, there is a clear steer in most of the current literature on an SPC's role in gaining entry, trust or buy-in from the coach, as opposed to an approach where the SPC has a primary relationship with the coach, providing them with services, and a secondary one with the team or individual players (Gardner, 1995). Whilst the receptiveness of the coach is a key factor here, the SPC's philosophy of practice will also determine their ways of working within the team context. At a youth level, Harwood's (2008) developmental work in academy soccer focused on the coach being the key service provider of psychological skills training in coaching sessions, and the clear aim of the programme was to enhance a coach's efficacy in delivering that role autonomously. Fifer *et al.* (2008) also remark on the importance of integrating mental skills or strategies into team practice sessions (see Sinclair and Sinclair, 1994), and this will require the support and understanding of the coach to help structure and reinforce such drills and processes as part of a training session's natural fabric. Jones *et al.* (2007) present the interesting case of a rugby coach who was training as a SPC under supervision from a senior practitioner. The coach adopted a dual role as coach–psychologist to a specific player in the team. The case presented some interesting ethical issues to manage, and noted the increased levels of stress as a result of multiple role conflict. Nevertheless, the case provides an insight into where the psychological input of coach might end, and where the psychological services of an impartial, "internal" consultant might begin. In summary, whilst the literature is lacking in bespoke consultant–coach interventions in teams, there is evidence from SPCs' experiences that working with a coach on their psychological skills, integration of mental skills in practice, emotional and behavioural self-management, and relationships with players forms a critical element to a successful holistic programme (see Higham *et al.*, 2005; Sinclair and Sinclair, 1994).

A final service that falls under the SPC's remit is the education and support of other key personnel in the athlete's environment. Within the team organisation, the multidisciplinary sports science team may have its own issues and conflicts to deal with. Reid *et al.* (2004) address some of the key issues that can arise amongst sports science and medical staff when multiple roles are engaged, decisions about athletes are made, resources are slim, limits of confidentiality and privacy are strained, and each specialist carries an opinion that they feel needs to be respected. Reid *et al.* (2004) note the importance of the SPC working with the team to collaboratively develop standard, agreed procedures for decision-making, and being available for honest and open discussions. Use of the MBTI or other psychometric instruments may also function to aid an awareness and understanding of individuals within the medical team so that greater harmony is facilitated.

Finally, for those SPCs who are drawn towards more holistic, integrated and social psychological models of practice, it is important to assess whether work with an athlete's family is appropriate in reinforcing some of the themes or strategies that characterise your work with the player or team. Botterill (1990) refers to educational sessions with the wives/partners of players when appropriate, as do other SPCs when working in large organisations. Family members can serve as important sources of social support for the player, and therefore a valuable secondary resource for the SPC. Clearly, the primary stage where family intervention may be most useful and appropriate is during youth sport (see Harwood, 2008; Holt and Dunn, 2004). In this context, the player is still in the process of understanding the psychological demands of the sport, experiencing new and often more challenging situations, developing his or her psychological skills, and learning about new strategies and coping techniques. The parent and family unit as a whole play key roles as providers of emotional and esteem support, and can supplement the work of a SPC through their adaptive behaviours and reinforcement of strategy use. It is evident from anecdotal reporting and selected literature (see Gould *et al.*, 2008) that parents can be viewed as problems more than resources. However, taking a more positive and humanistic perspective to "working with parents", as opposed to "dealing with parents", the SPC involved in a youth team sport might consider parent education and effective parenting as a key service objective for the programme (Gould *et al.*, 2008).

Concluding with consulting effectiveness

The final section of this chapter draws together some of the insights offered by SPCs in terms of evaluating the effectiveness of their work, as well as some observations from personal experience. This chapter has been intentionally systematic and linear in emphasising the importance of building relationships and selling one's model of practice; by selecting appropriate assessment methods and needs analysis techniques; and by implementing a range of services to a variety of team stakeholders in order to educate, improve performance, and maintain psychological well-being. In many ways, SPCs' evaluation of themselves and their work corresponds with the achievement of these three objectives, and this is reflected in the literature. Objective measures of evaluating a programme's success can be related to the final position or ranking of the team, as well as other statistical measures (Lidor *et al.*, 2007). Whilst this purely outcome evaluation alone might be the "harshest" yardstick, it is completely understandable in high-performance environments where results matter and where SPCs might be handsomely remunerated. Specific improvement in team-member performance, attributable to improved psychological skills, is a further semi-objective means of programme evaluation (Hardy and Parfitt, 1994). Indeed, Hardy and Parfitt point out astutely that, in order to provide a fully impartial service, the SPC should not be involved in conducting their own evaluation, and that this should be the responsibility of an external party. At the simplest level of evaluation, this amounts to the coach or organisation inviting the consultant back on a season-by-season basis (Halliwell, 1990; Lidor *et al.*, 2007).

The majority of consultants, however, would appear to conduct more subjective, process-oriented evaluations (Bull, 1995; Gordon, 1990; McCann, 2008). Some refer to using Partington and Orlick's (1987) Consultant Evaluation Form, which focuses on the athletes' and coaches' perceptions of positive consultant characteristics (e.g. knowledge, practical advice, trustworthiness, flexibility, positive presence, and fitting in) and whether they helped or hindered team performance. However, the limitation of the CEF is that it doesn't allow for a comprehensive evaluation of the specific strategies and services that represent a SPC's body of work with a team. Beyond ongoing informal feedback from players and coaches, examples of a more thorough programme evaluation are noted by Gordon (1990) and Ravizza (1990) in terms of gaining feedback on players' attitudes towards, and use of, particular strategies, as well as any self-reported improvements in their profiles. Shambrook (2009) also lists and asks some rigorous questions of himself, including the degree to which coaches and athletes are taking ownership of the key concepts delivered, as well as more session-specific personal reflections. In my (Harwood's) own season-end evaluation of work in professional soccer, players were questioned on the utility and value of each core service and strategy (e.g. pre-match primer, post-match review, use of DVD and video, MP3 imagery work) that had been implemented at a team or individual level. In addition, levels of interest in continuing receipt of these services were assessed, as well as proposals for additional services or changes to my focus of work. Players who had not received individual support were also offered the opportunity to disclose their interest (or not) in work during the forthcoming season. In this respect, an end-of-season consulting evaluation is as much about determining levels of "buy in" for the future as it is about receiving perceptions of past services. This approach to evaluation informs the SPC about their real value and effectiveness, given that players are being asked about how much they want you around in the future. The varying methods by which you make professional judgements about the impact of your work and the subsequent decisions that you make regarding your services are nicely articulated by Martindale and Collins (2005) in their position paper on professional judgement and decision-making.

Conclusion

The aim of this chapter has been to provide the reader with insights into some of the main professional practice issues, offered by the existing literature, which can be prominent when engaging in team sports. In terms of the processes that an SPC must go through, and the competencies that might be expected across the continuum of personnel involved, few jobs in sport psychology could be tougher. Yet few jobs could be as satisfying when one creates a trusted and effective foundation of performance-related and developmental services within the relationships formed across the team and staff. The overall literature on team-consulting experiences is fairly rich, yet when reviewing the body of academic work there has been less documented by professionals in the past ten years compared with case studies before the millennium. Although these early case experiences have stood the test of time, and the reflections of senior consultants have served as valuable education, there is certainly a need to update the literature with specific experiences of professionals in current-day practice. Hopefully, this chapter will serve as an impetus and framework for young professionals to share their challenges and innovative solutions when working in the complex dynamic of the team sport context.

References

Andersen, M. B. (ed.), (2000). *Doing sport psychology*. Champaign, IL: Human Kinetics.

Balague, G. (1999). Understanding identity, value and meaning when working with elite athletes. *The Sport Psychologist*, 13, 89–98.

Botterill, C. (1990). Sport psychology and professional hockey. *The Sport Psychologist*, 4, 358–368.

Buchko, K. J. (2005). Team consultation following an athlete's suicide: A crisis intervention model. *The Sport Psychologist*, 19, 288–302.

Bull, S. J. (1995). Reflections on a 5-year consultancy program with the England women's cricket team. *The Sport Psychologist*, 9, 148–163.

Butler, R. J. and Hardy, L. (1992). The performance profile: Theory and application. *The Sport Psychologist*, 6, 253–264.

Carron, A. V., Hausenblas, H. A., and Eys, M. A. (2005). *Group dynamics in sport* (3rd edn). Morgantown, WV: Fitness Information Technology.

Cecil, S., Brandon, R., and Moore, J. (2009). An integrated multi-disciplinary support service for an injured rugby union lock. In B. Hemmings and T. Holder (eds), *Applied sport psychology: A case-based approach* (pp. 203–222). Chichester, UK: Wiley-Blackwell.

Dorfman, H. A. (1990). Reflections on providing personal and performance enhancement consulting services in professional baseball. *The Sport Psychologist*, 4, 341–346.

Dunn, J. G. H. and Holt, N. L. (2003). Collegiate ice hockey players' perceptions of the delivery of an applied sport psychology program. *The Sport Psychologist*, 17, 351–368.

Dunn, J. G. H. and Holt, N. L. (2004). A qualitative investigation of a personal-disclosure mutual-sharing team building activity. *The Sport Psychologist*, 18, 363–380.

Eccles, D. W. and Johnson, M. B. (2008). Letting the social and cognitive merge: New concepts for an understanding of group functioning in sport. In S. D. Mellalieu and S. Hanton (eds), *Advances in applied sport psychology: A review* (pp. 281–316). London, UK: Routledge.

Fifer, A., Henschen, K., Gould, D., and Ravizza, K. (2008). What works when working with athletes. *The Sport Psychologist*, 22, 356–377.

Fletcher, D., Hanton, S., and Mellalieu, S. D. (2006). An organisational stress review: Conceptual and theoretical issues in competitive sport. In S. Hanton and S. D. Mellalieu (eds), *Literature reviews in sport psychology* (pp. 321–374). Hauppage, NY: Nova Science.

Gardner, F. L. (1995). The coach and the team psychologist: An integrated organisational model. In S. Murphy (ed.), *Sport psychology interventions* (pp. 147–175). Champaign, IL: Human Kinetics.

Giges, B. and Petitpas, A. (2000). Brief contact interventions in sport psychology. *The Sport Psychologist*, 14, 176–187.

Giges, B., Petitpas, A. J., and Vernacchia, R. A. (2004). Helping coaches meet their own needs: Challenges for the sport psychology consultant. *The Sport Psychologist*, 18, 430–444.

Gilbourne, D. and Richardson, D. (2006). Tales from the field: Personal reflections on the provision of psychological support in professional soccer. *Psychology of Sport and Exercise*, 7, 325–337.

Gipson, M., McKenzie, T., and Lowe, S. (1989). The sport psychology program of the USA women's national volleyball team. *The Sport Psychologist*, 3, 330–339.

Gould, D., Lauer, L., Rolo, C., Jannes, C., and Pennisi, N. (2008). The role of parents in tennis success: Focus group interviews with junior coaches. *The Sport Psychologist*, 22, 18–37.

Gordon, S. (1990). A mental skills training program for the Western Australian state cricket team. *The Sport Psychologist*, 4, 386–399.

Gutkind, S. M. (2004). Using solution-focused brief counselling to provide injury support. *The Sport Psychologist*, 18, 75–88.

Halliwell, W. (1990). Providing sport psychology consulting services in professional hockey. *The Sport Psychologist*, 4, 369–377.

Hardy, C. J. and Crace, R. K. (1997). Foundations of team building: Introduction to the team building primer. *Journal of Applied Sport Psychology*, 9, 1–10.

Hardy, L. and Parfitt, G. (1994). The development of a model for the provision of psychological support to a national squad. *The Sport Psychologist*, 8, 126–142.

Harwood, C. G. (2003). In the hot seat and with a goal in mind: 1st year consulting experiences in British Professional soccer. Colloquium presented at the Annual Meeting of the Association for the Advancement of Applied Sport Psychology. Philadelphia, October.

Harwood, C. G. (2008). Developmental consulting in a professional football academy: The 5Cs coaching efficacy program. *The Sport Psychologist*, 22, 109–133.

Higham, A., Harwood, C. G., and Cale, A. (2005). *Momentum in soccer: Controlling the game*. Leeds, UK: Coachwise/1st for Sport Publications.

Holt, N. L. and Dunn, J. G. H. (2004). Toward a grounded theory of the psychosocial competencies and environmental conditions associated with soccer success. *Journal of Applied Sport Psychology*, 16, 199–219.

Holt, N. L. and Dunn, J. G. H. (2006). Guidelines for delivering personal-disclosure mutual-sharing team building interventions. *The Sport Psychologist*, 20, 348–367.

Jones, L., Evans, L., and Mullen, R. (2007). Multiple roles in an applied setting: Trainee sport psychologist, coach and researcher. *The Sport Psychologist*, 21, 210–226.

Kirschenbaum, D. S., Parham, W. D., and Murphy, S. M. (1993). Provision of sport psychology services at Olympic events: The 1991 US Olympic Festival and beyond. *The Sport Psychologist*, 7, 419–440.

Lidor, R., Blumenstein, B., and Tenenbaum, G. (2007). Psychological aspects of training in European basketball: Conceptualisation, periodisation and planning. *The Sport Psychologist*, 21, 353–367.

Luft, J. and Ingham, H. (1955). *The Johari-window: A graphic model for interpersonal relations*. University of California, LA: Western Training Laboratory.

Marchant, D. and Gibbs, P. (2004). Ethical considerations in treating borderline personality in sport: A case example. *The Sport Psychologist*, 18, 317–323.

Martindale, A. and Collins, D. (2005). Professional judgement and decision making: The role of intention for impact *The Sport Psychologist*, 19, 303–317.

May, J. R. and Brown, L. (1989). Delivery of psychological services to the US alpine ski team prior to and during the Olympics in Calgary. *The Sport Psychologist*, 3, 320–329.

McCann, S. (2008). At the Olympics, everything is a performance issue. *International Journal of Sport and Exercise Psychology*, 6, 267–276.

Mellalieu, S. D. and Hanton, S. (2008). *Advances in applied sport psychology: A review.* London, UK: Routledge.

Meyers, A. W. (1997). Sport psychology service to the United States Olympic Festival: An experiential account. *The Sport Psychologist,* 11, 454–468.

Myers, I. B. (1962). *Manual: The Myers-Briggs Type Indicator.* Palo Alto, CA: Consulting Psychologists Press.

Neff, F. (1990). Delivering sport psychology services to a professional sport organisation. *The Sport Psychologist,* 4, 378–385.

Orlick, T. (1989). Reflections on sport psych consulting with individual and team sport athletes at the summer and winter Olympic Games. *The Sport Psychologist,* 3, 358–365.

Orlick, T. (1990). *In pursuit of excellence.* Champaign, IL: Leisure Press.

Pain, M. A. and Harwood, C. G. (2004). Knowledge and perceptions of sport psychology within English soccer. *Journal of Sports Sciences,* 22, 813–826.

Pain, M. A. and Harwood, C. G. (2007). The performance environment of the English youth soccer teams. *Journal of Sports Sciences,* 25, 1307–1324.

Pain, M. A. and Harwood, C. G. (2008). The performance environment in English youth soccer: A quantitative investigation. *Journal of Sports Sciences,* 26, 1157–1169.

Pain, M. A. and Harwood, C. G. (2009). Team building through mutual sharing and open discussion of team functioning. *The Sport Psychologist,* 23, 523–542.

Partington, J. and Orlick, T. (1987). The sport psychology consultant evaluation form. *The Sport Psychologist,* 1, 309–317.

Petitpas, A. J., Giges, B. and Danish, S. J. (1999). The sport psychologist-athlete relationship: Implications for training. *The Sport Psychologist,* 13, 344–352.

Ravizza, K. (1988). Gaining entry with athletic personnel for season-long consulting. *The Sport Psychologist,* 2, 243–254.

Ravizza, K. (1990). Sport psychology consultation issues in professional baseball. *The Sport Psychologist,* 4, 330–340.

Ravizza, K. and Hanson, T. (1995). *Heads-up baseball. Playing the game one pitch at a time.* Indianapolis, IN: Masters.

Reid, C., Stewart, E., and Thorne, G. (2004). Multidisciplinary sport science teams in elite sport: Comprehensive servicing or conflict and confusion? *The Sport Psychologist,* 18, 204–217.

Shambrook, C. (2009). Delivering sport psychology to Olympic rowers: Beyond psychological skills training. In B. Hemmings and T. Holder (eds), *Applied sport psychology: A case-based approach* (pp. 111–138). Chichester, UK: Wiley-Blackwell.

Sinclair, G. and Sinclair, D. (1994). Developing reflective performers by integrating mental management skills with the learning process. *The Sport Psychologist,* 8, 13–27.

Smith, R. E. and Johnson, J. (1990). An organisational empowerment approach to consultation in professional baseball. *The Sport Psychologist,* 4, 347–357.

Steiner, I. D. (1972). *Group process and productivity.* New York, NY: Academic Press.

Sullivan, P. (1993). Communication skills training for interactive sports. *The Sport Psychologist,* 7, 79–91.

Thelwell, R. (2009). Team goal setting in professional football. In B. Hemmings and T. Holder (eds), *Applied sport psychology: A case-based approach* (pp. 161–180). Chichester, UK: Wiley-Blackwell.

Thomas, P. R. (1990). *An overview of the performance enhancement processes in applied sport psychology.* Unpublished manuscript, US Olympic Training Centre, Colorado Springs.

Tonn, E. and Harmison, R. J. (2004). Thrown to the wolves: A student's account of her practicum experience. *The Sport Psychologist*, 18, 324–340.

Vernacchia, R. A., Reardon, J. P., and Templin, D. P. (1997). Sudden death in sport: Managing the aftermath. *The Sport Psychologist*, 11, 223–235.

Widmeyer, W. N., Brawley, L. R., and Carron, A. V. (1985). *The measurement of cohesion in sport teams: The Group Environment Questionnaire.* London, ON: Spodym.

Woodman, T. and Hardy, L. (2001). A case study of organisational stress in elite sport. *Journal of Applied Sport Psychology*, 13, 207–238.

Woods, B. and Thatcher, J. (2009). A qualitative exploration of the soccer substitute's experience. *The Sport Psychologist*, 23, 45–469.

5 Working with injured athletes

Research and practice

Ross Wadey and Lynne Evans

Abstract

The purpose of this chapter is to consider the challenges injured athletes typically experience, and their implications for professional practice. The narrative is informed by the psychology of sport injury empirical and professional practice literature and the authors' experiences from working with injured athletes. Underpinned by Wiese-Bjornstal and colleagues' (1998) integrated model and Brewer and colleagues' (2002) biopsychosocial model, this chapter is divided into three main sections. First, an overview of the models of injury response is provided. Second, three phases of recovery are considered: (a) injury onset, (b) rehabilitation, and (c) return to competitive sport. Within each of these phases, the common challenges injured athletes encounter are discussed alongside their implications for professional practice. The final section concludes the chapter by providing general guidelines for practitioners working with injured athletes.

Keywords: injury, rehabilitation, recovery, professional practice

Introduction

> After one particularly frustrating day, I suddenly felt as if I couldn't cope any longer. I stood in the bathroom of our room in the apartment, locked the door and stared at the mirror, feeling utterly miserable. I was crying uncontrollably but tried to drown out the sound by running the tap into the basin and keeping down the noise of my sobs. There was a pair of nail scissors in a cup on a shelf. To this day, I don't know what made me do this, but I picked them up, opened them and started to cut my left arm with one of the blades. One cut for every day that I had been injured. ... I stared at myself with hatred, wondering if anyone could have put a curse on me to cause this endless run of injuries, asking myself, "Why me? What have I done to deserve this hurt and disappointment?" ... I knew I needed help, but I

> didn't know where to find it. I had to try and cope with the negative feelings on my own – one of the hardest things I've had to do. … Those were the days when I reached rock bottom.
>
> (Kelly Holmes, 2005, pp. 210–211)

This quote from Dame Kelly Holmes provides a powerful illustration of the psychological effect that injuries can have, and, although extreme, it is not atypical; athletes commonly find injury to be a debilitating experience (see, for example, Appaneal *et al.*, 2009; Brewer *et al.*, 1995; Leddy *et al.*, 1994). With often unfamiliar and varied demands, responses, outcomes and implications, injury can pose a significant threat to athletes' coping resources. Indeed, without appropriate resources, recovery from injury can become an arduous and protracted experience, with potentially debilitating consequences (cf. Henderson, 2007; Petitpas and Danish, 1995; Smith and Milliner, 1994). Dame Kelly Holmes eventually returned to sport, and went onto win track gold medals in the 800 and 1,500 metres at the 2004 Olympic Games in Athens. However, not all athletes achieve such a successful outcome (e.g. Carey *et al.*, 2006; Evans *et al.*, 2000; Podlog and Eklund, 2006). It is vital, therefore, that coaches, medical practitioners, and sport scientists are cognisant of the challenges injured athletes face, and the ways in which they can be helped to deal with them to enable a successful return to competitive sport.

The purpose of this chapter is to consider some of the common challenges injured athletes experience, and the implications of these challenges for professional practice. The chapter is divided into three sections. First, it provides a brief overview of models of injury response, which underpin this field of research. Second, it considers three phases of recovery: (a) injury onset, (b) rehabilitation, and (c) return to competitive sport. Within each phase, its potentially stressful nature will be discussed together with the implications for professional practice. The final section, concluding comments, provides some general guidelines for sport psychology consultants (SPCs) working with, or intending to work with, injured athletes. Embracing an evidence-based philosophy, this chapter will largely be informed by empirical research. However, to further illuminate issues of central importance to the purpose of this chapter, it will also draw on anecdotal evidence from professional practice texts and the authors' consulting experiences of working with injured athletes.

A brief overview of models of injury response

Contemporary research into the psychology of sport injury has been guided by a number of theories and models, including the integrated model of response to sport injury (Wiese-Bjornstal *et al.*, 1998), biopsychosocial model of sport injury rehabilitation (Brewer *et al.*, 2002), stage-based grief response models (Kübler-Ross, 1969), self-determination theory (Ryan and Deci, 2000), cognitive-motivational relational theory of emotion (Lazarus, 2000), self-efficacy theory (Bandura, 1997), stage model of the return to sport (Taylor and Taylor, 1997), reversal theory (Apter, 1982), personal investment theory (Maehr and Braskamp, 1986), and protection motivation theory (Rogers, 1975). Although many of these models and theories merit further attention, the models that have received the most attention to date and which will provide the theoretical foundation for this chapter are Wiese-Bjornstal *et al.*'s integrated model and Brewer *et al.*'s biopsychosocial model.

Wiese-Bjornstal *et al.*'s (1998) integrated model suggests that both pre-injury and post-injury factors moderate one's cognitive, emotional, and behavioural responses to injury, mediated by the process of appraisal. Pre-injury factors comprise personality (e.g. hardiness and optimism), history of stressors (e.g. major life events and daily hassles), and coping resources (e.g. psychological skills and coping strategies). Post-injury factors comprise personal (e.g. gender and injury severity) and situational variables (e.g. rehabilitation environment and provision of social support). As a stress-process-based model that embraces the concept of change, physical and psychological recovery from injury is viewed as a dynamic, interactive process in which cognitions, emotions, and behaviours are explained within a cyclical framework. Although Wiese-Bjornstal *et al.*'s integrated model has yet to be examined in its entirety, a number of its central tenets have been supported. For example, researchers have observed pre-injury (e.g. major life events and the personality trait of hardiness) and post-injury variables (e.g. emotional climate and injury severity) to affect athletes' responses to injury (e.g. Albinson and Petrie, 2003; Brewer, 1993; Mankad *et al.*, 2009; Smith *et al.*, 1990; Wadey *et al.*, 2011a). Researchers have also found injured athletes' cognitive, emotional, and behavioural responses to change over time, and to influence one another additively and interactively (e.g. Carson and Polman, 2008; Daly *et al.*, 1995; Gallagher and Gardner, 2007; Podlog and Eklund, 2006; Udry, 1997). For example, Daly *et al.* found cognitive appraisal (i.e. evaluation of ability to cope with injury) was inversely correlated with mood disturbance, which in turn was inversely correlated with attendance at rehabilitation sessions. However, one limitation of the integrated model is that it fails to explain how injured athletes' responses affect rehabilitation outcomes. To address this concern and to more closely align with medical models of injury, Brewer *et al.* (2002) developed the biopsychosocial model.

Brewer *et al.*'s (2002) biopsychosocial model suggests specific mechanisms by which psychological factors (i.e. personality, cognition, emotions, and behaviour) might affect sport injury rehabilitation outcomes (e.g. functional performance and readiness to return to sport). Specifically, the model suggests that psychological factors affect sport injury rehabilitation outcomes directly or indirectly through intermediate biopsychological outcomes (e.g. range of motion and rate of recovery). Biological factors such as endocrine, metabolism, and immune functioning are also suggested to have a reciprocal relationship with psychological factors, and to mediate the relationship between psychological factors and intermediate biopsychosocial outcomes. But despite these purported direct, indirect, and reciprocal effects, researchers to date have tended to examine the direct relationship between psychological factors and sport injury rehabilitation outcomes or intermediate biopsychosocial outcomes. For example, a number of experimental studies have demonstrated the efficacy of psychological skills (e.g. goal-setting, imagery, and relaxation) in attaining desirable rehabilitation outcomes such as reduced pain and re-injury anxiety, and increased strength and self-efficacy (e.g. Cupal and Brewer, 2001; Johnson, 2000; Theodorakis *et al.*, 1996, 1997). Other studies have shown cognitive (e.g. cognitive appraisal), emotional (e.g. psychological distress), and behavioural responses (e.g. clinical ratings of adherence) to be correlated with rehabilitation outcomes such as functional ability, knee laxity, pain, and recovery time (e.g. Brewer *et al.*, 2000, 2004; Johnson, 1997; Tripp *et al.*, 2007). However, although these findings are encouraging and provide preliminary support for the biopsychosocial model, this area of research is still very much in its infancy. More experimental studies are required to examine the direct, indirect, and reciprocal effects of psychological factors on sport injury rehabilitation outcomes.

Underpinned by Wiese-Bjornstal *et al.*'s (1998) and Brewer *et al.*'s (2002) models, and consistent with post-injury temporal patterning (cf. Evans *et al.*, 2006a), the following section explores the full recovery process by examining three distinct but related phases: injury onset, rehabilitation, and return to competitive sport. For the purposes of this chapter, *injury onset* starts from the occurrence of injury, *rehabilitation* starts from the first physiotherapy appointment, and *return to competitive sport* starts from returning to full competitive training. It is important that SPCs are aware, however, that these phases are not discrete; athletes can oscillate between them, and their responses can carry over. In addition, some athletes may not progress through all the phases (e.g. career termination).

Phases of recovery

Injury onset

Of the three phases of recovery, this phase has received the least research attention to date. This limited research attention is surprising given that injured athletes' experience a myriad of cognitive, emotional, and behavioural responses during this phase, and that these responses are often more intense than those encountered in subsequent phases (e.g. Bianco *et al.*, 1999; Carson and Polman, 2008; Petitpas and Danish, 1995). The extant literature suggests that the most common features of injured athletes' experiences during this phase are the emotional turmoil, a lack of understanding of the injury and recovery process, the dilemma of whether to compete while injured, and loss of functional ability.

Although often short-lived, some of the most intense emotions that injured athletes' experience ensue soon after the injury occurs (e.g. Gallagher and Gardner, 2007; Quinn and Fallon, 1999; Wadey *et al.*, 2011a). Indeed, athletes report experiencing a rollercoaster of emotions during this time, with the most prevalent being shock, anger, depression, helplessness, and frustration (e.g. Grove and Cresswell, 2007; Johnston and Carroll, 1998a; Tracey, 2003; Wadey *et al.*, 2011b). The antecedents of these include physical pain, injury prognosis, timing of the injury in relation to the competitive season, missing training and competition, financial concerns, misdiagnosis, and flashbacks of the injury incident, as well as other real, perceived, and potential personal and contextual losses (e.g. Bianco *et al.*, 1999; Evans *et al.*, 2000, 2011; Gayman and Crossman, 2003; Gould *et al.*, 1997a; Krane *et al.*, 1997; Vergeer, 2006). These losses can include loss of identity, self-esteem, independence, fitness, and career (cf. Evans and Hardy, 1995). Not surprisingly, the latter appears particularly salient for professional athletes because of the threat injury poses to their livelihood (Bianco *et al.*, 1999; Carson and Polman, 2008; Evans *et al.*, 2000; Gould *et al.*, 1997a).

Unfortunately, the emotional turmoil following injury, which can be particularly challenging for many athletes, often lingers beyond what might be expected, because athletes all too frequently internalise their emotions and do not want (or find it too difficult) to communicate how they are feeling to others (e.g. Petitpas and Danish, 1995; Wadey *et al.*, 2011b). Perhaps not surprisingly, therefore, it is not uncommon for athletes to isolate themselves, in particular from those associated with their sport (e.g. Mankad *et al.*, 2009; Tracey, 2003). Consistent with the authors' own professional practice experiences, Mankad amd colleagues found that some injured athletes did not want to express their emotions because they felt that it would be seen as a sign of weakness that may in the future negatively affect their place in the team. As a result the athletes reported inhibiting and/or suppressing their injury-related emotions, and "Although many considered this inhibitive technique effective, some athletes felt that the unwanted, suppressed injury-related thoughts sometimes built up and got so intense that they could not stop themselves from reacting and lashing out emotionally" (Mankad *et al.*, 2009, p. 8).

During this phase athletes also experience a myriad of questions; for some these arise from a lack of understanding about their injury and its implications, for others simply the uncertainty about the situation and how to deal with being injured (e.g. Carson and Polman, 2008; Gould *et al.*, 1997a; Tracey, 2003; Wadey *et al.*, 2011b). Questions include: What have I done? How long will I be out? Do I need an operation? What will the rehabilitation involve? When will I be able to play again? Will it (the injured limb/body part) ever be the same again? Bianco *et al.* (1999) suggested that one of the most pertinent questions is whether to receive treatment or forego it to continue participating in sport (cf. Charlesworth and Young, 2004; Collins *et al.*, 2009; Shaffer and Wiese-Bjornstal, 1999). In some instances external pressures may influence this decision or take it out of the athletes' hands. For example, Krane *et al.* (1997) cites the experiences of an elite gymnast who continued practising and competing while seriously injured, largely because of the pressure placed on her by her coaches. However, the pressure can also come from the injured athletes themselves. Indeed, Bianco *et al.* (1999) interviewed three Canadian Alpine Ski Team members who faced the decision to race in an important event while injured; all said that they felt compelled to take the risk. In these circumstances, coaches and medical staff have been reported to provide short-term relief (e.g. pain killers and anti-inflammatory drugs) to enable athletes to play through their injuries, with full treatment being delayed until the end of the competitive season (e.g. Krane *et al.*, 1997; Mankad *et al.*, 2009). However, despite some athletes succeeding when injured (cf. Shaffer and Wiese-Bjornstal, 1999), underperformance and reinjury are also commonplace. For example, one athlete in Bianco *et al.*'s study commented:

> I was ranked top 10 in the world. I was the number one Canadian coming into the Olympics. I tore my ACL [anterior cruciate ligament], and I continued skiing without having it repaired. I wore a brace and went to the Olympics. Two days before the race, I fell and destroyed my knee ... and my career.
>
> (Bianco *et al.*, 1999, p. 163)

Clearly, the consequences of competing while injured can be traumatic. For those athletes who cannot or choose not to compete while injured, however, dealing with the loss of functional ability is one of the biggest challenges they will face during this phase. This loss of functional ability includes, for example, the inability to do everyday tasks (e.g. cooking, housework, shopping, and dressing themselves) and restricted mobility; losses that can heighten feelings of frustration and helplessness (e.g. Bianco, 2001; Carson and Polman, 2008; Johnson and Carroll, 1998a; Tracey, 2003).

From a professional practice perspective, a number of strategies can be adopted by SPCs to address the aforementioned features of this phase of recovery. One strategy that is recommended repeatedly in the empirical and professional practice literature is social support (e.g. Bianco and Eklund, 2001; Brewer and Petitpas, 2005). In terms of the emotional turmoil of injury, emotional support can help athletes eradicate or regulate their emotions by support-providers listening to athletes' concerns, offering emotional comfort by expressing empathy and encouragement, and, if appropriate, challenging emotions to help athletes rationalise their thoughts and feelings (e.g. Bianco, 2001; Johnston and Carroll, 1998b). In relation to the latter, it is important that SPCs recognise that the trauma of and loss associated with injury may cause athletes to become uncharacteristically irrational, in part because of the threat to their normal perceptions of control and goal attainment. Although the main providers of emotional support should be people who have a close relationship with the injured athlete (e.g. friends, family, and teammates; Bianco, 2001; Johnston and Carroll, 1998b), SPCs are ideally suited to provide emotional support, particularly where athletes do not feel comfortable disclosing their feelings to significant others. Where SPCs are called upon to provide emotional support, it is important that they create a climate of mutual trust (cf. Petitpas and Danish, 1995; Shaffer and Wiese-Bjornstal, 1999; Tracey, 2008). Petitpas and Danish (1995) emphasised that the most important consideration for SPCs is to understand injured athletes as individuals (i.e. attend to the person and not just the injury). Both creating a climate of mutual trust and attending to the person will in turn increase the likelihood of injured athletes disclosing their thoughts and feelings, which will facilitate short- and long-term recovery (e.g. Johnston and Carroll, 1998b; Tracey, 2003). Indeed, Wadey *et al.* (2011b) recently found that injured athletes who self-disclosed their emotions to others gained additional long-term perceived benefits (i.e. it improved their ability to understand, express, and regulate their emotions once they had returned to sport).

Other types of social support that have been observed to be effective during injury onset are informational and tangible support (e.g. Bianco, 2001; Johnston and Carroll, 1998b; Wadey *et al.*, 2011b). In terms of informational support, it is important that SPCs encourage athletes to seek answers to the questions they may have surrounding their injury and the recovery process; a feature that has been associated with successful recovery (e.g. Carson and Polman, 2008; Tracey, 2008). Both Bianco (2001) and Johnston and Carroll (1998b) emphasised the importance of obtaining this information from people with relevant expertise (e.g. medical personnel) and experience (e.g. other injured athletes); a process that can be facilitated by the SPC (e.g. by encouraging effective communication). However, some athletes may prefer to seek answers to questions by searching textbooks, journals, and reputable internet sites (Wadey *et al.*, 2011b).

With regard to the dilemma of whether to compete while injured, although it may be inappropriate (or indeed unethical) for SPCs to intervene in this decision, we recommend that they should strongly encourage athletes once again to seek informational support from medical personnel in order to raise their awareness of the potential long-term implications of competing while injured. From a professional practice perspective, consistent with the views of Shaffer and Wiese-Bjornstal (1999), we feel the overriding priority should be the health and well-being of the athlete. In essence, SPCs can play a key role in this decision-making process by helping to increase athletes' perception of available support from members in and outside their existing social network (e.g. doctors, athletic trainers, and physiotherapists), as well as mobilising the support that meets their specific needs – something that the athlete might otherwise not do.

Finally, tangible support has been shown to be effective in helping athletes to address the everyday demands that injured athletes find challenging (e.g. Carson and Polman, 2008; Gould *et al.*, 1997b; Tracey, 2003); this may include transportation to medical appointments, shopping, cooking, and housework. The SPC can help athletes to recognise who in their social support network can help and/or encourage them to mobilise their network by seeking out assistance and/or accepting the assistance offered to them by others. The main providers of tangible support appear to be teammates, family, and friends; in particular, people with whom the injured athlete lives or has regular contact, and who are willing and able to provide the necessary assistance (e.g. Bianco, 2001; Johnston and Carroll, 1998b). Wadey *et al.* (2011b) also found mobilising one's social support network can prove beneficial in the long term by increasing athletes' perception of social support and strengthening attachments to members of their support network upon their return to sport. It is important to acknowledge, however, that not all athletes will require or welcome tangible social support (e.g. those who have not lost their mobility or are just trying to maintain their independence). For these athletes, too much support, or support from those from whom it is not welcome, can be considered unhelpful, particularly if it poses a threat to self-esteem (e.g. Bianco, 2001; Johnston and Carroll, 1998b).

Rehabilitation

For many injured athletes rehabilitation can be extremely protracted, and a period characterised by uncertainty, frustration, and despair as they come to terms with the unpredictability of rehabilitation progress and subsequent recovery (e.g. Cecil *et al.*, 2009; Kolt, 2000; Petitpas and Danish, 1995). It is during this period that the majority of injured athletes will face the greatest number of challenges as they try to expedite their recovery and successful return to competitive sport (e.g. Bianco *et al.*, 1999; Evans *et al.*, 2000; Gould *et al.*, 1997a). The most common challenges during rehabilitation include those associated with physical incapacitation, isolation, contractual and financial issues, perceptions of control and autonomy, slowness of progress and setbacks, and the monotony of rehabilitation activities.

Typically, physical incapacitation and a lack of mobility, particularly during the early part of rehabilitation, will continue to disrupt athletes' ability to undertake normal daily activities (e.g. Evans *et al.*, 2000; Gould *et al.*, 1997a; Johnston and Carroll, 1998a). Indeed, the physical restriction imposed by the injury will heighten athletes' perceptions of loss and isolation, and feelings of frustration (e.g. Carson and Polman, 2008; Tracey, 2003; Udry *et al.*, 1997). During this time, while attending training and practice has the potential to help injured athletes maintain and strengthen important attachments to, for example, sources of self-identity, self-esteem, social support, and reinforcement and gratification, exposure to non-injured others' training and competing can also provide unwelcome reminders of a number of real and perceived losses (e.g. loss of status/role within the team, missed sporting opportunities, and loss of fitness and performance ability; Evans and Hardy, 1995; Evans *et al.*, 2011; Tracey, 2003; Wadey *et al.*, 2011). Indeed, the actual and perceived isolation caused by the injury can be a double-edged sword; it can remove athletes on the one hand from reminders of what they have lost as a result of injury, but on the other hand from important sources of support and motivation that might help them deal more effectively with the challenges associated with rehabilitation (e.g. Bianco, 2001; Carson and Polman, 2008; Gould *et al.*, 1997b).

Empirical research is equivocal on the effect of isolation on athletes' rehabilitation experience (e.g. Bianco *et al.*, 1999; Tracey, 2003; Udry *et al.*, 1997). The authors' own professional practice experience from working with injured athletes suggests that athletes should be encouraged to do what works for them. For some athletes this will mean withdrawing from all contact with their sport; for others, maintaining social contact; and for others, continued and full integration into the sporting environment. For professional athletes, however, contractual obligations may have some bearing on this decision (Bianco *et al.*, 1999; Evans *et al.*, 2000). For example, contractually athletes may be obliged to be in attendance at training and competitive games where they may be required to fulfil a team support role or meet and interact with sponsors. Fulfilling these and other obligations may be important, not least to alleviate the perceived threat that the injury may pose to their current professional contract or its renewal and, as a result, their future livelihood. Indeed, such obligations and incentives may impact not only on athletes' ability to cope with the demands of rehabilitation, but also on their adherence behaviours and subsequent rehabilitation outcomes (Brewer *et al.*, 2002; Wiese-Bjornstal *et al.*, 1998). For example, athletes may be more self-motivated to engage with and commit to a rehabilitation programme when a professional contract is at stake. On the flip side, however, obligations such as these may also detract from their perceptions of control and autonomy – a feature of athletes' rehabilitation experience that has been widely acknowledged to affect rehabilitation adherence (e.g. Brewer *et al.*, 2000; Laubach *et al.*, 1996; Murphy *et al.*, 1999).

Self-motivation is the factor most positively associated with athletes' rehabilitation adherence (e.g. Brewer *et al.*, 2003; Fields *et al.*, 1995; Levy *et al.*, 2008). Self-motivation and rehabilitation adherence are in turn influenced by a myriad of factors, including locus of control; task involvement; attributions for recovery to internal, stable and controllable factors; and an autonomy-supporting environment (cf. Brewer, 2007; Evans *et al.*, 2006a). The importance of these factors and their effect on rehabilitation outcomes is all the more salient because of the unpredictability of rehabilitation, the slowness of progress, and the potential for setbacks (e.g. Carson and Polman, 2008; Gould *et al.*, 1997a; Tracey, 2003). Indeed, one of the biggest challenges athletes face during rehabilitation is to avoid becoming disheartened by the slowness of rehabilitation progress. In addition, self-motivation to engage with rehabilitation programmes can be considerably reduced when athletes experience setbacks that threaten their rehabilitation goals and outcome expectancy. Both slowness of rehabilitation progress and setbacks can exacerbate athletes' preoccupation with the loss associated with injury, as well as their impatience to return to pre-injury levels of functioning (e.g. Bianco *et al.*, 1999; Evans *et al.*, 2000; Johnston and Carroll, 1998a). However, such concerns can also be manifested in the absence of setbacks and slowness of progress as a result of the monotony of rehabilitation activities, which can cause athletes to become demoralised and demotivated (e.g. Evans and Hardy, 2002a; Petitpas and Danish, 1995; Tracey, 2003). Indeed, research supports the need for variety within rehabilitation programmes to enhance not only athletes' self-motivation and rehabilitation adherence, but also their belief in the efficacy of their rehabilitation programme – features that are positively associated with rehabilitation outcomes (e.g. Molloy *et al.*, 2009; Thomee *et al.*, 2007).

Other factors that influence athletes' rehabilitation experience include the athlete's previous injury history, and their knowledge and understanding of their prescribed rehabilitation. On the one hand, previous experience of injury can facilitate coping through enhanced knowledge and understanding of what rehabilitation entails, and how to best deal with the associated challenges; on the other, it can prove disheartening and cause athletes to question their ability to either fully recover or remain injury free in the future (Bianco *et al.*, 1999; Evans *et al.*, 2000). In addition, knowledge and understanding of the prognosis and its implications for rehabilitation can help athletes cope more effectively with the challenges of injury, and prevent "over"- or non-adherence to prescribed activities (Bianco *et al.*, 1999; Carson and Polman, 2008; Gould *et al.*, 1997). The latter is important, because in their desire to expedite recovery injured athletes will mistakenly perceive more to be better in relation to completing rehabilitation activities. SPCs should alert injured athletes to the dangers of "over"-adherence, and the potential for experiencing setbacks and re-injury (Bianco, 2001; Evans *et al.*, 2000). In addition, greater knowledge and understanding is also likely to enhance athletes' perceptions of control, autonomy, and task involvement.

Based on the empirical research, professional practice literature, and our own experiences as SPCs, a number of approaches should be adopted and strategies employed to facilitate athletes' ability to cope with and successfully rehabilitate during this phase. During the early part of rehabilitation, the provision of emotional support and tangible assistance is essential to offset the detrimental effects of physical incapacitation, lack of mobility, and the associated disruption to athletes' ability to engage with and undertake normal daily activities (e.g. Bianco, 2001; Johnston and Carroll, 1998b; Rees *et al.*, 2010). Providers of this support should include family, friends, and, if appropriate, teammates. This support will also help to negate perceptions of isolation that may be caused by imposed or voluntary withdrawal from social and sport interaction. That said, support-providers should be cognisant of the athlete's need to withdraw from and avoid contact with the sporting environment and individuals associated with it, as opposed to welcome and indeed seek continued interaction and involvement (e.g. Bianco *et al.*, 1999; Evans *et al.*, 2000). Regardless, however, teammates and coaches will undoubtedly have an important role to play in the perception of available and provision of social support to enhance perceptions of belonging and worth within their sport, particularly if it conveys messages of esteem (e.g. Bianco and Eklund, 2001; Rees *et al.*, 2010).

As rehabilitation progresses, informational and tangible support that facilitates problem and/or task-focused coping has been reported to be particularly effective (e.g. Bianco, 2001; Evans *et al.*, 2000; Gould *et al.*, 1997b). Providers of this support will include coaches, medics, physiotherapists, and athletic trainers, and the focus of the support will be on treatment and rehabilitation regimes and activities, and sport-related activity and goals. For example, access to and information from physiotherapists and coaches have the potential to engender an autonomy-supporting, task-oriented environment that enhances athletes' knowledge and understanding of their injury, task involvement, perceptions of control and autonomy, and self-esteem. This in turn will promote treatment and rehabilitation efficacy, motivation, adherence, and rehabilitation outcomes – assuming, of course, the quality, timing, and appropriateness of the support messages conveyed (e.g. Bianco and Eklund, 2001; Green and Weinberg, 2001; Johnston and Carroll, 2000; Robbins and Rosenfeld, 2001). Indeed, both emotional and informational support has been found to be particularly important when rehabilitation progress is slow or setbacks are experienced (e.g. Bianco, 2001; Evans *et al.*, 2000). Information conveyed may include that relating to rehabilitation activities, feedback on rehabilitation progress relative to the original prognosis, and advice on conditioning and training activities that will facilitate subsequent return to training and competitive sport. Clearly, the most important feature of the support is that it is perceived to be supportive by the athlete and meets their specific needs – something that is frequently not the case (e.g. Bianco, 2001; Johnston and Carroll, 2000; Tracey, 2003).

In a number of studies, informational and technical support has taken the form of goal-setting (e.g. Evans *et al.*, 2000; Gilbourne *et al.*, 1996). Perhaps not surprisingly, there is much support in the injury literature for the use of goal-setting to enhance motivation and rehabilitation adherence through the creation of a task-oriented focus and environment (e.g. Carson and Polman, 2008; Duda *et al.*, 1989; Evans and Hardy, 2002b; Gould *et al.*, 1997b; Levy *et al.*, 2008; Taylor and May, 1993). Indeed, athletes who have demonstrated greater adherence have been found to be more goal-directed and self-motivated, and to place more emphasis on task- and/or mastery-involved goals. Alongside our own experiences as SPCs, research provides support for the use of both process and performance goals during rehabilitation (e.g. Evans and Hardy, 2002a; Evans *et al.*, 2000; Gould *et al.*, 1997b). The use of these goal types enhances a task-focused approach to rehabilitation and provides the basis of performance accomplishment information, which is essential for motivation and treatment and rehabilitation self-efficacy (e.g. Evans and Hardy, 2002b; Theodorakis *et al.*, 1996, 1997). Specifically, process goals can be used to focus on the correct execution of exercises during rehabilitation sessions, which will increase focus and self-confidence; and performance goals, which can centre on attaining specific standards within a specific time-frame (e.g. strength gains or increased range of movement), can be used to enhance motivation and self-confidence. However, a flexible approach to the use of goal-setting, wherein goals are regularly monitored and where necessary adjusted, is essential in accounting for the unpredictability of rehabilitation progress (e.g. Evans *et al.*, 2000; Evans and Hardy, 2002b); setting unrealistic goals or not achieving a goal can reduce motivation and self-efficacy (e.g. Evans and Hardy, 2002a; Johnston and Carroll, 1998a). Progress towards goals and adherence to rehabilitation programmes can be enhanced by the use of a daily diary, which provides athletes with an important evidence base to reinforce their rehabilitation progress. However, the use of goals will also serve to enhance athletes' treatment and rehabilitation efficacy and perception of control and autonomy through their involvement in the goal-setting process (cf. Kingston and Wilson, 2009). Importantly, it can also enhance communication and strengthen relationships between the athletes and treatment and rehabilitation providers, as well as coaches and conditioning personnel (Wadey *et al.*, 2011).

Adherence and the likelihood of attaining rehabilitation outcomes can also be enhanced through the use of psychological skills such as imagery, self-talk, relaxation, biofeedback, and stress inoculation training (e.g. Christakou and Zervas, 2007; Cupal and Brewer, 2001; Hare *et al.*, 2008; Johnson, 2000; Ross and Berger, 1996). Of these, we feel that imagery and self-talk, in particular, merit further attention here. Although there are some inconsistencies in the research that has explored the use of imagery during rehabilitation, the findings have generally provided support for the use of the cognitive, motivational, healing, and pain management functions of imagery (e.g. Driediger *et al.*, 2006; Evans *et al.*, 2006b; Law *et al.*, 2006; Sordoni *et al.*, 2000). Specifically, athletes have used imagery to image, for example, the damaged tissue healing, improved circulation around the point of injury, successful execution of rehabilitation exercises and activities, achieving short-term and long-term rehabilitation goals, and being confident and mentally tough. Using imagery in this way has been observed to increase athletes' understanding of the physiological basis of their injury and recovery process; motivation and rehabilitation adherence; positive attitude to rehabilitation; treatment and rehabilitation efficacy; and outcome expectancy. Informational support from, for example, physiotherapists, athletic trainers, and coaches can facilitate the effectiveness of imagery use through the provision of detailed written protocols, feedback on goal attainment, and visual images in the form of demonstrations, X-rays, and scans.

To date, self-talk has received limited research attention in the injury literature. However, drawing upon the extant literature (Gould *et al.*, 1997b; Ievleva and Orlick, 1991), anecdotal evidence (Shaffer and Wiese-Bjornstal, 1999; Smith, 1996), and our own professional practice experience, it appears that self-talk can serve a number of purposes during rehabilitation. Specifically, it can be used to direct attention during rehabilitation sessions to reinforce the correct execution of rehabilitation movements and techniques, and convey positive self-affirmations while pursuing, and following, goal attainment. In this regard, it can be used in conjunction with imagery to enhance motivation and self-efficacy. Sources of positive self-talk will include feedback from medical personnel and coaches, and the athletes' daily diary, which provides a record of goal achievement. In this way, self-talk can be used to offset the detrimental effects of slowness of rehabilitation progress and setbacks in recovery. Additional sources of self-talk to reinforce rehabilitation and treatment efficacy as well as outcome expectancy can include the use of other evidence bases, such as the results of scans, X-rays, and physiological tests demonstrating strength and range of movement gains. In essence, many of the sources of self-talk will also form the basis of informational support discussed earlier, which reinforces the importance of social support during rehabilitation.

Return to competitive sport

Research that has examined athletes' return to competitive sport suggests that the demands and responses experienced by injured athletes during this phase are often varied and complex (Andersen, 2001; Bianco, 2001; Brewer and Petitpas, 2005; Carson and Polman, 2008; Evans *et al.*, 2000; Podlog *et al.*, 2011; Podlog and Dionigi, 2010; Podlog and Eklund, 2005, 2006, 2007, 2009, 2010; Podlog *et al.*, 2010). That said, the literature can be synthesised round three recurrent themes: re-injury anxiety, the decision to return to sport, and returning to pre-injury levels of performance.

Of the aforementioned themes, the most salient for athletes during this phase is re-injury anxiety (e.g. Evans *et al.*, 2000; Johnston and Carroll, 1998a; Kvist *et al.*, 2005; Podlog and Eklund, 2007; Walker *et al.*, 2004). There are a number of demands and cognitions that precede re-injury anxiety; namely, lack of confidence in the injured body part, pain and soreness at the site of injury, performing the same skill in the same situation that the injury was incurred, concerns for potential setbacks, and the physical demands of training and competition (e.g. Bianco *et al.*, 1999; Cox, 2002; Podlog and Eklund, 2006). The resultant re-injury anxiety can manifest itself in several ways during athletes' return to training and competition, including holding back and not giving 100 per cent effort, avoiding situations that could cause (re-)injury, trying too hard and over-compensating in other aspects of training and performance, and questioning physical and psychological readiness to return – all of which can negatively impact sporting performance and increase the risk of (re-) injury (e.g. Andersen, 2001; Evans *et al.*, 2000; Johnston and Carroll, 1998a).

With regard to the decision to return to sport, although based traditionally on athletes' physical readiness, more recently researchers have acknowledged that physical readiness to return to sport is not necessarily synonymous with psychological readiness (e.g. Bauman, 2005; Evans *et al.*, 2000; Johnston and Carroll, 1998a; Kvist *et al.*, 2005; Podlog and Eklund, 2006, 2007). Put simply, athletes may be physically ready to return to sport well in advance of being psychologically ready. A number of factors will affect psychological readiness, including self-presentation concerns, feelings of disengagement and isolation from significant others (e.g. coaches and teammates), negative social comparison, re-injury anxiety, competitive anxiety, confidence in the injured body part and its ability to withstand sporting demands, fitness status (e.g. match/game fitness), prolonged time out from sport, time relative to the competitive season, reduced sport-confidence, and inadequate levels of emotional, informational, and esteem support (e.g. Gould *et al.*, 1997a; Kvist *et al.*, 2005; Podlog and Eklund, 2006, 2007; Udry *et al.*, 1997). For example, Podlog and Eklund (2006) found that athletes returning to sport had self-presentation concerns of not upholding their reputation and meeting the expectations of others, and perceiving that they will perform poorly in front of coaches, spectators, and fellow competitors. From the authors' professional practice experiences, these self-presentation concerns can be further intensified by, for example, losing their position in the team, and their non-injured counterparts making significant performance gains during their competitive absence.

The effect of internal and external demands should, however, not be underestimated in terms of athletes' decision to return to sport (e.g.

Bauman, 2005; Bianco *et al.*, 1999; Charlesworth and Young, 2004; Krane *et al.*, 1997; Murphy and Waddington, 2007; Podlog and Dionigi, 2010). Although extreme, Krane *et al.* described the experiences of a gymnast who reported insisting on returning to sport after rehabilitating from a career-threatening injury despite the doctors' assertions that another fall could render her permanently paralysed. This pressure to return can result from situational factors (e.g. proximity of important competitions and contractual obligations), the influence of significant others (e.g. coaches and family), and from within the athletes themselves (e.g. Bianco, 2001; Bianco *et al.*, 1999; Krane *et al.* 1997; Podlog and Eklund, 2009). Regardless of the source, however, the pressure can result in athletes returning prematurely and becoming (re-)injured (e.g. Johnston and Carroll, 1998a; Krane *et al.*, 1997; Podlog and Eklund, 2006). Interestingly, Gould *et al.* (1997) found that patience and taking it slowly was cited more by successful than unsuccessful recoverers from injury (i.e. those who returned to a performance level equal to, or exceeding, their pre-injury performance level). However, our own experiences as SPCs suggest that while "taking it slow" may facilitate a successful return, it might also be symptomatic of underlying concerns that have not been adequately addressed. Indeed, failure to achieve rehabilitation goals is likely to exacerbate self-doubts, which in turn can affect one's psychological readiness to return to sport.

Another challenge that injured athletes repeatedly experience during this phase is striving to attain pre-injury standards of performance – an important determinant of a successful return to sport (Podlog and Eklund, 2009). Unfortunately, injured athletes often have unrealistic expectations of their performance abilities when they initially return to sport (e.g. Bianco, 2001; Bianco *et al.*, 1999; Podlog and Eklund, 2007, 2009). For example, Bianco found:

> Some skiers naively believed that because they had worked so hard to recover and were disciplined in their rehabilitation, they would be able to perform at pre-injury levels. This erroneous belief led some skiers to have unrealistically high performance expectations for their return, and the failure to achieve these goals resulted in drops in confidence and doubts about regaining pre-injury form.
>
> (p. 383)

Indeed, a number of empirical studies have observed that the combination of high performance expectations and disappointing performances contributes to a decrease in athletes' self-confidence, which in turn leads to further decrements in performance as well as the potential for (re-) injury (e.g. Bianco *et al.*, 1999; Johnston and Carroll, 1998a; Podlog and Eklund, 2007). A number of factors can influence athletes' performance expectations, and the realisation of these expectations through performance attainment. These include the ability to regain their place on the team, secure opportunities to perform at pre-injury levels of competition (e.g. through selection processes), ensure teammates have confidence in their ability, withstand being targeted by players in opposing teams, the stigma of being a lesser athlete because of the injury, and meeting the performance expectations of others who may either have unrealistic expectations or be prejudiced against the player because of their time away as a result of the injury (e.g. supporters and media; Gould *et al.*, 1997a; Podlog and Eklund, 2007; Tracey, 2003). These factors have the potential to increase the pressure on athletes to return to pre-injury levels of performance while undermining confidence in their ability to achieve these levels. That said, it is important to acknowledge that some athletes may never return to pre-injury standards of performance (e.g. Carey *et al.*, 2006; Podlog and Eklund, 2006). For those who have the potential to return to pre-injury levels of functioning, research is equivocal as to how long it takes. Indeed, researchers have suggested it could take six weeks (Evans *et al.*, 2000), six months (Podlog and Eklund, 2006), 12 months (Bianco *et al.*, 1999), or even 24 months (Bianco, 2001) to regain pre-injury levels of performance. Obviously, the objective of the SPC is to help athletes set realistic performance expectations, and to work collaboratively with athletes, coaches, and medical staff to help expedite this process (Podlog and Eklund, 2009).

A number of strategies can be adopted by SPCs to address the aforementioned themes (e.g. Carson and Polman, 2009; Podlog and Dionigi, 2010; Podlog and Eklund, 2007). Strategies to lower and/or eradicate re-injury anxiety should focus on engendering confidence in the injury and the athlete's ability to meet the physical and technical demands of the sport. These strategies include emotional support, informational support, simulation training, and imagery (e.g. Bianco, 2001; Bianco *et al.*, 1999; Evans *et al.*, 2000; Johnston and Carroll, 1998a; Podlog and Eklund, 2006, 2007; Rotella and Campbell, 1983). Indeed, these strategies can help to provide an evidence base to eradicate or regulate any concerns that the athlete may have in their recovery and performance status during their return to sport. For example, informational support from medical personnel and coaches in relation to recovery status can help athletes overcome their re-injury anxiety by instilling confidence about the ability of the injury to withstand the demands associated with competitive sport, and, as a result, the potential for re-injury (e.g. Bianco, 2001; Carson and Polman, 2008; Podlog and Eklund, 2006, 2007). This informational support can take the form of verbal persuasion, based on evidence derived from X-ray and scan images and tests of physical function. Emotional support should take the form of listening to athletes' concerns, and providing empathy and reassurance. Simulation training should underpin athletes' return to sport to enable them to progressively approximate the demands of the competitive environment (e.g. Cox, 2002; Evans *et al.*, 2000; Podlog and

Eklund, 2007; Suinn, 1975). For example, Podlog and Eklund (2007) reported that coaches organised matches with lower-calibre opponents for athletes returning to sport in order to build their confidence, whereas Evans *et al.* (2000) reported using physical practice (e.g. static tackling with tackle bags to simulate training) and imagery (e.g. images of successfully achieving performance goals) to eradicate or regulate re-injury anxiety. Indeed, imagery could be used to complement simulation training by the athlete invoking images prior to and following simulated training and performance situations. For example, images of executing skills and strategies could reinforce correct technique and enhance self-confidence, whereas images of the injury withstanding injury-threatening situations, particularly the one in which the injury originally occurred, could offset re-injury anxiety.

Informational support can also help athletes to avoid returning prematurely and increasing their risk of re-injury (e.g. Bianco, 2001; Johnston and Carroll, 1998b; Podlog and Eklund, 2006, 2007). Indeed, Johnston and Carroll (1998a) found that the majority of the athletes they interviewed who returned prematurely received no informational support. Subsequent research has supported this finding, and observed that this support should be received from medical staff, coaches, and others with injury-specific knowledge and experience (e.g. Bianco, 2001; Podlog and Dionigi, 2010; Podlog and Eklund, 2007). The content of this support should include encouraging athletes not to rush their return, explicit instructions regarding what the athletes can and cannot do to facilitate their return, and learning from the experiences of others (e.g. athletes who re-injured themselves from returning to sport too soon, and those who made a successful transition back into competitive sport). SPCs can facilitate the provision of this support by enabling clear lines of communication between athletes, coaches, and medical staff that meet the needs of the athletes (Podlog and Dionigi, 2010; Podlog and Eklund, 2007). Finally, members of injured athletes' social support network (e.g. coaches and family members) should avoid pressurising them to return to sport too soon (cf. Krane *et al.*, 1997). Where athletes are tempted to return prematurely, the SPC should discuss with athletes, coaches, and parents the potentially detrimental effects of a premature return through, for example, the use of "what if?" scenarios (e.g. risk of re-injury and poor performance; Podlog *et al.*, 2011).

Athletes' aspirations once they return to sport are generally to attain pre-injury performance levels (Podlog and Eklund, 2009). However, it is essential that these aspirations are realistic and based on athletes' current physical, technical, tactical, and psychological status (e.g. Bianco, 2001; Cox, 2002; Podlog and Eklund, 2007). Collaboration between athletes and other members of the medical and coaching support team is essential to ensure the effectiveness of this process, which should be underpinned by goal-setting (e.g. Bianco *et al.*, 1999; Podlog and Dionigi, 2010;

Podlog and Eklund, 2007). Often informed by objective performance indicators, goals not only provide the stepping stones for attaining performance aspirations and increase a task focus, but also enhance self-confidence through performance accomplishment (e.g. Carson and Polman, 2008; Podlog and Eklund, 2006, 2007, 2009). Process goals in particular help focus athletes' attention on task-related activities and their requirements, as well as increasing self-confidence and motivation to set and achieve subsequent goals (e.g. Evans *et al.*, 2000; Podlog and Dionigi, 2010). Monitoring goal attainment as the basis for feedback is essential, given that previously injured athletes have reported taking between six weeks and 24 months to regain their self-confidence and pre-injury levels of performance (Bianco, 2001; Bianco *et al.*, 1999; Evans *et al.*, 2000; Podlog and Eklund, 2006). Indeed, goal attainment and the associated feedback can be used as the basis for verbal persuasion (e.g. positive self-talk) and imagery use (e.g. motivational imagery), which can enhance self-confidence and performance (e.g. Evans *et al.*, 2000; Hare *et al.*, 2008; Podlog and Eklund, 2006, 2007).

On a final note, it is increasingly becoming accepted that athletes can return to sport above and beyond their pre-injury levels of functioning (e.g. Bianco *et al.*, 1999; Podlog and Eklund, 2006, 2009; Udry *et al.*, 1997; Wadey *et al.*, 2011b). For example, Udry and colleagues found that 20 of the 21 injured US Ski Team members that they interviewed gained personal growth benefits (e.g. gaining a sense of perspective), psychological-based performance enhancements (e.g. increased mental toughness), and physical/technical development benefits (e.g. physical health improvement) following sport injury. Wadey *et al.* (2011b) recently extended this research by examining the mechanisms that led to these perceived benefits. These mechanisms included self-disclosure to others, mobilising one's social support network, taking the time to understand one's emotions, and reflective practice. In terms of the latter, the reflective practice literature emphasises the development of learning from experience (e.g. Ghaye and Ghaye, 1998; see also Chapter 12 in this book). Indeed, Ghaye and Ghaye suggested that reflection has the potential to empower individuals to become self-aware and implement change. It would therefore seem appropriate for SPCs to encourage injured athletes to foster a self-awareness that may help to generate a number of perceived benefits. Although there is no denying the suffering sport injury can cause, it is important that SPCs are cognisant that injury can provide an opportunity for growth and development for athletes.

Concluding comments

The purpose of this chapter has been to consider the challenges athletes experience when injured, and the implications for professional practice. Although the challenges reviewed in this chapter are not intended to be exhaustive, they purport to be some of the most prevalent experienced by injured athletes throughout their recovery. For many athletes, injury and the associated challenges pose a threat to the very core of their identity and ability to cope. This may mean that many athletes who normally respond well under stressful circumstances (e.g. the demands associated with competitive sport) think and behave in what are quite uncharacteristic ways that can be dysfunctional and maladaptive. However, with the appropriate support most athletes can make a successful return to competitive sport. The key to this successful return is to ensure that the support provided by practitioners meets the athlete's needs and facilitates coping. The SPC can play an important role in this process by providing support to athletes – and indeed other support-providers, such as medical personnel and coaches (e.g. enhancing their knowledge and understanding of the athlete's needs will help them more effectively meet those needs) – in terms of helping them mobilise support to meet their needs, and educating them about the use of specific skills and strategies. Of course this may require the SPC to initially help increase the athlete's awareness of their needs. Our goal within this chapter has been to enhance SPCs' knowledge and understanding of some of the ways in which they can help athletes deal with and overcome a number of challenges and potential barriers to progress, and in turn facilitate athletes' successful return to sport. By way of a summary, we conclude this chapter by synthesising the approaches that can be adopted and strategies employed with injured athletes during the three phases considered within this chapter.

Onset of injury

- Understand the athlete and not just the injury.
- Foster a working relationship with injured athletes that will enable them to disclose their thoughts and feelings.
- Provide emotional support and empathy by listening to the athletes' concerns – and reinforce that the intensity of these emotions is normal.
- Get athletes to consider the potential long-term consequences as well as the short-terms gains of competing while injured.
- Encourage athletes to learn about their injuries by speaking to knowledgeable others and seeking out information from other creditable sources (e.g. journals and credible internet sites).
- Raise athletes' awareness of who in their social support network can help them with everyday tasks, thereby increasing their perception of available social support.
- Encourage athletes to mobilise their social support networks to help them deal with the challenges that the injury presents – and reinforce that availing of support is a strength, not a weakness.

Rehabilitation

- Facilitate the provision of emotional support and get athletes to mobilise their support network to gain tangible support to help them with issues associated with mobility and doing normal daily activities.
- Discuss with athletes the potential for feeling isolated, and how best to deal with this.
- Encourage effective communication between athletes and medical and coaching personnel.
- Increase athletes' awareness of the unpredictability of rehabilitation progress and the potential for slowness of progress and setbacks (and reinforce the use of psychological skills and strategies to offset their potentially detrimental effects).
- Encourage a task- and mastery-oriented focus using process and performance goals.
- Create awareness with athletes and the medical support team of the need for goals to be flexible to account for the slowness of rehabilitation progress and setbacks.
- Encourage the use of a daily diary to monitor progress and provide a basis for feedback.
- Facilitate variety in the rehabilitation programme.
- Encourage the use of imagery and self-talk to facilitate healing, learn and refine rehabilitation skills and activities, and reinforce goal attainment.
- Increase the awareness of physiotherapists, athletic trainers, and coaches of the need to provide feedback that reinforces autonomy, progress, and goal attainment.
- Help athletes to become aware of the potential benefits they might gain during their injury experience.

Return to competitive sport

- Encourage members of injured athletes' support network to provide positive feedback to lower or eradicate re-injury anxiety.
- Provide athletes with informational support to prevent a premature return to sport.
- Facilitate clear lines of communication between athletes, coaches, and medical staff to ensure athletes are not rushing their return to sport.
- Challenge unrealistic performance expectations, and help athletes replace them with more realistic ones.
- Increase levels of self-confidence by drawing on available sources of self-efficacy (e.g. performance accomplishments and verbal persuasion).
- Encourage athletes through reflective practice to become self-aware of any potential long-term benefits they gained during their injury experience.
- Help injured athletes to physically and mentally simulate progressively the competitive environment, to reduce or eradicate re-injury anxiety.

References

Albinson, C. B. and Petrie, T. A. (2003). Cognitive appraisals, stress and coping: Pre-injury and postinjury factors influencing psychological adjustment to sport injury. *Journal of Sport Rehabilitation*, 12, 306–322.

Andersen, M. B. (2001). Returning to action and the prevention of future injury. In J. Crossman (ed.), *Coping with sports injuries: Psychological strategies for rehabilitation* (pp. 162–173). Melbourne, Victoria: Oxford University Press.

Appaneal, R. N., Levine, B. R., Perna, F. M., and Roh, J. (2009). Measuring postinjury depression among male and female competitive athletes. *Journal of Sport and Exercise Psychology*, 31, 60–76.

Apter, M. J. (1982). *The experience of motivation: The experience of psychological reversals*. London, UK: Academic Press.

Bandura, A. (1997). *Self-efficacy: The exercise of control*. New York, NY: Freeman.

Bauman, J. (2005). Returning to play: The mind does matter. *Journal of Clinical Sports Medicine*, 15, 432–435.

Bianco, T. (2001). Social support and recovery from sport injury: Elite skiers share their experiences. *Research Quarterly for Exercise and Sport*, 72, 376–388.

Bianco, T. and Eklund. R. C. (2001). Conceptual consideration for social support research in sport and exercise settings: The case of sport injury. *Journal of Sport and Exercise Psychology*, 23, 85–107.

Bianco, T., Malo, S., and Orlick, T. (1999). Sport injury and illness: Elite skiers describe their experiences. *Research Quarterly for Exercise and Sport*, 70, 157–169.

Brewer, B. W. (1993). Self-identity and specific vulnerability to depressed mood. *Journal of Personality*, 61, 343–364.

Brewer, B. W. (2007). Psychology of sport injury rehabilitation. In G. Tenenbaum and R. C. Eklund (eds), *Handbook of sport psychology* (3rd edn, pp. 404–424). Hoboken, NJ: Wiley.

Brewer, B. W., Linder, D. E., and Phelps, C. M. (1995). Situational correlates of emotional adjustment to athletic injury. *Clinical Journal of Sport Medicine*, 5, 241–245.

Brewer, B. W., Cornelius, A. E., Van Raalte, J. L., Petitpas, A. J., Sklar, J. H., Pohlman, M. H. *et al.* (2000). Attributions for recovery and adherence to rehabilitation following anterior cruciate ligament reconstruction: A prospective analysis. *Psychology and Health*, 15, 283–291.

Brewer, B. W., Andersen, M. B., and Van Raalte, J. L. (2002). Psychological aspects of sport injury rehabilitation: Toward a biopsychosocial approach. In D. L. Mostofsky and L. D. Zaichkowsky (eds), *Medical and psychological aspects of sport and exercise* (p. 41–54). Morgantown, WV: Fitness Information Technology.

Brewer, B. W., Cornelius, A. E., Van Raalte, J. L., Petitpas, A. J., Sklar, J. H., Pohlman, M. H. *et al.* (2003). Age-related differences in predictors of adherence to rehabilitation after anterior cruciate ligament reconstruction. *Journal of Athletic Training*, 38, 158–162.

Brewer, B. W., Cornelius, A. E., Van Raalte, J. L., Brickner, J. C., Sklar, J. H., Corsetti, J. R. *et al.* (2004). Rehabilitation adherence and anterior cruciate ligament outcomes. *Psychology, Health and Medicine*, 9, 163–175.

Brewer, B. W. and Petitpas, A. J. (2005). Returning to self: The anxieties of coming back after injury. In M. B. Andersen (ed.), *Sport psychology in practice* (pp. 93–108). Champaign, IL: Human Kinetics.

Carey, J. L., Huffman, G. R., Parekh, S. G., and Sennett, B. J. (2006). Outcomes of anterior cruciate ligament injuries to running backs and wide receivers in the National Football League. *American Journal of Sports Medicine*, 34, 1911–1917.

Carson, F. and Polman, R. C. J. (2008). ACL injury rehabilitation: A psychological case-study of a professional rugby union player. *Journal of Clinical Sport Psychology*, 2, 71–90.

Cecil, S., Brandon, R., and Moore, J. (2009). An integrated multi-disciplinary support service for an injured rugby union lock. In B. Hemmings and T. Holder (eds). *Applied sport psychology: A case-based approach* (pp. 203–222). Chichester, UK: John Wiley and Sons Ltd.

Charlesworth, H. and Young, K. (2004). Why English female university athletes play with pain: Motivations and rationalisations. In K. Young (ed.), *Sporting bodies, damaged selves: Sociological studies of sport related injury* (pp. 163–180). Oxford, UK: Elsevier.

Christakou, A. and Zervas, Y. (2007). The effectiveness of imagery on pain, edema, and range of motion in athletes with a grade II ankle sprain. *Physical Therapy in Sport*, 8, 130–140.

Collins, D. J., Moore, P. M., Mitchell, D., and Alpress, F. (2009). Role conflict and confidentiality in multidisciplinary athlete support programmes. *British Journal of Sports Medicine*, 33, 208–211.

Cox, R. (2002). The psychological rehabilitation of a severely injured rugby player. In I. Cockerill (ed.), *Solutions in sport psychology* (pp. 159–172). London, UK: Thompson.

Cupal, D. D. and Brewer, B. W. (2001). Effects of relaxation and guided imagery on knee strength, re-injury anxiety, and pain following anterior cruciate ligament reconstruction. *Rehabilitation Psychology*, 46, 28–43.

Daly, J. M., Brewer, B. W., Van Raalte, J. L., Petitpas, A. J., and Sklar, J. H. (1995). Cognitive appraisal, emotional adjustment, and adherence to rehabilitation following knee surgery. *Journal of Sport Rehabilitation*, 4, 23–30.

Driediger, M., Hall, C., and Callow, N. (2006). Imagery use by injured athletes: A qualitative analysis. *Journal of Sports Sciences*, 24, 261–271.

Duda, J. L., Smart, A. E., and Tappe, M. K. (1989). Predictors of adherence in rehabilitation of athletic injuries. *Journal of Sport and Exercise Psychology*, 11, 367–381.

Evans, L. and Hardy, L. (1995). Sport injury and grief responses: A review. *Journal of Sport and Exercise Psychology*, 17, 227–245.

Evans, L. and Hardy, L. (2002a). Injury rehabilitation: A qualitative follow-up study. *Research Quarterly for Exercise and Sport*, 73, 320–329.

Evans, L. and Hardy, L. (2002b). Injury rehabilitation: A goal-setting intervention study. *Research Quarterly for Exercise and Sport*, 73, 310–319.

Evans, L., Hardy, L., and Fleming, S. (2000). Intervention strategies with injured athletes: An action research study. *The Sport Psychologist*, 14, 188–206.

Evans, L., Mitchell, I., and Jones, S. (2006a). Psychological responses to sport injury: A review of current research. In S. Hanton and S. D. Mellalieu (eds), *Literature reviews in sport psychology* (pp. 289–319). Hauppage, NY: Nova Science.

Evans, L., Hare, R., and Mullen, R. (2006b). Imagery use during rehabilitation from injury. *Journal of Imagery Research in Sport and Physical Activity*, 1, 1–19.

Evans, L., Wadey, R., Hanton, S., and Mitchell, I. (2011). Stressors experienced by injured athletes. *Journal of Sports Sciences*, under review.

Fields, J., Murphy, M., Horodyski, M., and Stopka, C. (1995). Factors associated with adherence to sport injury rehabilitation in college-age recreational athletes. *Journal of Sport Rehabilitation*, 4, 172–180.

Gallagher, B. V. and Gardner, F. L. (2007). An examination of the relationship between early maladaptive schemas, coping, and emotional response to athletic injury. *Journal of Clinical Sport Psychology*, 1, 47–67.

Gayman, A. M. and Crossman, J. (2003). A qualitative analysis of how the timing of the onset of sports injuries influences athlete reactions. *Journal of Sport Behaviour*, 26, 255–271.

Gilbourne, D., Taylor, A. H., Downie, G., and Newton, P. (1996). Goal-setting during sports injury rehabilitation: a presentation of underlying theory, administration procedure, and an athlete case study. *Sports Exercise and Injury*, 2, 192–201.

Gould, D., Udry, E., Bridges, D., and Beck, L. (1997a). Stress sources encountered when rehabilitating from season-ending ski injuries. *The Sport Psychologist*, 11, 361–378.

Gould, D., Udry, E., Bridges, D., and Beck, L. (1997b). Coping with season ending injuries. *The Sport Psychologist*, 11, 379–399.

Ghaye, A. and Ghaye, K. (1998). *Teaching and learning through critical reflective practice*. London, UK: David Fulton.

Green, S. L. and Weinberg, R. S. (2001). Relationships among athletic identity, coping skills, social support, and the psychological impact of injury in recreational participants. *Journal of Applied Sport Psychology*, 13, 40–59.

Grove, J. R. and Creswell, S. L. (2007). Personality correlates of appraisal, stress, and coping during injury rehabilitation. In D. Pargman (ed.). *Psychological bases of sport injuries* (pp. 79–94). Morgantown, WV: Fitness Information Technology.

Hare, R., Evans, L., and Callow, N. (2008). Imagery use during rehabilitation from injury. A case study of an elite athlete. *The Sport Psychologist*, 22, 405–422.

Henderson, J. C. (2007). Suicide in sport: Athletes at risk. In D. Pargman (ed.), *Psychological bases of sport injuries* (pp. 267–289). Morgantown, WV: Fitness Information Technology.

Holmes, K. (2005). *Black, white and gold: My autobiography*. London, UK: Virgin Books Ltd.

Ievleva, L. and Orlick, T. (1991). Mental links to enhanced healing: An exploratory study. *The Sports Psychologist*, 5, 25–40.

Johnson, U. (1997). A three-year follow-up of long-term injured competitive athletes: Influence of psychological risk factors on rehabilitation. *Journal of Sport Rehabilitation*, 6, 256–271.

Johnson, U. (2000). Short-term psychological intervention: A study of long-term injured competitive athletes. *Journal of Sport Rehabilitation*, 9, 207–218.

Johnston, L. H. and Carroll, D. (1998a). The context of emotional responses to athletic injury: A qualitative analysis. *Journal of Sport Rehabilitation*, 7, 206–220.

Johnston, L. H. and Carroll, D. (1998b). The provision of social support to injured athletes: A qualitative analysis. *Journal of Sport Rehabilitation*, 7, 267–284.

Johnston, L. H. and Carroll, D. (2000). Coping, social support, and injury: Changes over time and the effects of level of sports involvement. *Journal of Sport Rehabilitation*, 9, 290–303.

Kingston, K. and Wilson, K. (2009). The application of goal setting in sport. In S. D. Mellalieu and S. Hanton (eds), *Advances in applied sport psychology: A review* (pp. 75–123). New York, NY: Routledge.

Kolt, G. S. (2000). Doing sport psychology with injured athletes. In M. Andersen (ed.), *Doing sport psychology* (pp. 223–236). Champaign, IL: Human Kinetics.
Krane, V., Greenleaf, C. A., and Snow, J. (1997). Reaching for gold and the price of glory: A motivational case study of an elite gymnast. *The Sport Psychologist*, 11, 53–71.
Kübler-Ross, E. (1969). *On death and dying*. London, UK: Tavistock.
Kvist, J., Ek, A., Sporrstedt, K., and Good, L. (2005). Fear of re-injury: A hindrance for returning to sports after anterior cruciate ligament reconstruction. *Knee Surgery, Sports Traumatology, Arthroscopy*, 14, 393–397.
Laubach, W. J., Brewer, B. W., Van Raalte, J. L., and Petitpas, A. J. (1996). Attributions for recovery and adherence to sport injury rehabilitation. *Australian Journal of Science and Medicine in Sport*, 28, 30–34.
Law, B., Driediger, M., Hall, C., and Forwell, L. (2006). Imagery use, perceived pain, limb functioning and satisfaction in athletic injury rehabilitation. *New Zealand Journal of Physiotherapy*, 34, 10–16.
Lazarus, R. S. (2000). How emotions influence performance in competitive sports. *The Sport Psychologist*, 14, 229–252.
Leddy, M. H., Lambert, M. J., and Oges, B. M. (1994). Psychological consequences of athletic injury among high-level competitors. *Research Quarterly for Exercise and Sport*, 65, 347–354.
Levy, A. R., Polman, R. C. J., and Clough, P. J. (2008). Adherence to sport injury rehabilitation programs: An integrated psychosocial approach. *Scandinavian Journal of Medicine and Sciences in Sports*, 18, 798–809.
Maehr, M. L. and Braskamp, L. A. (1986). *The motivation factor: A theory of personal investment*. Lexington, MA: D.C. Heath and Company.
Mankad, A., Gordon, S., and Wallman, K. (2009). Perceptions of emotional climate among injured athletes. *Journal of Clinical Sport Psychology*, 3, 1–14.
Molloy, G. J., Sniehotta, F., and Johnston, M. (2009). Two alternative models of health behaviour and recovery from activity limitations due to acute injury: A prospective study. *Psychology and Health*, 24, 271–285.
Murphy, G. C., Foreman, P. E., Simpson, C. A., Molloy, G. N., and Molloy, E. K. (1999). The development of a locus of control measure predictive of injured athletes' adherence to treatment. *Journal of Occupational and Organisational Psychology*, 72, 83–99.
Murphy, P. and Waddington, I. (2007). Are elite athletes exploited? *Journal of Sport and Social Issues*, 10, 239–255.
Petitpas, A. and Danish, S. J. (1995). Caring for injured athletes. In S. M. Murphy (ed.), *Sport psychology interventions* (pp. 255–282). Champaign, IL: Human Kinetics.
Podlog, L. and Dionigi, R. (2010). Coach strategies for addressing psychosocial challenges during the return to sport from injury. *Journal of Sports Sciences*, 28, 1197–1208.
Podlog, L. and Eklund, R. C. (2005). Return to sport after serious injury: A retrospective examination of motivation and psychological outcomes. *Journal of Sport Rehabilitation*, 14, 20–34.
Podlog, L. and Eklund, R. C. (2006). A longitudinal investigation of competitive athletes' return to sport following serious injury. *Journal of Applied Sport Psychology*, 18, 48–68.
Podlog, L. and Eklund, R. C. (2007). Professional coaches' perspectives on the return to sport following serious injury. *Journal of Applied Sport Psychology*, 19, 207–225.

Podlog, L. and Eklund, R. C. (2009). High-level athletes' perceptions of success in returning to sport following injury. *Psychology of Sport and Exercise*, 10, 535–544.

Podlog, L. and Eklund, R. C. (2010). Returning to competition after a serious injury: The role of self-determination. *Journal of Sports Sciences*, 28, 819–831.

Podlog, L., Lochbaum, M., and Stevens, T. (2010). Need satisfaction, well-being, and perceived return-to-sport outcomes among injured athletes. *Journal of Applied Sport Psychology*, 22, 167–182.

Podlog, L., Dimmock, J., and Miller, J. (2011). A review of return to sport concerns following injury rehabilitation: Practitioner strategies for enhancing recovery outcomes. *Physical Therapy in Sport*, 12, 36–42.

Quinn, A. M. and Fallon, B. J. (1999). The changes in psychological characteristics and reactions of elite athletes from injury onset until full recovery. *Journal of Applied Sport Psychology*, 11, 210–229.

Rees, T., Mitchell, I., Evans, L., and Hardy, L. (2010). Stressors, social support psychological response to sports injury in high and low-performance standard participants. *Psychology of Sport and Exercise*, 11, 505–512.

Robbins, J. E. and Rosenfeld, L. B. (2001). Athletes' perceptions of social support provided by their head coach, assistant coach, and athletic trainer, pre-injury and during rehabilitation. *Journal of Sport Behaviour*, 3, 277–297.

Rogers, R. W. (1975). A protection motivation theory of feat appeals and attitude change. *Journal of Psychology*, 91, 93–114.

Ross, M. J. and Berger, R. S. (1996). Effects of stress inoculation on athletes' post-surgical pain and rehabilitation after orthopaedic injury. *Journal of Consulting and Clinical Psychology*, 64, 406–410.

Rotella, R. J. and Campbell, M. S. (1983). Systematic desensitisation: Psychological rehabilitation of injured athletes. *Athletic Training*, 18, 149–152.

Ryan, R. and Deci, E. L. (2000). Self-determination theory and the facilitation of intrinsic motivation, social development and well-being. *American Psychologist*, 55, 68–78.

Shaffer, S. M. and Wiese-Bjornstal, D. M. (1999). Psychosocial interventions strategies in sports medicine. In R. Ray and D. M. Wiese-Bjornstal (eds), *Counselling in sports medicine* (pp. 41–54). Champaign, IL: Human Kinetics.

Sordoni, C., Hall, C., and Forwell, L. (2000). The use of imagery by athletes during rehabilitation. *Journal of Applied Sport Psychology*, 3, 329–338.

Smith, A. M. (1996). Psychological impact of injuries in athletes. *Sports Medicine*, 9, 352–369.

Smith, A. M. and Milliner, E. K. (1994). Injured athletes and the risk of suicide. *Journal of Athletic Training*, 29, 337–341.

Smith, A. M., Scott, S. G., O'Fallon, W. M., and Young, M. L. (1990). Emotional responses of athletes to injury. *Mayo Clinic Proceedings*, 65, 38–50.

Suinn, R. M. (1975). *Behavior modification for athletic injury.* Fort Collins, CO: Colorado State University.

Taylor, A. H. and May, S. (1996). Threat and coping appraisal as determinants of compliance to sports injury rehabilitation: An application of protection motivation theory. *Journal of Sports Sciences*, 14, 471–482.

Taylor, J. and Taylor, S. (1997). *Psychological approaches to sport injury rehabilitation.* Gaithersburg, MD: Aspen.

Theodorakis, Y., Malliou, P., Papaioannou, A., Beneca, A., and Filactakidou, A. (1996). The effect of personal goals, self-efficacy, and self-satisfaction on injury rehabilitation. *Journal of Sport Rehabilitation*, 5, 214–223.

Theodorakis, Y., Beneca, A., Malliou, P., and Goudas, M. (1997). Examining psychological factors during injury rehabilitation. *Journal of Sport Rehabilitation*, 6, 355–363.

Thomee, P., Wahrborg, M., Borjesson, R., Thomee, R., Eriksson, B. I., and Karlsson, J. (2007). Self-efficacy, symptoms and physical activity in patients with an anterior cruciate ligament injury: A prospective study. *Scandinavian Journal of Medicine and Science in Sports*, 17, 238–245.

Tracey, J. (2003). The emotional response to the injury and rehabilitation process. *Journal of Applied Sport Psychology*, 15, 279–293.

Tracey, J. (2008). Inside the clinic: Health professionals' role in their clients' psychological rehabilitation. *Journal of Sport Rehabilitation*, 17, 413–431.

Tripp, D. A., Stanish, W., Ebel-Lam, A., Brewer, B. W., and Birchard, J. (2007). Fear of re-injury, negative affect, and catastrophising predicting return to sport in recreational athletes with anterior cruciate ligament injuries at 1 year postinjury. *Rehabilitation Psychology*, 52, 74–81.

Udry, E. (1997). Coping and social support among injured athletes following surgery. *Journal of Sport and Exercise Psychology*, 19, 71–90.

Udry, E., Gould, D., Bridges, D., and Beck, L. (1997). Down but not out: Athlete responses to season-ending injuries. *Journal of Sport and Exercise Psychology*, 19, 229–248.

Vergeer, I. (2006). Exploring the mental representation of athletic injury: A longitudinal case study. *Psychology of Sport and Exercise*, 7, 99–114.

Wadey, R., Evans, L., Hanton, S., and Neil, R. (2011a). Examining hardiness throughout the sport injury process. *British Journal of Health Psychology*, in press.

Wadey, R., Evans, L., Evans, K., and Mitchell, I. (2011b). Examining the antecedents and mechanisms underlying the perceived benefits following sport injury. *Journal of Applied Sport Psychology*, 23, 142–158.

Walker, N., Thatcher, J., Lavallee, D., and Golby, J. (2004). The emotional response to athletic injury: Re-injury anxiety. In D. Lavallee, J. Thatcher, and M. V. Jones (eds), *Coping and emotion in sport* (pp. 91–103). Hauppauge, NY: Nova Science.

Wiese-Bjornstal, D. M., Smith, A. M., Shaffer, S. M., and Morrey, M. A. (1998). An integrated model of response to sport injury: Psychological and sociological dynamics. *Journal of Applied Sport Psychology*, 10, 46–69.

6 Professional practice issues in athlete burnout

Kate Goodger and Göran Kenttä

Abstract

At some point, you may find yourself in a situation of trying to support an athlete struggling with something that seems to be a case of burnout. Perhaps you pick up a book chapter or journal article to learn more about the phenomenon, and how to work with the athlete. Unfortunately, you will instead find that things are not so straightforward when it comes to working with cases of burnout. The field has been plagued by conceptual confusion and conflict (Cresswell and Eklund, 2006a; Hodge *et al.*, 2008), and, not surprisingly, burnout is poorly understood as an applied area (Raedeke *et al.*, 2002). This chapter supports professionals by exploring the guts of the athlete burnout literature in order to raise awareness of the issues that challenge professional practice. The field's historical development; conceptual confusion around definitions, measurement, explanations of burnout, and related constructs (e.g. overtraining and depression); and pertinent research and theories framed under *types* of athlete burnout (i.e. social-psychologically driven and physically driven) are all discussed. Implications for professional practice towards diagnosis, assessment, prevalence, and intervention approaches are considered in the conclusion to the chapter, alongside the presentation of a novel screening tool that can be employed in cases of physically-driven burnout.

Keywords: burnout, overtraining, recovery, stress, job stress, depression, fatigue/exhaustion, health, well being, motivation, engagement, commitment, perfectionism, identity, screening-tool, prevention, rehabilitation

Introduction to the chapter and conceptual area

At some point in time, you may find yourself in a situation trying to support an athlete struggling with something that seems to be a case of burnout. Likely, you want to know more about the phenomenon – so what do you do? Perhaps you will attempt to pick up a book chapter or journal article on athlete burnout in order to find some solid knowledge and answers. Unfortunately, you will instead find that things are not so straightforward when it comes to working with cases of burnout. The field has been plagued by conceptual confusion and conflict (Cresswell and Eklund, 2006a; Hodge *et al.*, 2008), and, not surprisingly, burnout is poorly understood as an applied area (Raedeke *et al.*, 2002). Author George Kohlrieser (2006) offers the metaphor "Put the fish on the table" as a tool to resolve mudded and conflicted issues. He explains that each time we want to eat a fish supper, someone has to clean and prepare the fish. If a fish is left under the table it will start to rot and smell, and leaving it there means that things will simply only get worse. Kohlrieser encourages that we put the fish on the table and go through the mess of cleaning it (the conflict or issue) in order to have a delicious fish supper (solution). When we accepted the invitation to write this chapter, we saw it as an exciting opportunity to support practitioners in the field of sport. Our intention is to put the fish *on* the table and examine the guts of athlete burnout. This will be done with the purpose of raising awareness of how various issues of burnout impact professional practice.

The chapter begins with a brief look at the historical development of burnout before moving on to pick our way through the conceptual confusion that has plagued the field. Specifically, we explore the challenges around defining, measuring, and explaining burnout. To continue in our attempt to offer professionals greater clarity in working with burnout, the next section of the chapter distinguishes burnout and related constructs, including overtraining, recovery, depression, and job stress. An overview of the athlete burnout literature including pertinent research and theories is then presented in line with Gould *et al.*'s (1996a) types of athlete burnout (i.e. social-psychologically driven and physically driven). Professional practice issues are then brought together in a final section that looks at implications for both applied practice and research. Diagnosis, assessment, prevalence, and intervention approaches are examined, together with the presentation of a novel screening tool that practitioners can use in the one-to-one consultancy setting with cases of physically-driven burnout.

A short history of burnout

Traditionally, researchers have described burnout as an enduring experiential syndrome that manifests as a reaction to chronic psychological and psychosocial stressors (Cresswell and Eklund, 2006b; Maslach *et al.*, 2001; Schaufeli and Salanova, 2007). At its core is the gradual depletion and erosion of an individual's intrinsic energetic resources. Due to the prolonged nature of the process, Shirom (2009) and Etzion (1987) proposed that burnout can remain undetected for some time, and, as a consequence, is rarely subject to any coping efforts.

Burnout originated with, and was initially restricted to, those who did "people work" of some kind (Maslach *et al.*, 2001; Schaufeli and Salanova,

2007). Contemporary researchers and practitioners consider Herbert Freudenberger (1974) to be the founding father, when he first coined the term to label a type of exhaustion he observed in young volunteers experiencing energy depletion and loss of motivation and commitment when he was working in a New York Free Clinic for drug addicts. Although scholarly enquiry began in human care settings, Freudenberger (1975) did not consider burnout to be exclusive to this domain but rather that it was likely to exist in other settings, including sport. The concept has subsequently broadened to span all occupations (Maslach *et al.*, 2001), and its introduction to sport began through the work of Caccese and Mayerberg (1984) examining burnout amongst coaches. Later, Cohn (1990) and Silva (1990) made the first empirical attempts to study burnout in the population of athletes. Interestingly, by 1952 the Swedish media were already claiming that one of the greatest endurance athletes, Gunder Hägg, was burned out. He was a middle-distance runner who, between the years 1939 and 1945, broke a number of world records at distances between 1,500 and 5,000 metres. This was possibly the first mention ever of sport-related burnout in the media.

Conceptual confusion

The purpose of this section of the chapter is to clarify some issues that have previously been unclear and confusing. From its inception "burnout" has had an evocative power, and quickly became (and continues to be) a highly popularised term. In health- and work-related psychology it is a major area of research, with more than 5,000 publications recorded, but it is also something that resonates with the layman and is a colloquialism of modern culture. The media have been instrumental in popularising burnout, yet the concept has generated much more than this. The term "burnout" captures the realities of people's experiences of the stresses and strains of modern life, and is simply something that each individual can identify and relate to in their own way. Therein, however, lies the Achilles heel of the burnout research field, and the origin of our confusion.

Maslach (1993) explains that the original appeal of burnout was that it provided an explanation for a phenomenon that was not unknown but was rarely acknowledged and discussed openly. At the time there was denial surrounding these types of experiences within people's professional lives, and it was a taboo subject in some occupations (a situation that is still evident in some professional sport: see, for example, Cresswell and Eklund, 2007a). Schaufeli and Enzmann (1998) describe the rapid and widespread commercial and media interest in burnout as the "booming burnout business", during which a proliferation of workshops, seminars, and self-help strategies designed to help combat burnout emerged. This was also set against the backdrop of Freudenberger's (1974) clinical perspective of burnout that emphasised a focus on symptoms of burnout and mental health issues. The resulting impact was that early work in the field was based upon unsystematic observation that had no clear conceptual underpinning, which led to descriptive, impressionistic, and selective accounts of burnout (Schaufeli and Enzmann, 1998). The emphasis on symptoms in particular generated a "laundry list approach" (i.e. a list of more than 200 symptoms), which risked the concept becoming blurred and all-encompassing, meaning very different things to different people, and, potentially, in danger of hardly meaning anything at all (Schaufeli and Buunk, 2003).

With some irony, then, Maslach and Leiter (1997) commented that the popularity of burnout actually left the concept vulnerable to burning out from overuse, and it is therefore possible to see how this early history contributed to conceptual underpinnings that lacked rigor and robustness. Although it is fair to say research has moved on since, and demonstrates considerably greater methodological rigor and more comprehensive conceptual approaches (Schaufeli and Buunk, 2003), three main threads of confusion continue to challenge the field. These have hindered progress in the parent domain of professional burnout as well as sport, and include (1) how burnout is defined, (2) how it is measured, and (3) how it can be explained.

Defining burnout

The absence of a universal definition of burnout has most hindered advancements to the understanding of the concept (Cox *et al.*, 2005; Cresswell and Eklund, 2006a; Shirom, 2005). The lack of agreement has meant simply that, operationally, scholars and practitioners are not necessarily looking at the same phenomenon. The attainment of a consensus on how burnout is defined has been exacerbated by three key issues, namely: (1) difficulty in identifying clear boundaries that distinguish it from related conditions (i.e. anxiety, depression, and overtraining); (2) authors confusing antecedents, characteristics, and consequences of burnout; and (3) the applicability of definitions of professional burnout transferred to the sport context. The issues of burnout and related conditions, and the confusion relating to antecedents, characteristics, and consequences, will be examined in more detail later in the chapter.

Initial work investigating athlete burnout (e.g. Coakley, 1992, Cohn, 1990, Gould *et al.*, 1996b) employed the popular definition by Smith (1986) of burnout as a "psychological, emotional and at times physical withdrawal from a formerly pursued and enjoyable activity in response to excessive stress or dissatisfaction" (p. 39), and led to burnout being conceptualised as a withdrawal-based phenomena. Since the late 1990s researchers have begun to move away from this definition, citing that it fails to differentiate adequately between athletes who withdraw from sport because of burnout versus other reasons for leaving sport (Raedeke and

Smith, 2001). An alternative definition by Raedeke (1997) has gained significant support in recent years (e.g. Creswell and Eklund, 2006b; Goodger *et al.*, 2007a; Raedeke *et al.*, 2002) and is based upon an original conceptualisation of professional burnout advanced by Maslach and Jackson (1984). Maslach and Jackson described burnout as, "a psychological syndrome of emotional exhaustion, depersonalisation, and reduced sense of performance accomplishment that can occur among individuals who work with people in some capacity" (1984, p. 134). This definition has become one of the most widely utilised within the professional domain, and, as research has extended across an increasing number of occupations, has been modified to encapsulate a crisis in one's relationship with work in general, rather than a crisis in one's relationship with people at work. Concern has been expressed that the transference of conceptualisations of burnout from the professional domain to sport has previously shown little consideration of how it might manifest differently based upon the demands of the athletic environment (Cresswell and Eklund, 2006c), and Maslach and Schaufeli (1993) also warn that there is danger in transplanting Maslach and Jackson's conceptualisation uncritically to different contexts. Heeding this advice, Raedeke (1997) applied the same strategy as the original authors to shape an athlete-specific definition of burnout by identifying common signs and symptoms associated with the phenomenon in the athletic context, and aligning these with the core element of sport: performance. The output of Raedeke's work resulted in the modification of the three original dimensions to describe athletic burnout as "a syndrome of physical/emotional exhaustion, sport devaluation, and reduced athletic accomplishment" (p. 398). Physical and emotional exhaustion is associated with the demands of intense training and competition schedules, and experiences of a reduced sense of accomplishment with an athlete's skills and abilities, where they may be unable to achieve personal goals, or perform below expectations. Depersonalisation was not identified as salient to athlete burnout, and instead the dimension of *sport devaluation* emerged; this is characterised by a loss of interest, and negative attitudes such as a "don't care" attitude, and resentment. In comparison, burnout in domains outside of the traditional service-provider relationship has been defined as a crisis in one's relationship with work, not necessarily as a crisis in one's relationships with people at work. This is reflected in replacing depersonalisation with cynicism that describes a pronounced distant attitude towards work (Maslach *et al.*, 1996).

Measuring burnout

It is reasonable, if we struggle to know what burnout is, that we would also struggle to know how to measure it. The attainment of a valid and reliable approach to assess burnout among athlete populations has been a longstanding quest within empirical research (Dale and Weinberg, 1990; Fender,

1989), and has led to variability in the rigor of research designs (Goodger *et al.*, 2007a). In addition, there has been long standing criticism of a bias towards cross sectional designs and the pre-dominance of self-report measures over other approaches (Cresswell and Eklund, 2006a; Goodger *et al.*, 2007a). There have, however, been significant strides made in the last decade towards the advancement of an athlete-specific measure of burnout.

The widespread acceptance of Maslach and Jackson's (1984) three-dimensional conceptualisation of burnout is due in part to its operationalisation through the development of the Maslach Burnout Inventory (MBI; Maslach and Jackson, 1981), a self-report tool that measures burnout across the three dimensions. Although not devoid of critics, this instrument has "almost been universally accepted as the gold standard" in assessing burnout (Schutte *et al.*, 2000, p. 53). Following Maslach and Jackson's (1984) lead, Raedeke (1997) has sought to operationalise his three dimensions of athlete burnout through the development of the Athlete Burnout Questionnaire (ABQ; Raedeke and Smith, 2001, 2009). The ABQ comprises three five-item subscales that assess physical and emotional exhaustion, sport devaluation, and reduced sense of athletic accomplishment. Responses to each item are scored on a five-point Likert scale ranging from 1 (Almost never) to 5 (Almost always). To date, researchers employing the ABQ have reported acceptable internal consistency (alphas between 0.85 and 0.91), test–retest reliability, and construct validity (Creswell and Eklund, 2005a, 2005b; Raedeke and Smith, 2001, 2004). Furthermore, Cresswell and Eklund (2006c) conducted an analysis to assess the convergent, discriminant, and construct validity of the ABQ, the MBI-General Survey (MBI-GS; Schaufeli *et al.*, 1996), and the Depression Anxiety Stress Scales (DASS; Brown *et al.*, 1997). The researchers made comparisons between these measures in particular because Schaufeli and colleagues specifically designed the MBI-GS for the assessment of burnout outside helping professions, and there has been ongoing debate as to how to discriminate between burnout and depression and other negative affective states, due to shared symptomology. Findings reported acceptable convergent validity and satisfactory internal discriminant validity for the ABQ and MBI-GS, and adequate discrimination between the concepts of burnout and depression, and the authors concluded that the ABQ should be the recommended self-report measure for athlete burnout.

The utility of the MBI has been aided by the establishment of norms and cut points indicating low, moderate, and high levels of burnout (Maslach *et al.*, 1996). In addition, efforts have been undertaken to employ the MBI as a diagnostic tool, and to provide clinical cut points mainly in the Netherlands (Roelofs *et al.*, 2005; Schaufeli *et al.*, 2001). With reference to the ABQ manual (2009), there are at present no established or suggested diagnostic criteria. Instead, Raedeke and Smith (2009) suggest careful interpretation of scores that rest upon evaluation of the magnitude of scores for each individual, since there are no formal norms available.

Unfortunately, the potential to compare and evaluate norms between MBI and ABQ is limited, since response scales are different (i.e. the MBI scale ranges from 1 to 7, and the ABQ scale ranges from 1 to 5). Consequently, both practitioners and researchers are advised to proceed cautiously when classifying athletes as having high or low burnout (Hodge *et al.*, 2008).

Explaining burnout

In an article exploring burnout in college sports, Coakley (2009) likens research and theories in the field to the parable of the blind men and the elephant. In the story, each of the men encounters a different part of the elephant – one encounters a leg and describes it as a tree, another feels the trunk and relates it to a snake, and yet another grasps the tail and says it is similar to a rope. The Raja who arranged the scenario and introduced the elephant to the men takes great pleasure in the conflict between their explanations, as this confirms his argument that scholars often study reality from different vantage points but insist that their explanation is the most accurate and objective. This story is not so far removed from the situation relating to explanations of athlete burnout. The confusion overshadowing burnout as a construct has led to criticism that commentaries lack commonality in essential parameters such as shared terminology (i.e. what is and what is not burnout), the nature and attributes of burnout (i.e. characteristics, antecedents, and consequences), and the causal ordering of relevant burnout–related constructs (i.e. dropout and overtraining: Cresswell and Eklund, 2006a). A further criticism is that theoretical frameworks need to be tested (Hodge *et al.*, 2008). To date, there has been a dearth of studies that have systematically assessed the merits of existing explanations of athlete burnout (e.g. Cresswell and Eklund, 2006b, 2007a; Gould *et al.*, 1996a; Raedeke, 1997). More recent research efforts have in fact devoted more attention to assessing the efficacy of applying alternative frameworks from outside the sport domain to athlete burnout, such as Ryan and Deci's (2000) Self-Determination Theory (e.g. Cresswell and Eklund, 2005a; Hodge *et al.*, 2008; Lemyre *et al.*, 2007, Lonsdale and Hodge, 2011; Lonsdale *et al.*, 2009).

In summarising the confusion that has been pervasive in the athlete burnout field, the lack of conceptual consensus on what burnout actually is means that both researchers and practitioners should view findings cautiously, and be mindful of whether commentaries are actually talking about burnout or about related constructs (e.g. overtraining and dropout). There is also a recursive relationship between this conceptual confusion and measurement shortcomings, in that the failure of researchers to provide a precise operational definition of burnout has led to the absence of a valid and reliable measurement method that is conceptually grounded (Cresswell and Eklund, 2006a). That said, the work of Raedeke and colleagues (Raedeke, 1997; Raedeke and Smith, 2001) has created an opportunity for greater consensus through a conceptualisation of athlete burnout that is closely aligned with and informed by professional burnout, but which has also been sensitive to contextual interference in its application to the sport context. Moreover, the authors offer a measure that is conceptually linked and has been subject to systematic testing. There is a continued need for further validation of Raedeke's (1997) conceptualisation, but we would advocate that this endeavour is worthwhile, and pivotal to overcoming the barriers that have historically limited progress.

Clarifying related constructs

Creswell and Eklund (2006b) describe burnout as a multidimensional psychosocial syndrome. A syndrome refers to a group of signs and symptoms that occur together and characterise a particular abnormality (Shirom, 2005). Burnout does, however, have a number of complications with regard to its symptomatology. Symptoms associated with burnout are as wide-ranging as they are varied, and also exhibit commonality with related conditions, including job stress, anxiety, and depression, leading some authors to question whether it is a distinct psychological phenomenon or merely "old wine in new bottles" (Schaufeli and Buunk, 2003, p. 388). There is also ambiguity around what comprises a symptom versus a consequence, as a number of factors can manifest as either (e.g. decreased motivation, increased anxiety, and fatigue). In a study by Goodger *et al.* (2007b) that specifically examined symptoms and consequences associated with Raedeke's (1997) three dimensions of athlete burnout, symptoms were defined as physical or mental characteristics of burnout, and consequences as the result or outcome of burnout. The reader is also referred to a "practitioner's guide" of athlete burnout by Cresswell and Eklund (2003), which pragmatically differentiates between early signs, symptoms, and potential consequences.

Burnout is an enduring state, rather than a transitory experience (Cresswell and Eklund, 2006b). It is also a chronic developmental process (i.e. burning out: Cherniss, 1980), which is to say that an athlete does not simply wake up one morning with burnout. Emotional exhaustion is considered to be the central component of burnout, and represents the stress dimension. It is the result of a gradual depletion of emotional resources due to emotionally overtaxing work (Toppinen-Tanner *et al.*, 2002). The salience of exhaustion to burnout is not only that it is a significant experiential state, but also that it prompts action by the affected individuals to emotionally and cognitively distance themselves from work (Maslach *et al.*, 2001). This distancing is identified as a coping strategy that is part of the second dimension of burnout, depersonalisation (sport devaluation), and is associated with a negative attitude towards work, loss of interest, and motivational change. The third dimension of reduced accomplishment has been marginalised in comparison to the other dimensions in the work setting, with authors being less clear on its relationship to the other dimensions (Cox *et al.*, 2005). In contrast, athlete burnout research suggests a more significant role for this dimension within the sport context (e.g. Cresswell and Eklund, 2006b; Goodger *et al.*, 2007b; Gustafsson *et al.*, 2007). Raedeke (1997) observed that the core element of this social context was performance; therefore, this finding does not seem unsurprising. The salience of exhaustion has brought about debate as to whether the other dimensions are needed (Schaufeli and Taris, 2005), but proponents of the three dimensions argue that a unidimensional perspective creates the potential for losing "sight of the phenomenon entirely" (Maslach *et al.*, 2001, p. 403). Therefore, we advocate that burnout is the development and enduring experience of all three dimensions in combination.

Overtraining

The basic idea behind training principles builds upon the notion that the body will respond to training-induced disturbance of homeostasis. During recovery, homeostasis is restored, biological adaptations occur, and an increased functional capacity for greater exercise intensity and volume results (Viru, 1994). Consequently, brief periods of positive overtraining (i.e. functional overreaching) followed by adequate recovery will increase performance. In contrast, a process of negative overtraining (i.e. dysfunctional overreaching) with inadequate recovery will decrease performance and develop overtraining syndrome. Overtraining represents the process whereas overtraining syndrome defines the maladaptive outcome. Overtraining syndrome (OTS) is regarded as a consequence of an ongoing imbalance between a total stress load (i.e. training and non-training stress) and total recovery in relation to a total capacity to tolerate and cope with stress (Kenttä and Hassmén, 1998). Burnout and OTS do share some common characteristics. OTS is best described by the key feature as displayed by the loss in capacity to train and perform at a normal level (i.e. a state of underperformance). In addition, mood disturbance and prolonged fatigue have been reported as key symptoms during OTS (cf. Urhausen and Kindermann, 2002). A large body of research, conducted mainly within sports medicine and exercise physiology, has further reported sleep disturbance, loss of appetite, muscle soreness, feelings of heaviness in the muscles, and increased perception of effort during training at a given work load, and a reduced ability for adaptation during recovery. The primary distinction between overtraining syndrome and burnout noted in the literature is based on the quality and level of motivation. Athletes experiencing overtraining syndrome can still be motivated to train, compete, and stay involved in sport, whereas athletes suffering from burnout have developed a cynical attitude to their previously beloved sport and may have fully or partially withdrawn from sport participation. It is further suggested that frequently or prolonged overtraining syndrome may develop into burnout.

Recovery

A fundamental biological principal in stress research is that the more activity a living organism is exposed to, the greater the need for recovery. Lack of recovery is more often regarded as a major contributor to overtraining syndrome and burnout. In fact, Kellmann (2002) suggested that overtraining syndrome could perhaps better be understood, from a different perspective, as an "under-recovery syndrome". Nevertheless, research in general has generated far more knowledge relevant to understanding stress and exhaustion as compared to recovery. In sport science, Kuipers noted in 1996 that relatively little is known about recovery, and that this was explained by the absence of assessment methods and instruments. Kenttä and Hassmén (1998) published a conceptual model on stress and recovery including the Total Quality Recovery Scale (TQR) as a tool to assess both recovery actions (i.e. nutrition and fluid, sleep and rest, relaxation and emotional support, active recovery) and a global perception of recovery. Kellmann and Kallus (2001) developed a questionnaire that simultaneously assesses stressful and restful events over a period of three days and nights. The Recovery-Stress Questionnaire for Athletes (RESTQ) includes general recovery scales that assess success, social recovery, physical recovery, general well-being, and sleep quality. In addition, some sport-specific recovery scales assess being in shape, personal accomplishment, self-efficacy, and self-regulation. Most recently, Lundqvist and Kenttä (2010) developed the Emotional Recovery Questionnaire (EmRecQ). Recovery was further defined as the psychosocio-physiological process of eliminating all levels of fatigue and regaining vitality. The questionnaire can be seen as an important contribution, since various emotional states play an important role in terms of their potential to either enhance or interfere with the process of recovery (Sonnentag and Fritz, 2007). Furthermore, the Emotional Recovery Questionnaire can be regarded as an extension of Fredrickson and colleagues "undoing hypothesis". More specifically, research has supported the notion that positive emotions undo the cognitive and physiological effects of stress and negative emotions, thus enhancing recovery for the body and the mind (Fredrickson and Joiner, 2002). In conclusion, increasing training loads and intensified psychosocial demands will further advance the challenge to understand, monitor, and meet individual recovery needs among athletes (Kenttä *et al.*, 2006).

Depression

A common symptomatology (i.e. low physical and emotional energy is associated with both concepts) and shared aetiology has led researchers to use the constructs of depression and burnout interchangeably (Hemingway and Marmot, 1999; Shirom, 2005). However, there is equally significant research that presents them as distinct conditions. In a meta-analysis of 18 studies, Glass and McKnight (1996) concluded that, despite shared variance across studies, they are not redundant concepts. Furthermore, factor analysis studies examining items measuring both conditions have generally reported that loading on different factors suggests again that they are different constructs (Schaufeli and Enzmann, 1998). In distinguishing between depression and burnout, Freudenberger (1983) explains that burnout tends (initially at least) to be associated with the social environment at work (or, in the case of athletes' burnout, sport). In contrast, depression is seen to be more pervasive, and generalises across all aspects of an individual's environment. Sadness, guilt, hopelessness, and feelings of worthlessness are also considered basic features of depression, but are not associated with burnout (Shirom, 2005). In order to combat the possible impact of depression in studies of burnout, Shirom advocates that researchers include a measure of depressive symptomatology in the research design.

Job stress

Occupational or job stress is a generic term that refers to, "any affect-laden negative experience that is caused by an imbalance between job demands and the response capability of the worker" (Schaufeli and Enzmann, 1998, p. 8). Burnout is viewed as one potential reaction to chronic stress (Dale and Weinberg, 1990), and as such it is considered to be a special type of prolonged job stress that results particularly from interpersonal demands at work (Schaufeli and Buunk, 2003). It is also distinguished from job stress through its symptomatology in that burnout represents a multidimensional stress response characterised by negative, dysfunctional, job-related attitudes and behaviours not covered by the traditional job stress concept (Schaufeli and Enzmann, 1998).

Stress is explained as a process in which the situation is initially appraised with respect to demands and an individual's ability to cope with these demands. Burnout is considered to be a "particular slice across the stress process", and the dominant view in burnout research is that a "causal chain exists in which the experience of stress contributes to the aetiology of burnout, which in turn is related to negative job perceptions, lack of organisational commitment, and withdrawal behaviour such as absence and leaving" (Cox *et al.*, 1993, p. 183).

Theories and models of athlete burnout

Within the extant literature, theoretical explanations of athlete burnout have been variously grouped into different categories, such as traditional versus contemporary, stress induced versus non-stress induced, motivational, and so on. To aid the utility of these explanations for professional practice, we discuss the major theoretical perspectives in relation to different "strains" or "types" of burnout, as originally proposed by Gould and colleagues (1996a). More specifically, this research suggests two types of burnout: social-psychologically driven, and physically driven. The social-psychologically driven strain was identified as the more dominant of the two, and could be further subdivided into "athletic perfectionism" and "situational pressure". Typically, athletes exhibiting these strains of burnout had low physical training loads, and either exhibited a perfectionist personality disposition that predisposed them to burnout and/or were placed in situations of tremendous psychological stress (e.g. parental pressure). In contrast, in physically driven cases of burnout athletes find themselves unable to meet physical demands placed upon them. This in turn causes significant physical and psychological stress, and leads to eventual burnout. We begin our journey through the explanations posited within the extant literature for athlete burnout by looking at the physically driven strain.

Physically driven burnout

Burnout as a negative response to excessive training loads

One of the earliest explanations of athlete burnout was advanced by Silva (1990) as the Negative Training Stress Response Model. The model proposes that burnout is the end result of a series of maladaptive responses to training. Physical training places stress on the athlete that can be both positive and negative. Positive stress results in adaptations and training gains, whilst negative stress, such as too much training, can lead to maladaptation and negative training responses. Silva stated that these negative responses include staleness ("an initial failure of the body's adaptive mechanisms to cope with psycho-physiological stress," p. 10), overtraining ("detectable psycho-physiological malfunctions characterised by easily observed changes in the athletes' mental orientation and physical performance", p. 10), and burnout ("an exhaustive psycho-physiological response exhibited as a result of frequent, sometimes extreme, but generally ineffective efforts to meet excessive training and sometimes competitive demands", p. 11), and that they lie on a psycho-physiological continuum. Initial negative responses to training demands result in staleness, which, if unmanaged, progresses to overtraining as the body's adaptive mechanisms fail to respond effectively, and burnout is the end consequence of overtraining occurring when the body's response system is depleted and becomes exhausted. Support for Silva's model has been limited to date (e.g. Gould *et al.*, 1996a). Criticism has been levied at it for presenting possible antecedents or consequences of burnout rather than the key characteristics of the experience itself (Cresswell and Eklund, 2006a), as well as the proposition Silva makes that withdrawal from sport is inevitable, which other authors have suggested is not always the case (e.g. Cresswell and Eklund, 2007b; Gould *et al.*, 1996a; Raedeke, 1997).

Although support has been limited, tenets of Silva's work with reference to the impact of training and physical demands placed upon athletes have been adopted more recently within a stress–recovery approach to burnout, and the related concepts of overtraining and burnout.

Burnout as a result of a stress–recovery imbalance

The stress–recovery approach advocates that burnout is the product of accumulating stress (which is both training and non-training based) without appropriate recovery (Kallus and Kellmann, 2000). The reader is referred to Kellmann (2002) for a comprehensive overview of this work. Overtraining occurs when an athlete is exposed to stress and is unable to recover sufficiently from this exposure. Progressively, this imbalance of stress and recovery leads to staleness and then burnout. To advance research and to enable early identification of athletes at risk, Kellmann and Kallus (2001) developed a multidimensional self-report measure: the Recovery Stress Questionnaire (RESTQ). This instrument contains stress and recovery subscales and assesses the stress–recovery state of individuals, which indicates the extent to which they are physically and/or mentally stressed, and whether or not they are capable of using individual strategies for recovery, as well as which strategies are used. The authors advise a multidimensional intervention approach encompassing physiological, emotional, cognitive, behavioural/performance, and social aspects.

A second stress–recovery perspective which emphasises the importance of sufficient (and quality) recovery in preventing burnout is that of Kenttä and Hassmén (1998). The authors propose a conceptual model of under-recovery and overtraining, together with a monitoring tool to assess the quality and amount of recovery (TQR – Total Quality Recovery). The model is grounded in a psychosocio-physiological framework, and promotes that conditions such as overtraining, staleness, and burnout are a product of three subsystems affecting the individual — physiology, psychology, and sociology. An individual's adaptation or maladaptation to training is affected by the balance between total stress (training and non-training) and total recovery (quality and amount) in relation to total stress tolerance (capacity of the individual to cope with stress) which manifest through these subsystems.

Although the stress–recovery perspective is not exclusively an explanation of athlete burnout, in that it applies to staleness and overtraining as well, the value of this perspective is that it offers practitioners the opportunity to be proactive in safeguarding against incidences of insufficient or under-recovery. Burnout is considered to be the depletion and eventual exhaustion of an individual's resources, and hence recovery must be considered a key factor in prevention. We return to this approach through a novel screening tool that suggests possible intervention strategies, later in the chapter.

Burnout as a consequence of chronic exposure to psychosocial stress

One of the most comprehensive explanations of athlete burnout that can be applied to both social-psychologically driven and physically driven strains of burnout is Smith's (1986) Cognitive–Affective Model. Smith proposed a four-stage model of stress and burnout in which stress is the causal factor, and burnout is conceptualised as a process that involves physical, psychological, and behavioural components. These components are also influenced by personality and motivational factors. The first stage of the process comprises situational demands that the athlete is placed under. These demands are cognitively appraised, in the second stage, against the athlete's personal resources (i.e. perceived ability to meet demands). This appraisal in turn governs the nature and intensity of emotional responses, and, if negative (i.e. perceived imbalance between demands and resources), initiates physiological responses in the third stage. The final stage, behavioural responses, is characterised by types of coping and task behaviour. A recursive relationship is proposed to exist between stages, as well as behavioural responses feeding back into the situational demands stage (Gould *et al.*, 1996a). In the case of burnout, the process is initiated through a perceived imbalance between demands and resources over time (i.e. a sense of chronic overload or conflict between demands and resources), and manifests as physiological responses such as lethargy, tension, fatigue, or illness. Ultimately, behavioural responses are observed as performance decrements and eventual withdrawal.

Smith's model is conceptually grounded in Thibaut and Kelley's (1959) Social Exchange Theory (SET). The principles of this theory propose that human behaviour is governed by the desire to maximise positive experiences and minimise negative experiences. Individuals participate in activities as long as they are favourable, and this favourability is determined by the balance of costs and rewards, and how these compare to the outcomes of alternative activities (Weinberg and Gould, 2003). If activities fall below the comparison level for alternatives, individuals are likely to withdraw in the hope of pursuing alternative activities. For the individual who experiences burnout, Smith asserts that withdrawal results from an increase in stress-induced costs for the present activity, and the previously enjoyed activity becomes an aversive source of stress.

In their original work Gould and colleagues (1996a) concluded that Smith's model could be applied effectively to most cases of athlete burnout, and as such was the most useful explanation of the syndrome available. They cited its comprehensiveness, which incorporated both personal and situational factors, together with a premium being placed on the athlete's interpretation of events causing chronic stress, as the strength underpinning its utility. More recently, Cresswell and Eklund (2006a) argued that Smith's model (Smith, 1986) fits with extant descriptions of burnout within the wider literature, and that it has made important conceptual contributions to the understanding of burnout in sport (e.g. Harlick and McKenzie, 2000; Raedeke and Smith, 2004).

Social-psychologically driven burnout

As stated previously Smith's model (Smith, 1986) can be applied equally to social-psychologically or physically driven cases of burnout. With the exception of Smith's model, other explanations of social-psychologically driven burnout are also described as non-stress induced perspectives; that is, stress is not considered to be the causal factor. For some authors stress is seen as a symptom of burnout (e.g. Coakley, 1992), whilst others argue that burnout perceived as exclusively related to stress restricts understanding of the uniqueness of the phenomenon, and it is simply another perspective on stress (Raedeke, 1997).

Burnout through identity foreclosure and loss of autonomy

Coakley's (1992) Unidimensional Identity Development and External Control Model applies a sociological perspective to athlete burnout, and proposes burnout is a social problem that is the product of the organisation of sport. Specifically, organisational constraints prevent the development of a multifaceted identity. Exclusive involvement in sport instead results in young athletes being unable to explore and develop other aspects of their identity, and experiencing identity foreclosure. They become identified and recognised by others through sport, and identity becomes hinged upon sporting success. Furthermore, the organisation of the sport constricts the athlete's sense of autonomy, with decision-making in the hands of others. Coakley argues that burnout stems from stress associated with the creation of a unidimensional identity and a lack of control over one's own life. Unlike the professional literature, the exploration of the role of organisations in athlete burnout has been limited, but research has supported the tenets of Coakley's model and the role of identity, control, and the sport organisation in athlete burnout (Black and Smith, 2007; Cresswell and Eklund, 2007b; Gould *et al.*, 1996a; Gustafsson *et al.*, 2007).

Burnout as a consequence of entrapment

Schmidt and Stein (1991) offer a commitment-based explanation for athlete burnout in their Sport Commitment Model. They contend that athlete commitment is determined by three factors, and that athletes who experience burnout are committed to sport for reasons that differ from those of athletes who do not experience burnout. The determinants of commitment are satisfaction (rewards and costs), attractiveness of alternative options, and resources invested. The incidence of burnout it proposed to be more likely in athletes who display an entrapment-based commitment profile, where they are participating in the sport because they "have to" rather than "want to" (Raedeke, 1997). This occurs when athletes experience high costs and low rewards, but remain in the sport because they feel they have invested significant resources and perceive a lack of attractive alternatives (i.e. high investment and low alternatives). The model has accrued significant interest, and is empirically supported through findings by Raedeke and colleagues (e.g. Raedeke, 1997; Raedeke and Smith 2001). It should be noted, however, that it is a correlation-based association that has been reported in research between burnout and entrapment, and not causality. Cresswell and Eklund (2006a) advocate that a commitment approach to burnout has much to offer, but further research is warranted to understand the role of commitment more fully.

Burnout and motivation

Motivation that is burning out is a signature feature of burnout. Changes in motivation from an intense drive, desire, and investment to succeed, to a psychological and physical distancing and eventual disengagement, is a palpable characteristic of athlete burnout. Gould (1997) describes this as a situation in which "motivation has gone awry", and Raedeke and colleagues (Raedeke *et al.*, 2002) reference the metaphor of "a candle that once glowed brightly, began to flicker, and eventually extinguished". The premise here is that for individuals to burn out, they must first be on fire (highly motivated; Pines, 1993). Interestingly, despite the significance of motivation to the burnout experience, research findings have been inconclusive in explaining the association between the two concepts (Goodger *et al.*, 2007a). Moreover, theoretical explanations of the syndrome have made little direct reference to motivation until recently. Gould *et al.* (1996b) originally proposed that burnout research could benefit from employing motivational theories such as Deci and Ryan's (1985) intrinsic motivation and Self-Determination Theory (SDT). However, it was not until almost a decade later that this approach was adopted (e.g. Cresswell and Eklund, 2005a, 2005b; Lemyre *et al.*, 2006) in a bid to understand the motivational determinants of athlete burnout. Self Determination Theory (Ryan and Deci, 2000) has since become something of a hot topic in athlete burnout research, with a steady flow of studies emerging since 2005.

According to SDT, the basis of human well-being and personal growth is the satisfaction of three basic needs (i.e. autonomy, competence, and relatedness), and that, conversely, a state of ill-being (e.g. depression) is the result of chronic failure to satisfy these needs. In addition, the level of perceived need satisfaction also influences individuals in an achievement setting to adopt a more or less self-determined motivational style. Motivational styles are proposed to lie on a continuum, with athletes who are more self-determined experiencing more control over their own behaviour and a greater likelihood of an adaptive outcome in the achievement setting. For athletes who are more externally regulated than self-determined, they will feel less in control and are vulnerable to maladaptive outcomes such as overtraining and burnout (Lemyre *et al.*, 2006, 2007). The application of SDT to cases of athlete burnout offers the opportunity not only for further conceptual understanding, but also to inform applied practice. Hodge *et al.* (2008) advocate that practitioners may help to offset the incidence of burnout through encouraging need satisfaction, and in working with coaches to use a need-supporting coaching style. Work by Lemyre *et al.* (2008) has also proposed that motivation in cases of burnout should not simply be considered as a reduced level, but also a qualitative shift in motivation from adaptive to maladaptive (i.e. more or less self-determined). Furthermore, it is also valuable to identify an athlete's achievement motivation and the meaning they place on achievement. They argue that if achievement motivation is maladaptive (i.e. high ego and low task-oriented), this can predispose an athlete to burnout.

In summary of the explanations that have been advanced for athlete burnout, we advocate that the separation of cases of burnout into different types is a useful approach, in that it may help practitioners with their formulation and intervention. However, it may emerge that contributory factors and the burnout experience for the individual do, in practice, exhibit overlap across the types. In addition, it is important that professionals are mindful that systematic testing of explanations of athlete burnout within the extant literature has been limited to date, and this remains a pertinent area of enquiry within the field (Hodge *et al.*, 2008).

Athlete burnout research

As mentioned previously, Cohn (1990) and Silva (1990) published the first empirical investigations of burnout in athletes. Cohn conducted a qualitative study exploring sources of stress in high-school golfers and possible causal links to burnout, and Silva's study examined the relationship between training and burnout, which resulted in the advancement of his Negative Training Stress Response Model. Similarly, another noteworthy early analysis of athlete burnout was Coakley's (1992) study, which shaped the development of the Unidimensional Identity Development and External Control Model. In addition to the model development, Coakley's work is significant in that it was one of the first (and remains one of the few) to employ a qualitative approach in the exploration of athlete burnout.

Gould and colleagues' study of junior tennis players remains one of the most in-depth explorations of athlete burnout to date (Gould *et al.*, 1996a, 1996b, 1997). Commissioned by the Sport Science Division of the US Tennis Association (USTA), the study arose from concern over competitive pressures confronting junior players, and the consequences of such pressure. The study expressly sought to contrast the experiences of players who had experienced burnout with those of equivalent players who had not experienced burnout. In so doing, the authors intended to learn more about burnout from those who had actually lived with it, while also gathering information to inform future preventative and management strategies.

The study employed a mixed method approach of quantitative survey data and qualitative interview follow-up, and resulted in a series of three publications (Gould *et al.*, 1996a, 1996b, 1997). A considerable amount of data was generated and systematically presented under the following areas: a contrast of the responses of burned out versus non-burned out players across a battery of psychological and social-psychological variables (Gould *et al.*, 1996b); in-depth accounts from burned out players on the physical and mental characteristics of burnout and recommendations for prevention; an examination of the utility of existing theoretical explanations applied to actual cases of athlete burnout (Gould *et al.*, 1996a); and idiographic profiles of three individual burned out players as case studies (Gould *et al.*, 1997). The importance of this study's contribution is not only in the questions asked, but also in the design employed. A shortcoming and a major challenge in burnout research is locating individuals who have actually experienced the syndrome. By its very nature, burnout dictates that these individuals reach a point where they no longer wish to be part of the activity, and, as a consequence, choose to withdraw involvement. The authors actively sought out individuals who had lived with burnout in order to learn from them.

The direction of contemporary athlete burnout research has been most fundamentally influenced by the contributions of Raedeke and colleagues (Raedeke, 1997; Raedeke and Smith, 2001). The significance of this work is that it has begun to pave the way for potential future conceptual agreement on what actually comprises burnout, and how it is measured. Defining athlete burnout as a multidimensional syndrome comprising physical and emotional exhaustion, sport devaluation, and reduced athletic accomplishment is both conceptually well grounded, given the extent of the utilisation of these dimensions in research within the parent domain of work psychology, as well as Raedeke's sensitivity to contextual interference in transposing the original definition to the sport context and managing any divergence. Studies have continued to further cement the utility of Raedeke's dimensions by exploring the nature and characteristics of athlete burnout and assessing if these dimensions do indeed capture the essence of athlete burnout (e.g. Cresswell and Eklund, 2006c; Goodger *et al.*, 2007a; Gustafsson *et al.*, 2007; Raedeke *et al.*, 2002). The advancement of the Athlete Burnout Questionnaire (ABQ; Raedeke and Smith, 2001) and, through it, the operationalisation of Raedeke's three dimensions has been welcomed by researchers and is quickly becoming the instrument of choice, as evidenced by the number of studies employing this measure. Researchers have not gone blindly into using the ABQ, but rather have subjected it to systematic testing (Cresswell and Eklund, 2006b) and have acknowledged the limitations associated with the remaining absence of appropriate cut-offs (Hodge *et al.*, 2008). This will continue to be an important area of future research to ensure the ABQ is robust.

Two researchers who have championed Raedeke's three dimensions of athlete burnout in particular are Scott Cresswell and Bob Eklund. Through a funded research project exploring burnout in professional rugby players in New Zealand, and later in the UK, the authors have made a rapid and significant contribution to the empirical base of athlete burnout research (Cresswell and Eklund, 2003, 2004, 2005a, 2005b, 2006a, 2006b, 2006c, 2007a, 2007b). Moreover, they have returned to the professional literature repeatedly to challenge conceptual thinking in the sport context and heighten methodological rigor in research undertaken. The acknowledgment of their contribution to the field in this chapter has more to do with what their work has to offer to the practitioner in that there is much that can be applied in professional practice. They offer guidance on possible early warning signs of burnout (Cresswell and Eklund, 2003, 2004) and the opportunity to identify at-risk athletes (Cresswell, 2009), as well as characteristics associated with burnout versus other related complaints (e.g. transitory exhaustion) and temporal changes associated with the syndrome (Cresswell and Eklund, 2007a). As discussed previously, Cresswell and Eklund (2005a, 2005b) have also engaged a new perspective to motivation and burnout through Self-Determination Theory (Ryan and Deci, 2000). Finally, by undertaking their research within the demanding environment of professional rugby, the authors have given valuable insight into environmental and organisational factors associated with burnout (Cresswell and Eklund, 2007b).

A further area of advancement that has implications for the practitioner is the stress–recovery approach that has been applied to athlete burnout. The importance placed upon burnout (and overtraining and staleness) as a combination of psychological, sociological, and physiological factors stemming from both training and non-training stress highlights that it is a phenomenon, which is personal and situational in nature. Although Gould *et al.* (1996a) made this observation more than a decade ago, the stress–recovery perspective provides an approach in which both the characteristics of the athlete and the environment (in which the athlete lives) can be considered in combination. The RESTQ-Sport instrument developed by Kallus and Kellmann (2000) has supported the monitoring and identification of incidences of stress and under-recovery in the lead up to and during major competitions (Kellmann and Gunther, 2000).

Implications for professional practice – screening protocol

The development of the ABQ has made an important contribution to the field of athlete burnout in enhancing conceptual understanding of the syndrome, and in providing a valid assessment tool that has become increasingly employed across empirical studies, facilitating opportunity for comparison. In the applied context, however, the ABQ was not primarily developed as a diagnostic tool, or to be used in a consulting setting as an interview guide. A further compounding issue for practitioners in relation to physically driven burnout in particular is the potential overlap between burnout and overtraining. Presented below is a diagnostic questionnaire designed specifically to be used as a screening tool in any suspected case of overtraining syndrome or burnout.

Go through the following nine items step by step with an athlete in a phase that allows sufficient time for reflection about each response. At the end of the screening protocol some guidelines are outlined, with the purpose of enhancing interpretation and intervention development – i.e. what to do about the findings from a professional practice viewpoint:

1a Do you currently experience an extended performance slump (i.e. you are underperforming)? Yes – No
1b Do you experience difficulty to perform up to the level of your normal capacity? Yes – No
1c Do you feel that you perform below your normal capacity? Yes – No
1d Have you been struggling more than usual to reach your normal performance capacity? Yes – No

Comment: If you have answered "yes" to any of these questions, it is worthwhile answering the rest of the questions. Even if the overall results at the end indicate no serious concerns, you should try to maximise the lessons learned from the current situation. The answers will also serve as a benchmark for future similar situations.

2a Is your assessment derived from *objective* measurable performances or from your own *subjective* assessment of performances? Measurable (objective) – Experience (subjective)
2b Do you have a coach who knows you well and who shares your view that you are performing under your normal capacity? Yes – No
2c Is your assessment derived from *sports-specific* performances or less sport-specific performances? Sport-specific – Less sport-specific
2d Does your assessment build on submaximal or maximal performance? Submaximal – Maximal

Comment: The only test with full validity and reliability that is applicable of an elite athlete is a maximal competition or game performance.

Long-term underperformances during competitions/games should be investigated thoroughly. Unfortunately, it is difficult to reliably measure that type of performance in many sports. Nor is it desirable to expose an overly exhausted person to a maximum performance for the sole purpose of an evaluation.

It should therefore be acknowledged that athletes (and managers/trainers/coaches) who regularly reflect on their performances often develop a good ability to subjectively assess their own performance. It is thus wise to listen to and respect the athlete's subjective assessments that indicate a sense of reduced performance capacity. It is furthermore particularly important to have a thorough discussion of the meaning of a significant reduction in performance.

3a Do you feel that your difficulties to perform up to your normal level have continued for more than a week? Yes–No
If yes, for how long has it been a problem? Specify as precisely as possible.

3b Can you rule out other possible explanations for your performance slump (i.e. state of underperformance)? For instance, illness, injury, poor nutrition, poor hydration, poor sleep, external factors such as problems with equipment, environment etc? Yes–No (Try to really rule out all possible causes.)

3c Do you feel that your state of underperformance is mainly due to too much and too hard training, combined with insufficient recovery? Yes–No

3d Do you feel that there are things in your life outside your physical training (i.e. non-training stressors) that demand energy and impair your recovery? Yes–No

Comment: If it turns out that the problems lasted for less than five to seven days, the chances for recovery to a normal level within a relatively short time are good. If problems have occurred during a longer continuous period (more than 10–14 days), there should also be a thorough medical examination as a complement to these questions as soon as possible. The medical investigation is of particular importance with respect to the exclusion of medical explanations (infections, low haemoglobin, etc.). It should also be noted that some clinical medical findings may be symptoms in an overtraining or burnout syndrome.

Question 3c can favourably be verified by training diaries, where the focus should be to examine the weekly training load in relation to recovery (is there a full day of rest each week?). If possible, a longer period of training history should be explored, with particular attention to excessively rapid increase in the total workout volume and intensity, or, alternatively, monotonous training. Question 3c should also be related to

Question 3d in order to interpret the total training load and recovery, and thereby determine whether the main cause of fatigue can be explained by the training load or stress load in life (i.e. non-training stressors) and/or lack of recovery.

4 Have you been more frequently ill during the last six months than usual? Yes–No

Comment: The answer should, if possible, be supported by any documented training history where illness is recorded. A large part of the immune function is impaired due to the overtraining syndrome, and this often results in recurrent upper respiratory infections, mouth ulcers, allergic reactions, etc.

5 Consider the past week of training, and rate your overall perceived effort for the whole weekly training load (combine your overall perception of number of training sessions, time and intensity in training). Mark on the scale below:

0	Nothing at all
0.3	
0.5	Extremely low/Barely perceptible
0.7	
1	Very low
1.5	
2	Low/Easy
2.5	
3	Moderate
4	Somewhat hard
5	Hard/Heavy
6	
7	Very hard
8	
9	
10	Extremely hard/Maximal
11	
+	Absolute maximum

(Borg, 1982)

6 Consider your experiences with feeling recovered as an athlete. How do you feel that you are recovering from the fatigue of training sessions generally during the past week? Pay particular attention to how you recover during days of rest. Consider both physical (physical) and mental (psychological) cues when you rate your ability to recover from fatigue. Highlight on the scale below:

0	No recovery at all
0.3	
0.5	Extremely poor recovery
0.7	
1	Very poor recovery
1.5	
2	Poor recovery
2.5	
3	
4	Moderate recovery
5	
6	Good recovery
7	
8	Excellent recovery
9	
10	Extremely good recovery
11	
+	Absolute maximum/optimum recovery

Comment: Together, Items 5 and 6 are essential in interpreting how the stress load placed upon the athlete is perceived in relation to recovery. The total demand for recovery is largely a direct consequence of how extensive the overall stress load is, often to a large extent derived from the training load. Moreover, research suggests that the body's ability to "respond to recovery" significantly deteriorates when suffering from overtraining or burnout syndrome. During further investigation, this variable, used properly, can be the single most reliable source of information. For example, if you choose to apply a total rest from training for about three or four days, then you should carefully monitor how your body responds to rest. Do you experience an improved recovery (physically and mentally) in combination with reduced fatigue? If yes, that is a good sign of adaptation to recovery – you have received a positive response. You are on the right track! If you fail to achieve a positive response, an in-depth investigative is recommended and necessary.

7 Consider the following statements and think about how you have felt the past week.

> Please circle one number for each claim.
>
> The numbers represent: (1) Not at all, (2) A little bit, (3) Moderately, (4) A lot, (5) Very much
>
> (1 2 3 4 5) Cannot not sleep well (difficulty falling asleep and wake up a lot)
> (1 2 3 4 5) Lost my appetite for eating
> (1 2 3 4 5) Muscle soreness
> (1 2 3 4 5) Feeling heavy and slow
> (1 2 3 4 5) Training feels harder (heavier) than it normally should
> (1 2 3 4 5) My self-confidence is negatively influenced
> (1 2 3 4 5) I am unsure of my performance
> (1 2 3 4 5) Exhausted mentally (drained of mental energy)
> (1 2 3 4 5) Exhausted physically (drained of physical energy)
>
> Please indicate here if you experienced any other problems during your form slump:
>
> ____
>
> ____
>
> __________

Comment: The above is a selection of the most common symptoms associated with overtraining and burnout syndrome. Sleep and appetite problems are generally less pronounced, while other symptoms are usually rated close to the score of 4 in the average of individuals classified as being overtrained. "Training felt heavier than normal" is usually the single most pronounced feature.

8 Below is a list of words that describe different feelings we might have. Please read one word at a time very carefully, then circle the option that best describes the feeling that you've had the past week.

> The numbers represent: (1) Not at all, (2) A little bit, (3) Moderately, (4) A lot, (5) Very much
>
> (1 2 3 4 5) Friendly
> (1 2 3 4 5) Worthless

(1 2 3 4 5) Miserable
(1 2 3 4 5) Helpful
(1 2 3 4 5) Bad-tempered
(1 2 3 4 5) Guilty
(1 2 3 4 5) Unworthy
(1 2 3 4 5) Peeved
(1 2 3 4 5) Cheerful
(1 2 3 4 5) Sad

Comment: The above is a condensed version of the Profile of Mood States (McNair *et al.*, 1992). This version, labelled the Training Distress Scale (TDS), was originally developed by Raglin and Morgan (1994) and has been widely used in overtraining studies. Mood disturbance is one of the most common symptoms associated with overtraining and burnout syndrome. To score the TDS, you calculate negative mood scores by removing the positive adjectives (friendly, helpful, and cheerful). Previous studies have shown that overtrained individuals on average had 21 points in the negative mood score. Interestingly, research shows that that the same individuals in the context of very hard training without signs of overtraining syndrome (i.e. during functional overreaching) showed a significantly lower degree of negative mood (an average of 13 points).

9 Think about how your motivation has been in general during the last week.
9a I lost interest and motivation to continue training. Yes–No
9b I was still highly motivated to continue training. Yes–No
9c I lost interest and motivation to continue competing/playing matches (games) in my sport. Yes–No
9d I was still motivated to compete/play matches (games). Yes–No
9e I get negative and unpleasant feelings when I think about my sport. Yes–No

Comment: The motivational pattern is essential in the assessment and potential discrimination between overtraining syndrome and burnout, since both phenomena share the aetiology of a pronounced and enduring exhaustion. A high degree of sustained motivation implies that it is chiefly an overtraining syndrome. In contrast, a high degree of loss of motivation is associated with sport devaluation and a more serious condition of burnout.

Treatment and impact on training and competition

Interpretation of responses

Once all questions are answered thoroughly and methodically, it is advisable to collect all the impressions and do an overall assessment. If there are a lot of answers indicating a serious overtraining syndrome, seek immediate professional help for further investigation. If the answers indicate that it is a matter of normal fatigue, then begin by resting three or four days as a precaution. If the answers indicate an emerging overtraining syndrome, the first action should be to bring full focus on recovery and rest for a slightly longer period, tentatively one to two weeks. The same questions should be answered and re-evaluated after the period of recovery.

This means that the responses from both the first and the second occasion need to be compared in order to monitor a positive reaction to a longer recovery. When everything is indicating a full recovery, it is prudent to gradually step up training to a normal level in the same way as after an extended injury or illness.

Treatment

The following proposals on measures and treatment are particularly suitable for maladaptive states at risk of developing into overtraining and burnout syndrome, but the content is also relevant in less severe cases where an extended recovery need is evident. The choice of action should always be adjusted based on individual needs and current conditions for achieving the best effect of treatment.

1. Reduce the total training load (frequency, volume/duration, intensity).

   Training your way out of a performance slump caused by excessive training and inadequate recovery is impossible. However, it may in some cases be sufficient to reduce the overall training load; how much will depend on the current state. It is likely that the athlete can recover faster with a larger reduction, or choose a slower recovery with a slightly smaller reduction. If you are uncertain of the state, begin by sharply reducing (or removing) all high-intensity training that has elements of anaerobic processes. Also, reduce the actual training time so that no single workout exceeds 30–45 minutes.
2. Cancel all competitions (contests and games).

   Athletes should, if possible, refrain from competitions if there is any concern about an emerging maladaptive syndrome. This is important, since competitions and games in general are associated with the highest demands, both physically and mentally. However, this is easier said than done – after all, the athletes choose for themselves to play matches and compete – so you should be extra vigilant so that the state does not worsen.

3 Ensure genuine rest from training.

Generally, a full day off per week without exercise and physical activity is recommended. However, this may be insufficient if an extended recovery need is identified. In this case, the athlete must be careful and not train too many consecutive days without rest. It may also be useful to assemble several full days of rest so that a longer period of rest and recovery is achieved. Also, try to minimise the physical activity on the day of rest. Many athletes experience anxiety associated with absence of training, especially when it is involuntary. Unfortunately, recovery is hampered by the negative emotions associated with an inner compulsion to exercise (i.e. exercise dependency) – hence the next paragraph.

4 Suggest alternative physical activity with a "therapeutic" purpose.

A "training ban" is usually a great mental strain, although rest is recommended with the best of intentions. For this reason, it may be advantageous to suggest some form of low-intense physical activity that mainly serves a therapeutic purpose and focuses on recovery. The activity should be less than 30 minutes. It should be dynamic and pleasurable, and anything other than a competitive sport. Be creative. There is an added value if it is possible to perform the activity outdoors in an environment that is perceived as peaceful and unconditional.

5 Focus fully on recovery.

Aim for optimum recovery of all systems: physiological, nutritional, immunological, psychosocial, mental, emotional, and cognitive. Exploit people and environments in the vicinity that create a peaceful and relaxed situation as well as provide energy. Encourage the athlete to engage in mentally uplifting activities of "feel-good" character.

6 Take advantage of professional help.

Do not hesitate to seek professional help at an early stage. It is not a sign of weakness. On the contrary – to ask for help shows courage and wisdom! Having problems with sleep? Contact a cognitive behavioural therapist. Need help with energy and nutrient intake? Contact a nutrition counsellor. There are several categories of sports, medical, and professional support that you should contact when the specific need is identified.

7 Evaluate the impact on future training and competitions/matches.

Have you ever experienced an incipient overtraining syndrome and an increased need for recovery and managed to reverse the situation? Learn from your experience and realise that overtraining syndrome is considered to be an unfortunate and temporary interruption of training. It can happen to anyone. Then, you know that next time it might be wiser to rest one day too many than to rest a day too few.

To quote the US Olympic Committee leaders in their theme issue on overtraining and recovery: "It is not always how hard you train, but how well you recover that determines the results!"

Conclusion

It is well documented that the construct of athlete burnout remains a relatively poorly understood area both in academic and in applied terms (Cresswell and Eklund, 2006a; Hodge *et al.*, 2008; Raedeke *et al.*, 2002). This presents very real challenges to professional practitioners, and, more specifically, exactly what a practitioner does when faced with a potential case of athlete burnout. Research focused on athlete burnout in the past decade, however, has begun to pave the way for greater clarity and the development of a knowledge base with greater consensus to inform applied practice.

In order to act as a useful guide for professionals, this chapter has expressly set out to "put the fish on the table" and explore the guts of the issues in athlete burnout. The intention here is to raise awareness of the issues, and to enable an appreciation of what is known and not known in the field. By presenting the existent knowledge base as social-psychologically driven and physically driven types of burnout (Gould *et al.*, 1996a), practitioners can consider potential contributory factors and appropriate interventions tailored to the individual rather than a one-model-fits-all approach. At the core of the syndrome are the three dimensions of physical and emotional exhaustion, sport devaluation, and reduced athletic accomplishment. Critical also to the case of athlete burnout is that it is an enduring state and not transitory. It takes time to develop and may go unnoticed at first, but, equally, there are no quick-fix solutions to recovery from burnout. Ultimately, the best intervention is prevention.

References

Black, J. M. and Smith, A. L. (2007). An examination of Coakley's perspective on identity, control, and burnout among adolescent athletes. *International Journal of Sport Psychology*, 38, 417–436.

Brown, T. A., Chorpita, B. F., Korotitsch, W., and Barlow, D. H. (1997). Psychometric properties of the Depression Anxiety Stress Scales (DASS) in clinical samples. *Behaviour Research and Therapy*, 35, 79–89.

Caccese, T. M. and Mayerberg, C. K. (1984). Gender differences in perceived burnout of college coaches. *Journal of Sport and Exercise Psychology*, 6, 279–288.

Cherniss, C. (1980). *Staff burnout: Job stress in the human services*. Beverley Hills, CA: Sage.

Coakley, J. A. (1992). Burnout amongst adolescent athletes: A personal failure or social problem? *Sociology of Sport Journal*, 9, 271–285.

Coakley, J. A. (2009). From the outside in: Burnout as an organisational issue. *Journal of Intercollegiate Sports*, 2, 35–41.

Cohn, P. (1990). An exploratory study on sources of stress and athlete burnout in youth golf. *The Sport Psychologist*, 4, 95–106.

Cox, T., Kuk, K., and Leiter, M. P. (1993). Burnout, health, work stress and organisational healthiness. In W. B. Schaufeli, C. Maslach, and T. Marek (eds), *Profes-*

sional burnout: Recent developments in theory and research (pp. 84–101). Washington DC: Taylor & Francis.

Cox, T., Tisserand, M. and Taris, T. (2005). The conceptualisation and measurement of burnout: Questions and directions. *Work and Stress*, 19, 187–191.

Cresswell, S. L. (2009). Possible early signs of athlete burnout: A prospective study. *Journal of Science and Medicine in Sport*, 12, 393–398.

Cresswell, S. L. and Eklund, R. C. (2003). The athlete burnout syndrome: A practitioner's guide. *New Zealand Journal of Sports Medicine*, 31, 4–9.

Cresswell, S. L. and Eklund, R. C. (2004). The athlete burnout syndrome: Possible early warning signs. *Journal of Science and Medicine in Sport*, 7, 481–487.

Cresswell, S. L. and Eklund, R. C. (2005a). Motivation and burnout among top amateur rugby players. *Medicine and Science in Sports and Exercise*, 37, 469–477.

Cresswell, S. L. and Eklund, R. C. (2005b). Changes in athlete burnout and motivation over a 12-week league tournament. *Medicine and Science in Sports and Exercise*, 37, 1957–1966.

Cresswell, S. L. and Eklund, R. C. (2006a). Athlete burnout: Conceptual confusion, current research, and future directions. In S. Hanton and S. D. Mellalieu (eds). *Literature reviews in sport psychology* (pp. 91–126). Hauppage, NY: Nova Science.

Cresswell, S. L. and Eklund, R. C. (2006b). The nature of athlete burnout: Key characteristics and attributions. *Journal of Applied Sport Psychology*, 18, 219–239.

Cresswell, S. L. and Eklund, R. C. (2006c). The convergent and discriminant validity of burnout measures in sport: A multi-method multi-trait analysis. *Journal of Sports Sciences*, 24, 209–212.

Cresswell, S. L. and Eklund, R. C. (2007a). Athlete burnout: A longitudinal qualitative study. *The Sport Psychologist*, 21, 1–20.

Cresswell, S. L. and Eklund, R. C. (2007b). Athlete burnout and organisational culture: An English rugby replication. *International Journal of Sport Psychology*, 38, 365–387.

Dale, J. and Weinberg, R. S. (1990). Burnout in sport: A review and critique. *Journal of Applied Sport Psychology*, 2, 67–83.

Deci, E. L. and Ryan, R. M. (1985). *Intrinsic motivation and self-determination in human behavior.* New York, NY: Plenum Press.

Etzion, D. (1987). *Burnout: The hidden agenda of human distress.* IIBR Series of Organisational Behaviour and Human Resources, Working Paper No. 930/87. Tel Aviv, Israel: Tel Aviv University, The Israel Institute of Business Research, Faculty of Management.

Fender, L. K. (1989). Athlete burnout: Potential for research and intervention strategies. *The Sport Psychologist*, 3, 63–71.

Fredrickson, B. L. and Joiner, T. (2002). Positive emotions trigger upward spirals toward emotional well-being. *Psychological Science*, 13, 172–175.

Freudenberger, H. J. (1974). Staff burnout. *Journal of Social Issues*, 30, 159–165.

Freudenberger, H. J. (1975). The staff burnout syndrome in alternative institutions. *Psychotherapy Theory, Research, and Practice*, 12, 73–82.

Freudenberger, H. J. (1983). Hazards of psychotherapeutic practice. *Psychotherapy in Private Practice*, 1, 83–89.

Glass, D. C. and McKnight, J. D. (1996). Perceived control, depressive symptomatology, and professional burnout: A review of the evidence. *Psychology and Health*, 11, 23–48.

Goodger, K. I., Lavallee, D. E., Gorely, P. J., and Harwood, C. G. (2007a). Burnout in sport: A systematic review. *The Sport Psychologist*, 21, 127–151.

Goodger, K. I., Wolfenden, L., and Lavallee, D. (2007b). Symptoms and consequences associated with three dimensions of burnout in junior tennis players. *International Journal of Sport Psychology*, 38, 342–364.

Gould, D. (1997). Burnout: Personal motivation gone awry. *Journal of Applied Sport Psychology*, 7, 176–189.

Gould, D., Tuffey, S., Udry, E., and Loehr, J. (1996a). Burnout in competitive junior tennis players: II. Qualitative analysis. *The Sport Psychologist*, 10, 341–366.

Gould, D., Udry, E., Tuffey, S., and Loehr, J. (1996b). Burnout in competitive junior tennis players: I. A quantitative psychological assessment. *The Sport Psychologist*, 10, 322–340.

Gould, D., Udry, E., Tuffey, S., and Loehr, J. (1997). Burnout in competitive junior tennis players: III. Individual differences in the burnout experience. *The Sport Psychologist*, 11, 257–276.

Gustafsson. H., Kentta, G., Hassmen, P., Lundqvist, C., and Durand-Bush, N. (2007). The process of burnout: A multiple case study of three elite endurance athletes. *International Journal of Sport Psychology*, 38, 388–416.

Harlick, M. and McKenzie, A. (2000). Burnout in junior tennis: A research report. *New Zealand Journal of Sport Medicine*, 28, 36–39.

Hemingway, H. and Marmot, M. (1999). Psychosocial factors in the aetiology and prognosis of coronary heart disease: Systematic review of prospective cohort studies. *British Medical Journal*, 318, 1460–1467.

Hodge, K., Lonsdale, C., and Ng, J. (2008). Burnout in elite rugby: Relationships with basic psychological needs fulfilment. *Journal of Sports Sciences*, 26, 835–844.

Kallus, K. W. and Kellmann, M. (2000). Burnout in athletes and coaches. In Y. L. Hanin (ed.), *Emotions in sport* (pp. 209–230). Champaign IL: Human Kinetics.

Kellmann, M. (ed.), (2002). *Enhancing recovery: Preventing underperformance in athletes.* Champaign, IL: Human Kinetics.

Kellmann, M. and Gunther, K. (2000). Changes in stress and recovery in elite rowers during preparation for the Olympic Games. *Medicine and Science in Sport and Exercise*, 32, 676–683.

Kellmann, M. and Kallus, K. W. (2001). *Recovery-stress questionnaire for athletes: User manual.* Champaign IL: Human Kinetics.

Kenttä, G. and Hassmén, P. (1998). Overtraining and recovery: A conceptual model. *Sports Medicine*, 26, 1–16.

Kenttä, G., Hassmén, P., and Raglin, J. S. (2006). Mood state monitoring of training and recovery in elite kayakers. *European Journal of Sport Science*, 4, 245–253.

Kohlrieser, G. (2006). *Hostage at the table. How leaders can overcome conflict, influence others, and raise performance.* San Francisco, CA: Jossey-Bass.

Kuipers, H. (1996). How much is too much? Performance aspects of overtraining. *Research Quarterly for Exercise and Sport*, 67, 65–69.

Lemyre, N., Roberts, G. C., and Treasure, D. (2006). Influence of athlete variability in motivation and affect on burnout. *Journal of Sport and Exercise Psychology*, 28, 32–48.

Lemyre, P. N., Roberts, G. C., and Stray-Gundersen, J. (2007). Motivational, overtraining and burnout: Can self-determined motivation predict overtraining and burnout in elite athletes. *European Journal of Sport Sciences*, 7, 115–126.

Lemyre, P. N., Hall, H. K., and Roberts, G. C. (2008). A social cognitive approach to burnout in elite athletes. *Scandinavian Journal of Medicine and Sciences in Sport*, 18, 221–234.

Lonsdale, C. and Hodge, K. (2011). Temporal ordering of motivational quality and athlete burnout in elite sport. *Medicine and Science in Sport and Exercise*, 43, 913–921.

Lonsdale, C., Hodge, K., and Rose, E. A. (2009). Burnout in elite sport: A self-determination perspective. *Journal of Sports Sciences*, 27, 785–795.

Lundqvist, C. and Kenttä, G. (2010). Positive emotions are not simply the absence of the negative ones: Development and validation of the Emotional Recovery Questionnaire (EmRecQ). *The Sport Psychologist*, 24, 468–488.

Maslach, C. (1993). *Burnout: A multidimensional perspective.* In W. B. Schaufeli, C. Maslach, and T. Marek (eds), *Professional burnout: Recent developments in theory and research* (pp. 19–32). Washington DC: Taylor & Francis.

Maslach, C. and Jackson, S. E. (1981). The measurement of experienced burnout. *Journal of Occupational Behaviour*, 2, 99–113.

Maslach, C. and Jackson, S. E. (1984). Burnout in organisational settings. In S. Oskamp (ed.), *Applied social psychology annual: Applications in organisational settings* (Vol. 5, pp. 133–153). Beverly Hills, CA: Sage.

Maslach, C. and Leiter, M. P. (1997). *The truth about burnout.* San Francisco CA: Jossey-Bass.

Maslach, C. and Schaufeli, W. B. (1993). Historical and conceptual development of burnout. In W. B. Schaufeli, C. Maslach, and T. Marek (eds), *Professional burnout: Recent developments in theory and research* (pp. 1–16). Washington DC: Taylor & Francis.

Maslach, C., Jackson, S. E., and Leiter, M. P. (1996). *Maslach Burnout Inventory Manual* (3rd edn). Palo Alto, CA: Consulting Psychologists Press.

Maslach. C., Schaufeli, W. B., and Leiter, M. P. (2001). Job burnout. *Annual Review of Psychology*, 52, 397–422.

McNair, D. M., Lorr, M., and Droppleman, L. F. (1992). *Revised manual for the profile of mood states.* San Diego, CA: Educational and Industrial Testing Services.

Pines, A. (1993). Burnout: An existential perspective. In W. B. Schaufeli, C. Maslach and T. Marek (eds), *Professional burnout: Recent developments in theory and research* (pp. 33–51). Washington DC: Taylor & Francis.

Raedeke, T. D. (1997). Is athlete burnout more than just stress? A sport commitment perspective. *Journal of Sport and Exercise Psychology*, 19, 396–417.

Raedeke, T. D. and Smith, A. L. (2001). Development and preliminary validation of an athlete burnout measure. *Journal of Sport and Exercise Psychology*, 23, 281–306.

Raedeke, T. D. and Smith, A. L. (2004). Coping resources and athlete burnout: An examination of stress mediated and moderation hypothesis. *Journal of Sport and Exercise Psychology*, 26, 525–541.

Raedeke, T. D. and Smith, A. L. (2009). *The athlete burnout questionnaire manual.* Morgantown, WV: Fitness information Technology.

Raedeke, T. D., Lunney, K., and Venables, K. (2002). Understanding athlete burnout: Coach perspectives. *Journal of Sport Behaviour*, 22, 181–206.

Raglin, J. S. and Wilson. G. S. (2000). Overtraining in athletes. In Y. L. Hanin (ed.) *Emotions in sport* (pp. 191–207). Champaign, IL: Human Kinetics.

Roelofs, J., Verbraak, M., Keijsers, G. P. J., de Bruin, M. B. N., and Schmidt, A. J. M. (2005). Psychometric properties of a Dutch version of the Maslach Burnout Inventory General Survey (MBI-DV) in individuals with and without clinical burnout. *Stress and Health*, 1, 17–25.

Ryan, R. M. and Deci, E. L. (2000). The darker and brighter sides of human existence: Basic psychological needs as a unifying concept. *Psychological Inquiry*, 11, 319–338.

Schaufeli, W. B. and Buunk, B. P. (2003). Burnout: An overview of 25 years of research and theorising. In M. J. Schabracq, J. A. M. Winnubst, and C. L. Cooper (eds), *The handbook of work and health psychology* (2nd edn, pp. 383–425). Chichester, UK: Wiley.

Schaufeli, W. B. and Enzmann, D. (1998). *The burnout companion to study and practice: A critical analysis.* London, UK: Taylor & Francis.

Schaufeli, W. B. and Salanova, M. (2007). Efficacy or inefficacy, that's the question: Burnout and engagement, and their relationships with efficacy beliefs. *Anxiety, Coping and Stress*, 20, 177–196.

Schaufeli, W. B. and Taris, T. W. (2005). Commentary: The conceptualisation and measurement of burnout: Common ground and worlds apart. *Work and Stress*, 19, 256–262.

Schaufeli, W. B., Leiter, M. P., Maslach, C., and Jackson, S. E. (1996). Maslach Burnout Inventory – General survey. In C. Maslach, S. E. Jackson, and M. P. Leiter (eds), *The Maslach Burnout Inventory – Test Manual* (3rd edn, pp. 200–237). Palo Alto, CA: Consulting Psychologists Press.

Schaufeli, W. B., Bakker, A. B., Hoogdum, K., Schaap, C., and Klader, A. (2001). On the clinical validity of the Maslach Burnout Inventory and the Burnout Measure. *Psychology and Health*, 16, 565–582.

Schmidt, G. W. and Stein, G. L. (1991). A commitment model of burnout. *Journal of Applied Sport Psychology*, 8, 323–345.

Schutte, N., Toppinen, S., Kalimo, R., and Schaufeli, W. (2000). The factorial validity of the Maslach Burnout Inventory – General Survey (MBI-GS) across occupational groups and nations. *Journal of Occupational and Organisational Psychology*, 73, 53–66.

Shirom, A. (2005). Reflections on the study of burnout. *Work and Stress*, 19, 263–270.

Shirom, A. (2009). Burnout and health: Expanding our knowledge. *Stress and Work*, 25, 281–285.

Silva, J. M. (1990). An analysis of the training stress syndrome in competitive athletics. *Journal of Applied Sport Psychology*, 2, 5–20.

Smith, R. E. (1986). Toward a cognitive-affective model of athlete burnout. *Journal of Sport Psychology*, 8, 36–50.

Sonnentag, S. and Fritz, C. (2007). The Recovery Experience Questionnaire: Development and validation of a measure for assessing recuperation and unwinding from work. *Journal of Occupational Health Psychology*, 12, 204–221.

Thibaut, J. W. and Kelley, H. H. (1959). *The social psychology of groups.* New York, NY: John Wiley & Sons.

Toppinen-Tanner, S., Kalimo, R., and Mutanen, P. (2002). The process of burnout in white-collar and blue-collar jobs: Eight-year prospective study of exhaustion. *Journal of Organisational Behaviour*, 23, 555–570.

Urhausen, A. and Kindermann, W. (2002). Diagnosis of overtraining–What tools do we have? *Sports Medicine*, 32, 95–102.

Viru, A. (1994). Molecular cellular mechanisms of training effects. *Journal of Sports Medicine and Physical Fitness*, 34, 309–322.

Weinberg, R. S. and Gould, D. (2003). *Foundations of sport and exercise psychology* (4th edn). Champaign, IL: Human Kinetics.

7 Working with athletes in career transitions

Natalia B. Stambulova

Abstract

In this chapter an evolution of the topic of athletes' career transitions in sport psychology is traced though a meta-review of two books and eight review papers, in which theoretical, empirical, and applied aspects of the topic have been thoroughly addressed. Based on this meta-review, a conceptual model for assistance in career transitions (ACT model) is suggested. Within the ACT model, seven major types of career transition interventions – career planning, lifestyle management, life skills training, identity development, cultural adaptation, crisis-coping educational, and clinical – are described in greater depth. Further, anticipated challenges for both career transition research and practice are outlined.

Keywords: athletes' careers, career assistance, career transition, transition interventions

Introduction

Career development and transition research in sport psychology has a long past but a short history, in that initial interest in studying athletes' careers was generated in the 1950s and 1960s (see, for example, Weinberg and Arond, 1952; Bookbinder, 1955; Mihovilovic, 1968), but an essential increase in research and applications in the topic has referred mainly to the past two decades. Review types of publications on athletes' career transitions appeared at the end of the 1990s, after a solid body of knowledge on the topic had been accumulated. As stated by Mellalieu and Hanton, "A review of literature functions as an initial vehicle for a topic organisation, reorganisation, and defined structure" (2009, p. 1). Therefore, evolution of the topic can be traced through analysis of major publications such as books and review papers, to observe how the structure of the topic has been organised and reorganised. Two books and eight review papers on athletes' career transitions were selected to provide a meta-review of the topic (Alfermann and Stambulova, 2007; Gordon *et al.*, 2005;

Hackfort and Huang, 2005; Lavallee and Wylleman, 2000; Petitpas *et al.*, 2009; Stambulova, 2010a; Stambulova *et al.*, 2009; Taylor and Ogilvie, 2001; Wylleman *et al.*, 1999, 2004). Because this meta-review was intended to facilitate development of the conceptual model of assistance in career transitions (ACT model), the selection process was designed to prioritise: (a) the most recent review papers (since the end of 1990s) to provide an updated view of the career transition topic in sport psychology, (b) papers written by authors representing different countries and various traditions in career research and assistance to cover cultural diversity in the topic, and (c) papers in which a link between career research and assistance was clearly articulated. Below, the selected papers will be briefly analysed in their chronological order, followed by a summary of the meta-review, and further practical implications.

The first selected review-type publication on athletes' career transitions was the European Federation of Sport Psychology (FEPSAC) monograph *Career Transitions in Competitive Sports*, authored by 11 European and North American researchers and practitioners (Wylleman *et al.*, 1999). The authors were also members of the career transition special interest group organised in 1995, during the Ninth European Congress of Sport Psychology, to share knowledge and expertise in the area. This collective monograph provided a broad picture of the topic of career transitions in sport psychology, based on the theory-to-practice approach. Athletic career was described as a sequence of "specific stages and transitions" (1999, p. 6), with a transition defined as "an event or non-event [which] results in a change in assumptions about oneself and the world, and thus requires a corresponding change in one's behaviour and relationships" (Schlossberg, 1981, p. 5). At the same time, the authors proposed that a transition should be considered as a process and not as a single event. Transitions were classified in terms of their high or low degree of predictability, and their origin in athletes' athletic, psychological, psychosocial, or academic/vocational development. The authors provided a brief overview of predictable athletic transitions, such as transition into sport specialisation, transition to intensive training, transition to elite sports, and transition out of elite sports. Among non-athletic transitions, those in athletes' psychosocial and academic-vocational development were emphasised. Theoretical frameworks used to study athletes' transitions (mainly, athletic retirement) were reported to be not sport-specific, and borrowed from social gerontology, thanatology, and counselling psychology; research was both qualitative and quantitative, and, most often, retrospective. The authors called for sport-specific theoretical frameworks, as well as for multi-method, longitudinal, "in vivo" studies of the transition process from multiple perspectives (those of athletes, coaches, parents, etc.). The applied aspect of the topic of career transitions was termed "career assistance", and was represented by an overview of career assistance interventions (mainly life skills training and counselling) and programmes. Career assistance programmes (CAPs), such as the Olympic Athlete Career Centre (Canada), the Athlete Career and Education Program (Australia), and others, were summarised as encompassing five major topics: (1) social/relationship issues, (2) balancing lifestyle, (3) personal management skills, (4) educational/vocational guidance, and (5) athletic retirement issues. To briefly sum up, the FEPSAC monograph contributed to the literature by structuring the topic as having investigative and applied parts; defining an athletic career and career transitions; suggesting two classifications of transitions; and calling for sport-specific theoretical frameworks, variety in research methodologies, and theory/research-driven interventions.

The next big step in structuring the topic of career transitions in sport was a book, *Career Transitions in Sport: International Perspectives*, authored by 29 European, North American, and Australian experts in the area, and edited by Lavallee and Wylleman (2000). This book organised the career transition topic into three major parts, complemented by a bibliography on career transition literature with 270 annotated references. The first part was devoted to theory and research on athletes' career transitions, with foci on: (a) a shift from non-sport to sport-specific models employed to study athletic retirement, (b) self-identity and athletic identity issues in relation to career transitions, and (c) factors involved in athletes' adaptation in retirement. The conceptual model of athletic career termination (Taylor and Ogilvie, 1994) was introduced as a sport-specific framework to study the transition from sports to the post-sports life. The second part of the book introduced a range of CAPs around the world and services provided by them, practical recommendations for developing such programmes, and particular career transition intervention strategies (life skills training, information processing, mentoring, and existential counselling). In the third part of the book, the theory-to-practice approach was adopted in describing transitions of special populations, such as young athletes, disabled athletes, dancers, and athletes who were forced to terminate their involvement in sport because of an organisational decision. All in all, this book advocated theory/research-driven practice in helping athletes in career transitions. It emphasised that transitions vary in terms of the demands they put on athletes and also in terms of athletes' reactions to the demands and career assistance interventions. As noted by Petitpas and Champagne, "Athletes have a variety of experiences and come from diverse educational, cultural, and socio-economic backgrounds. As a result,... sport psychology practitioners are often required to use creative and adaptive approaches when working with this highly specialised population." (2000, p. 93).

The year after the book edited by Lavallee and Wylleman came out, Taylor and Ogilvie (2001) provided a review focused on only one aspect of the career transition topic; that is, athletes' career termination and retirement. The authors introduced their conceptual model of athletic career termination, along with related research findings and practical implications.

The process of athletes' adaptation to retirement was described with respect to: (1) causes of career termination, (2) factors that affect post-career adaptation, (3) resources available to facilitate retirement, (4) quality of adaptation, and (5) interventions. The authors provided a body of research findings on causes of career termination (age, de-selection, injury, free choice), and emphasised that normally several factors are responsible for an athlete's decision to terminate. Research confirmed that high and exclusive athletic identity (i.e. the degree of identification with the athlete's role), loss of athletic status and popularity, and lack of control over termination (i.e. involuntary or forced retirement) generate retirement difficulties. On the other hand, it was shown that multiple personal identities, positive experiences in roles other than the athletic role (e.g. in a student role), and perceived control over termination facilitate the retirement process. The same was also confirmed with regard to coping skills/strategies, retirement planning, and social support. Quality of adaptation was described as two potential outcomes of the transition; namely, healthy transition and transition distress or crisis. Analysing relevant literature, the authors did not find consensus between researchers in terms of what percentages of former athletes experienced retirement as a healthy transition and as a crisis. This lack of consensus in research findings could be a consequence of a lack of consensus among the researchers about how to measure the quality of the post-career adaptation. Some researchers measured it through athletes' adaptation difficulties and distress, while others considered life satisfaction and attitudes towards work. Research findings on factors and resources facilitating or debilitating the transition showed them to be a basis for career transition interventions. The authors classified interventions as having preventive (e.g. retirement planning) and distress/crisis treatment (e.g. dealing with identity problems) perspectives. They also classified career transition interventions as cognitive (e.g. cognitive reframing, positive imagery), emotional (e.g. stress management skills), behavioural (e.g. exploring new social roles), and social (e.g. expanding their social support system). Unlike the two books outlined above, Taylor and Ogilvie's chapter did not organise the whole career transition topic, but structured its athletic retirement subtopic, which dominated for years in the area and served as a basis for CAPs and interventions.

In 2004, *Psychology of Sport and Exercise* published a special issue on career transitions in sport. Wylleman, Alfermann, and Lavallee opened that issue with a review paper, "Career transitions in sport: European perspectives". This paper focused on several new developments in the topic, related to career transition terminology, theoretical frameworks, and applied work with transitional athletes. The authors stated that conceptual changes in the topic had led to a new theoretical framework and opened new directions and perspectives in both career transition research and interventions. Major conceptual developments included: (a) researchers' reappraisal of a career termination from “social death” to “social rebirth”, (b) a shift from understanding a transition as a single life event to seeing it as a process in which different spheres of one’s life are intertwined, and (c) fixing the terms normative and non-normative for predictable and less predictable (idiosyncratic) transitions, correspondingly. These conceptual changes led to a holistic lifespan perspective in understanding athletes’ development, “which spans the athletic and post-athletic career and which includes transitions occurring in the athletic career as well as those occurring in other domains of athletes’ lives” (Wylleman *et al.*, 2004, p. 7). The holistic lifespan perspective was embodied in the developmental model of transitions faced by athletes (Wylleman and Lavallee, 2004). In this model, stages and normative transitions in four domains of athletes’ lifespan development – athletic, psychological, psychosocial, and academic/vocational – were outlined and roughly aligned with chronological ages. The authors called for new research directions within the holistic lifespan perspective, such as athletic within-career transitions (e.g. from junior to senior sports), non-athletic transitions (e.g. from school to college), non-normative transitions (e.g. injury), premature dropout from sports, and others. In the applied part of the review it was mentioned that career transition interventions in parallel with the developments at the conceptual level showed a shift from therapeutic interventions dealing with traumatic retirement experiences to preventive and educational interventions (e.g. life skills training) helping athletes to develop coping resources. Last, but not least, the authors provided an updated list of 12 CAPs around the world, and stated the importance of comprehensive evaluation of the effectiveness of such programmes and career transition interventions. Briefly, this review demonstrated the whole topic reorganisation due to reappraisal of athletes’ transitions from the holistic lifespan perspective.

The two next review papers were published in 2005, following one another in the book edited by Hackfort *et al.* (2005). The first was authored by Gordon *et al.* (2005), and the second, by Hackfort and Huang (2005).

Gordon and colleagues provided an in-depth review of CAPs. They began with a brief rationale for such programmes, proceeded with an overview of existing CAPs, and completed the paper with analysis, and discussion of the future directions in research evaluating the effectiveness, of CAPs. Based on the literature and their own professional experiences, the authors stated that many athletes find themselves unprepared for career transitions (even for such inevitable one as athletic retirement), and to successfully cope with transitions need professional assistance provided by, for example, CAPs. Arguments for the significance of CAPs for athletes’ successful career development in sport and in the post-sport life were also found in the analysis of some forecast tendencies of elite and professional sports – for example, early sport specialisation, sport’s commercialisation and globalisation, athletes’ international migration, and elevated public visibility of sport stars – which put additional pressure on athletes and increase their potential vulnerability in career transitions. Four major CAPs, including the International Olympic Job Opportunities Program, the United States' Career Assistance Program for Athletes, the Canadian Olympic Athlete Career Centre, and the Athlete Career and Education Programme that operated in Australia and the United Kingdom, were described in terms of their content, target groups, and style of service delivery. From their descriptions, the CAPs looked like programmes that should be really helpful to athletes, providing a good addition to the athletes' coping resources. However, the authors strongly advocated for evidence-based research demonstrating effects of the programmes and transition services/interventions involved. Discussing three studies on evaluation of CAPs (Bobridge *et al.*, 2003; Gorely *et al.*, 2001; UK Sport, 2001), the authors concluded that such studies were rare but also highly descriptive in nature, with foci on services used (and not used) and the clients' satisfaction. To sum up, a research–practice–research cycle is visible in the overall structure of this paper, meaning that development of CAPs is informed by research, and after the programmes are established, research methods should be applied again to evaluate their effectiveness. In the evaluative studies the authors recommended using a longitudinal design and multi-method approach to assess changes in athletes' behaviours, perceptions, attitudes, etc., and also to consider as mediating factors athletes' career stage and readiness for career assistance.

In the review of Hackfort and Huang (2005), the topic of career transitions was organised using the action theory (e.g. Nitsch, 2000) as an embracing and integrative framework: "The action theory offers a holistic approach including goal-directed and purposeful behaviour in a person–environment–task constellation" (Hackfort and Huang, 2005, p. 246). Taking this perspective, a career was defined as "a result of actions organised in a number of situations over a long period of time" (2005, p. 251). In line with the action theory, the authors suggested adopting the concepts "external career" (progress measured by objective categories established by society or organisation) and "internal career" (individuals' own concepts of their progress) in athletes' career research. Further, an overview of existing career transition studies was provided, and an interpretation from the point of view of action theory was offered. When applying the action theory to a career transition, "task" represented transition demands an athlete had to cope with; "person", the athlete's personal resources; and "environment", environmental contexts of the transition. Indeed, all these three aspects were visible in the career transition research analysed in the paper, but in the studies they were often considered separately. Moving to an applied perspective, the authors emphasised "obvious yet complex" relationships between elite athletes and related sport organisations/systems. The authors recommended that the typical utilitarian nature of these relationships be replaced by three deontological principles of treating athletes in sport organisations and CAPs: (1) autonomy, with an intention to help athletes become autonomous; (2) beneficence – that is, helping them to realise their interests; and (3) non-maleficence, with an obligation not to intentionally inflict any harm. Further, it was suggested that task, person, and environment form a frame to structure career counselling and CAPs. All in all, the authors advocated for the action theory's potential to enrich both career transition research and career assistance.

Alfermann and Stambulova (2007) contributed a review in which the topic of career transitions in sport was further organised in terms of its conceptual/theoretical, empirical, and applied aspects. The authors defined key terms in the topic, classified relevant theoretical frameworks, summarised research issues, and provided a set of major principles and a summary of career transition interventions and CAPs. Athletic career was defined as: (a) "a multi-year sport activity voluntarily chosen by the person and aimed at achieving his/her individual peak in athletic performance in one or several sport events" (2007, p. 713), (b) a succession of stages and transitions, and (c) related only to competitive sports but on all its levels, including local, national, and international, as well as amateur and professional. Applied to athletic careers, transitions were defined as normative or non-normative turning phases in the course of a career characterised by "a set of specific demands related to practice, competitions, communication, and lifestyle that athletes have to cope with in order to continue successfully in sport or to adjust to the post-career" (2007, p. 713). The major structural contribution of this review paper was a classification and an overview of career-related models used in sport psychology research and applied work with athletes. Three types of models were identified: (1) descriptive career stage models, (2) explanatory career transition models, and (3) intervention models. Descriptive models (e.g. Bloom, 1985; Côté, 1999; Salmela, 1994; Stambulova, 1994; Wylleman and Lavallee, 2004) provided a sequence of career stages and predicted a set of athletes' normative transitions derived from the logic of the career development process. In spite of the fact that descriptive models were created based on research in various sociocultural contexts, it was possible to identify a common pattern in a sequence of stages, including preparatory/initiation/sampling stage, development/specialisation stage, mastery/investment/culmination stage, final/maintenance stage, and discontinuation stage of an athletic career with normative transitional phases between them. Presenting the descriptive models, the authors emphasised that such models could predict the existence of particular transitions, but could not explain the process of transition. The transition process, outcomes, and factors involved were major foci of career transition explanatory models (Schlossberg, 1981; Stambulova, 2003; Taylor and Ogilvie, 1994, 2001). Among these models, the athletic career transition model

(Stambulova, 2003) was introduced in more detail. In this model, a transition was depicted as a process of coping with a set of transition demands. Effectiveness of coping was seen as dependent on a dynamic balance between the coping resources and barriers. "Resources" referred to the various internal and external factors that facilitated the transition (e.g. athlete's knowledge, competencies and skills, social support, etc.), and "barriers" referred to the various internal and external factors that interfered with the coping process (e.g. lack of certain competencies and skills, lack of financial or social support). The model entailed two primary transition outcomes: successful transition (in the case of a good fit between demands and the athlete's coping resources) and crisis transition. Crisis transition was conceptualised as a transition the athlete had to make but was not able to cope with independently, and for which the athlete perceived a need for psychological assistance. Further, according to the model, the crisis transition could have two possible secondary outcomes: delayed successful transition (in the case of effective intervention) and unsuccessful transition (in the case of no or ineffective intervention), associated with negative long-term consequences of not coping with a crisis (e.g. premature dropout, neuroses, overtraining, eating disorders, substance abuse, etc.). Each outcome dictated a distinct set of career transition interventions, such as preventive, crisis-coping, and negative-consequences coping interventions. The authors used this classification of interventions, with related models and strategies, to structure the applied part of the review paper. A new aspect included here was the integration of ten major principles of assisting athletes in career transitions. These principles included:

1 a whole-career approach, to help athletes cope with both normative and non-normative transitions throughout the whole course of an athletic career;
2 a whole-person approach, to help them deal with transitions in various spheres of life;
3 a developmental approach, to help athletes link their past career experiences, present situation, and perceived future;
4 an activity-specific approach, to take into account not only common but also type-of-sport-specific demands in each athletic transition;
5 a culture-specific approach, to help athletes adjust within a particular sport system and culture;
6 an individual approach, to accommodate the athletes' perceptions of the transition and their idiosyncratic resources and barriers;
7 a transferable skills approach, to teach them life skills applicable both in and outside sport;
8 a multidimensional approach, to provide enhancement, support, counselling, and other kinds of interventions, depending on the needs of the athlete;

9 a multilevel approach, to address both traumatic symptoms and the issues behind the symptoms (e.g. perceptions, decisions, attributions, attitudes, etc.); and
10 an empowerment approach, to help athletes develop coping resources and strategies, allowing them to become autonomous after the intervention.

Discussing CAPs, the authors stated some typical problems in their administration, including financial difficulties, low profile of CAPs among athletes and coaches, and a lack of empirically based evidence of their effectiveness. In the future directions, calls for longitudinal and cross-cultural studies on athletic and non-athletic transitions, and thorough assessment of CAPs, were articulated.

In the next review paper, Petitpas *et al.* (2009) organised theoretical, empirical, and applied perspectives in the subtopic of transitions of student-athletes. The authors stated that a transition from high school to college puts a set of demands on the incoming students. The students have to meet new academic requirements and the challenges of living far from home, create relationships, and manage their time and energy. Also, joining a sport programme, they have to adjust to demanding sport participation at the intercollegiate level and new teammates and coaches, as well as athletic career termination upon graduation from the college. Potential non-normative athletic transitions of student-athletes include injury and de-selection from the team. The authors mentioned that in spite of the obvious importance of student-athletes' transitions, very limited research was conducted on this specific population, and existing studies focused mainly on their retirement from sports. Research in this area based on the human adaptation to transition model (Schlossberg, 1981) and the life development intervention (LDI) model (Danish *et al.*, 1993) showed several parallels with athletic retirement research findings obtained in a broader athletic population. For example, career-ending injury and high athletic identity were found to interfere with successful adaptation to the post-career phase, while retirement planning was confirmed as a resource in this transition. The LDI framework was also suggested as a basis for assisting student-athletes in transitions. According to the LDI model, "transitions or 'critical life events' are not discrete but are processes that commence when individuals begin to anticipate them and continue through their occurrence until the post-transition aftermath has been determined" (Petitpas *et al.*, 2009, p. 289). Therefore, three types of transition interventions were outlined: (1) pre-transition enhancement interventions, educating student-athletes about the forthcoming transitions; (2) during transition, supportive interventions, helping athletes to develop coping resources and support networks; and (3) post-transition counselling interventions, assisting student-athletes to cope with potential negative consequences (e.g. substance abuse) of not coping with the transition. These types of interventions were well illustrated through presentation of the CHAMPS/Life skills program of the US National Collegiate Athletic Association. This program was designed to support student-athletes in five areas, namely academics, athletics, personal development, career planning, and community service, and it covered four years of college education, with new tasks and content each year. For example, while the first-year students were involved in self-exploration and development of communication skills, the final-year students were focused on preparing for termination in sport and a transition from college to the workplace. The authors concluded that any intervention programme for student-athletes should not only enhance their ability to cope with relevant transitions, but also help them in personal growth.

Recently, Stambulova *et al.* (2009) presented the International Society of Sport Psychology Position Stand on athletes' career development and transitions, using a sociocultural diversity of athletes, researchers, and practitioners as a principle to organise the paper. The authors emphasised that career models just reflect common patterns in athletes' careers and transitions. Depending on age, gender, type of sport, level in sport, and individual profile, as well as related sport system and culture, individual athletes' careers and transitions can vary considerably. Various personal characteristics (e.g. innate potential or athletic identity) and features of sociocultural contexts (e.g. public visibility of sport, jobs available in a sport system for retired athletes, etc.) can work as resources and/or barriers in different transitions across athletes' careers. Further, analysing a body of knowledge of the topic from an international perspective, the authors stated that career development and transition research is currently spread around the world, and the researchers normally internalise their research foci from relevant sociocultural contexts. Four major scientific traditions in career research and assistance – North American, West European, Australian, and East European – were identified and briefly described. It was shown that, due to a resemblance between sociocultural contexts in the respective countries (democratic society structures and individualist cultures), the first three traditions are rather similar to each other and share three major research interests: (1) athletic retirement and athletic identity, (2) stages in career (talent) development, and (3) transitions of student-athletes. The East European tradition, represented mainly by Russian studies, was shown to be infused with hierarchical and collectivist Russian culture, having within-career transitions (especially, the transition to elite sports) and athletes' crises among its major research topics. As examples of increased exchange and cooperation between West and East European researchers, brief summaries of research on the transition from junior to senior sports (e.g. Pummel *et al.*, 2008; Stambulova, 1994, 2009; Vanden Auweele *et al.*, 2004) and the European Perspectives on Athletic Retirement Project were provided. In this summary the transition from junior to senior sports was depicted as: (a) crucial for the athletes who want to reach the elite level in sport; (b) bringing demands related not only to a sport context but also to the athletes' psychological, psychosocial, and academic/vocational development; and (c) characterised by high life stress. Career planning, balancing lifestyle, stress/time/energy management, effective recovery, and continuity in social support were recommended to facilitate athletes' coping with this transition. The aforementioned European Perspectives on Athletic Retirement Project involved a series of cross-cultural studies on athletes' adaptation to the post-career (Alfermann *et al.*, 2004; Stambulova *et al.*, 2007). The researchers found common and nation-specific patterns in athletes' retirement, and attracted the attention of other researchers and practitioners to the multilevel sociocultural context as an important mediating factor in the transition. In the applied part of the paper, the authors emphasised globalisation tendencies in modern sport with the high international migration of athletes, coaches, and sport psychologists, and called for a multicultural approach to career assistance – that is, the practitioners' "ability to work with individuals who are of a different culture" (Gill, 2007, p. 837). All in all, this review paper contributed a new way to structure the topic of career transition by putting culturally informed career research and assistance on the agenda.

Recent focus on cultural/multicultural issues in the career literature is related to a new trend in sport psychology, termed "the cultural turn" (see Ryba *et al.*, 2010). Within the cultural turn perspective, Stambulova (2010a) provided a review paper on the professional culture of career assistance. In this paper, career assistance was defined as a rapidly developing discourse in applied sport psychology, focused on helping athletes with various issues related to their careers in and outside of sport. Helping athletes to cope with career transitions was shown to be essential part of career assistance provided by private career consultants (educational and clinical) and CAPs. The author introduced a new term, "professional culture of career assistance"; that is, "a system of related concepts, underlying theoretical frameworks and research, consultants' shared values, principles and ethical norms, as well as the typical working issues and professional strategies/tools used in consultants' work with athlete-clients" (2010a, p. 286). A multiple metaphor approach (Morgan, 1986) and, more specifically, nine career archetypical metaphors – inheritance, cycle, journey, action, fit, relationship, role, resource, and story (Inkson, 2006) – were applied in this paper to organise career development and transition research and practice in sport psychology. For example, in analysing the athletic career as a journey, three alternative athletic career trajectories defined by the developmental model of sport participation (Côté *et al.*, 2007) were introduced: (1) early sport specialisation and deliberate practice (i.e. high in structure/efforts and low in enjoyment) leading to top performance in one chosen sport; (2) early sampling and deliberate play (i.e. more flexible and diverse sport involvement) with transition to deliberate practice and top performance in one chosen sport; and (3) early sampling and deliberate play followed by transition to recreational sport. In the same way, other career frameworks, typical working issues, and intervention tools were associated with the relevant career metaphors. Based on such an overview, the career assistance professional culture was further defined as an open system with certain components (e.g. common and culture-specific values, principles, frameworks, tools, etc.), structural relationships (e.g. theory/research-driven practice), development in terms of content and delivery of the culture to the next generations in the profession, and systemic functions related to consultants' professional identification, clients' protection, and interventions' quality assurance. All in all, this review paper provided a message for career practitioners that, in order to win more visibility in applied sport psychology, they should increase awareness of their professional identification and culture, promote career assistance professional issues among applied sport psychology students, and ensure athletes and coaches are well informed about their services.

Summary

Ten review papers presented above described the topic of career transition in sport psychology in similar, but also different, ways. Among them, six papers (Alfermann and Stambulova, 2007; Hackfort and Huang, 2005; Lavallee and Wylleman, 2000; Stambulova *et al.*, 2009; Wylleman *et al.*, 1999, 2004) analysed the topic of athletes' career transitions as a whole; two reviews (Petitpas *et al.*, 2009; Taylor and Ogilvie, 2001) focused on the subtopics, such as transitions of student-athletes and athletic retirement; and two papers were devoted mainly to career assistance (Gordon *et al.*, 2005; Stambulova, 2010a).

Because a review of literature is aimed at organising and reorganising the topic of interest (Mellalieu and Hanton, 2009), the structures of the papers come into focus. Authors in five reviews (Alfermann and Stambulova, 2007; Petitpas *et al.*, 2009; Taylor and Ogilvie, 2001; Wylleman *et al.*, 1999, 2004) organised the content of the whole topic or particular subtopic in a traditional way, including concepts, theoretical frameworks, research methodologies and major findings, applied issues, and future directions. Authors of the other five papers used non-traditional ways to organise the topic, such as research-practice-specific populations in transitions (Lavallee and Wylleman, 2000), a research–practice–research cycle (Gordon *et al.*, 2005), the action theory perspective (Hackfort and Huang, 2005), a cultural diversity perspective (Stambulova *et al.*, 2009), and a multiple metaphor approach (Stambulova, 2010a). Comparing these five papers with each other and with the other five papers organised in the traditional way, it is possible to see career transition concepts, theories, research findings, and applied issues in new associations, enriching our overall understanding of the career phenomena. For example, applying the cultural diversity perspective allowed Stambulova *et al.* to identify major traditions in career transition research and applied work, to stimulate researchers around the world not to blindly adopt internationally recognised theoretical frameworks but dare to create culture-specific frameworks, as well as to introduce a multicultural approach for career assistance.

Summarising all the papers included in this meta-review, an evolution of the career transitions topic in sport psychology can be described through the following major shifts: (1) from defining a transition as an event to seeing it as a process; (2) from perceiving athletic retirement as a social death to seeing it as a social rebirth; (3) from particular focus on athletic retirement research to the holistic lifespan perspective in studying athletic and non-athletic, normative, and non-normative transitions; (4) from theoretical frameworks developed in other disciplines to frameworks specific to sport; (5) from career description to explanation of a transition process, and then to career assistance interventions and CAPs; and (6) from perceiving a body of career transition knowledge as universal and applicable to any culture to more culturally informed career research and interventions. Tracing the papers from the earliest to the latest, it is also possible to see that what were mentioned as future directions in earlier reviews often appeared among new developments/shifts in the later reviews (e.g. transition as a process, evaluation of CAPs). At the same time, some other repetitive calls in the reviews (e.g. for longitudinal and experimental design studies, for studies of non-normative transitions) were not really heard, with some rare exceptions (e.g. Lally, 2007; Lavallee, 2005; Stephan *et al.*, 2003).

To conclude, the current status of the career transition topic in sport psychology is characterised by: (a) sport-specific definitions of key concepts (e.g. athletic career, career transition, career assistance); (b) classifications of athletes' transitions, related theoretical frameworks, and interventions; (c) holistic lifespan perspective and a solid body of knowledge about athletes' transitions and the factors involved; (d) professional practice experiences accumulated in CAPs; and (e) principles, values, intervention strategies/tools, etc., integrated into the professional culture of career assistance. In the other word, the topic is "mature" enough to provide practitioners with a set of guidelines for working with athletes in career transitions. Below, these guidelines are integrated into the conceptual model for assistance in career transitions.

Professional practice issues: conceptual model for assistance in career transitions

Professional practice issues derived from the meta-review of the career transition literature and the author's professional experiences of working with transitional athletes are summarised in the conceptual model for assistance in career transitions (ACT model). Figure 7.1 presents a schematic illustration of the ACT model with eight interrelated components: (1) foundations, (2) client's characteristics and mediating factors, (3) goals, (4) contexts, (5) time-frames, (6) basic methods, (7) perspectives and content, and (8) assessment. These components and their relationships are considered below, followed by a summary of the ACT model.

Foundations for assistance in career transitions

Foundations in the ACT model address the question: What is assistance in transitions based on? In other words, how and why should practitioners

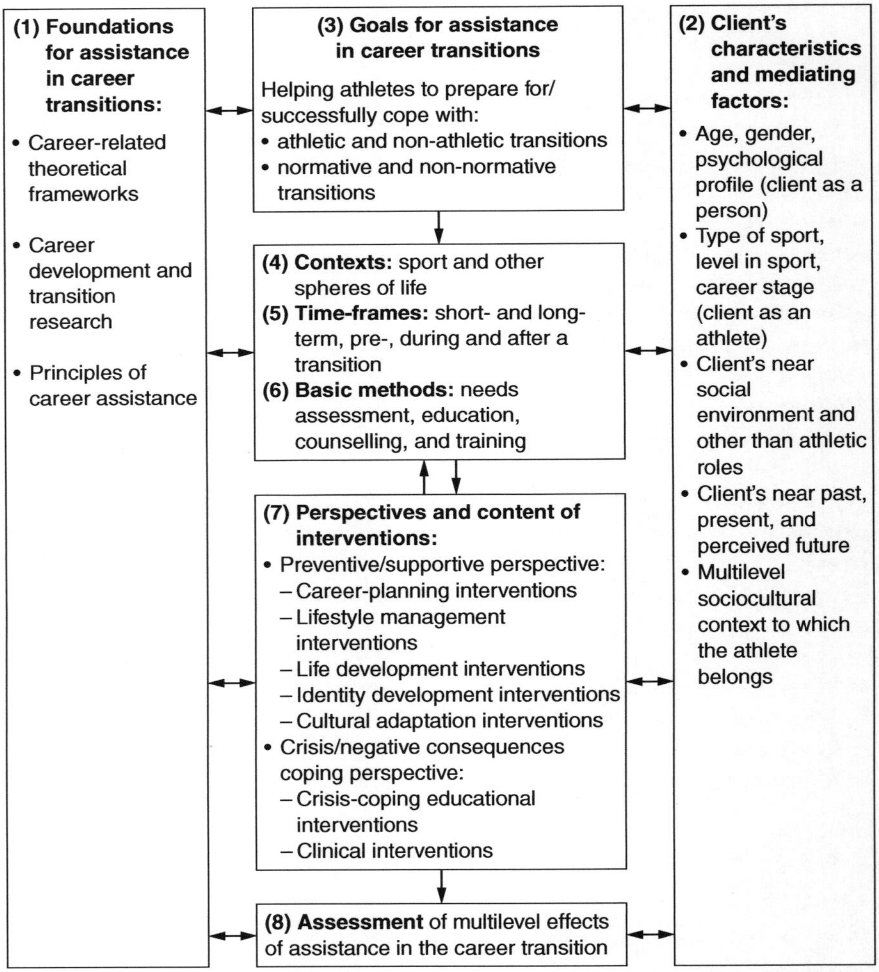

Figure 7.1 The conceptual model for assistance in career transitions (ACT model).

work with transitional athletes? Theory/research-driven practice can be seen as a common marker in the review papers analysed above, demonstrating how changes in conceptualisation of career transitions, theories used in the career research, and new research findings on athletes' transitions stimulated changes in principles and approaches used in the career assistance. Therefore, foundations for assistance in career transitions include career-related theoretical frameworks, career development and transition research, and principles of career assistance. These are what consultants dealing with transitional athletes are expected to be familiar with before starting their applied work. Theoretical frameworks (descriptive, explanatory, and intervention models – see the meta-review above and also Alfermann and Stambulova, 2007, for more details) – function as maps, helping to set goals and define the contexts, time-frames, methods, perspective, and content of the intervention, as well as factors to take into account to individualise the intervention, and assessment strategies. For example, descriptive models, such as the developmental model of transitions faced by athletes (Wylleman and Lavallee, 2004) or the developmental model of sport participation (Côté *et al.*, 2007), can be helpful to predict the athlete's forthcoming normative transitions in athletic and non-athletic contexts, while one of the career transition models (e.g. Schlossberg, 1981; Stambulova, 2003, 2009; Taylor and Ogilvie, 1994, 2001) should be used to further deal with the athlete's transition demands, resources, barriers, and coping strategies. When selecting particular frameworks for the intervention, priority should be given to culturally relevant models, if available (Stambulova *et al.*, 2009). Research findings on career transitions might also help practitioners to become oriented to the transition process and related phenomena. Besides, working with athletes experiencing a particular transition – for example, from junior to senior sport, from school to college, from sports to the post-sport life – it is beneficial to become acquainted with the research findings on these transitions to know their specific features (see Petitpas *et al.*, 2009; Stambulova *et al.*, 2009; Taylor and Ogilvie, 2001). Principles of career assistance, such as a whole-career approach, a whole-person approach, and others described in the meta-review above (see Alfermann and Stambulova, 2007; Hackfort and Huang, 2005; Stambulova, 2010a), should be applied in transition interventions and also complemented by basic ethical principles of helping people (non-maleficence, beneficence, informed consent, confidentiality, competence, referral, autonomy, and others).

Client's characteristics and mediating factors

The theoretical foundations can help practitioners to plan career transition interventions only in a combination with thorough information about their clients. In the review papers analysed above, several clients' characteristics, such as age, gender, individual profile, type of sport, level in sport, career stage, type of transition, and perception of the career situation, were shown useful to take into account in the career transition interventions (e.g. Gordon *et al.*, 2005; Lavallee and Wylleman, 2000; Stambulova *et al.*, 2009). In the ACT model, based on the literature and the author's practical experiences of assisting transitional athletes (e.g. Stambulova, 2008), clients' characteristics are structured in several blocks: (a) client as a person (age, gender, psychological profile, etc.); (b) client as an athlete (type of sport, level in sport, career stage, etc.); (c) client's near social environment (e.g. coach, teammates, parents, partner, peers, etc. and relationships with them) and other than athletic roles (e.g. student, friend, worker, family member, etc.); and (d) client's near past (perception of preconditions for the present situation), present situation in sport and life, and perceived future. This set of clients' characteristics is clearly grounded in the whole-person approach (or a holistic view of an athlete not only as an athletic performer but also as a person doing sport and other things in life), and may help practitioners to individualise the next components of the ACT model (i.e. goals, contexts, time-frames, etc.) and further increase the effectiveness of the intervention.

Among factors mediating effectiveness of career transition interventions, the literature stimulates practitioners to keep in mind influences of the multilevel sociocultural context in which athletes are imbedded, such as club/team organisational culture, sport/event-specific culture, youth culture, and national culture (Henriksen, 2010; Henriksen *et al.*, 2010a, 2010b; Ryba *et al.*, 2010; Schinke and Hanrahan, 2009; Stambulova and Alfermann, 2009). Keeping contextual factors in mind might help practitioners to implement culturally appropriate, and hence more effective, intervention strategies (Mio *et al.*, 2006).

Goals for assistance in career transitions

Goals in the ACT model address the question: What are the major directions of assisting athletes in career transitions? Based on the holistic lifespan perspective, the goals for assisting athletes in career transitions are defined as helping them to prepare for and successfully cope with athletic and non-athletic transitions, both normative and non-normative. Athletic transitions are outlined by several career-stage models (see Alfermann and Stambulova, 2007), and the developmental model of transitions faced by athletes (Wylleman and Lavallee, 2004) complements athletic transitions with non-athletic ones in athletes' psychological (e.g. from adolescence to adulthood), psychosocial (e.g. from parents' family to own family), and academic/vocational (e.g. from school to college or university) development. Because normative transitions are predictable, it is possible to help athletes to prepare for their demands in advance. For example, athletes of 16–17 years old, who in many sports are approaching the transition from junior to senior sports, are often unaware of what to expect at the senior level. Therefore, practitioners grounded in related models and research findings might help them to learn about forthcoming demands (e.g. coordination of sport goals and other life goals; more intense, competitive, and tough practices and competitions; identity formation; professional choice; and others) and assist them in developing relevant coping resources (e.g. career planning skills, time/stress/energy management skills, self-exploration experiences, etc.). In contrast, demands of non-normative transitions (e.g. injury, moving to a big city or other country, parents' divorce, etc.) most often find athletes unprepared, and practitioners are expected to help them to develop all necessary resources to cope. For example, in working with injured athletes, practitioners might assist them in developing rehabilitation skills, social support networks, and attitudes adequate to meet the rehabilitation routines, as well as in planning a comeback to practices and competitions. Further individualisation of the intervention goals is only possible based on analysing the client's characteristics and related contextual factors.

Contexts, time-frames, and basic methods of assistance in career transitions

Contexts in the ACT model are defined based on the whole-person approach, reflecting the question of "where" the assistance can be provided, and involving sport practices, competitions, and other spheres of the athlete's life, such as studies, work, family, friends, etc.

Time-frames in the model address two questions: "when" interventions are delivered (before, during, or after the transition), and "for how long" (short-term interventions with few sessions, or long-term cooperation for one season or several years). Answering these two questions might help a practitioner to identify major perspectives in the intervention (preventive or crisis-coping), prioritise working issues, and select intervention tools. For example, if the athlete-client approaches career termination and goes for a short-term collaboration with the practitioner, career planning intervention will be the most suitable; however, if the athlete is ready for a long-term collaboration, career planning can be well complemented by identity development and life development interventions.

Basic methods in the ACT model answer the question of "how" to help athletes, and include needs assessment, education, counselling, and training. Needs assessment consists of interviewing athletes and (if possible) their significant others, observation, and psychological inventories (e.g. questionnaires, tests, surveys) to collect information about athletes and their needs and current situations (see above client's characteristics component of the ACT model). Among psychological inventories useful in needs assessment, the athletes' retirement decision inventory (ARDI; Fernandez *et al.*, 2006) is a good example. The ARDI examines four groups of factors influencing the athlete's decision-making process when retiring from sport: (1) anti-pull (overall risk and cost aspects relating to the post-career life); (2) pull (perceived positive aspects of post-career life); (3) anti-push (attachment to sport, difficulty ending the athletic career); and (4) push (negative considerations about the athlete's present life). The authors emphasise that the ARDI provides "a comprehensive view of how each athlete oscillates between Push, Pull, Anti-Push, and Anti-Pull factors" (Fernandez *et al.*, 2006, p. 418) in the multifaceted and idiosyncratic decision-making process. They further state that this tool can be used in career assistance as "a relatively rapid screening device to clarify the diagnosis" (2006, p. 418) and help to determine appropriate directions in further psychological education, counselling, and/or training. Psychological education implies aiding athletes to enrich their psychology knowledge in different areas, such as coping resources and effective communication. Psychological counselling in its individual form can be defined as a dialogue between consultant and client, aimed at exploring and/or dealing with the client's experiences and needs. Transferring this to a group of athletes with similar needs/problems (e.g. retired or injured athletes) supports them in understanding their situations better and, consequentially, finding ways to cope. Psychological training involves individual or group sessions with exercises and regular practice on mental/life skills. The CHAMPS/Life skills program for collegiate athletes introduced in the meta-review above is a good example (Petitpas *et al.*, 2009). These four methods are called "basic", because career transition interventions most often include all of them to various degrees and in different ways, depending, among other factors, on what perspective and type(s) of intervention are going to be applied.

Major perspectives in, and content-related types of, career transition interventions

Perspectives in the ACT model help to further specify the intervention goals, and content-related types of interventions address the question: What is the intervention about? Based on comparing review papers presented above, two major perspectives in career transition interventions, the preventive/supportive and crisis/negative-consequences coping perspectives, have been included in the ACT model. The preventive/supportive perspective covers interventions aimed at enhancing athletes' awareness about forthcoming/current transition demands and aiding timely development of all necessary resources for effective coping. These interventions may assist the athlete's readiness for a normative career transition (Alfermann *et al.*, 2004) and/or support the athlete during the transition process. This perspective is represented by career planning interventions, lifestyle management interventions, life development interventions, identity development interventions, and cultural adaptation interventions, with related professional strategies and tools. The crisis/negative-consequences coping perspective covers interventions assisting athletes to analyse their crisis/traumatic situations and to find the best available ways to cope, and consists of crisis-coping educational interventions and clinical interventions. Below, each type of career transition intervention is presented in more detail, based on the analysis of related literature.

Career planning interventions

Career planning interventions are delivered in the form of individual counselling, and aimed at helping athletes to increase their self-awareness, to set realistic career goals bridging their past, present, and future, and to prepare in advance for the forthcoming transitions. The significance of career planning for transitional athletes is supported mostly by athletic retirement studies, where retirement planning was shown to be a factor facilitating adaptation to the post-career (e.g. Alfermann *et al.*, 2004; Stambulova *et al.*, 2007; Taylor and Ogilvie, 2001). There are two types of career planning strategies currently used to assist athletes in transitions. The first one is influenced by a work psychology approach, and aimed at helping retiring and retired athletes to find and start a new vocational career. The athlete's guide to career planning (Petitpas *et al.*, 1997) is an example. In this strategy career planning is presented as a three-phase process, with self-exploration, career exploration, and career acquisition (phase 1), planning for transition (phase 2), and career action planning (phase 3). The authors provide detailed advice on how to proceed through the process and make a sequence of effective decisions related to professional education, career choice and planning. The second type of career planning strategy is based on developmental psychology, and aimed at helping athletes to plan for a life career. The five-step career planning strategy (Stambulova, 2008, 2010b) can serve as an example. The five steps in this strategy deal with the client's past experiences, current situation, and perceived future in various spheres of life, followed by bridging the past with the present and the present with the future. The authors of both strategies reported that the career planning interventions were effective in increasing athletes' self-awareness and decision-making (Petitpas *et al.*, 2009; Stambulova, 2010b).

Lifestyle management interventions

Lifestyle management interventions consist of counselling, education, and training aimed at helping athletes to combine sport and other activities in life, to prioritise between them, and to manage time and energy in a way that helps athletes to maintain good health and well-being. More specifically, these interventions involve individual or group counselling sessions analysing athletes' current lifestyle and the most stressful areas in it, education on healthy lifestyle and related issues, and elements of life skills training with an emphasis on time/energy/stress management skills.

Lifestyle management interventions are based on the holistic lifespan perspective and supported by a number of research findings. For example, studies on the transition from junior to senior sports showed that athletes in this transition often try to coordinate sport, studies and/or work, friends, and loved ones, all resulting in high life stress (e.g. Stambulova, 2009). In a meta-review (Lindner and Johns, 2004) on the reasons for athletes' dropout from sports in adolescent years, "other things to do" ranked first. Athletic retirement research in relation to lifestyle management (e.g. North and Lavallee, 2004) confirmed that athletes having other than athletic interests are better prepared for career termination. The European Forum on Lifestyle Management of Elite Athletes collected information across Europe about conditions created for athletes in different countries to coordinate their sport and studies/work, and provided recommendations supporting dual career programmes, such as sport-oriented schools and support programmes for university student-athletes (Wylleman, 2004). Such programmes help athletes to organise a lifestyle that allows them to do sport and other things in life, and also to see their sport project as a part of the life project. Good examples of dual career research with practical implications are provided by Elbe and Beckmann (2006) with regard to the German cultural context, and by Henriksen *et al.* (2011) in relation to the Scandinavian context.

Life development interventions/life skills training

Life development interventions/life skills training (LDIs) consist of needs assessment, education, and training with regard to sets of transferable life skills that are skills applicable in both sports and other spheres of life (Danish *et al.*, 1993; Gould and Carson, 2008; Petitpas *et al.*, 2009). Such skills add to athletes' coping resources in transitions, and are expected to fit current or forthcoming demands.

Life development interventions are based on the LDI model (Danish *et al.*, 1993) and are also supported by the holistic lifespan perspective outlined by the developmental model of transition faced by athletes (Wylleman and Lavallee, 2004). Extensive literature describes and classifies life skills, and furthermore, provides recommendations on how to teach them to athletes (e.g. Ahlgren-Bedics and Monda, 2009; Carr and Bauman, 2002; Danish, 2001; Mayocchi and Hanrahan, 2000). The content of LDIs depends on the athletes' age, athletic and educational status, and individual and/or group needs. For example, "life skills through sport programmes" for young athletes (Danish, 2001) focus on skill modules, such as managing emotions in stressful situations, communicating effectively, setting reachable goals, making effective decisions, overcoming roadblocks, and handling success and failure. Life skills programmes for college student-athletes emphasise educational and social adjustment skills, substance abuse prevention, financial planning, resumé writing, and others (Carr and Bauman, 2002). LDIs for retiring and retired athletes help them to identify skills that they developed in sport but can also apply in other spheres of life (Lavallee, 2005, Mayocchi and Hanrahan, 2000). According to Danish (2001), principles of effective life skills teaching include: (a) explain the concept first; (b) provide examples for use of the skill in both sport and non-sport settings; (c) apply and practice in sport settings; (d) apply and practice in other domains; and (e) review and discuss successes and failures in applying skills in various domains. LDIs were evaluated and their effectiveness was confirmed for athletes' personal growth and, more specifically, for facilitating adaptation of student-athletes and retired athletes (e.g. Lavallee, 2005; Petitpas *et al.*, 2009).

Identity development interventions

Identity development interventions include counselling, education, and training aimed at helping athletes in self-exploration and development of multidimensional personal identities. These interventions are based on athletic identity and athletic retirement research, and especially on the research findings demonstrating that athletic identity foreclosure (i.e. one's exclusive focus on sport) might lead to athletes' one-sided development and also cause an identity crisis upon their career termination (Cecić Erpič *et al.*, 2004; Lally, 2007; Lavallee *et al.*, 1997; Petitpas, 1978; Stambulova, 2009; Stephan and Brewer, 2007; Warriner and Lavallee, 2008). Therefore, identity development interventions work to prevent athletic identity foreclosure in athletes, through counselling and education that stimulate their identity exploration and awareness, as well as through practical exploration of new social and professional roles. One example of such self-exploration training is so-called "shadow programmes", providing athletes with the opportunity "to explore career options by shadowing professionals in the field of their choice" (Gordon *et al.*, 2005, p. 235). Sport clubs might give athletes an opportunity to spend a couple of days accompanying a professional in sport – for example, a coach, a club manager, or a masseur – observing their everyday work and fitting these professional roles to themselves. Moreover, based on agreements between the sport clubs (or CAPs) and various business settings, athletes might have an opportunity to shadow professionals in areas outside of sport and enrich their ideas about various professional occupations and related roles. As stated by Lavallee and Andersen, "helping athletes establish a sense of who they are beyond sport is a useful intervention that can occur anytime in an athletic career, even several years before retirement" (2000, p. 254).

Cultural adaptation interventions

Cultural adaptation interventions consist of needs assessment, counselling, education, and training aimed at helping athletes adjust to the new sociocultural environment when moving to another country to play sports or to do both sport and studies. These types of interventions are relatively new, but their significance has been recently emphasised in the literature (Schinke *et al.*, 2007; Stambulova and Alfermann, 2009; Tenenbaum *et al.*, 2003). One approach in cultural adaptation interventions is based on Fiske's (2004) five core needs as the vehicles to adaptation: belonging, understanding, controlling, self-enhancement, and trusting. Practitioners should help athletes to increase their awareness of the new culture, and develop knowledge, competencies, and skills to satisfy the core needs. Another "cultural praxis" approach (Ryba, 2009a, 2009b) considers adaptation as a dynamic process of negotiation between maintaining a psychological homeostasis, and engagement in sociocultural everyday practices of the host site. Practitioners taking this approach are expected to help athletes to find consensus between their previous values, perceptions, habits, etc. and ones required/expected by people in the new culture.

Crisis-coping educational interventions

Typically, assistance in crisis is associated with clinical interventions. However, some educationally oriented strategies can be helpful, especially at the beginning phase of the crisis when athletes feel distressed and disoriented, but still do not experience any real clinical symptoms. An information-processing approach based on account-making in response to the transition distress, and especially complemented by mentoring (see Gordon *et al.*, 2005; Lavallee *et al.*, 2000), is one example. Another example is the "mobilisation" model of counselling in crisis transitions (Stambulova, 2000, 2008), helping athletes to change their perception of the crisis situation from "being at a dead end" to "being at a crossroad" by applying three strategic alternatives (termed "rejection", "acceptance", and "fighting") in the analysis of a crisis transition, followed by the athlete's selection of the best one, with further planning for its realisation. Crisis-coping educational interventions were reported to be effective for reducing stress and increasing athletes' awareness of, and self-efficacy in, a crisis transition (Lavallee *et al.*, 2000; Stambulova, 2000, 2011).

Clinical interventions

Clinical interventions should be applied in career transitions when athletes experience clinical symptoms related to overtraining, neuroses, psychosomatic illnesses, substance abuse, negative identities, eating disorders, anger and aggression, grieving, clinical depression, and suicidal thoughts. These interventions are mostly counselling interventions based on various psychotherapeutic approaches, such as psychoanalysis, existential therapy, cognitive-behavioural therapy, and others (Andersen, 2001; Barney and Andersen, 2000; Brewer and Petrie, 1996; Cogan, 2000; Eyal, 2001; Goodger *et al.*, 2010; Petrie and Trattner Sherman, 2000, Stainback and Taylor, 2005). For example, Petrie and Trattner Sherman demonstrated how behavioural, psychodynamic, and cognitive-behavioural perspectives can be used in treating athletes with eating disorders, followed by a case example where they applied "a flexible cognitive-behavioural perspective that focuses on changing clients' behaviours and thoughts as they relate to the disorder" (2000, p. 122).

Overlap between various types of interventions

Tracing various types of career transition interventions, it is easy to see some obvious overlaps between them. For example, exploring new social roles as a part of identity development interventions also contributes to the athlete's lifestyle management and life skills training. LDIs can be even seen as "cementing" different types of transition interventions. Such overlaps are not surprising, because all the interventions deal with various aspects of the transition process and adopt the holistic view of an athlete as a person doing sport and other things in life. These overlaps also facilitate combining various types of interventions to best meet the particular needs of the athlete.

Assessment

Last but not least, the ACT model directs practitioners to plan and to assess multilevel effects of career transition interventions, considering changes in athletes' personal growth and development, performance in sport and other activities, lifestyle, and well-being. In other words, and as recommended by Hackfort and Huang (2005), both external and internal career changes should be assessed.

Summary of the ACT model

The ACT model is derived from the meta-review presented in the first half of the chapter, and incorporates major contemporary ideas of athletes' career development and transitions, especially the holistic lifespan perspective. Briefly summing up, assistance in career transitions is viewed in the ACT model as a system with related components, structure, development, and functions. Obviously, it is an open system, because the model can be developed further – for example, as soon as new intervention types are identified.

The ACT model serves several functions. First of all, the model is created to integrate existing knowledge about assistance to athletes in career transitions, and can be seen as one more way to structure/restructure the career transition topic. Second, the ACT model provides a framework/guidance to plan an individual career transition intervention with its individualised goals, contexts, time-frames, content, and so forth. The client's characteristics are crucial to define the individual intervention goals and the perspective in the intervention (preventive or crisis-coping), while contextual mediating factors are important to adapt the intervention strategies to the client and his or her environment. Third, the ACT model is created for educational purposes to introduce assistance in career transitions to applied sport psychology students. Fourth, the ACT model might stimulate performance enhancement practitioners to adopt the holistic lifespan perspective in working with their clients, and add assistance in career transitions to their professional repertoires.

Keeping in mind that the meta-review is the author's interpretation of several previous interpretations of the topic, it is clear that the ACT model is also driven by her professional and living background and experiences. Therefore, other researchers and practitioners have to test/validate it in their own practices (Jarvis, 1999), which is to say, the question of "who will listen?" is no less crucial than the question of "who is speaking?" (Spivak, 1990, cited in Smith, 1999).

Future challenges for career transition research and applied work

Some future challenges for career transitions research are not new, and, once again, it is important to emphasise that more research with preferably longitudinal design and concurrent perspective should be done on the athletic within-career normative and non-normative transitions in their overlap with non-athletic transitions in athletes' psychological, psychosocial, and academic/vocational development. The topic of career transitions can also be enriched by means of more cooperation with related areas. For example, in the sport injury literature, an injury most often is considered as an event isolated from the career development process. The fields of both injury and transition can only benefit by incorporating a career perspective into injury research – that is, to view it as a non-normative transition with preconditions in the career development/situation, rehabilitation process, and short-term and long-term consequences for the rest of the career. In the case of such cooperation between these areas, it can be expected that injury-coping interventions will find their place in the ACT model. A relatively new challenge for the transition research is to incorporate "a cultural mindset" – that is, "cultural and cross-cultural psychology approaches to further improve both mono-cultural and cross-cultural studies" (Stambulova and Alfermann,

2009, p. 302) – and also the related holistic ecological perspective shifting focus from studying individual athletes in career transitions to studying the transition environment, as is shown, for example, in Henriksen (2010).

There are also several future challenges for the applied part of the career transition topic. First of all, practitioners should promote career assistance as a distinct discourse in applied sport psychology, mainly through professional publications and symposia/workshops at major conferences, with participants further negotiating and promoting the professional culture of career assistance. Second, a big challenge is to attract young professionals and applied sport psychology students to practise in the career transition area. To facilitate young professionals' applied work, career/transition issues should become an essential part of applied sport psychology education. Also, more articles and books describing particular strategies of career transition interventions (e.g. career planning or cultural adaptation counseling tools), with case examples complemented by the consultants' lessons learned and clients' feedback, should be written by experienced practitioners to help novices in the field to enrich their professional toolboxes. A third challenge for career practitioners is to adopt the cultural mindset; that is, to increase their cultural reflexivity and apply cultural and multicultural perspectives in career transition interventions. Fourth is the challenge to further develop CAPs, treating the athlete as a whole person and providing high-quality services to meet the athlete's individual needs. Effective assistance in career transitions may not only aid athletes to cope with one or a set of interrelated transitions, but also help them to live a long and happy life in sports, find the best moment to terminate, and then adjust successfully to the post-sports career.

References

Ahlgren-Bedics, R. and Monda, S. (2009). Life skills for collegiate student-athletes: Defining the need and model practices. In E. F. Etzel (ed.), *Counselling and psychological services for college student-athletes* (pp. 113–142). Morgantown, WV: Fitness Information Technology.

Alfermann, D. and Stambulova, N. (2007). Career transitions and career termination. In G. Tenenbaum and R. C. Eklund (eds), *Handbook of sport psychology* (3rd edn, pp. 712–736). New York, NY: Wiley.

Alfermann, D., Stambulova, N., and Zemaityte, A. (2004). Reactions to sports career termination: A cross-national comparison of German, Lithuanian, and Russian athletes. *Psychology of Sport and Exercise*, 5, 61–75.

Andersen, M. B. (2001). When to refer athletes for counselling or psychotherapy. In J. Williams (ed.), *Applied sport psychology* (4th edn, pp. 401–414). Mountain View, CA: Mayfield.

Barney, S. T. and Andersen M. B. (2000). Looking for help, grieving love lost: The case of C. In M. B. Andersen (ed.), *Doing sport psychology* (pp. 139–150). Champaign, IL: Human Kinetics.

Bloom, B. S. (1985). *Developing talent in young people.* New York, NY: Ballantine Books.

Bobridge, K., Gordon, S., Walker, A., and Thompson, R. (2003). Evaluation of a career assistance program for youth-aged cricketers. *Australian Journal of Career Development*, 12, 19–27.

Bookbinder, H. E. (1955). Work histories of men leaving a short lifespan occupation. *Personnel and Guidance Journal*, 34, 164–167.

Brewer, B. W. and Petrie, T. A. (1996). Psychopathology in sport and exercise. In J. L. Van Raalte and B. W. Brewer (eds), *Exploring sport and exercise psychology* (pp. 275–286). Washington, DC: American Psychological Association.

Carr, C. and Bauman, N. J. (2002). Life skills for collegiate student-athletes. In E. Etzel, A. Ferrante, and J. Pinkney (eds), *Counselling college student-athletes: Issues and interventions* (pp. 281–308). Morgantown, WV: Fitness Information Technology.

Cecić Erpič, S., Wylleman, P., and Zupančič, M. (2004). The effect of athletic and non-athletic factors on the sport career termination. *Psychology of Sport and Exercise*, 5, 45–60.

Cogan, K. D. (2000). The sadness in sport: Working with a depressed and suicidal athlete. In M. Andersen (ed.), *Doing sport psychology* (pp. 107–120). Champaign, IL: Human Kinetics.

Côté, J. (1999). The influence of the family in the development of talent in sport. *The Sport Psychologist*, 13, 395–417.

Côté, J., Baker, J., and Abernethy, B. (2007). Practice and play in the development of sport expertise. In G. Tenenbaum and R. C. Eklund (eds), *Handbook of sport psychology* (3rd edn, pp. 184–202). New York, NY: Wiley.

Danish, S. J. (2001). Frameworks for developing personal and performance excellence. In A. Papaioannou, M. Goudas, and Y. Theodorakis (eds), *Proceedings of the 10th World Congress of Sport Psychology* (Vol. 2, p. 315). Thessaloniki, Greece: Christodoulidi Publications.

Danish, S. J., Petitpas, A. J., and Hale, B. D. (1993). Life development intervention for athletes: Life skills through sports. *The Counselling Psychologist*, 21, 352–385.

Elbe, A. M. and Beckmann, J. (2006). Motivational and self-regulatory factors and sport performance in young elite athletes. In D. Hackfort and G. Tenenbaum (eds), *Essential processes for attaining peak performance* (pp. 137–157). Oxford, UK: Meyer and Meyer Sport.

Eyal, N. (2001). Reflections on sport psychology practice: A clinical perspective. In G. Tenenbaum (ed.), *The practice of sport psychology* (pp. 169–196). Morgantown, WV: Fitness Information Technology.

Fernandez, A., Stephan, Y., and Fouquereau, E. (2006). Assessing reasons for sports career termination: Development of the athletes' retirement decision inventory (ARDI). *Psychology of Sport and Exercise*, 7, 407–421.

Fiske, S. T. (2004). *Social beings: A core motives approach to social psychology.* Hoboken, NJ: Wiley.

Gill, D. (2007). Gender and cultural diversity. In G. Tenenbaum and R. C. Eklund (eds), *Handbook of sport psychology* (3rd edn, pp. 823–844). New York, NY: Wiley.

Goodger, K., Lavallee, D., Gorely, T., and Harwood, C. (2010). Burnout in sport: Understanding the process—from early warning signs to individualised interventions. In J. M. Williams (ed.), *Applied sport psychology* (6th edn, pp. 492–511). New York, NY: McGraw-Hill.

Gordon, S., Lavallee, D., and Grove, J. R. (2005). Career assistance program interventions in sport. In D. Hackfort, J. Duda, and R. Lidor (eds), *Handbook of research in*

applied sport and exercise psychology: International perspectives (pp. 233–244). Morgantown, WV: Fitness Information Technology.
Gorely, T., Lavallee, D., Bruce, D., Teale, B., and Lavallee, R. (2001). A sampling of perceptions of potential users of the Australian Athlete Career and Education program. *Academic Athletic Journal*, 15, 11–21.
Gould, D. and Carson, S. (2008). Life skills development through sports: Current status and future directions. *International Review of Sport and Exercise Psychology*, 1, 58–78.
Hackfort, D. and Huang, Z. (2005). Considerations for research on career counselling and career transition. In D. Hackfort, J. Duda, and R. Lidor (eds), *Handbook of research in applied sport and exercise psychology: International perspectives* (pp. 245–255). Morgantown, WV: Fitness Information Technology.
Hackfort, D., Duda, J., and Lidor, R. (eds), (2005). *Handbook of research in applied sport and exercise psychology: International perspectives.* Morgantown, WV: Fitness Information Technology.
Henriksen, K. (2010). *The ecology of talent development in sport.* Unpublished doctoral dissertation, University of Southern Denmark, Odense, Denmark.
Henriksen, K., Stambulova, N., and Roessler, K. K. (2010a). Holistic approach to athletic talent development environment: A successful sailing milieu. *Psychology of Sport and Exercise*, 11, 212–222.
Henriksen, K., Stambulova, N., and Roessler, K. K. (2010b). Successful talent development in athletics: Considering the role of environment. *Scandinavian Journal of Science and Medicine in Sport*, 20, 122–132.
Henriksen, K., Stambulova, N., and Roessler, K. K. (2011). Riding the wave of an expert: A successful talent development environment in kayaking. *The Sport Psychologist*, in press.
Inkson, K. (2006). *Understanding careers: The metaphors of working lives.* Thousand Oaks, CA: Sage.
Jarvis, P. (1999). *The practitioner-researcher. Developing theory from practice.* San Francisco, CA: Jossey-Bass.
Lally, P. (2007). Identity and athletic retirement: A prospective study. *Psychology of Sport and Exercise*, 8, 85–99.
Lavallee, D. (2005). The effect of a life development intervention on sports career transition adjustment. *The Sport Psychologist*, 19, 193–202.
Lavallee, D. and Andersen, M. B. (2000). Leaving sport: Easing career transitions. In M. B. Andersen (ed.), *Doing sport psychology* (pp. 249–260). Champaign, IL: Human Kinetics.
Lavallee, D. and Wylleman, P. (eds), (2000). *Career transitions in sport: International perspectives.* Morgantown, WV: Fitness Information Technology.
Lavallee, D., Gordon, S., and Grove, R. (1997). Retirement from sport and the loss of athletic identity. *Journal of Personal and Interpersonal Loss*, 2, 129–147.
Lavallee, D., Nesti, M., Borkoles, E., Cockerill, I., and Edge, A. (2000). Intervention strategies for athletes in transition. In D. Lavallee and P. Wylleman (eds), *Career transitions in sport: International perspectives* (pp. 111–130). Morgantown, WV: Fitness Information Technology.
Lindner, K. J. and Johns, D. P. (2004). Factors in withdrawal from youth sport: A proposed model. *Journal of Sports Behaviour*, 14, 3–16.
Mayocchi, L. and Hanrahan, S. J. (2000). Transferable skills for career change. In D. Lavallee and P. Wylleman (eds), *Career transitions in sport: International perspectives* (pp. 95–110). Morgantown, WV: Fitness Information Technology.

Mellalieu, S. D. and Hanton, S. (2009). Introduction. In S. D. Mellalieu and S. Hanton (eds), *Advances in applied sport psychology. A review.* (pp. 1–4). New York, NY: Routledge.

Mihovilovic, M. A. (1968). Status of former sportsmen. *International Review of Sport Sociology*, 3, 73–93.

Mio, J. S., Barker-Hackett, L., and Tumambing, J. (2006). *Multicultural psychology: Understanding our diverse communities.* Boston, MA: McGraw-Hill.

Morgan, G. (1986). *Images of organisation.* Beverly Hills, CA: Sage.

Nitsch, J. R. (2000). Handlungstheoretische grundlagen der sportpsychologie [Action theory fundamentals for sport psychology]. In H. Gabler, J. R. Nitsch, and R. Singer (eds), *Introduction to sport psychology* (Pt 1, pp. 43–164). Schorndorf, Germany: Hofmann.

North, J. and Lavallee, D. (2004). An investigation of potential users of career transition services in the United Kingdom. *Psychology of Sport and Exercise*, 5, 77–84.

Petitpas, A. J. (1978). Identity foreclosure: A unique challenge. *Personnel and Guidance Journal*, 56, 558–561.

Petitpas, A. and Champagne, D. (2000). Practical considerations in implementing sport career transition programs. In D. Lavallee and P. Wylleman (eds), *Career transitions in sport: International perspectives* (pp. 81–93). Morgantown, WV: Fitness Information Technology.

Petitpas, A., Champagne, D., Chartrand, J., Danish, S., and Murphy, S. (1997). *Athlete's guide to career planning: Keys to success from the playing field to professional life.* Champaign, IL: Human Kinetics.

Petitpas, A. J., Brewer, B. W., and Van Raalte, J. L. (2009). Transitions of the student-athlete: Theoretical, empirical, and practical perspectives. In E. F. Etzel (ed.), *Counselling and psychological services for college student-athletes* (pp. 283–302). Morgantown, WV: Fitness Information Technology.

Petrie, T. A. and Trattner Sherman, R. (2000). Counselling athletes with eating disorders: A case example. In M. B. Andersen (ed.), *Doing sport psychology* (pp. 121–137). Champaign, IL: Human Kinetics.

Pummel, B., Harwood, C., and Lavallee, D. (2008). Jumping to the next level: A qualitative examination of within career transition in adolescent event riders. *Psychology of Sport and Exercise*, 9, 427–447.

Ryba, T. V. (2009a). Understanding your role in cultural sport psychology. In S. J. Hanrahan and R. J. Schinke (eds), *Cultural sport psychology* (pp. 33–44). Champaign, IL: Human Kinetics.

Ryba, T. V. (2009b). The bricolage of cultural adaptation. *Proceedings of the 24th Annual Conference of the Association for Applied Sport Psychology* (p. 22). Madison, WI: Association for Applied Sport Psychology.

Ryba, T. V., Schinke, R. J., and Tenenbaum, G. (eds), (2010). *The cultural turn in sport psychology.* Morgantown, WV: Fitness Information Technology.

Salmela, J. H. (1994). Phases and transitions across sports career. In D. Hackfort (ed.), *Psychosocial issues and interventions in elite sport* (pp. 11–28). Frankfurt, Germany: Lang.

Schinke, R. J. and Hanrahan, S. (eds), (2009). *Cultural sport psychology.* Champaign, IL: Human Kinetics.

Schinke, R. J., Gauthier, A. P., Dubuc, N. G., and Crowder, T. (2007). Understanding athlete adaptation in the National Hockey League through an archival data source. *The Sport Psychologist*, 21, 277–287.

Schlossberg, N. K. (1981). A model for analysing human adaptation to transition. *The Counselling Psychologist*, 9, 2–18.

Smith, L. T. (1999). *Decolonising methodologies: Research and indigenous peoples*. Dunedin, New Zealand: University of Otago Press.

Stainback, R. D. and Taylor, R. E. (2005). Facilitating change: Alcohol and violence among athletes. In M. B. Andersen (ed.), *Sport psychology in practice* (pp. 135–158). Champaign, IL: Human Kinetics.

Stambulova, N. (1994). Developmental sports career investigations in Russia: A post-perestroika analysis. *The Sport Psychologist*, 8, 221–237.

Stambulova, N. (2000). Athlete's crises: A developmental perspective. *International Journal of Sport Psychology*, 31, 584–601.

Stambulova, N. (2003). Symptoms of a crisis-transition: A grounded theory study. In N. Hassmén (ed.), *SIPF Yearbook 2003* (pp. 97–109). Örebro, Sweden: Örebro University Press.

Stambulova, N. (2008). *Methods and tools for career assistance*. Paper presented at the 2nd ASPIRE Conference, Doha, Qatar, January.

Stambulova, N. (2009). Talent development in sport: A career transitions perspective. In E. Tsung-Min Hung, R. Lidor, and D. Hackfort (eds), *Psychology of sport excellence* (pp. 63–74). Morgantown, WV: Fitness Information Technology.

Stambulova, N. (2010a). Professional culture of career assistance to athletes: A look through contrasting lenses of career metaphors. In T. V. Ryba, R. J. Schinke, and G. Tenenbaum (eds), *The cultural turn in sport psychology* (pp. 285–314). Morgantown, WV: Fitness Information Technology.

Stambulova, N. (2010b). Counselling athletes in career transitions: The five-step career planning strategy. *Journal of Sport Psychology in Action*, 1, 95–105.

Stambulova, N. (2011). The mobilization model of counseling athletes in crisis-transitions: An educational intervention tool. *Journal of Sport Psychology in Action*, in press.

Stambulova, N. and Alfermann, D. (2009). Putting culture into context: Cultural and cross-cultural perspectives in career development and transition research and practice. *International Journal of Sport and Exercise Psychology*, 7, 292–308.

Stambulova, N., Stephan, Y. and Järphag, U. (2007). Athletic retirement: A cross-national comparison of elite French and Swedish athletes. *Psychology of Sport and Exercise*, 8, 101–118.

Stambulova, N., Alfermann, D., Statler, T., and Côté, J. (2009). ISSP Position Stand: Career development and transitions of athletes. *International Journal of Sport and Exercise Psychology*, 7, 395–412.

Stephan, Y. and Brewer, B. W. (2007). Perceived determinants of identification with the athlete role among elite competitors. *Journal of Applied Sport Psychology*, 19, 67–79.

Stephan, Y., Bilard, J., Ninot. G., and Delignières, D. (2003). Bodily transition out of elite sport: A one-year study of physical self and global self-esteem among transitional athletes. *International Journal of Sport and Exercise Psychology*, 1, 192–207.

Taylor, J. and Ogilvie, B. C. (1994). A conceptual model of adaptation to retirement among athletes. *Journal of Applied Sport Psychology*, 6, 1–20.

Taylor, J. and Ogilvie, B. C. (2001). Career termination among athletes. In R. N. Singer, H. A. Hausenblas, and C. M. Janelle (eds), *Handbook of sport psychology* (2nd edn, pp. 672–691). New York, NY: Wiley.

Tenenbaum, G., Jones, C. M., Kitsantas, A., Sachs, D. N., and Berwik, J. P. (2003). Failure adaptation: An investigation of the stress response process in sport. *International Journal of Sport Psychology*, 34, 27–62.

UK Sport (2001). *Athletes' lifestyle and ACE UK: A survey of athletes' experience of sport, education and work, and the role of the ACE UK programme*. London, UK: Author.

Vanden Auweele, Y., De Martelaer, K., Rzewnicki, R., De Knop, P., and Wylleman, P. (2004). Parents and coaches: A help or harm? Affective outcomes for children in sport. In Y. Vanden Auweele (ed.), *Ethics in youth sport* (Vol. 2., pp. 85–102). Leuven, Belgium: Lannoocampus.

Warriner, K. and Lavallee, D. (2008). The retirement experiences of elite female gymnasts: Self-identity and the physical self. *Journal of Applied Sport Psychology*, 20, 301–317.

Weinberg, S. K and Arond, H. (1952). The occupational culture of the boxer. *The American Journal of Sociology*, 57, 460–469.

Wylleman, P. (2004). Athletic career development and the relevance of lifestyle management to elite athletes. *Proceedings of the European forum on lifestyle management for elite athletes* (cd-rom). London, UK: UK Sport.

Wylleman, P. and Lavallee, D. (2004). A developmental perspective on transitions faced by athletes. In M. Weiss (ed.), *Developmental sport and exercise psychology: A lifespan perspective* (pp. 507–527). Morgantown, WV: Fitness Information Technology.

Wylleman, P., Lavallee, D., and Alfermann, D. (eds), (1999). *Career transitions in competitive sports*. Biel, Switzerland: FEPSAC.

Wylleman, P., Alfermann, D., and Lavallee, D. (2004). Career transitions in sport: European perspectives. *Psychology of Sport and Exercise*, 5, 7–20.

8 Psychological preparation in early phases of talent development in sport

Ronnie Lidor and Gal Ziv

Abstract

The main purpose of this chapter is to review a series of studies (a) focusing on psychological characteristics of young athletes engaged in individual and team sports, and (b) examining the use of psychological interventions in young athletes involved in these sports. The main findings that emerge from the reviewed studies are: (a) motivation to participate in sport is more intrinsic than extrinsic; (b) gender differences exist in some, but not all, psychological characteristics; (c) the use of imagery is common among young athletes, but the content of the imagery and the reasons to use imagery vary; (d) the combination of using imagery and arousal adjustment can improve the performance of free-throw shots in basketball; (e) imagery and biofeedback can improve both swimming technique and performance; and (f) both psychological skills training and mental toughness training can promote mental toughness in young football players. Six methodological concerns and research limitations associated with the reviewed studies are discussed, among them the lack of longitudinal studies and the lack of interventional studies. Seven practical implications for sport psychology consultants are discussed, among them teaching the young athlete various psychological techniques, focusing on what the sport psychology consultant is capable of doing best, and cooperating regularly with the professional staff working with the young athlete.

Keywords: talent development, psychological characteristics, psychological interventions, individual sports, team sports

Introduction

Talent detection and early development in sport have been perceived as valuable phases in any long-term sport programme aimed at developing elite-level athletes, and are also considered as being dynamic and interrelated (see Abbott and Collins, 2004; Côté *et al.*, 2009; Lidor *et al.*, 2009). Various genetic (e.g. psychological traits or the structure of the skeletal muscles) and environmental (e.g. the quality of the training programme, coaching, and family support) factors associated with achieving a high level of proficiency in sport are involved in early phases of talent detection and development (Davids and Baker, 2007). Each factor, as well as the interactions among the factors, influence the chances of the young athlete achieving a high level of excellence in sport in the future.

The typical training programme used for helping the young athlete attain proficiency is composed of three properties – physical, psychological, and social (Brown, 2001). Although researchers are not always in agreement as to the relative importance of each aspect (e.g. Falk *et al.*, 2004), it can be argued that these aspects, if appropriately planned and integrated, will enable coaches to develop effective training programmes that provide their athletes with the required conditions to improve their athletic skills.

The current chapter focuses on one aspect of early sport development programmes – the *psychological* aspect. This chapter has five purposes: (1) to define the terms *talent detection, talent identification, talent selection,* and *talent development,* and to briefly discuss two approaches of talent detection and talent development in sport; (2) to review a series of studies that focus on psychological characteristics of young athletes engaged in individual and team sports; (3) to review a series of studies examining the use of psychological interventions in young athletes involved in individual and team sports; (4) to outline a number of methodological concerns and research limitations associated with the reviewed studies; and (5) to provide a number of recommendations (a) to researchers on how to strengthen the design of studies collecting data on psychological interventions in prospects in sport, and (b) to practitioners on the effective use of psychological techniques when working with prospective young athletes in sport.

We included in our chapter a total of 31 articles that focused on young athletes aged 14 years or younger. The reason for this age selection is that many researchers in the area of talent detection and early development in sport (e.g. Baker *et al.*, 2009; Côté *et al.*, 2006) consider the age of 14 as the final year of the athlete's *developmental years,* a phase reflecting his or her early involvement in sports. After the age of 14, talented athletes typically begin their *specialisation years,* namely the years that they focus solely on one sport activity, and devote a considerable amount of practice to refining specific athletic skills (Côté *et al.*, 2006, 2009).

Definition of terms

A number of terms associated with the early development phase in sport have been used in the literature – talent detection, talent identification, talent selection, and talent development (Bompa, 1999; Lidor *et al.*, 2009). As discussed by Williams and Reilly (2000), the term *talent detection* refers to the discovery of potential performers who are currently *not* involved in any sport programme. The term *talent identification* refers to the process of recognising individuals currently involved in sport, who have the potential to become elite athletes. The term *talent selection* involves the ongoing process of identifying athletes *at various stages* of the training programme; references to *a specific task* (i.e. a test) and *sport activity* are decisive. Finally, the term *talent development* implies that the athletes are being provided with the appropriate *environmental and contextual conditions* that enable them to realise their potential in a specific sport.

In this chapter we discuss psychological characteristics and sport psychology interventions of athletes who are already engaged in a sport activity. The athletes who participated in the reviewed studies were part of the processes of talent identification, talent selection, or talent development. However, since data on psychological characteristics of young athletes are discussed in the current chapter, coaches and sport psychology consultants (SPCs) can also benefit from these data in the process of talent detection. That is, when coaches search for a talented child who has not yet been involved in an organised sport programme, information on the psychological characteristics of those who are already involved in the early phases of sport development can help them in their detection process.

Approaches of talent detection and early development – a brief review

Two approaches of talent selection and early development in sport have been discussed in the literature: the traditional Eastern European (practised mostly in Eastern Europe) approach and the more current Western approach. Traditional sport training theories proposed by sport scientists from the former Soviet bloc countries (e.g. Bompa, 1999; Matveyev, 1981) emphasised the use of scientific tools and testing devices by sport professionals (e.g. coaches, instructors, and physical educators) in the searching process (i.e. talent detection) for the talented child. Data on the anthropometrics of the child as well as on his or her physical and psychological abilities were collected and carefully analysed. Profiles of physical and psychological characteristics were developed for each sport, serving as a reference for comparing the achievements of the selected child with those of children who were already part of the training programme. The obtained data were also used to help coaches predict the future athletic ability of the child. Those children who were selected for the sport-training programme were carefully monitored and trained (i.e. talent identification). A specialisation approach was adopted in the early phases of sport development; at an early age the young athlete was directed to one specific sport activity and assigned a specific task (i.e. talent selection). As soon as the athlete was assigned to a sport activity and task, the main objective was to enhance his or her performance to achieve the best results.

In contrast to the Eastern approach, current Western approaches, developed mainly in North America, are characterised in early phases of sport development by free selection of the sport activity/activities and having fun with the activity itself. For example, Côté (1999) proposed a four-stage sport developmental model: in Stage 1, the sampling years, the young athlete participates in different sports for fun and enjoyment; in Stage 2, the specialising years, he or she focuses on one or two sport activities; in Stage 3, the investment years, the athlete attempts to achieve proficiency in one or two sport activities; and in Stage 4, the recreational years, he or she participates in a number of sport activities, not for achieving proficiency but mainly for fun and good health. In this model, an emphasis is made on the contribution of supportive environments – the family members of the young athlete, his or her coaches, the school, and the community at large – to the long-term talent development process (i.e. sport development).

A comparison between the Eastern and Western approaches of talent detection and early development in sport indicates that there has been a shift in emphasis from talent detection and talent identification (as seen in the Eastern approach) to talent development (as seen in the Western approach; Lidor *et al.*, 2009). However, regardless of the approach adopted by policy-makers in talent detection and early development in sport, coaches, instructors, and SPCs should be aware of the psychological characteristics required for achievement in sport as well as the interventional techniques that should be practised, in order to help the young athletes to achieve his or her best.

Psychological characteristics of young athletes

In this section, we review the findings of 25 studies describing psychological characteristics of young athletes from various sports, including basketball, gymnastics, hockey, soccer, and wrestling. We categorised the reviewed studies into seven groups according to the nature of the study or the described characteristics: social-psychological aspects of competition; gender differences; persistence; motivational aspects; anxiety, stress and worries; imagery; and coping skills.

Social-psychological aspects of competition

A series of four studies performed between the years 1984 and 1986 examined social-psychological aspects of competition in young wrestlers (age 9–14 years) who were members of the California Age Group Wrestling Association. More specifically, these studies attempted to predict competitive stress (Scanlan and Lewthwaite, 1984), performance outcomes (Scanlan *et al.*, 1984), personal performance expectancies (Scanlan and Lewthwhite, 1985), and enjoyment (Scanlan and Lewthwaite, 1986) in young talented wrestlers. A number of questionnaires were administered pre-tournament, post weigh-in, pre-combat (rounds 1 and 2), and post-combat (rounds 1 and 2), assessing trait and state anxiety, adult influences, enjoyment, competitive stress, perceived expected outcomes, perceived ability, and perceived discrepancies between expected and achieved performance.

In general, pre-competition stress was predicted by competitive trait anxiety and personal performance expectancies, while win or loss and the amount of fun experienced were predictors of post-competition stress (Scanlan and Lewthwaite, 1984). The strongest and most stable predictors of performance outcomes were competitive experience and pre-competition performance expectancies. Win or loss was successfully predicted in 78 per cent and 80 per cent of the cases for round 1 and round 2, respectively (Scanlan *et al.*, 1984). Personal performance expectancies were divided into generalised expectancies and specific expectancies, the latter being expectations to win a specific combat. High generalised expectancies were predicted by high self-esteem, greater success in the preceding tournament, perception of parental and coach satisfaction, and the lack of non-contingent performance reactions by parents (Scanlan and Lewthwhite, 1985). Lastly, enjoyment was predicted by greater parental and coach satisfaction, less maternal pressure and fewer negative maternal reactions, and more positive adult sport involvement and interaction (Scanlan and Lewthwaite, 1986). These predictors accounted for 38 per cent of the variance in the participants' enjoyment.

The ability to predict both negative (e.g. competitive trait anxiety) and positive (e.g. enjoyment) affective responses in youth sport could provide a means for creating a positive climate for participants. In a study of 207 male and female basketball players (age 9–13 years), it was found that in both boys and girls the strongest predictors of enjoyment were high intrinsic motivation and low parental pressure (r^2=0.24–0.25; Brustad, 1988). When the participants were divided into groups of high, medium, and low competitive trait anxiety, it was found that the high competitive trait anxiety group reported greater performance and evaluative worry than the two other groups.

Gender differences

One qualitative study examined gender differences in psychosocial factors of young athletes (Holt and Morley, 2004). The children were identified as being athletically talented by their physical education teachers, and competed at the county level or above. Results revealed that 74.4 per cent of the children attributed their success to how much they practised. Gender differences were numerous. For example, girls reported professional/international ambitions less often than boys. In contrast, girls reported enjoyment as a motive for playing sports more often than boys.

Quite expectedly, more boys than girls were socialised into sport by their father/brother. In addition, more boys than girls attributed their success to physical factors. It is suggested that coaches take into account gender differences and incorporate this knowledge into their early development training programmes.

Persistence

In one study of 50 male gymnasts (age 8–13 years), general persistence was assessed and compared to a group of non-athletes of similar ages (Lufi and Tenenbaum, 1991). It was found that athletes were more persistent than non-athletes in a variety of tasks. Specifically, statistically significant differences were found in persistence in "what I do", duration of chess playing, duration of stay at a boring movie, and working on mathematical problems until a solution is found. The authors suggested that choosing gymnasts who are persistent may reduce dropout rates.

Motivational aspects

The relationships between perceived physical ability and the motives for participating in sport were examined in one study of 123 ninth-grade students participating in organised sports (Ryckman and Hamel, 1993). Three questionnaires were used: the Participation Motivation Inventory (Gill *et al.*, 1983), the Perceived Physical Ability (PPA) Scale (McAuley and Gill, 1983), and the Social Desirability Scale (Reynolds, 1982). Athletes higher in PPA more often reported skill development, team affiliation, fun, excitement of game, liking to compete, and liking to do something they're good at as important motives for participating in sport as compared to the number of times these were reported by athletes low in PPA. No differences were found between male and female athletes. From these results, it appears that many reasons for participating in sports are intrinsic rather than extrinsic. Hence, emphasising winning as the ultimate goal of sport participation does not always make sense (Ryckman and Hamel, 1993).

The relationships between competitiveness, motivation, perceived purposes of sport, and sportsmanship were examined in a study of 319 young athletes (mean age 12.65 years; Ryska, 2003). A number of questionnaires were used, and multiple regression models were performed with four sportsmanship factors as the dependent variables: (1) social convention, (2) respect for opponent, (3) full commitment, and (4) rules and officials. Adjusted R^2 ranged from 0.26 when respect for opponent was the dependent variable to 0.43 when full commitment was the dependent variable. This study suggested that athletes participating in sports for intrinsic reasons (e.g. learning new skills, enhancing self-esteem) exhibit better sportsmanship compared to athletes participating in sports for extrinsic reasons (e.g. enhancing social status, obtaining a college scholarship). However, while extrinsically motivated athletes had a tendency to be disrespectful to their opponents, they showed high sportsmanship relating to rules and officials. This can be explained by the fact that the extrinsically motivated athletes benefit from unsportsmanlike conduct towards opponents as well as from respecting rules and officials, since both deliver competitive advantages.

Another study (Nieuwenhuis *et al.*, 2002) examined physiological and psychological attributes of 14- to 15-year-old hockey players from the two most successful teams and the two least successful teams in the South African North West Province field hockey league. No anxiety differences were observed between the more successful and less successful teams. However, athletes from the more successful teams showed a higher level of motivation to achieve success when compared to athletes from the less successful teams. Similarly, a longitudinal study that examined physical, physiological, technical, and psychological attributes of elite and sub-elite male and female field hockey players suggested that by the age of 14 future elite players excel in tactical skills, interval endurance capacity, and high motivation and confidence, especially the female athletes (Elferink-Gemser *et al.*, 2007).

The relationships between goal orientation and beliefs about the causes of success, perceived ability, and degree of enjoyment were examined in 57 young basketball players (32 males and 25 females; mean age 11.3 years) during a summer basketball camp (Hom *et al.*, 1993). Task orientation was related to the belief that success was a result of motivation and hard work ($r=0.34$), and ego orientation was related to the belief that success was due to possessing high ability ($r=0.56$) and to deception ($r=0.31$). High task orientation was also linked to a de-emphasis of the role of deception in success. Children who had both high task and high ego orientation viewed themselves as having more ability in basketball. Lastly, young athletes who were high in perceived ability and strong in both task and ego orientation reported being satisfied with basketball as their chosen sport.

Another study (Elferink-Gemser *et al.*, 2004) revealed differences in tactical, technical, and psychological, but not physiological, characteristics in 126 male and female elite (mean age 13.2 years) and sub-elite (mean age 14.2 years) players. The psychological assessment tool was the Psychological Skills Inventory for Sports (Bakker, 1995). This tool assesses motivation, confidence, anxiety control, mental preparation, team emphasis, and concentration. Statistically significant differences between elite and sub-elite players were found only in motivation.

Motivational profiles of young athletes were also examined in a group of 413 children (mean age 13.7 years) from 28 sport schools in Spain (Murcia *et al.*, 2007). A cluster analysis based on a number of sport psychology questionnaires revealed three distinct motivational profiles:

(1) self-determined, (2) non-self-determined, and (3) low self-determined, low non-self-determined. While 53.5 per cent of the athletes belonged to the self-determined profile, 32.7 per cent belonged to the non-self-determined profile, and 13.8 per cent of the athletes belonged to the low self-determined, low non-self-determined profile. This last group of athletes had the lowest scores on all variables in the study. As the authors of this study suggested, the fact that almost 50 per cent of the athletes did not have a self-determined profile should be addressed by the coaches. In this study, it was more likely that males participating in team sports, and athletes training fewer days a week, had undesirable motivational profiles.

Differences in intrinsic motivation between boys and girls who were beginners at track and field were studied in a group of Croatian primary school students (n=246; Baric *et al.*, 2002). It was found that while boys were more ego-oriented than girls, girls were more task-oriented than boys. In addition, girls reported enjoyment/interest as an intrinsic motivation to participate in sports more than boys did. In contrast, boys reported pressure/tension as an intrinsic motivation to participate more than girls.

Differences in perceived motivation climate, perceived peer relationships, and motivationally-related responses were examined in young male soccer players (age 9–12 years), based on their goal orientation profiles (Smith *et al.*, 2006a). A cluster analysis revealed four distinct groups: (1) low ego/high task, (2) high ego/low task, (3) high ego/moderate task, and (4) moderate ego/low task. Players with lower task goal orientation exhibited fewer adaptive responses to motivation climate, peer relationships, and enjoyment. For example, those with a high ego/low task profile reported lower task-involving climate, soccer enjoyment, and satisfaction with performance and team compared to those with a high ego/moderate task profile. The results of this study suggest that goal orientation in young athletes is related to their motivational climate, peer relationship, and enjoyment.

One of the problems with self-reports and questionnaires is that individuals tend to answer in a culturally accepted manner (Furr and Bacharach, 2008). This was termed *social desirability*, and was incorporated into a study of goal orientation in young male and female recreational basketball players (Grossbard *et al.*, 2007). Similar to previous studies, females scored higher on task and lower on ego orientation compared to males. Ego orientation positively correlated with somatic anxiety, concentration disruption, and worry, both in males and in females. In contrast, task orientation negatively related to somatic anxiety and concentration disruption only in males, and to concentration disruption only in females. However, the r values were relatively low, and ranged from 0.17 to 0.41. In female players, the correlations between goal orientation and performance anxiety were attenuated when social desirability was taken into consideration.

In another study of 493 young athletes (age 12–17 years), the perceptions of coach- and peer-created motivational climate (MC) on affective (e.g. self worth, enjoyment, trait anxiety) and behavioural (e.g. exerted effort) responses were examined (Vazou *et al.*, 2006). In general, peer task MC was the strongest predictor of physical self worth, and coach ego MC was the strongest predictor of trait anxiety. In addition, coach task MC was the strongest predictor of effort. It should be noted that all R^2 values were low (i.e. values under 0.18).

Anxiety/stress/worries

The relationships between competitive trait anxiety (CTA) and perceptions of competence were examined in baseball (male) and softball (female) players (age 9–13 years; Brustad and Weiss, 1987). The children were divided into three CTA groups: low, medium, and high. Measures of perceived competence included baseball/softball competence, perceived control, frequency of evaluative worry, frequency of performance worry, and self-esteem. Results showed that self-esteem and frequency of performance worry significantly contributed to the differences between the high and low CTA groups in boys. However, no differences were found between the CTA groups of girls. It appears, at least for boys, that CTA is partially related to worry. However, the high CTA group did not differ from other groups in measures such as baseball competence and frequency of evaluative worry.

One study of 11- to 12-year-old swimmers (77 boys and 66 girls) examined the relationships between trait and state worries and confidence (Psychountaki and Zervas, 2000). Trait and state questionnaires of competitive worries and sport confidence were administered, and several relationships were found between state and trait characteristics. As expected, the level of trait confidence was negatively related to the level of state competitive worries.

Competitive anxiety was assessed in a group of young male and female athletes (age 9–14 years) participating in several team sports (e.g. baseball, basketball, hockey, rugby, soccer; Grossbard *et al.*, 2009). An age-appropriate Sport Anxiety Scale (SAS-2; Smith *et al.*, 2006b) was administered. This instrument has three subscales: somatic anxiety, worry, and concentration disruption. Older athletes (12–14 years old) showed higher scores for worry compared to younger athletes (9–11 years old). Compared to boys, girls showed higher worry but less concentration disruption. However, the gender and age differences were modest and were not likely to be practically significant. Nevertheless, as the authors of this study suggested, these differences are in line with previous studies, and may encourage theoretical interest in developing models for anxiety. Specifically, concentration disruption is of importance since it can directly affect competitive performance. In the context of the SAS-2, concentration disruption measures difficulties in focusing on task-relevant cues, such as the coach's instructions.

Relationships between anxiety and performance were also examined in a group of young wrestlers (age 13–14 years) during a tournament (Gould *et al.*, 1991). A number of questionnaires addressing trait and state anxiety, pre-combat cognitions, parental pressure, and achievement orientation were administered right after entry to the combat. In addition, a state-anxiety questionnaire was administered 10–20 minutes before competing and immediately after competing in two combats. A factor analysis exposed three factors from the pre-combat cognition questionnaire: please self and others, adult failure worries, and father evaluation worries. Discriminant analysis was conducted to differentiate between won and lost combats. The biggest contributors to the between-group differences were years of experience, perception of ability, and pre-combat state anxiety. Pre- and post-combat state anxiety was predicted by trait anxiety, pre-combat performance expectancies, and parental-pressure-to-wrestle items ($R^2=0.27$). It should be noted that individual variability in feelings of anxiety and worry can be relatively high, and practitioners would be well advised to examine the relationships between these attributes and performance over time in each individual athlete (Gould *et al.*, 1991).

Imagery

The use of imagery was examined in a qualitative study of 110 male and female young athletes aged 7–14 years playing 22 different sports (Munroe-Chandler *et al.*, 2007). Athletes were divided into four age groups: 7–8 years, 9–10 years, 11–12 years, and 13–14 years. Interviews regarding when and why athletes used imagery were conducted in focus groups for each age group. It was found that athletes from all age groups used imagery during practice and competition. In addition, all age groups except for the 7–8 years age group used imagery after practice or after competition. As suggested in this study, it is possible that the youngest age group did not use imagery outside practice or competition because at these ages most children are sampling different sports and do not spend much time focusing on one sport (Munroe-Chandler *et al.*, 2007a). The reasons for the use of imagery were of both a cognitive and a motivational nature. For example, all groups reported using imagery for developing game strategy. The youngest age group (7–8 years) appeared to use imagery for individual goals only, while the oldest group (13–14 years) used imagery for both individual and team goals. Boys did not report using imagery relating to arousal and anxiety, but girls did. In addition, girls reported using imagery to improve self-confidence and mental toughness, while boys did not. These gender differences can be attributed to the boys' reluctance to admit their anxiety and their need to exhibit mental toughness.

Another qualitative study by the same group of researchers reported on the content of imagery in the same four age groups (Munroe-Chandler *et al.*, 2007b). All participants used imagery spontaneously. Five imagery content categories emerged: imagery sessions (i.e. duration, frequency, and type of session), the effectiveness of imagery, the nature of imagery, the surroundings, and the type of imagery. These categories were similar to those in previous studies of adult athletes. Types of imagery used were visual, auditory, kinaesthetic, and tactile, while the nature of imagery was either negative or positive. While several differences were found between age groups and between males and females, at least some aspects of imagery were used by all participants.

In another study (Munroe-Chandler *et al.*, 2008), the relationships between imagery and confidence and between imagery and self-efficacy were examined in young male and female soccer players between the ages of 11 and 14 years. Imagery use was assessed using the Sport Imagery Questionnaire for Children (SIQ-C; Hall *et al.*, 2009), confidence was assessed using the Competitive State Anxiety Inventory–2 for Children (CSAI-2C; Stadulis *et al.*, 2002), and self-efficacy was assessed using the Self-efficacy Questionnaire for Soccer (SEQ-S; a modified questionnaire used by Mills *et al.*, 2001). Regression analysis revealed that using imagery for motivation-general mastery (MG-M) accounted for 50.6 per cent and 39.6 per cent of the total variance in confidence in recreational and competitive players, respectively. In addition, MG-M accounted for 51.6 per cent and 57 per cent of the variance in self-efficacy in recreational and competitive players, respectively.

Coping skills

Young elite athletes may experience stress and anxiety during training and competition, and several types of coping skills can help them in alleviating these feelings. A study of young soccer players from the Olympic Developmental Programme in the US found that a group of under-15-year-olds used concentration as a coping skill more than a group of under-14-year-olds (Meyers *et al.*, 2008). In addition, higher use of body awareness and lower use of avoidance was seen in the under-15 group when compared to the under-14 group. No differences were found between players who played different positions. The higher avoidance response in the younger players may have been due to attempts at dissociating themselves from the stressful experience rather than embracing and working through it. The older players' usage of coping skills, such as body awareness and concentration, may have been due to their higher level of seriousness and to their understanding that they had a limited window of opportunity for being selected for the national team (Meyers *et al.*, 2008).

This section decribed a number of studies focusing on psychological characteristics of young athletes. The psychological characteristics included the social-psychological aspects of competition, persistence to participate in sport, motivational aspects, gender differences, stress and anxiety, the use of imagery, and athletes' coping skills. Some of the studies were quantitative and some were qualitative in nature. Based on these studies, it was concluded that: (a) motivation to participate in sport is more intrinsic than extrinsic; (b) gender differences exist in some, but not all, psychological characteristics; and (c) the use of imagery is common among young athletes, but the content of the imagery sessions and the reasons for using imagery vary. In addition, it was observed that there is a lack of studies regarding persistence and coping skills of young athletes.

Psychological interventions

Four intervention (experimental) studies are discussed in this section. In intervention studies, the researcher can manipulate treatments or conditions that have the potential to enhance behaviour (Thomas and Nelson, 2005). One of the objectives in the described intervention studies was to examine the effectiveness of sport psychology techniques on sport performance in young athletes. Among the examined interventions were self-regulation and imagery, mental toughness, and decision-making.

In one study examining the effectiveness of cognitive strategies on free-throw shots in basketball (Wrisberg and Anshel, 1989), 40 boys with a mean age of 11.6 years were assigned to four experimental groups: (1) imagery, (2) arousal adjustment, (3) combined imagery and arousal adjustment, and (4) control (no strategy). Each participant watched a model demonstrate the correct technique of the shot, and then made 20 free-throw shots with 45 seconds in between. During the 45-second breaks, participants read sections of a book entitled *Basketball for Young Champions*. Each group was then instructed on its assigned cognitive intervention in two 15-minute sessions, one on each of two consecutive days. The control group received only extra written instructions. This was followed by a post-test of 20 shots. Results showed that the combined group performed better at the post-test than the arousal adjustment and the control groups. While it was difficult to explain why the arousal adjustment participants performed poorly, it was clear that certain cognitive strategies can improve the accuracy of free-throw shots.

The effects of mental training with biofeedback on swimming technique and performance were examined in another study on a group of 45 Israeli swimmers (age 11–14 years; Bar-Eli *et al.*, 2002). The swimmers were divided into an intervention group and a control group. The intervention lasted 14 weeks: in the first seven weeks the swimmers were taught a number of self-regulation techniques, including imagery and biofeedback, and during the last seven weeks they were asked to identify the self-regulation techniques that worked best for them and to practise these techniques in a simulated competitive stress setting. In order to prevent a Hawthorne Effect (a change in participants' behaviour due to the participants' awareness of being studied; Jones, 1992) as a potential explanation for the effectiveness of the learned interventions, the control group underwent a series of relaxing activities during the seven-week training period. Swimming technique was assessed by three experts, and while both groups improved over time, the intervention group showed a greater improvement than the control group. Similar results were found in the performance of a 50-m freestyle swimming test. A programme of mental training that included biofeedback was shown to be useful in improving swimming performance in a group of 11- to 14-year-old swimmers.

In another study of 75 under-15 Australian footballers, the effects of two six-week training programmes on mental toughness were examined (Gucciardi *et al.*, 2009). Participants were assigned to three groups: (1) psychological skills training (PST), (2) mental toughness training (MTT), and (3) control (no psychological training). The players in the PST and the MTT groups received a weekly two-hour training session. The PST group sessions involved self-regulation, arousal regulation, mental rehearsal, attentional control, self-efficacy, and ideal performance state. The MTT group sessions involved direct and indirect key mental toughness characteristics. The control group did not receive any training, and had no contact with the researchers. Results showed that both PST and MTT group participation led to an increased subjective view of mental toughness, resilience, and flow states, compared to the control group. Members of the coaching staff and a parent of each player participated in the study by completing the same questionnaires. Similar results were found in the parental and coaches' ratings. While differences existed between the PST and MTT groups, both were equally useful in promoting mental toughness. The control group in this study did not receive any intervention, and thus a Hawthorne Effect cannot be ruled out as a cause for the differences between the intervention groups and the control group. Future research should ensure that the control group receives some kind of technical enrichment, matching the sessions of the interventional groups in frequency and duration.

Finally, one study examined the decision-making skills of young soccer players between the ages of 13.0 and 15.8 years (Vaeyens *et al.*, 2007). The players were divided into three intervention groups according to their skill level: (1) elite players (in first-division clubs), (2) sub-elite players (on the provincial level), and (3) regular players (on the regional level). A fourth group of non-athletes served as control. Films of simulated offensive situations were shown to the participants. The offensive situations included games of two players versus one player, three versus one, three versus two, four versus three, and five versus three. The participants were asked to answer as quickly as possible what their next action would be when they got the ball (the model in the film that simulated the participant was clearly marked). An eye-tracking device was used to record search behaviour, and the decisions made by the participants were assessed by expert soccer coaches. Overall, decision time (DT) and response accuracy (RA) were higher in the three interventional groups than in the control group. In addition, DT increased and RA decreased when more players were on the scene. No differences in DT and RA between the three soccer groups were found in the two vs one situation. Differences in RA were seen only in the five vs three situation. Elite players were more accurate than regular players, and both elite and sub-elite players were more accurate than controls. In the two vs one and three vs one conditions, fixations were mostly directed at the person with the ball. In situations involving more players, fixations were directed to other location zones (e.g. attacker, defender). The authors concluded that visual search behaviours and decision-making skills vary based on the situation (e.g. number of players), skill level, and playing experience. In addition, the more players that were presented in the scene, the greater were the cognitive demands. Importantly, differences were found between the elite and sub-elite players and the regular players. This information may help in searching for talent during early phases of talent development.

This section discussed four studies examining the use of psychological interventions in young athletes. Based on these studies, it was observed that: (a) the combination of using imagery and arousal adjustment can improve the performance of free-throw shots in baskatball; (b) imagery and biofeedback can improve both swimming technique and performance; and (c) both psychological skill training and mental-toughness training can promote mental toughness in young football players.

Psychological interventions – a case study approach

We found two studies in which a case study approach was used. The objective of these studies was to describe the process of learning psychological techniques in a small number of athletes. The first study described the use of a breath-centring technique as part of a pre-performance routine performed prior to free-throw shots in basketball in five junior basketball players (two females and three males, age 10–11 years; Haddad and Tremayne, 2009). After a baseline period of two to three weeks during which free-throw performance was assessed until participants were ready for the intervention (i.e. reached a consistent free-throw performance), the intervention began. Each participant received a 20-minute session explaining the procedure of breath centring prior to the shooting act. During the post-intervention period participants practised at least twice a week, and were instructed to keep a training diary. All participants completed eight free-throw sessions in which they were asked to use the newly taught breath-centring technique. Performance during the post-intervention period improved for all participants, but with great variance. The smallest improvement in free-throw percentage was 4 per cent and the largest improvement was 25 per cent. This variance could have been due to the initial free-throw abilities of the participants. The participant that improved the most had the lowest free-throw percentage values at baseline (21.25 per cent), while the participant that improved the least had the highest free-throw percentage values at baseline (82.5 per cent). Since the researchers of this study used a single-subject design, they could not rule out the multiple-testing effect. Therefore, it was difficult to explain the improvement in accuracy of shooting only by the use of the learned breath-centring technique.

The second study looked at the use of an eight-week imagery programme on affective responses in three competitive swimmers (two 15-year-old females and one 13-year-old male; McCarthy, 2009). A 30-minute session explaining motivational general-mastery (MG-M) imagery was conducted with each swimmer, and they each received a booklet on mental imagery. The swimmers practised a few minutes at a time during imagery practice and in a practice at home before going to bed. Positive affects (e.g. the extent to which a person feels enthusiastic, active, and alert) and negative affects (e.g. reflecting distress and unpleasantness) of swimming were assessed using two ten-item subscales: the positive affects subscale had emotions such as interested, alert, and excited, and the negative affects subscale contained emotions such as scared, nervous, and upset. The swimmers rated each emotion on a scale of one to five. They increased their score on the positive affects subscale by 15–30 per cent, while no differences were found in the negative affects subscale. All three swimmers reported an increase in imagery use after the intervention. However, while the focus of the intervention was on MG-M, no changes were observed before or after the intervention in this specific type of imagery. In fact, the increases were observed in visual and kinaesthetic imagery. Hence, it was not clear what caused the reported increases.

Methodological concerns and research limitations

The studies reviewed in the latter three sections of the current chapter provide useful information for both researchers and SPCs on psychological characteristics of young athletes, as well as on intervention techniques used with this population. However, six methodological concerns and research limitations associated with the reviewed studies are discussed.

1 The lack of longitudinal studies. Most of the studies reviewed in our chapter were cross-sectional. None of the studies examined the psychological aspects of early development in sport over a number of years. In the majority of the intervention studies, no replicated measurements over time were performed. In order to effectively examine psychological characteristics of elite young athletes, or the usefulness of sport psychology interventional techniques given to young athletes, a longitudinal approach should be adopted. In this approach, one group of individuals is observed over a long period of time (Thomas

and Nelson, 2005), enabling the researcher to obtain qualitative and quantitative data on various dependent variables relating to the training process and performance outcome. In the case of early development in sport, data should be collected during a time period of five to six years. The information obtained during these years would result in improving the ability of coaches, instructors, and SPCs to more effectively plan training programmes for the young athlete.

2 The lack of interventional studies. Only four out of 31 studies reviewed in our chapter were intervention-based (experimental) in nature. While descriptive data on psychological characteristics of young athletes are important, they cannot lead to a cause-and-effect relationship. Intervention studies are essential for examining the actual contribution of sport psychology programmes to performance enhancement. Data emerging from intervention studies on elite adult performers may not be applicable when working with the young talented population, for a number of reasons. Among these are: (a) the different developmental stages of the two populations, (b) their different skill levels, and (c) their different levels of experience. Therefore, additional intervention studies should be conducted on athletes in their early years of sport development, to increase our knowledge on the effectiveness of sport psychology interventions during this period of time.

3 The lack of qualitative studies. Only two qualitative studies in which a case study approach was used were found. As indicated above, intervention studies are needed for examining the contribution of psychological interventions to performance enhancement in young athletes. However, in qualitative studies, data on psychological aspects related to the training process – such as feelings, perceptions, and thoughts of the young athlete – can be gathered. This information, typically collected by observation, in-depth interviews, and written materials (e.g. coach's progress report) on the young athlete, is rarely obtained in interventional studies. By collecting these data, coaches and SPCs can better understand the specific needs of the individual athlete and subsequently develop better training programmes.

4 The inherent limitations of self-report. Most of the descriptive studies reviewed in our chapter used self-report. Different questionnaires were given to the young athletes in order to obtain information relating to their psychological characteristics. The process of self-report has inherent limitations, one of which is the faking of responses, known as the Social Desirability Response Bias. This tendency is defined as, "the tendency for a person to respond in a way that seems socially appealing, regardless of his or her true characteristics" (Furr and Bacharach, 2008, p. 246). It is assumed that in studies on young athletes this is manifested when they falsify their inventory responses in order to be consistent with the wishes of their coach or parents, rather than providing honest responses. In order to cope with this

methodological limitation, additional in-depth interviews and observations should be carried out when collecting data on young athletes.

5 The lack of differentiation between ages and levels of experience of athletes participating in the same study. Data were collected in the same study on athletes of different age groups (e.g. 7–14 years and 11–14 years) and different levels of sport experience (e.g. beginning athletes and athletes having two or three years of experience). These two variables – age and experience – can obviously influence the results obtained in the reviewed studies. The selected research methodology used by the researchers should account for this limitation. For example, in the same study, data should be collected on athletes who were born in the same year and those who have a similar level of experience.

6 The extensive use of correlational studies. Most of the studies reviewed in the section on psychological characteristics of young athletes were of a correlational or descriptive nature, implying certain possible conclusions; thus, they can by no means suggest causality. Correlational studies can only provide associations among variables, and cannot entirely explain any variation in the results obtained. In addition, some of the correlational relationships discussed in our chapter yielded low *r* values. Therefore, a careful approach should be used when applying data from these studies.

Implications for practice

Based on the studies reviewed and the methodological concerns discussed in this chapter, as well as on our own experience working with young athletes in a number of sports such as basketball (females and males), judo (females and males), soccer (males), and volleyball (females and males), a number of practical implications are discussed for SPCs who provide consultations to athletes in early phases of talent development. The practical implications are as follows.

Teaching the young athlete various psychological techniques

The young athlete should practise a number of psychological techniques in order to be familiar with the basic principles of each technique, as well as to be able to select in the future those techniques that most fit his or her professional needs. Basic principles of psychological techniques, such as focusing attention, imagery, and relaxation, should be taught in early phases of talent development. The SPC should not only explain to the young athlete how to use the technique, but also provide him or her with the rationale of why psychological preparation is necessary for achieving a high level of proficiency in sport. Only after becoming familiar with the foundations of the techniques will the young athlete be able to select those techniques that fit his or her professional needs.

Focusing on what the SPC is capable of doing best

SPCs should focus on what they are capable of doing best. A variety of psychological techniques is available in the sport psychology literature and can be adopted by SPCs, and we suggest that SPCs develop their own approach using some of these techniques, based on their professional knowledge, experience, and expertise. SPCs cannot present every psychological intervention discussed in the literature; instead, they should use the psychological techniques with which they are familiar. Having experience in delivering a core number of psychological techniques over long periods of time will enable SPCs to develop expertise in practising these techniques. In addition, they will be able to better convince their athletes that the practised psychological techniques can help them improve their athletic skills.

Cooperating regularly with the professional staff working with the young athlete

Psychological preparation is only one type of preparation used when working with young athletes. There are other preparations, such as physical, technical, and tactical (see Bompa, 1999), which may be perceived by the athletes and coaches as more important than psychological preparation. SPCs should understand the objectives of each of the other preparations, and cooperate with other professionals working with the young athlete, among them coaches, athletic trainers, strength and conditioning coaches, and physicians. They should attend practices, games, and competitions in order to observe the young athletes performing in real-life sport situations. In addition, they should listen to requests made by the other professionals, particularly the coaching staff (e.g. to work with injured athletes, to talk with players who have lost interest in their sport, or to help athletes effectively manage their free time). It is our assumption that the psychological preparation should be naturally synthesised into the training programme of young athletes. The involvement of the SPC with the other professionals who are working with the young athlete may help him or her to get to know the athlete better, and therefore to be able to plan the psychological programme for a particular athlete in an optimal way.

Creating a dialogue with the family members of the young athlete

The family of the young athlete plays a major role in his or her journey to sporting excellence (see Côté, 1999). SPCs should create an open dialogue with the family members of the young athlete, particularly with the parents. The SPC should inform the parents about the work he or she is doing with their child, and in what ways the child is expected to benefit from the psychological preparation given. SPCs should also listen to the parents' requests (e.g. helping them to convince the child to invest more time on school assignments and preparation for exams). If required, SPCs should serve as a channel of communication between the parents and the coaching staff. The parents may have difficulties approaching the coaches, and therefore they can ask the SPC to convey their feelings and thoughts to the coaches.

Providing the athlete with appropriate learning environments

SPCs should create stimulating learning environments for the young athlete, so that he or she will be willing to allocate time to practise the learned psychological techniques. A major goal of the SPC is to convince young athletes that their psychological skills need to be as developed and refined as their motor/physical skills. Therefore, in addition to the individual/group sessions that SPCs regularly conduct with the athletes, they have to find appropriate opportunities within the training programme for the athletes to practise the psychological techniques they have been taught. We offer a number of activities that can provide young athletes with additional instructional opportunities to practise their psychological techniques as part of the training programme:

1 Warm-up sessions – when readying themselves for the practice/competition/game by performing warm-up activities such as jogging and stretching, the young athlete can simultaneously perform psychological techniques such as imagery, focusing attention, and self-talk.
2 Cooling-down sessions – at the end of the practice/competition/game, while the athlete performs cooling-down activities such as stretching, he or she can also use psychological techniques such as breathing and relaxation;
3 Home assignments – young players can be asked to practise their psychological interventions at home, in a quiet and relaxed atmosphere. Practising psychological techniques such as imagery, focusing attention, self-talk, or relaxation at home can increase the athlete's awareness of the appropriate use of the psychological techniques he or she learned during individual or group sport psychology consultation sessions. It is true that SPCs cannot ensure that the athlete will indeed perform the assigned psychological techniques at home; however, we believe that it is the responsibility of young athletes to make the effort to practise these techniques at home as part of their commitment to achieving the best that they are capable of.

Adopting an "open door" approach

SPCs should regularly use an "open door" approach and a "listening to the athlete" approach when working with young athletes. They should speak with their athletes more often, or go over their training diaries (if permission is granted), in order to learn more about their feelings and thoughts. SPCs should encourage their athletes to consult them at any time, not only during formal consultation. A lack of information on what the athlete feels about his or her involvement in the early phases of talent development may hinder the ability of the SPC to match relevant interventions to the actual needs of the individual athlete.

Collecting information for assessing the effectiveness of the psychological preparation

SPCs should assess the consultation process with the young athlete by collecting both quantitative and qualitative data related to different aspects of their practical work together. They should collect data on the individual achievements of the athlete (e.g. final ranking in a competition, individual records, or playing ability in a ball game), and evaluate the contribution of the interventional techniques practised by the athlete to his or her achievements. They should also gather information from all those involved during the training programme (e.g. the coaches, the parents) on how they perceive the actual contribution of the psychological programme to the development of the athlete. In addition, they may talk with the young athlete about his or her feelings and thoughts on the use of the psychological techniques in the training programme. In this respect, it is suggested that SPCs use various retrospective methods, such as: (a) conducting a detailed retrospective interview (e.g. with the athlete) reflecting the collection of measures of performance and measurable improvements in performance; (b) obtaining information about the amount and structure of practice-related activities and training resources as a function of the development of athletes; and (c) developing an interview procedure to map out longitudinal changes of sport participation patterns and various training activities (see Côté *et al.*, 2005), as part of their effort to assess the effectiveness of their professional practice.

Summary

Psychological preparation is an essential aspect of any sport programme aimed at developing talent in young athletes (Bompa, 1999). When planning short- or long-term psychological preparation, SPCs should integrate empirical and applied knowledge into their programmes in order to help their young athletes achieve a high level of proficiency. The reviewed studies in our chapter on the psychological characteristics of young athletes, as well as on the effectiveness of the psychological interventions they use, can help SPCs in their planning process. The discussion on methodological concerns and research limitations associated with the reviewed studies that are discussed in our chapter can help SPCs in adopting a careful approach when implementing the findings of these studies. Finally, the quantitative and qualitative data presented in the sport psychology literature can be applied by SPCs in their programmes to help their young athletes fulfil their athletic potential.

References

Abbott, A. and Collins, D. (2004). Eliminating the dichotomy between theory and practice in talent identification and development: Considering the role of psychology. *Journal of Sports Sciences*, 22, 395–408.

Baker, J., Schorer, J., Cobley, S., Schimmer, G., and Wattie, N. (2009). Circumstantial development and athletic excellence: The role of birth date and birth place. *European Journal of Sport Science*, 9, 329–339.

Bakker, F. (1995). Ontwikkeling van tests op het terrein van de sportpsychologie in Nederland en Vlaanderen [Development of tests for the field of sport psychology in the Netherlands and Belgium]. *Sportpsychologie Bulletin*, 6, 13–15.

Bar-Eli, M., Dreshman, R., Blumenstein, B., and Weinstein, Y. (2002). The effect of mental training with biofeedback on the performance of young swimmers. *Applied Psychology: An International Review*, 51, 567–581.

Baric, R., Erpic, S. C., and Babic, V. (2002). Intrinsic motivation and goal orientation in track-and-field children. *Kinesiology*, 34, 50–60.

Bompa, T. (1999). *Periodisation: The theory and methodology of training* (4th edn). Champaign, IL: Human Kinetics.

Brown, J. (2001). *Sport talent: How to identify and develop outstanding athletes*. Champaign, IL: Human Kinetics.

Brustad, R. J. (1988). Affective outcomes in competitive youth sport: The influence of intrapersonal and socialisation factors. *Journal of Sport and Exercise Psychology*, 10, 307–321.

Brustad, R. and Weiss, M. R. (1987). Competence perceptions and sources of worry in high, medium, and low competitive trait-anxious young athletes. *Journal of Sport Psychology*, 9, 97–105.

Côté, J. (1999). The influence of the family in the development of talent in sport. *The Sport Psychologist*, 13, 395–417.

Côté, J., Ericsson, K. A., and Law, M. P. (2005). Tracing the development of athletes using retrospective interview methods: A proposed interview and validation procedure for reported information. *Journal of Applied Sport Psychology*, 17, 1–19.

Côté, J., MacDonald, D. J., Baker, J., and Abernethy, B. (2006). When "where" is more important than "when": Birthplace and birthdate effects on the achievement of sporting expertise. *Journal of Sports Sciences*, 24, 1065–1073.

Côté, J., Lidor, R., and Hackfort, D. (2009). To sample or to specialise? Seven postulates about youth sport activities that lead to continued participation and elite performance. *International Journal of Sport and Exercise Psychology*, 9, 7–17.

Davids, K. and Baker, J. (2007). Genes, environment and sport performance: Why the nature–nurture dualism is no longer relevant. *Sports Medicine*, 37, 961–980.

Elferink-Gemser, M. T., Visscher, C., Lemmink, K. A. P. M., and Mulder, T. W. (2004). Relation between multidimensional performance characteristics and level of performance in talented youth field hockey players. *Journal of Sports Sciences*, 22, 1053–1063.

Elferink-Gemser, M. T., Visscher, C., Lemmink, K. A. P. M., and Mulder, T. (2007). Multidimensional performance characteristics and standard of performance in talented youth field hockey players: A longitudinal study. *Journal of Sports Sciences*, 25, 481–489.

Falk, B., Lidor, R., Lander, Y., and Lang, B. (2004). Talent identification and early development of elite water-polo players: A 2-year follow-up study. *Journal of Sports Sciences*, 22, 347–355.

Furr, R. M. and Bacharach, V. R. (2008). *Psychometrics: An introduction*. Thousand Oaks, CA: Sage.

Gill, D., Gross, J., and Huddleston, S. (1983). Participation motivation in youth sports. *International Journal of Sport Psychology*, 14, 1–14.

Gould, D., Eklund, R. C., Petlichkoff, L., Peterson, K., and Bump, L. (1991). Psychological predictors of state anxiety and performance in age-group wrestlers. *Pediatric Exercise Science*, 3, 198–208.

Grossbard, J. R., Cumming, S. P., Standage, M., Smith, R. E., and Smoll, F. L. (2007). Social desirability and relations between goal orientations and competitive trait anxiety in young athletes. *Psychology of Sport and Exercise*, 8, 491–505.

Grossbard, J. R., Smith, R. E., Smoll, F. L., and Cumming, S. P. (2009). Competitive anxiety in young athletes: Differentiating somatic anxiety, worry, and concentration disruption. *Anxiety, Stress and Coping*, 22, 153–166.

Gucciardi, D. F., Gordon, S., and Dimmock, J. A. (2009). Evaluation of a mental toughness training program for youth-aged Australian footballers: I. A quantitative analysis. *Journal of Applied Sport Psychology*, 21, 307–323.

Haddad, K. and Tremayne, P. (2009). The effects of centering on the free-throw shooting performance of young athletes. *The Sport Psychologist*, 23, 118–136.

Hall, C. R., Munroe-Chandler, K. J., Fishburne, G., and Hall, N. D. (2009). The sport imagery questionnaire for children (SIQ). *Measurement in Physical Education and Exercise Science*, 13, 93–107.

Holt, N. L. and Morley, D. (2004). Gender differences in psychosocial factors associated with athletic success during childhood. *The Sport Psychologist*, 18, 138–153.

Hom, J. H. L., Duda, J. L., and Miller, A. (1993). Correlates of goal orientations among young athletes. *Pediatric Exercise Science*, 5, 168–176.

Jones, R. G. (1992). Was there a Hawthorne effect? *American Journal of Sociology*, 98, 451–468.

Lidor, R., Côté, J., and Hackfort, D. (2009). To test or not to test? The use of physical skill tests in talent detection and in early phases of sport development. *International Journal of Sport and Exercise Psychology*, 7, 131–146.

Lufi, D. and Tenenbaum, G. (1991). Persistence among young male gymnasts. *Perceptual and Motor Skills*, 72, 479–482.

Matveyev, L. (1981). *Fundamentals of sports training*. Moscow, Russia: Progress.

McAuley, E. and Gill, D. (1983). Reliability and validity of the physical self-efficacy scale in a competitive sport setting. *Journal of Sport Psychology*, 5, 410–418.

McCarthy, P. J. (2009). Putting imagery to good affect: A case study among youth swimmers. *Sport and Exercise Psychology Review*, 5, 27–38.

Meyers, M. C., Stewart, C. C., Laurent, C. M., LeUnes, A. D., and Bourgeois, A. E. (2008). Coping skills of Olympic developmental soccer athletes. *International Journal of Sports Medicine*, 29, 987–993.

Mills, K. D., Munroe, K. J., and Hall, C. R. (2001). The relationship between imagery and self-efficacy in competitive athletes. *Imagination, Cognition, and Personality*, 20, 33–39.

Munroe-Chandler, K. J., Hall, C. R., Fishburne, G. J., and Hall, N. (2007). The content of imagery use in youth sport. *International Journal of Sport and Exercise Psychology*, 2, 158–174.

Munroe-Chandler, K. J., Hall, C. R., Fishburne, G. J., and Strachan, L. (2007). Where, when, and why young athletes use imagery: An examination of developmental differences. *Research Quarterly for Exercise and Sport*, 78, 103–116.

Munroe-Chandler, K., Hall, C., and Fishburne, G. (2008). Playing with confidence: The relationship between imagery use and self-confidence and self-efficacy in youth soccer players. *Journal of Sports Sciences*, 26, 1539–1546.

Murcia, J. A. M., Gimeno, E. C., and Coll, D. G. C. (2007). Young athletes' motivational profiles. *Journal of Sports Science and Medicine*, 6, 172–179.

Nieuwenhuis, C. F., Spamer, E. J., and van Rossum, J. H. (2002). Prediction function for identifying talent in 14- to 15-year-old female field hockey players. *High Ability Studies*, 13, 21–34.

Psychountaki, M. and Zervas, Y. (2000). Competitive worries, sport confidence, and performance ratings for young swimmers. *Perceptual and Motor Skills*, 91, 87–94.

Reynolds, W. M. (1982). Development of a reliable and valid short form of the Marlowe-Crowne social desirability scale. *Journal of Clinical Psychology*, 18, 112–119.

Ryckman, R. M. and Hamel, J. (1993). Perceived physical ability differences in the sport participation motives of young athletes. *International Journal of Sport Psychology*, 24, 270–283.

Ryska, T. A. (2003). Sportsmanship in young athletes: The role of competitiveness, motivational orientation, and perceived purposes of sport. *Journal of Psychology*, 137, 273–293.

Scanlan, T. K. and Lewthwaite, R. (1984). Social psychological aspects of competition for male youth sport participants: I. Predictors of competitive stress. *Journal of Sport Psychology*, 6, 208–226.

Scanlan, T. K. and Lewthwhite, R. (1985). Social psychological aspects of competition for male youth sport participants: III. Determinants of personal performance expectancies. *Journal of Sport Psychology*, 7, 389–399.

Scanlan, T. K. and Lewthwaite, R. (1986). Social psychological aspects of competition for male youth sport participants: IV. Predictors of enjoyment. *Journal of Sport Psychology*, 8, 25–35.

Scanlan, T. K., Lewthwaite, R., and Jackson, B. L. (1984). Social psychological aspects of competition for male youth sport participants: II. Predictors of performance outcomes. *Journal of Sport Psychology*, 6, 422–429.

Smith, A. L., Balaguer, I., and Duda, J. L. (2006a). Goal orientation profile differences on perceived motivational climate, perceived peer relationships, and motivation-related responses of youth athletes. *Journal of Sports Sciences*, 24, 1315–1327.

Smith, R. E., Smoll, F. L., Cumming, S. P., and Grossbard, J. R. (2006b). Measurement of multidimensional sport performance anxiety in children and adults: The Sport Anxiety Scale-2. *Journal of Sport and Exercise Psychology*, 29, 39–59.

Stadulis, R. E., MacCracken, M. J., Eidson, T. A., and Severance, C. (2002). A children's form of the competitive state anxiety inventory: The CSAI-2C. *Measurement in Physical Education and Exercise Science*, 6, 147–165.

Thomas, J. R. and Nelson, J. K. (2005). *Research methods in physical activity* (5th edn). Champaign, IL: Human Kinetics.

Vaeyens, R., Lenoir, M., Williams, A. M., Mazyn, L., and Philippaerts, R. M. (2007). The effects of task constraints on visual search behavior and decision-making skill in youth soccer players. *Journal of Sport and Exercise Psychology*, 29, 147–169.

Vazou, S., Ntoumanis, N., and Duda, J. L. (2006). Predicting young athletes' motivational indices as a function of their perceptions of the coach- and peer-created climate. *Psychology of Sport and Exercise*, 7, 215–233.

Williams, A. M. and Reilly, T. (2000). Talent identification and development in soccer. *Journal of Sports Sciences*, 18, 657–667.

Wrisberg, C. A. and Anshel, M. H. (1989). The effect of cognitive strategies on the free throw shooting performance of young athletes. *Sport Psychologist*, 3, 95–104.

9 Working with coach–athlete relationships

Their quality and maintenance

Daniel J. A. Rhind and Sophia Jowett

Abstract

This chapter aims to highlight theory, research, and practice that concern the quality of the coach–athlete relationship and its maintenance. The 3+1Cs model of relationship quality and the COMPASS model of relationship maintenance are discussed. Research associated with these models is summarised while highlighting their applied implications. Validated measurement tools that allow the assessment of the quality of coach–athlete relationships and the strategies used to maintain the effectiveness of these relationships are also discussed. Case studies are used to show the ways in which these models can inform sport psychology consultants working with coaches and athletes. Key practical issues are also considered.

Keywords: coach–athlete, relationship maintenance, man management

Setting the scene

One only needs to tune in to a sports bulletin, read the autobiography of a successful sports person or turn to the back pages of most newspapers to find compelling anecdotal evidence of the importance of the role played by the coach–athlete relationship in sport. We often hear successful head coaches being described as "great man managers", with elite players attributing successful performance to the support, guidance, direction, attention, interest, belief, and trust showed by their coaches. For example, Wayne Rooney discussed the good relationships that the England players had with their then manager Sven-Goran Eriksson: "There is a feeling we should win the World Cup for Sven, he is a great manager … all of the players like him and respect him, he respects us and, more importantly, he trusts us" (BBC News, 2006). Similarly, Geoff Hurst, the hat-trick scoring hero of England's 1966 world cup final victory, gives great credit to the influence that the relationship he had with his coaches, Ron Greenwood and Sir Alf Ramsey, had in facilitating the success he achieved during his career (Hurst, 2001).

It is not just athletes but also coaches who acknowledge the importance of the coach–athlete relationship. In his autobiography, Sir Alex Ferguson (2000), a highly successful manager of Manchester United Football Club, explained that loyalty and commitment are key elements of effective coaching. Another prolific coach, Sir Clive Woodward (2004), who led the England Rugby team to winning the 2003 World Cup, reported in his autobiography that the partnership between the coach and the athlete was a key ingredient in a winning team. The relationships coaches and athletes develop in the course of their athletic partnership can continue even when the coach or athlete has left the sports club. For instance, Jose Mourinho, the recently appointed manager of Real Madrid, stated that "It is normal that as a consequence of the relationship that I have with my players, almost all of them want to work with me in the future", in response to transfer speculation linking him with players from his previous club, Chelsea (*Independent*, 2008).

The importance of this relationship may be most clearly demonstrated when it starts to break down. The disintegration of many high-profile coach–athlete relationships has been played out in the media. For example, David Beckham explained that

> I had been there since 15 and the manager had total control over all the young lads, but the fact was I'd grown and he didn't see me as a man instead of a boy. It wasn't a matter of respect. I just think he felt he didn't have control of me...
>
> (*Scotsman on Sunday*, 2003)

Another example comes from Craig Bellamy, who spoke publicly after Graeme Souness, his then Newcastle United manager, had claimed that Bellamy had feigned injury to avoid playing in a different position. Bellamy stated that "When I heard what the manager was saying, I was in shock ... I thought not only has he gone behind my back, he's lying" (BBC News, 2005). It was shortly after this incident that Bellamy left Newcastle United to join Blackburn Rovers, who were managed by Mark Hughes, a coach that Bellamy had worked for and formed a good relationship with whilst playing for the Welsh national team. More recently, Albert Riera highlighted the importance of communication when discussing his fall out with his then Liverpool manager, Rafael Benitez:

> I have been here two years and I know how he is. He has never sorted out a situation with a player by talking with him.... If I'm doing something badly and you are my boss, and you value me, then you are going to come and tell me what I have to do to play again.
>
> (*Daily Telegraph*, 2010)

Further examples can be drawn from individual sports, such as tennis: "We just decided it was not working. It was probably a question of understanding what kind of person I am" (Novak Djocovic talking about Todd Martin; Fox Sports, 2010).

These real-life examples illustrate the need for sport psychology consultants to acknowledge their important role in helping facilitate the development and maintenance of successful and effective relationships, as well as helping prevent their breakdown. This leads one to ask the following questions, all of which will be addressed in this chapter:

- What makes a good-quality or an effective coach–athlete relationship?
- How is the quality of the coach–athlete relationship measured, and can we diagnose effective from ineffective relationships?
- What are the functions of the coach–athlete relationship?
- How can the quality and effectiveness of the coach–athlete relationship be maintained?
- What strategies can a sport psychologist use to help a coach and athlete optimise the quality of their relationship?

The conceptual basis of the coach–athlete relationship

Within the coaching context, the relationship that is developed between the coach and the athlete is viewed as paramount (Lyle, 1999). Lyle (1999) explained the importance of the coach–athlete relationship by arguing that it is at the very heart of coaching, and that coaches who fail to acknowledge the importance of it risk not developing their athletes to their full potential. Jowett (2005a) supported this assertion by arguing that "The coach–athlete relationship is not an add-on to, or by-product of, the coaching process ... instead it is the foundation of coaching", and that the relationship is therefore "...embedded in the dynamic and complex coaching process and provides the means by which coaches' and athletes' needs are expressed and fulfilled" (p. 412). Moreover, Côté and Sedgwick (2003) have highlighted that the coach–athlete relationship is of significant importance to both the coach and the athlete, and that it is therefore an issue which merits the attention of theory and research relevant to coaching, coaches, and athletes. Subsequently, if the relationship that is developed between coaches and athletes is a central aspect of coaching and, in turn, to skill development and performance success, then it is a key issue for sport psychology and sport psychologists alike. It may be important that sport psychologists who work closely with coaches and athletes acknowledge the importance of this relationship if they wish to achieve success in their consultancy.

What makes a good-quality or an effective coach–athlete relationship?

The first step to understanding the coach–athlete relationship is to provide a clear definition. Jowett and Poczwardowski (2007) define the coach–athlete relationship as "...the situation in which a coach's and an athlete's cognitions, feelings, and behaviours are mutually and causally interrelated" (p. 4). In line with this definition, Jowett (2007a, 2007b) proposed the 3+1C conceptualisation of the coach–athlete relationship. This conceptualisation comprises four key constructs: closeness (i.e. interpersonal feelings), commitment (i.e. interpersonal cognitions), complementarity (i.e. interpersonal behaviours), and co-orientation (i.e. perceptually interconnected).

Closeness refers to the affective element of the coach–athlete relationship. It relates to the interpersonal feelings that the coach and the athlete associate with their sporting partnership. Closeness in relationships is characterised by coaches and athletes who like, trust, appreciate, and respect each other. In contrast, lack of closeness in a relationship is evident when a coach or an athlete dislike, distrust, and disrespect their sporting partner. Overall, closeness reflects the strength of the affective bond or ties within a given coach–athlete dyad.

Commitment reflects the cognitive element of the coach–athlete relationship. It relates to the dyadic members' thoughts regarding their intentions or plans to maintain an athletic relationship that is close over time, both at the present time and in the future. Committed dyad members are more likely to be motivated to work with their sporting partner in the medium and longer term. A lack of commitment may be shown by a coach or an athlete thinking that they no longer want or desire to work with their athlete or coach, and hence they may be considering terminating the relationship.

Complementarity concerns the behavioural aspect of the coach–athlete relationship. This construct refers to the members' cooperative and corresponding behaviours of affiliation as these unfold in training sessions and competitions. Such cooperative and corresponding behaviours include being responsive, prepared, relaxed, and open in the presence of one another. In sporting terms, an example of complementarity may be the case in which an athlete turns up on time and is kitted appropriately for training, and a coach is happy to hear the athlete's thoughts or feedback. Lack of complementarity may therefore be manifested as arriving late for training, or adopting a hostile, distant, or aggressive stance.

The "+1C" of the 3+1Cs model reflects the "interrelated" element of the definition. *Co-orientation* captures coaches and athletes' interrelated feelings, thoughts, and behaviours captured via coaches and athletes' interpersonal perceptions of Closeness, Commitment, and Complementarity (3Cs). Based on the broader construct of Co-orientation (see Newcomb, 1953; Laing *et al.*, 1966), Jowett (2006, 2007b, 2009a) explained that the quality of the relationship is shaped not only by how members directly perceive their connections with others, known as the *direct perspective*, but also by how they believe others' perceive these connections, known as *meta-perspective*.

The *direct perspective* therefore focuses on how a coach/athlete feels, thinks, and behaves regarding their sporting relationship (as this is defined by the 3Cs). It therefore consists of direct closeness (e.g. I like my coach/athlete), direct commitment (e.g. I am committed to my coach/athlete) and direct complementarity (e.g. I am responsive to my coach/athlete). The *meta-perspective* focuses on how a coach/athlete believes their athlete/coach feels, thinks, and behaves relative to them within the context of the sporting relationship (as this is defined by the 3Cs). It therefore consists of meta-closeness (e.g. My coach/athlete likes me), meta-commitment (e.g. My coach/athlete is committed to me) and meta-complementarity (e.g. My coach/athlete is responsive).

In summary, closeness (feelings), commitment (thoughts), and complementarity (behaviours) are the 3 Cs within the 3+1C conceptualisation, with co-orientation being represented by the "+1". The 3+1C model integrates these three constructs to suggest that athletes and coaches feelings (Closeness), thoughts (Commitment), and behaviours (Complementarity) are causally and mutually interconnected (Co-orientation). Therefore, the feelings, thoughts, and behaviours of a coach are theorised to influence, and are influenced by, the feelings, thoughts and behaviours of their athlete, and vice versa.

How is the quality of the coach–athlete relationship measured, and can we diagnose effective from ineffective relationships?

A series of qualitative studies have been conducted in relation to this conceptualisation. For example, interviews have been conducted with Olympic medallists (Jowett and Cockerill, 2003), typical (Jowett, 2003; Jowett and Frost, 2007; Jowett and Timson-Katchis, 2005) and atypical (Jowett and Meek, 2000; Jowett *et al.*, 2007) relationships, elite Swiss swimmers (Philippe and Seiler, 2006), and elite Hungarian coaches and athletes from individual sports (Trzaskoma-Bicserdy *et al.*, 2007). Each of these studies has supported the utility of the 3+1Cs to conceptualise the quality and nature of the coach–athlete relationship whilst highlighting some of its functions (i.e. how the presence of such relational constructs and properties facilitates athletic performance and subjective well-being).

Building upon the earlier qualitative research work, Jowett and Ntoumanis (2004) initially developed the Coach–Athlete Relationship Questionnaire (CART-Q). This is an 11-item self-report measure that assesses respondents' *direct perceptions* of the quality of the coach–athlete relationship in terms of closeness (four items; e.g. "I respect my coach/athlete"), commitment (three items; e.g. "I am committed to my coach/athlete") and complementarity (four items; e.g. "When I am coached by/coaching my coach/athlete, I am ready to do my best"). The athlete and coach versions of the CART-Q are practically the same, with only the target of the items being altered depending on the respondent. This affords the opportunity to compare the perceptions of both members of the dyad.

Moreover, Jowett (2009a) developed and gained validity evidence for a *meta-perspective* version of the 11-item CART-Q. The meta-perspective version is very similar to the direct version, but the items are reworded such that they involve participants reporting how they believed their sporting partner feels, thinks, and behaves. It therefore measures meta-closeness (e.g. "My coach/athlete likes me"), meta-commitment (e.g. "My coach/athlete is committed to me") and meta-complementarity (e.g. "When I am coached by/coaching my coach/athlete, he/she is ready to do his/her best"). The items of the direct and meta-perspectives of the CART-Q are displayed in Table 9.1.

More recently, Rhind and Jowett (2010a) developed and validated a longer version of the Coach–Athlete Relationship Questionnaire (CART-Q Long). This also measures direct closeness (seven items; e.g. "I value my coach/athlete"), direct commitment (ten items; e.g. "I cannot imagine ending my relationship with my coach/athlete in the next year") and direct complementarity (12 items; e.g. "I am organised"). A meta-version of the long CART-Q has also been developed and validated. Both short and long versions of the direct and meta-perspective CART-Q have demonstrated content, factorial, and criterion validity, as well as internal consistency (see Jowett, 2009a, 2009b; Jowett and Ntoumanis, 2004; Rhind and Jowett, 2010a).

The inclusion of the direct and meta-perspective versions of the CART-Q affords the assessment of three dimensions of co-orientation: actual similarity, assumed similarity, and empathic understanding (see Jowett, 2005b, 2006, 2007b, 2009a). First, *actual similarity* involves the comparison of a coach and an athlete's direct perspectives of the 3Cs and therefore assesses whether the members of a given dyad feel, think, and behave in similar ways. Second, *assumed similarity* concerns how similar a member perceives their feelings, thoughts, and behaviours (as defined by the 3Cs) are to those of their coach/athlete. It involves the comparison of an individual's direct and meta-perspectives. Third, *empathic understanding* refers to how accurate an individual is in terms of reporting how the coach/athlete is feeling, thinking, and behaving (as defined by the 3Cs) relative to him/her. For example, an athlete's direct perspective (e.g. "I like my coach") is compared with their coach's equivalent meta-perception (e.g. "My athlete likes me") such that the correspondence (or lack thereof) between these two views can be assessed. Overall, assessments of the three dimensions of co-orientation can be plotted in "dyad maps" (see Jowett, 2005b) in order to provide visual information about the quality of the relationship and the degree to which it appears to function effectively or optimally.

Table 9.1 Sample items in the long version of the Coach–Athlete Relationship Questionnaire (CART-Q).

Sub-scale	*Direct perspective*	*Meta-perspective*
Closeness	*I trust my coach	*My coach trusts me
	*I respect my coach	*My coach respects me
	I value my coach	My coach values me
	I care about my coach	My coach cares about me
Commitment	*I am committed to my coach	*My coach is committed to me
	*I think that my sport career is promising with my coach	*My coach thinks that his/her sport career is promising with me
	I cannot imagine ending my relationship with my coach in the next year	My coach cannot imagine ending his/her relationship with me in the next year
	I expect to be close to my coach the season after this one	My coach expects to be close to me the season after this one
Complementarity	*I am at ease	*My coach is at ease
	*I am ready to do my best	*My coach is ready to do his/her best
	*I am responsive to his/her efforts	*My coach is responsive to my efforts
	I know how to approach him/her	My coach knows how to approach me
	I am focused on the task in hand	My coach is focused on the task in hand
	I readily seek my coach's views and opinions	My coach readily seeks my views and opinions

Note
Items with asterisks denote original items from the current short CART-Q.

What are the functions of the coach–athlete relationship? Research employing the CART-Q

A wide range of studies has employed the direct and/or meta-perspective versions of the CART-Qs. These studies will briefly be outlined in relation to the intrapersonal, interpersonal, and environmental factors that have been investigated over recent years. Research regarding *intrapersonal factors* has indicated links between respondents' perceptions of the quality of their coach–athlete relationship and their levels of satisfaction (Jowett and Nezlek, 2011; Jowett and Ntoumanis, 2004; Lorimer, 2009), physical self-concept (Jowett, 2008a), passion for sport/coaching (Lafraniere *et al.*, 2008), achievement goals and intrinsic motivation (Adie and Jowett, 2010), fear of failure (Sagar and Jowett, 2010), burnout (Gustaffson and Jowett, 2010), and perceived performance (Rhind and Jowett, 2010a). Overall, this research highlights that athletes and coaches who have formed relationships that are close, committed, and complementary are likely to be more physically competent, intrinsically motivated, harmoniously passionate for sport/coaching, satisfied with sport, and less likely to experience fear of failure and burnout.

The CART-Qs have also been used to investigate how relationship quality is related to *interpersonal factors*. For instance, Jowett and Clark-Carter (2006) investigated the three dimensions of co-orientation. Athletes were found to show higher levels of empathic understanding in terms of closeness relative to coaches. It was also reported that athletes and coaches forming newly developed relationships were also found to have higher levels of empathic understanding. Female athlete respondents were found to have higher levels of assumed similarity relative to their male counterparts.

Further research has focused on exploring empathy within the coach–athlete relationship. Lorimer and Jowett (2009) filmed 56 coach–athlete dyads during training sessions. The participants then viewed clips of their training and reported how they had felt and thought at different times, as well as making inferences about how their coach/athlete had been feeling and thinking. Empathic accuracy, as defined as the ability to accurately infer how one's sporting partner is feeling and thinking, was then assessed through a comparison of these self-reports and inferences. A positive association was found between participants' meta-perceptions of the quality of their coach–athlete relationship and their level of empathic accuracy.

Moreover, there is also research to suggest that the 3Cs of the coach–athlete relationship associate positively with support supplied by the coach, and negatively with interpersonal conflict (e.g. disagreements, misunderstandings; see Jowett, 2009b). More recently, the quality of the relationship has been linked with athletes' and coaches' attachment orientations, with insecure attachments (avoidance attachment style) predicting ineffective coach–athlete relationships or relationships that lack in closeness, commitment, and complementarity (Davis and Jowett, 2011). Another study highlights that lack of commitment is negatively related to disorderly eating behaviours through lower levels of self-esteem (Shanmugam and Jowett, 2010).

Links have also been found between relationship quality and *environmental factors*. For example, the quality of the coach–athlete relationship has been found to be associated with team cohesion (Jowett and Chaundy, 2004), collective efficacy (Jowett *et al.*, 2011), and coach-created motivational climate (Olympiou *et al.*, 2008). While these findings appear to suggest that the context within which a coach and an athlete interact may influence, and be influenced by, the quality of their relationship, they also highlight potential functions of the dyadic athletic relationship that may be particularly important for achieving performance success and a sense of personal fulfilment.

It is important to acknowledge that many of the studies discussed above explore relationships between different self-report measures. These are clearly limited due to the fact that they rely on the perceptions of the respondents. More research is required which investigates the links between these self-report measures and other measures of related outcomes. One good example of this is provided by the work of Lorimer and Jowett (2009), who used videos of real-life training sessions to explore levels of empathy. There is scope to expand such work to employ other innovative measures of relationship outcomes. A quantitative example may include observational analyses of various aspects of performance. There is also scope to more utilise qualitative methods, such as ethnography and personal diaries, to capture the intricacies of such dyads.

Although research has started to enhance our understanding of the antecedents and consequences of the coach–athlete relationship, as well as how it is experienced, it is important to continue exploring such important factors as coaches' and athletes' individual difference characteristics (e.g. cultural background, experience) and relationship characteristics (e.g. relationship length). Further studies in this area will help to elucidate the extent to which the 3+1C conceptualisation and the CART-Qs are applicable to all forms of this relationship. To date, a large body of evidence supports the validity of the constituent elements of the coach–athlete relationship (3+1Cs) and its accompanied measures (CART-Qs) by highlighting their applicability across a range of intrapersonal, interpersonal, and environmental factors.

How can the quality and effectiveness of the coach–athlete relationship be maintained?

The body of theoretical and empirical as well as anecdotal evidence suggests that the coach–athlete relationship is associated with physical and psychological growth and development. This has contributed to a growing interest in trying to understand how one can make the most from developing athletic relationships that are effective and beneficial.

In the context of sport, coaches and athletes formulate and maintain their athletic relationship motivated by such goals as improving performance and achieving success (Jowett and Poczwardowski, 2007). Since performance accomplishments rarely occur overnight, coaches and athletes are usually required to establish a working partnership that is long term, stable and satisfying, and thus requires maintenance over time (Durand-Bush and Salmela, 2002). Maintenance of the coach–athlete relationship is not simple, and may necessitate conscious effort from both parties; in some instances it may necessitate the assistance and intervention of a sport psychology consultant.

Relationship maintenance can be defined as the strategies used by coaches and athletes to keep their relationship in a specified state (Rhind and Jowett, 2010b). The importance of maintaining effective relationships in sport has been highlighted by previous research with elite athletes, coaches, and coach–athlete dyads. For example, Greenleaf *et al.* (2001) conducted a study to investigate which factors Olympic athletes viewed as having the biggest impact on the effectiveness of their coach. Effective coaching was found to be exemplified by the ability to develop trust and friendship within the coaching relationship, providing appropriate feedback, and ensuring that there is sufficient contact between the coach and the athlete. Gould *et al.* (2002) conducted a similar study to investigate what Olympic athletes viewed as important elements of effective coaching. Questionnaires were administered to 379 athletes who had participated in an Olympic Games. Respondents highlighted the importance of developing trust in their coach, and of their coach showing that they are committed to them. They also highlighted the benefit of being familiar with one's coach and having realistic expectations, as well as the potentially negative effect that conflict can have on their performance.

In a more recent study, Gould *et al.* (2007) interviewed ten American football coaches who had all received awards for their ability to facilitate their athletes' personal development. They were all found to have good interpersonal or communication skills. In the interviews, these coaches emphasised the importance of having open lines of communication with their athletes, possessing clear expectations, and holding their players accountable to them, avoiding punishment or criticisms that were directed to their players' character or personality, and showing that they cared, trusted, and respected their players as people. Trzaskoma-Bicserdy and colleagyes' (2007) study involving 12 international Hungarian coaches and three international Hungarian athletes highlighted in their interviews the importance of supporting behaviours as well as having clear expectations and an ongoing exchange of information through regular communication.

These results seem to be consistent with Côté and Sedgwick's (2003) study. They conducted interviews with ten coach–athlete dyads that participated in rowing at an elite level. A number of themes emerged characterising an effective coaching relationship, including: creating a positive training relationship, promoting goal-setting, building athlete confidence, recognising individual differences, and establishing rapport with each athlete. Moreover, in a study carried out by sport pedagogists (Jones *et al.*, 2003), an elite football coach was interviewed. Over a series of five in-depth interviews, the importance of generating mutual respect and of creating a positive learning environment was highlighted. The coach was able to develop relationships with the athletes that were based on respect, trust, and having confidence in each other's abilities. These strong relationships were said to be associated with the coach's positive approach and cooperative philosophy towards coaching. The importance of communication in the development of effective relationships was identified.

Finally, research focusing on coaches' behaviours has consistently illustrated that supportive and encouraging coaches are more likely to have a positive impact on their athletes' development (Coatsworth and Conroy, 2006), particularly when their athletes are less confident about themselves (Smith and Smoll, 1990). A common thread that runs through these research studies is the combination of positive interpersonal factors, including openness, acceptance, empathy or understanding, and adaptability, that appear to characterise the interactions and relationships between coaches and athletes. This supports the suggestion of Saliminen and Liukkonen (1996), who stated that "The coach who considers the feelings and opinions of their athletes seems to have the best relationships with their athletes" (p. 65). The importance of social support, both perceived and received, has also been emphasised (Rees, 2007).

While communication that is effective, appropriate, adaptive, supportive, positive, and open is likely to enhance and maintain the quality of the coach–athlete relationship and interaction, lack of it is likely to lead to ineffective and distractive partnerships. As discussed earlier, research has shown that lack of relationship maintenance can be linked with interpersonal conflict, fear of failure, and burnout. Moreover, poor relationships have been linked to poor performances. For example, Gould *et al.* (1999) studied four teams who took part in either the Atlanta or the Nagano Olympics and who did not achieve the performance that they had expected when going into the games. The athletes within these teams attributed a range of factors to their disappointing performances. These factors primarily related either to the relationship they had developed with their coach or to the coaching that they had received. The relational factors included having to work with an unfamiliar coach or not having sufficient contact with the coach, which led to there being a lack of insight within the relationship. They also suggested that there was poor communication within their coach–athlete relationship, which contributed to there being a lack of trust and the presence of conflict within the dyad. The athletes also reported that their underperforming was associated with their coach having unrealistic expectations, not showing enough confidence in their athletes, not providing sufficient support, and "over-coaching" the athletes.

Furthermore, Greenleaf *et al.* (2001) reported that ineffective coaching was characterised by frequent coach–athlete conflict, and insufficient contact between the coach and the athlete. Other research has suggested that a discrepancy between the perceptions of a coach and an athlete within a dyad can be associated with negative outcomes (e.g. Jowett, 2003). More recently, Jowett (2009b) found that athletes' perceptions of interpersonal conflict (e.g. arguments, disagreements) with their coaches were associated with lower levels of closeness (e.g. respect, trusting the coach), commitment, and complementarity (e.g. being responsive and prepared). In addition, athletes' perceptions of interpersonal conflict with the coach were negatively related to their physical self-concept (Jowett and Cramer, 2010). Thus, athletes who perceive conflict in the coaching relationship are likely to feel a less competent and skilful performer. Despite the detrimental impact ineffective coach–athlete relationships and interaction can have on individuals' physical and psychological well-being, it is only recently that attempts have been made to develop a conceptual model of relationship strategies that aims to maintain an effective coach–athlete relationship.

The compass model

In an attempt to investigate coaches' and athletes' perceptions of the strategies they use to maintain relationship quality, Rhind and Jowett (2010b) conducted 12 one-to-one interviews, with six coaches and six athletes. The interviews were structured based on Jowett's (2007b) 3+1C conceptualisation of coach–athlete relationship quality (i.e. closeness, commitment, complementarity, and co-orientation). Deductive and inductive content analysis revealed seven main categories: conflict management, openness, motivation, positivity, advice, support, and social networks. These categories reflected relationship maintenance strategies that were employed by both coaches and athletes.

Subsequently, Rhind and Jowett (2011) developed the Coach–Athlete Relationship Maintenance Questionnaire (CARM-Q, see Table 9.2). This is a 28-item self-report instrument that measures a coach and/or an athlete's use of specific relationship maintenance strategies. The results from the statistical analyses suggested that two original categories of the COMPASS model should be revised, with Positivity and Advice being replaced by Preventative and Assurance strategies to better reflect the collection of items within these two dimensions. Thus, the seven key strategies which can be used to maintain relationship quality, and which comprise the COMPASS model (Figure 9.1), are:

- Conflict management – identifying, discussing, resolving and monitoring potential areas of disagreement;
- Openness – promoting open lines of communication;
- Motivation – providing reasons for one's sporting partner to stay in the relationship;
- Preventative – discussing expectations and what should happen if these are not met;
- Assurance – showing one's commitment to the relationship;
- Support – helping the coach or athlete through difficult times;
- Social networks – socialising together to maintain a common social network.

The model theorises that the use of these strategies helps to maintain close, committed, complementary, and co-oriented relationships (i.e. better quality relationships). It also suggests that the absence of these strategies can lead to relationships that are characterised by distance, low commitment or indifference, lack of cooperation, and common ground or discrepant views.

Rhind and Jowett (2011) administered the Coach–Athlete Relationship Maintenance Questionnaire (CARM-Q) to 146 athletes and 105 coaches. Correlational analysis revealed that closeness was strongly associated with the use of openness and social network strategies. Thus, the more individuals reported having open lines of communication and regularly socialising with their coach/athlete, the higher the level of direct and meta-closeness they associated with the relationship. Levels of commitment were most strongly associated with the use of motivational, assurance, and support strategies. In other words, if individuals worked to sustain clear reasons for both partners to remain in the relationship,

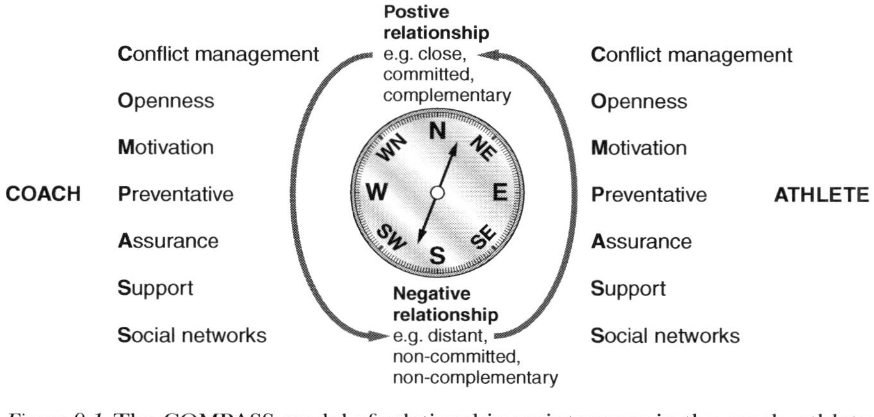

Figure 9.1 The COMPASS model of relationship maintenance in the coach–athlete relationship.

Table 9.2 Items from the Coach–Athlete Relationship Maintenance Questionnaire (CARM-Q)

Sub-scale	*Items*
Conflict management	I try not to lose my temper during disagreements
	I am patient during disagreements
	I am understanding during disagreements
	I listen to my coach/athlete during disagreements
	I cooperate in how I handle disagreements
Openness	I state my opinion when we are setting goals
	I give my coach/athlete constructive feedback
	I give my coach/athlete praise when appropriate
	I am open about my feelings
Motivation	I show that I am motivated to work hard with my coach/athlete
	I show my ability as a coach/athlete
	I show that I am motivated to achieve
	I work hard to achieve our goals
	I show that I am passionate about our sport
Preventative	I tell my coach/athlete what I expect from him/her
	I talk about where we stand
	I tell my coach/athlete when he/she has/has not met my expectations
	I like to have regular talks about our relationship
Assurance	I show my coach/athlete that he/she can rely on me even when things are not going well
	I show my coach/athlete that he/she can count on me
	I show my coach/athlete that he/she can talk to me about anything
Support	I give my coach/athlete support when he/she is going through difficult times
	I am considerate of events in my coach's/athlete's personal life
	I give my coach/athlete support when things are not going well
Social networks	I like to spend time with our mutual friends
	I socialise with my coach/athlete
	I spend time outside of training with my coach/athlete
	I talk about our mutual friends and affiliations

showed their partner that they could count on them, and supported their partner when required, they would be likely to perceive higher levels of direct and meta-commitment within the dyad. In terms of complementarity, this was found to be linked with the use of conflict management and preventative strategies. Therefore, coaches and athletes who discussed their expectations and managed areas of disagreement were likely to report higher levels of direct and meta-complementarity within the relationship.

Further analysis revealed that conflict management and assurance were found to play more significant roles for coaches than athletes. In other words, coaches' perceptions of the quality of their relationship were more significantly associated with the extent to which disagreements were effectively managed, and whether both members of the partnership could count on each other. This may be explained by the nature of the coaches' role. Managing conflict and assuring the athlete may play more of a central role for a coach, and is therefore less salient to the requirements of the athlete.

The associations found between the COMPASS relationship enhancement strategies and the 3Cs may also be explained using well-established theoretical frameworks. According to the basic tenets and constructs of Achievement Goal Theory (Ames, 1992; Nichols, 1989), the social situation created by significant others, such as coaches, varies in terms of the achievement goals emphasised. Subsequently, when athletes' perceive their coaches investing in them by supplying interesting training sessions, and showing their commitment, enthusiasm, supportiveness, and acceptance (COMPASS strategies), then they are also more likely to perceive the environment in which they train as more task-involving (e.g. perceived coaching emphasis placed is on personal achievement). In fact, Olympiou *et al.* (2008) have shown that the 3Cs and the task-involving motivational climate are positively associated, while the 3Cs and the ego-involving motivational climate (e.g. perceived coaching emphasis is placed on outperforming others) are negatively associated. It may be that these reported links can be explained through the COMPASS relationship enhancement strategies coaches are likely to use. This conjecture merits investigation.

Another well-established framework within sport psychology is Self-Determination Theory (SDT; Deci and Ryan, 2000). Self-determination theory proposes that social contexts provide the necessary conditions for the satisfaction of three basic needs (i.e. autonomy, relatedness, and competence) that in turn lead to the enhancement of psychological well-being (e.g. positive affect, vitality). Olympiou *et al.* (2005) have supplied preliminary evidence to suggest that the three basic needs can be satisfied within the context of the coach–athlete relationship as defined by the 3Cs. This study highlights that, through this relationship, individuals can satisfy their key needs. When a coach or athlete feels a sense of belongingness, competence and autonomy within the relationship, he or she is likely to be clearer about the role he/she has been assigned to fulfill within the team. Consequently, it could be possible that the COMPASS strategies associate (directly or indirectly) with the satisfaction of basic needs. Future research is warranted in this area.

What strategies can a sport psychologist use to help a coach and athlete optimise the quality of their relationship?

A number of applied implications can be highlighted based on the research related to the 3+1C conceptualisation of relationship quality and the COMPASS model of relationship maintenance and enhancement. These implications can impact how, when, and why sport psychology consultants work with coaches and athletes, but can also provide resources to guide their practice. This section will consider these points in more detail before outlining seven different case studies which underline the dimensions of the COMPASS model.

Think dyadically

In line with Jowett's (2007b) 3+1C conceptualisation, sport psychology consultants should be able to understand clearly and accurately the viewpoints of both the coach and the athlete. They are encouraged to "think dyadically" when working with their clients (cf. Berscheid, 1999, p. 261), and thus consider both the effect that a coach has on an athlete as well as the effect that an athlete has on a coach. Relationships are reciprocal, and hence it will only be through analysing a coach and an athlete as a dyad that a comprehensive impression of the relationship would be made possible.

Think multidimensionally

The 3+1Cs model also encourages sport psychologists to view relationships as multidimensional. As such, coach–athlete relationships are comprised of a number of dynamic and interconnected parts. Through considering both the coach and the athlete's feelings (closeness), thoughts (commitment), behaviours (complementarity), and interconnections (co-orientation), a sport psychologist will be better able to identify areas of strength or weakness within the dyad. Thus, simply concluding that a relationship is "good" or "bad" may be too simplistic and uni-dimensional, and will only serve to condense the multiple aspects of the relationship into a relatively useless label. A coach and an athlete may experience low, moderate or high levels of closeness, commitment, complementarity, and co-orientation, and hence each of these dimensions merits consideration.

Think dynamically

Sport psychologists should also note that coach–athlete relationships are dynamic, and hence are potentially in a constant state of change. This should inform the development of any intervention which is designed to develop or maintain the quality of a coach–athlete relationship. As such, it is critical that any interventions focus on the *processes* that govern the relationship. The coach–athlete relationship, as mentioned earlier, has been defined as a situation (Jowett and Poczwardowski, 2007), and therefore its quality is expected to change over time. The quality of the relationship is often prone to important transitional events, such as injury, burnout, success or failure, and so on. Such events are likely to trigger conflict that can imbalance the state of the relationship, and thus if a coach and an athlete are having a disagreement, it will be more effective in the longer term for a sport psychologist to work with the dyad to implement effective conflict management processes rather than to just focus on resolving the specific argument.

In combination, the 3+1C conceptualisation and COMPASS model represent useful tools which can guide psychological practice in sport. This may be through providing frameworks to guide sport psychology consultants' observations, or interviews that may inform their needs analysis. They can similarly provide the foundation for any educational intervention, which may be developed to suit the needs and requirements of a coach–athlete dyad, sports team, or organisation as a whole.

In conjunction with these conceptualisations, the CART-Q and CARM-Q offer useful psychometric and diagnostic tools that can provide quantitative measures of the quality of a coach–athlete relationship, as well as the current perceived levels of the use of the seven key relationship maintenance strategies. As a result, they can be used in combination as initial diagnostic tools for highlighting areas of possible weakness, or of particular strength, within a relationship. Beyond this, however, they also have an important role to play in evaluating the effects of an intervention. For instance, through administering the measures before, during, and after an initial attempt to enhance relationship quality, one can obtain a numerical evaluation of whether any quantitative changes have taken place.

Promoting relationship maintenance

The research in this area is at an early stage, and hence studies are yet to be conducted regarding the utility of using these strategies to enhance relationship quality. However, based on the growing body of qualitative and quantitative evidence, the seven strategies within the COMPASS model appear to play important roles. Therefore, based on our experience of working with coaches and athletes, we can offer a number of preliminary techniques that may help to promote the use of these strategies within a coach–athlete dyad.

Promoting conflict management

In the Rhind and Jowett (2010b) study, effective coach–athlete dyads were not characterised by an absence of conflict, but rather by the presence of effective processes for managing conflict. Sport presents an environment in which there is a plethora of potential areas of disagreement. These may include issues related to training (e.g. content, feedback, goals), competition (e.g. tactics, team selection, underperformance), the organisation (e.g. clarity of roles, expectations, and contracts), or private lives (see, for example, stories in the media about inappropriate behaviour). With this wide range of possible sources of disagreement, it is important that the sport psychologist helps the dyad to approach and manage conflict rather than to avoid it.

For example, imagine a coach and an athlete who are constantly arguing over a range of issues, such as training strategies, tactics, and the overall performance of the team. The player has given an interview to a national paper to voice his unhappiness and to hint that he is looking to leave the club. You are brought in as the sport psychologist; what would you do?

In this case, it is important to explore and identify the underlying problems that are being manifested in these disagreements. Thus, one should identify the source of the conflict rather than focus on treating the symptoms. When you talk to the coach, he reports that the athlete is not committed to the team and only has his self-interest at heart. In contrast, when you talk to the athlete, he reports that the key problem is that the coach does not treat him with any respect. The player feels that he is a striker but is always played out of position on the right wing, and he feels that this is not getting the best out of him for the team. You decide that the conflict within the dyad is not being managed effectively. You therefore arrange to meet with both the coach and the athlete to discuss these issues and identify the key discrepancies in their perceptions of the relationship. Moreover, the CART-Qs suggested lack of meta-commitment from the coach and lack of meta-closeness perceived from the player. Possible solutions can then be discussed. For example:

- the athlete is convinced by the coach's position and realises what he can bring to the team as a winger;
- the player consents to start on the bench, with an agreement to have chances as a striker;
- the player agrees to drop down to the reserve team, prove himself in the striker role and win his place in the first team.

Inevitably, there will be a wide range of possible solutions. It is important that the coach and the player are encouraged to explore all of the options, no matter how appropriate or practical, and to mutually agree on a solution. For example, they may agree that the player will play for the reserves as a striker over the next month to show his capability to be effective in this role. The situation will be reviewed on a weekly basis over this period.

In some cases it may be that the conflict is so fundamental that it cannot be resolved, as in the case of Kevin Pietersen (England Cricket Captain) and Peter Moores (England Head Coach). Hugh Morris, Managing Director of the English Cricket Board, said, "This has become an impossible situation given the irretrievable breakdown of the relationship between captain and coach" (BBC Sport, 2009). This will happen in some cases, but it is still important that the process is managed such that the relationship can be maintained at an amicable level and does not disrupt the functioning of the squad.

Promoting openness

Communication is at the heart of coaching, and consequently it is important that the coach and the athlete are able to have open lines of communication and feel able to share relevant information. This may particularly be the case for a newly formed relationship. For instance, imagine an 18-year-old rugby union player who has just been called up to represent his national team and to work with a very experienced and successful coach. Your observations from working with this dyad, and the results of completed CARM-Qs, suggest that there are low levels of openness within the relationship, and that this may be preventing the development of closeness (i.e. mutual trust, respect, appreciation, and interpersonal liking).

A potentially useful strategy in this case may be an adapted version of the Personal Disclosure Mutual Sharing task developed by Dunn and Holt (2004). Traditionally this approach has been used with squads as a whole, and involves each member disclosing his or her reason for wanting to be on the team. It has been reported that this approach can be very emotional and even life-changing, as people disclose very personal information (Dunn and Holt, 2004; Holt and Dunn, 2006).

A similar approach could be implemented with the coach and player in a private setting. Through facilitating the disclosure of these personal feelings and thoughts, a sport psychologist may be able to significantly enhance the use of openness within the dyad and potentially help to develop the closeness experienced by the coach and player. As always, however, it is important that processes are changed to promote permanent rather than short-term changes based on one-off events. Therefore, in combination with the PDMS, weekly one-on-one meetings can be arranged between the coach and each of the players. These may just be for five or ten minutes, but they will provide important opportunities for open lines of communication to be developed and maintained, promoting openness within all of the coach–player relationships in the squad.

Promoting motivation

Motivation is clearly a well-researched topic within sport psychology. However, it is important to make the distinction here that motivational strategies are designed to motivate one's sporting partner to remain in the relationship, not to motivate them in a more general sense. This is a subtle yet important difference, as a coach, for instance, can motivate the athlete, but this may not necessarily mean that they are being motivated to continue working with the coach. In fact, they may become so motivated that they wish to progress and work with another coach.

Motivational strategies therefore focus on providing reasons to stay in the relationship. Take the scenario of a tennis player and her coach. The player is developing her talent and is moving up the rankings. She is therefore happy with her performance. However, the interactions with the coach are becoming mundane and predictable. As a result, whilst the player is very motivated to continue playing tennis, she is losing motivation to stay in the relationship.

After observing a few training sessions, you notice how the same drills are regularly used, and that the coach and the athlete never seem to enjoy training. This surprises you, as they both seem to be enthusiastic people with a good sense of humour off the court. In this case, the relationship may start to break down through a developing lack of commitment – hence it appears necessary to promote the use of motivational strategies.

A possible intervention may focus on enhancing the level of enjoyment within training. Through basic conditioning, if training sessions are constantly uninspiring then one's level of anticipation when thinking about coach–athlete interactions is bound to decline. There are many ways in which the same skills can be developed during training whilst also ensuring that the training is enjoyable. For example, the use of forfeits has been reported within Andy Murray's training groups. Games such as football tennis are played, with the loser having to perform a forfeit. After losing one such bet, Andy reportedly had to wear a women's pink luminous tracksuit for a few days (*Daily Mail*, 2010).

Clearly, such forfeits may not be appropriate for certain dyads. However, the broader point of making coaching interactions fun may have great potential as a tool for enhancing the quality of a coach–athlete relationship. Previous research has also highlighted the challenges faced by a coach and athlete after great success. Jowett (2003) reports a case study of a coach–athlete dyad which had experienced some relational problems after the athlete had won an Olympic medal. Although some evidence of the 3Cs was salient, these appeared to be outweighed by a number of negative interpersonal factors. It was revealed that the relationship was characterised by feelings of distance (e.g. not feeling part of the relationship), lack of co-orientation (e.g. disagreements and no longer sharing the same goals), and lack of complementarity (e.g. anger and frustration as well as there being an inequality in terms of the influence that the coach and athlete had on each other). Poor communication and an increase in the number of negative interactions characterised the dyad, and this ultimately led to the coach and athlete terminating their sporting relationship (Jowett, 2003). It is important in such cases that a sport psychologist is able to work with the dyad to help set new goals which ensure that there is a reason for both members to sustain the relationship. Once the key focus for the partnership has been achieved, there will be potential for the relationship to break down unless the future direction is discussed, defined, and agreed.

Promoting prevention

Traditionally, efforts to optimise the quality of close relationships have taken a "cure" rather than a "prevention" approach. Relationship problems were usually treated through therapy when negative consequences for the relationship members or significant others became salient issues (Hahlweg and Markman, 1988). More recently, the focus has shifted towards emphasising "prevention" rather than "cure". It is likely that sport psychologists will benefit from adopting a similarly proactive approach. Preventative strategies within the COMPASS model focus on establishing clear expectations, and the consequences if these are not met.

Imagine the situation in an elite American Football squad where the previous head coach has just lost his job. There was a general perception of a lack of discipline within the team, with players regularly being portrayed in the media as being drunk and out at parties until the early hours prior to important matches. When the previous head coach dropped a star player after one such incident, a number of other players came out in support of the player and questioned the judgement of the head coach, saying that they had lost respect for him and that he had "lost the dressing room". A new coach has been brought in and has asked you, as a sport psychologist, how he should approach this situation.

In this instance, the use of preventative strategies may be particularly effective. The coach and players can meet and discuss what is expected of everyone on the team, and the consequences if these expectations are not met. For example, there may be a general agreement that a player should not be going out the night before a match, and that if he does then he will be dropped from the game. A series of key points can be identified, and used to compile an *expectations contract*. Each member of the squad, including the coaches, players and support staff, can sign this agreement, and it can be posted on the dressing-room wall each time the team trains or competes. With this in place, everyone should be much clearer, and accountable for their actions. Should the situation arise again where a player is pictured partying before a key match, then the coach will be more justified in dropping them from the team and should subsequently receive the support of the squad.

Promoting assurance and support

Although distinct within the COMPASS model, assurance and support are related concepts. Assurance refers to a sense that the coach or athlete will be there should the need arise, whilst support relates to the actual provision of help in difficult times. These concepts correspond to those labelled as perceived and received support, described by Rees (2007). Imagine a case where a player within a netball team has a long-term injury. She feels that the coach has not been there for her and has not showed an interest in her well-being; only in when she will be able to play again. CARM-Qs have been given to the squad. The injured player reports low levels of meta-support (i.e. she does do not feel that the coach is supporting her) whilst many of the other players indicate low levels of meta-assurance (i.e. they do not feel that the coach would be there for them should the need arise).

One evidence-based and empirically evaluated programme that has purported to enhance social support between coaches and their athletes is Coach Effectiveness Training (CET; Smith and Smoll, 2007). This involves the provision of a two-hour workshop that emphasises the importance of creating a coaching environment that is supportive, nurturing, and encouraging. Subsequently, the training that coaches receive educates them in terms of the importance of exhibiting supportive and positive behaviours. CET is perhaps the only intervention programme that has been subjected to numerous empirical evaluations since its conception. For example, Smith *et al.* (1979) found that coaches in the experimental group who had received CET used more reinforcement behaviours, which were linked to increases in their athletes' self-esteem relative to the control group who had received no training.

More recently, Coatsworth and Conroy (2006) delivered an adapted CET to coaches working in a youth swimming league. It was found that the swimmers reported significant increases in their level of self-esteem after a seven-week period, with the effect being stronger for girls who started the season with low self-esteem. They concluded that "training coaches in psychosocial and behavioural principles is an effective way of altering coach behaviour and of enhancing the athlete–coach relational context" (p. 173). Although this assertion may be possible, it is notable that research regarding the CET programme has not employed measures of perceived relationship quality. Clearly, research is required in order to provide evidence upon which confident conclusions can be drawn regarding the effects of such interventions on relationship quality. However, CET may inform an intervention designed to enhance feelings of assurance and support. It is also important to note that this chapter emphasises the bi-directional nature of dyadic relationships, and therefore it may be beneficial to involve both coaches and athletes within an intervention.

Promoting social networks

One area that has been the focus of a number of evaluative studies is the enhancement of group cohesion. This relates to social networks, as, through strengthening the links around the coach and athlete, it may be possible to enhance their dyadic relationship. These interventions tend to be implemented through activities that involve guiding the recipients to complete a task, or through a programme of workshops. For example, Martin and Davis (1995) delivered a five-day army training course to 22 elite soccer players, and found that it had a significant impact on the players' well-being and social cohesion. More recently, Dunn and Holt (2004) presented the Personal Disclosure Mutual Sharing programme (discussed above). It has reportedly enhanced cohesion as well as understanding (both of self and others), confidence, and the motivation to work with each other (Dunn and Holt, 2004; Holt and Dunn, 2006).

These strategies may be most appropriate when working with newly formed relationships or teams that do not regularly interact, such as national squads. Team-building activities and social situations can be used to promote interaction and develop relationship quality. Selection of the most appropriate activities will be based on an understanding of the characteristics of the client group. Some examples may include playing a round of golf, attending a horse racing event, go-carting, going to the the cinema, or watching an alternative sporting event.

Imagine that you are working with a basketball team. Your observations, and the results of CART-Qs and CARM-Qs, reveal that relationships between the coach and the athletes are weak, and that there are currently low levels of the use of social networks. As the team is currently not working well as a unit, a potential option would be to organise a social event to have fun whilst also observing an effective team at work. You may therefore arrange to attend a Formula 1 grand prix and pay particular attention to watching the pit stops of the elite teams. This may provide the players and coaches with an opportunity to interact and develop their relationships, whilst also potentially identifying some elements of effective team functioning that can be transferred into their squad.

Practice issues

Whenever working with a coach–athlete dyad, there is a range of practice issues that require consideration. The wide range of intrapersonal, interpersonal, and environmental variables ensures that every dyad will be unique. As such, the composition of the dyad and the situation in which they interact must be assessed such that any interventions can be tailored to meet these specific requirements. For example, you need to consider the composition of the coach and athlete that you are working with. In many cases you may be working with a dyad of people who are only connected through their sporting relationship. In contrast, in other cases a coach and an athlete are not only sporting partners but also have another significant relationship. For instance, as well as being coach–athlete, they may also have a familial relationship (e.g. father and daughter, or brother and sister), a romantic relationship (e.g. they are a dating or married couple), or a professional relationship (e.g. business colleagues or lecturer and student). Examples of such coach–athlete relationships within the tennis world are provided by Richard Williams (father), who has coached Venus and Serena Williams (daughters), and Tony Nadal (uncle), who has coached Rafael Nadal (nephew).

Jowett and Meek (2000) conducted a study involving four Greek coach–athlete dyads who were also married. The potential for there to be a difficulty in differentiating between these dual connections was identified. The coach–athlete relationship was found to impact on the husband–wife relationship, resulting in conflictual interactions at home. Jowett (2008b) also conducted research with an elite swimmer and her coach, who was also her father. Difficulties were highlighted in distinguishing between the coach–athlete and the father–daughter relationship. A sport psychologist can help the coach and athlete to distinguish between their dual roles, to facilitate the management of any tensions which may arise.

The gender of those within the relationship may also have an important role to play. For example, research reported by Lorimer and Jowett (2010) found that female coaches were more accurate than male coaches in inferring the feelings and thoughts of their athletes. In terms of athletes, the highest empathic accuracy was reported for female athletes working with male coaches, with the lowest scores being associated with all female coach–athlete dyads. This illustrates how the gender of the coach and athlete, as well as the composition of the dyad, needs to be taken into consideration when working as a sport psychologist.

The composition of the dyad also relates to the race of the coach and athlete. Jowett and Frost (2007) conducted semi-structured interviews with elite black professional footballers who had white coaches. The players' race was found to impact upon the quality of their relationships with their coaches. For instance, in terms of closeness, the footballers reported that they did not perceive that their coaches afforded them the respect they had earned. Participants also revealed that they viewed coach–player communication as being important, but that they believed the level of openness between themselves and their coach was inhibited due to the fact that they perceived there to be a risk that they would be misunderstood. They also felt that the coach did not provide them with the level of support that was required. Although race was found to impact closeness, communication, and support, it was reported that it did not have an influence on the players' level of commitment within their dyadic relationships. The growth of the international transfer market over recent years ensures that many teams at the elite level are comprised of coaches and athletes from a wide range of racial, ethnic, and cultural groups. It is thus important that a sport psychologist considers how this may be impacting the interactions between a given coach and athlete.

As has been previously alluded to, there is clearly a wide range of individual differences which can impact the quality of the relationship and the ways in which this is maintained. For example, one's attachment style has been found to be associated with the quality of the coach–athlete relationship (Davis and Jowett, 2011). Moreover, the extent to which a coach or an athlete's personality is extrovert, neurotic, conscientious, agreeable, or open will have the potential to have a significant influence on perceptions, interactions, and their experiences of the relationship. Yang and Jowett (2011) have started exploring the impact of personality factors on coaches' and athletes' perceptions of relationship quality. Their findings suggest that not only do certain personality factors (e.g. neuroticism) influence one's own perceptions of relationship quality, but also athletes' personality in particular is likely to influence their coaches' perceptions of relationship quality. This clearly has implications for practice, as coaches need to be aware that their athletes' actions and interactions or their preferences for interaction may reside in innate idiosyncrasies. Thus, relationships are as complex as the people comprising them, and this has to be taken into account in assessments.

Moreover, the relationship does not exist in isolation, and therefore a number of social factors will need to be considered. One such influence, particularly within youth sport, may come from the parent(s). Jowett and Timson-Katchis (2005) conducted the first study within the coach–athlete research domain that involved the interviewing of triads. Five athletes were interviewed, along with their coach and a parent. The parent was found to provide informational, opportunity, and emotional support. The informational support may relate to the parent finding out information about local clubs and competitions, and helping to plan the athlete's sport participation. Parents were also found to provide their children with the opportunity to participate and compete in sport, and to be part of the coach–athlete relationship. This may involve financial support (e.g. the buying of equipment and the paying of membership fees) or temporal support (e.g. taking the child to training sessions or competitions, and spending time supporting their child). Emotional support may be exemplified by the parent listening to and encouraging the child during difficult times. It was concluded that the parent can significantly influence the coach–athlete relationship but that the influence must be maintained at an appropriate level, and that over-involvement or under-involvement may result in significant problems for the coach–athlete relationship. The sport psychologist must therefore consider the role played by significant others, such as parents, to ensure that any potential positive influences are maximised while any possible negative influences are mitigated.

Recent years have witnessed a number of cases in which the chairmen of football clubs have impacted the coach–player relationship. Whether it is uncertainty about the ownership of the club, the buying or selling of players, or team selection, there is great scope for people in significant managerial roles at the club to impact coach–player relationships, both in a positive and a negative way. The sport psychologist needs to be aware of this broader context, and that any problems within the dyad may be environmental as well as intrapersonal or interpersonal. As a result, interventions to enhance relationship quality may involve taking steps to change the situation around the coach and athlete rather than always focusing on the dyad itself.

Conclusion

This chapter contributes to the drive towards creating coach–athlete relationships that are not only successful but also effective, such that they can promote coaches' and athletes' athletic as well as personal development (Jowett and Poczwardowski, 2007). It highlights the need to consider not only which properties constitute relationship quality, but also how relationship quality can be maintained. As is often argued in sport, staying at the top is often as hard as getting there. Interpersonal relationships in sport may be viewed in a similar way, with maintaining a successful and effective relationship being as important as having a good relationship at a given moment in time. In 2000, Wylleman argued that the coach–athlete relationship is an "... unchartered territory" (p. 555). Since this time, significant strides have been made in starting to charter this research domain. The CART-Qs and the CARM-Qs alongside their respective models of 3+1Cs and COMPASS represent tools that can aid the further navigation of this territory, and should prove valuable in facilitating a successful journey.

References

Adie, J. and Jowett, S. (2010). Athletes' meta-perceptions of the coach–athlete relationship, multiple achievement goals and intrinsic motivation among track and field athletes. *Journal of Applied Social Psychology*, 40, 2750–2773.

Ames, C. (1992). Achievement goals, motivational climate, and motivational processes. In G. C. Roberts (ed.), *Motivation in sport and exercise* (pp. 161–176). Champaign, IL: Human Kinetics.

BBC News (2005). *Newcastle fine Bellamy after row*. Retrieved 9 August 2007, from http://news.bbc.co.uk/sport1/hi/football/eng_prem/4194437.stm.

BBC News (2006). *England's 2006 World Cup in quotes*. Retrieved 1 July 2008, from http://news.bbc.co.uk/sport1/hi/football/world_cup_2006/teams/england/5113360.stm.

BBC Sport (2009). *England captain Pietersen resigns*. Retrieved 20 May 2010, from http://news.bbc.co.uk/sport1/hi/cricket/england/7815038.stm.

Berscheid, E. (1999). The greening of relationship science. *American Psychologist*, 54, 260–266.

Coatsworth, J. D. and Conroy, D. E. (2006). Enhancing the self-esteem of youth swimmers through coaching training: Gender and age effects. *Psychology of Sport and Exercise*, 7, 173–192.

Côté, J. and Sedgwick, W. (2003). Effective behaviours of expert rowing coaches: A qualitative investigation of Canadian athletes and coaches. *International Sports Journal*, 7, 62–77.

Daily Mail (2010). Andy Murray's lively, fun and he doesn't hate England. Retrieved 20 July 2010, from www.dailymail.co.uk/sport/tennis/article-1247168/AUSTRALIAN-OPEN-2010-Andy-Murrays-lively-fun-humble–doesnt-hate-England.html.

Davis, L. and Jowett, S. (2011). *Relational processes associated with attachment styles in coach–athlete dyads*, under review.

Deci, E. L. and Ryan, R. M. (2000). The "what" and "why" of goal pursuits: Human needs and the self-determination of behaviour. *Psychological Enquiry*, 11, 227–268.

Dunn, J. G. H. and Holt, N. L. (2004). A qualitative investigation of a personal-disclosure mutual sharing team-building activity. *The Sport Psychologist*, 18, 363–380.

Durand-Bush, N. and Salmela, J. H. (2002). The development and maintenance of expert athletic performance: Perceptions of world and Olympic champions. *Journal of Applied Sport Psychology*, 14, 154–171.

Ferguson, A. (2000). *Managing my life: My autobiography*. London, UK: Hodder and Stoughton.

Fox Sports (2010). Novak Djocovic splits from coach Todd Martin. Retrieved 20 May 2010, from http://msn.foxsports.com/tennis/story/djokovic-ends-relationship-with-coach-martin-041210.

Gould, D., Guinan, D., Greenleaf, C., and Medbery, R. (1999). Factors affecting Olympic performance: Perceptions of athletes and coaches from more or less successful teams. *The Sport Psychologist*, 13, 371–394.

Gould, D., Greenleaf, C., Chung, Y., and Guinan, D. (2002). A survey of US Atlanta and Nagano Olympians: Variables perceived to influence performance. *Research Quarterly for Exercise and Sport*, 73, 175–186.

Gould, D., Collins, K. B., Louer, L. A., and Chung, Y. C. (2007). Coaching life skills through football: A study of award-winning high-school coaches. *Journal of Applied Sport Psychology*, 19, 16–37.

Greenleaf, C., Gould, D., and Dieffenbach, K. (2001). Factors influencing Olympic performance: Interviews with Atlanta and Nagano US Olympians. *Journal of Applied Sport Psychology*, 13, 154–184.

Gustaffson, H. and Jowett, S. (2010). *Exploring the association of burnout within the coach–athlete relationship context*, unpublished manuscript.

Hahlweg, K. and Markman, H. J. (1988). Effectiveness of behavioural marital therapy: Empirical studies of behavioural techniques in preventing and alleviating marital distress. *Journal of Consulting and Clinical Psychology*, 56, 440–477.

Holt, N. L. and Dunn, J. G. H. (2006). Guidelines for delivering personal-disclosure mutual sharing team-building interventions. *The Sport Psychologist*, 20, 348–367.

Hurst, G. (2001). *1966 and all that*. London, UK: Headline.

Independent (2008). *Mourinho charms Italy to prove his specialness in any language.* Retrieved 1 July 2008, from www.independent.co.uk/sport/football/news-and-comment/frank-dunne-mourinho-charms-italy-to-prove-his-specialness-in-any-language-839513.html.

Jones, R. L., Armour, K., and Potrac, P. (2003). Constructing expert knowledge: A case study of a top-level professional soccer coach. *Sport, Education and Society*, 8, 213–229.

Jowett, S. (2003). When the honeymoon is over: A case study of a coach–athlete relationship in crisis. *The Sport Psychologist*, 17, 444–460.

Jowett, S. (2005a). The coach–athlete partnership. *The Psychologist*, 18, 412–415.

Jowett, S. (2005b). On repairing and enhancing the coach–athlete relationship. In S. Jowett and M. Jones (eds), *The psychology of coaching* (pp. 14–26). Leicester, UK: The British Psychological Society.

Jowett, S. (2006). Interpersonal and structural features of Greek coach–athlete dyads performing in individual sports. *Journal of Applied Sport Psychology*, 18, 69–81.

Jowett, S. (2007a). Coach–athlete relationships ignite groupness. In M. Beauchamp and M. Eys (eds), *Group dynamics advances in sport and exercise psychology* (pp. 63–77). New York, NY: Routledge.

Jowett, S. (2007b). Interdependence analysis and the 3+1Cs in the coach–athlete relationship. In S. Jowett and D. Lavallee (eds), *Social psychology in sport* (pp. 15–27). Champaign, IL: Human Kinetics.

Jowett, S. (2008a). Moderators and mediators of the association between the coach–athlete relationship and physical self-concept. *International Journal of Coaching Science*, 2, 43–62.

Jowett, S. (2008b). Outgrowing the familial coach–athlete relationship. *International Journal of Sport Psychology*, 39, 20–40.

Jowett, S. (2009a). Factor structure and criterion validity of the meta-perspective version of the Coach–athlete Relationship Questionnaire (CART-Q). *Group Dynamics: Theory, Research and Practice*, 13, 163–177.

Jowett, S. (2009b). Validating coach–athlete relationship measures with the nomological network. *Measurement in Physical Education and Exercise Science*, 13, 1–18.

Jowett, S. and Chaundy, V. (2004). An investigation into the impact of coach leadership and coach–athlete relationship on group cohesion. *Group Dynamics: Theory, Research and Practice*, 8, 302–311.

Jowett, S. and Clark-Carter, D. (2006). Perceptions of empathic accuracy and assumed similarity in the coach–athlete relationship. *British Journal of Social Psychology*, 45, 617–637.

Jowett, S. and Cockerill, I. M. (2003). Olympic medallists' perspective of the athlete-coach relationship. *Psychology of Sport and Exercise*, 4, 313–331.

Jowett, S. and Cramer, D. (2010). The prediction of young athletes' physical self from perceptions of relationships with parents and coaches. *Psychology of Sport and Exercise*, 11, 140–147.

Jowett, S. and Frost, T. C. (2007). Race/ethnicity in the all male coach–athlete relationship: Black footballers' narratives. *Journal of International Sport and Exercise Psychology*, 3, 255–269.

Jowett, S. and Meek, G. A. (2000). The coach–athlete relationship in married couples: An exploratory content analysis. *The Sport Psychologist*, 14, 157–175.

Jowett, S. and Nezlek, J. (2011). Relationship interdependence and satisfaction with important outcomes in coach–athlete dyads. *Journal of Social and Personal Relationships*, in press.

Jowett, S. and Ntoumanis, N. (2004). The Coach–Athlete Relationship Questionnaire (CART–Q): Development and initial validation. *Scandinavian Journal of Medicine and Science in Sports*, 14, 245–257.

Jowett, S. and Poczwardowski, A. (2007). Understanding the coach–athlete relationship. In S. Jowett and D. Lavallee (eds), *Social psychology in sport* (pp. 3–14). Champaign, IL: Human Kinetics.

Jowett, S. and Timson-Katchis, M. (2005). Social networks in sport: The influence of parents on the coach–athlete relationship. *The Sport Psychologist*, 19, 267–287.

Jowett, S., Shanmugam, V., and Caccoulis, S. (2011). Collective efficacy as a mediator of the link between interpersonal relationships and athlete satisfaction in team sports. *International Journal of Sport and Exercise Psychology*, in press.

Jowett, S., Timson-Katchis, M., and Adams, R. (2007). Too close for comfort? Dependence in the dual role of parent/coach–child/athlete relationship. *International Journal of Coaching Science*, 1, 59–78.

Lafrenière, M. A. K., Jowett, S., Vallerand, R. J., Donahue, E. G., and Lorimer, R. (2008). Passion in sport: On the quality of the coach–athlete relationship. *Journal of Sport and Exercise Psychology*, 30, 541–560.

Laing, R. D., Phillipson, H., and Lee, A. R. (1966). *Interpersonal perception: A theory and a method of research*. New York, NY: Harper and Row.

Lorimer, R. (2009). Coaches' satisfaction with their athletic partnerships. *International Journal of Coaching Science*, 3, 57–66.

Lorimer, R. and Jowett, S. (2009). Empathic accuracy in coach–athlete dyads who participate in team and individual sports. *Psychology of Sport and Exercise*, 10, 152–158.

Lorimer, R. and Jowett, S. (2010). The influence of role and gender in the empathic accuracy of coaches and athletes. *Psychology of Sport and Exercise*, 11, 206–211.

Lyle, J. (1999). Coaching philosophy and coaching behaviour. In N. Cross and J. Lyle (eds), *The coaching process: Principles and practice for sport* (pp. 25–46). Oxford, UK: Butterworth-Heineman.

Martin, R. and Davis, K. (1995). The effects of group development techniques on a professional athletic team. *The Journal of Social Psychology*, 135, 533–535.

Newcomb, T. M. (1953). An approach to the study of communicative acts. *Psychological Review*, 60, 393–404.

Nicholls, J. G. (1989). *The competitive ethos and democratic education*. Cambridge, MA: Harvard University Press.

Olympiou, A., Jowett, S., and Duda, J. L. (2005). *Psychological needs as mediators of social contexts and role ambiguity*. Symposium on Interpersonal Relationships in Sport and Exercise. Annual Conference of the British Psychological Society, Abstracts (p. 27). Manchester, UK.

Olympiou, A., Jowett, S., and Duda, J. L. (2008). The psychological interface of the coach-created motivational climate and the coach–athlete relationship. *The Sport Psychologist*, 22, 423–438.

Philippe, R. A. and Seiler, R. (2006). Closeness, co-orientation and complementarity in coach–athlete relationships: What male swimmers say about their male coaches. *Psychology of Sport and Exercise*, 7, 159–171.

Rees, T. (2007). Influence of social support on athletes. In S. Jowett and D. Lavallee (eds) *Social psychology in sport* (pp. 223–233). Champaign, IL: Human Kinetics.

Rhind, D. J. A. and Jowett, S. (2010a). Initial evidence for the criterion-related and structural validity of the long versions of the direct and meta-perspectives of the Coach–Athlete Relationship Questionnaire. *European Journal of Sport Science*, 10, 359–370.

Rhind, D. J. A. and Jowett, S. (2010b). Relationship maintenance strategies in the coach–athlete relationship: The development of the COMPASS model. *Journal of Applied Sport Psychology*, 22, 106–121.

Rhind, D. J. A. and Jowett, S. (2011). Linking maintenance strategies to the quality of coach–athlete relationships. *International Journal of Sport Psychology*, 42, 55–68.

Sagar, S. and Jowett, S. (2010). *Relationship quality and self-control as determinants of fear of failure in the context of sport*, unpublished manuscript.

Saliminen, S. and Liukkonen, J. (1996). Coach–athlete relationship and coaching behaviour in training sessions. *International Journal of Sport Psychology*, 27, 59–67.

Scotsman on Sunday (2003). Beckham admits Ferguson intimidated him. *Scotsman on* Sunday, 13 August 2003. Accessed at http://scotlandonsunday.scotsman.com/davidbeckham/Beckham-admits-Ferguson-intimidated-him.2457637.jp on August 12th, 2011.

Shanmugam, V. and Jowett, S. (2010). *The links between coach–athlete relationship quality and athletes' disorderly eating: An examination of mediators*. Unpublished data.

Smith, R. E. and Smoll, F. L. (1990). Self-esteem and children's reactions to youth sport coaching behaviours: A field study of self-enhancement processes. *Developmental Psychology*, 26, 987–993.

Smith, R. E. and Smoll, F. L. (2007). Social-cognitive approach to coaching behaviours. In S. Jowett and D. Lavallee (eds), *Social psychology in sport* (pp. 75–90). Champaign, IL: Human Kinetics.

Telegraph (2010). Alan Smith: "Albert Reera fall-out shows Rafael Benitez man-management style needs tweak. Retrieved 20 May 2010, from www.telegraph.co.uk/sport/football/leagues/premierleague/liverpool/7482445/Alan-Smith-Albert-Riera-fall-out-shows-Rafael-Benitez-man-management-style-needs-tweak.html.

Trzaskoma-Bicserdy, G., Bognar, J., Revesz, L., and Geczi, G. (2007). The coach–athlete relationship in successful Hungarian individual sports. *International Journal of Sports Science and Coaching*, 2, 485–495.

Woodward, C. (2004). *Winning: The story of England's rise to rugby world cup glory*. London, UK: Hodder and Stoughton.

Wylleman, P. (2000). Interpersonal relationships in sport: Uncharted territory in sport psychology research. *International Journal of Sport Psychology*, 31, 555–572.

Yang, X. and Jowett, S. (2011). *Effects of Big-Five personality traits on the quality of relationship and satisfaction in coach–athlete dyads*, under review.

10 Developing life skills in athletes

Martin I. Jones

Abstract

In this chapter, I will examine the theoretical and applied developments in the life skills literature. I will discuss the key issues related to the definition of life skills, theoretical foundations, and applied strategies. The chapter will describe and examine models of life skills development from sport psychology (i.e. the life development intervention; Danish *et al.*, 1993) and developmental science (e.g. Larson, 2000; Lerner *et al.*, 2006) to provide practitioners with an understanding of how life skills may be developed through sport. The chapter provides scholars and practitioners with summary conclusions of the research, including the need to examine the transferability of life skills across life domains and to understand that sport participation correlates with several positive (and negative) outcomes, but this relationship may not be causal. Furthermore, sport may not provide a homogenous experience or a panacea for life skills development. Specifically, not all sports will develop the same skills in the same way, and therefore researchers and practitioners need to explore the individual nuances of ranges of sports, coaching styles, and developmental climates. Finally, scholars and practitioners can use different teaching strategies, including direct systematic teaching strategies and experiential learning strategies, to develop life skills.

Keywords: life skills, athletes, positive development

Introduction

The position that sport teaches life skills is not new. Philosophers, politicians, religious leaders, educators, and sports people have all described the benefits of sport on the development of the person. For example, current President of the International Olympic Committee (at the time of publication), Jacques Rogge (2004), said, "The world of sport is not separate from the rest of the world. Sport breaks down barriers, promotes self-esteem, and can teach life skills and healthy behaviour". Similarly, Sir Phillip

Craven MBE (2006), President of the International Paralympics Committee, said, in a press release: "Sport teaches life skills you don't get anywhere else and you don't get them by watching TV or downloading stuff off a computer. It's about exercising the body as well as the mind. That's what makes sport crucial." From these anecdotal reports, it seems evident that sport teaches athletes "life skills" in addition to physical skills. However, sport, in and of itself, does not produce positive developmental outcomes (Petitpas *et al.*, 2005). Participation in sport has also been associated with negative behaviours, such as increased use of alcohol and performance-enhancing drugs (Eccles and Barber, 1999; Siegenthaler and Gonzalez, 1997). Additionally, participation in sport may also interfere with moral development (Shields and Bredemeier, 1995), while youth sport participants have reported higher levels of stress and social exclusion compared with participants from other organised activities (Larson *et al.*, 2006). Therefore, scholars and practitioners need to be able to direct athletes toward the positive outcomes associated with sport participation (e.g. life skills) and away from the potential negatives. It is also important to understand how to teach life skills, because the World Health Organisation (1999) suggested that the development of life skills is essential for the promotion of healthy development, and for preparing young people for their changing social circumstances. To this end, the purpose of this chapter is to review the existing literature and provide guidelines for developing life skills.

Defining life skills

Life skills may be physical skills (e.g. proper posture), behavioural skills (e.g. effective communication), or cognitive skills (e.g. effective decision-making; Danish and Donohue, 1995; Danish and Nellen, 1997). In addition to this classification, several other definitions of life skills exist. These definitions stem from the sport psychology literature, developmental psychology literature, health and wellness literature, and international policy documents. Given the ranges of research and policy areas that use life skills as an operational term, there is some overlap and conceptual confusion regarding the definition of life skills. For example, UNICEF (United Nations Children Fund) defines life skills as a large group of psychosocial and interpersonal skills which can help people make informed decisions, communicate effectively, and develop coping and self-management skills that may help them lead a healthy and productive life (UNICEF, n.d.). The World Health Organisation (1999) defines life skills as the abilities for adaptive and positive behaviour that enable individuals to deal effectively with the demands and challenges of everyday life. The Life Skills Center defines life skills simply as the skills that enable us to succeed in the environments in which we live (Life Skills Center, n.d.). The range of definitions could mean that virtually every skill could be included under this broad umbrella term. The potential vague and confusing definitions of what a life skill is or is not led Jones and Lavallee (2009a) to eschew existing definitions and to develop a participant-centred definition of life skills that is relevant to athletes and key stakeholders in an athlete's life. Specifically, Jones and Lavallee conducted group interviews with adolescent athletes, coaches, and experts in sport psychology, and found that participants defined life skills as ranges of transferable skills needed for everyday life, by everybody, that help people thrive. Moreover, Jones and Lavallee provided examples of life skills that are particularly pertinent to athletes. For example, group interview participants revealed that athletes needed to develop social skills, respect, leadership, interactions with the family, communication skills, self-organisation skills, discipline, the ability for self-reliance, goal-setting ability, managing performance outcomes, motivation, and identity exploration. A criticism levied at this range of skills could be that some positive outcomes are not necessarily skills (e.g. identity exploration). Despite this criticism, the research by Jones and Lavallee extended previous potentially ambiguous definitions by also listing important life skills that athletes need to learn.

What is unambiguous is that there are several shared concepts across definitions. Specifically, it is clear that life skills can help people live a good and productive life by helping them manage the demands of life. It is clear that life skills also help people succeed and to thrive beyond normal requirements. Finally, for skills to be classified as life skills they need to be transferable across life domains. For example, the ability to coordinate the unique movements and skills patterns involved in taking a penalty in football is a sport skill (because athletes rarely need these skills outside of a sporting context). The abilities of managing a training schedule to allow a player to practise penalty taking, of concentrating on the ball, blocking out external distractions, and controlling the anxiety associated with taking a penalty are life skills (because time management, concentration, and anxiety management are useful skills in multiple scenarios that help people thrive). Consequently, practitioners need to actively encourage and stimulate transfer of skills across life domains, and, where possible, evaluate transfer. For example, a practitioner may discuss the use of sport-based life skills in other life domains (e.g. public-speaking skills developed from media interviews to public speaking in a business setting) or may provide opportunities for controlled experimentation of life skills in non-sport settings (e.g. setting up talks to school children regarding personal career highlights and training).

Which life skills can athletes learn through sport?

Danish *et al.* (1993) suggested that sport was particularly suited to teaching several life skills, including (but not limited to) performing under pressure, organisation, communication, patience, risk-taking, commitment, self-control, self-evaluation, decision-making, goal-setting, and motivation.

Similarly, Larson (2000) stated that sport was a particularly salient context for positive development because it is a rule-bound and volitional activity that involves reciprocal relationships with non-familial adults, over a prolonged period. Larson also suggested that youth are motivated and intensely involved in enjoyable activities, like sport, and therefore organised sport provides an environment for life-skill learning. Despite these endorsements, scholars do not know which life skills athletes can learn. Rather, researchers have provided a wealth of evidence that shows that sport participation correlates with several positive outcomes. For example, sport participation is associated with personal and social responsibility, physical, cognitive, emotional, and social well-being, improved self-knowledge, improved self-esteem, emotional regulation, problem-solving, goal attainment, coping, team work, and skill development, and provides opportunities for learning moral behaviours (Barber *et al.*, 2001; Brustad, 1992; Eccles and Barber, 1999; Fox, 2004; Hansen *et al.*, 2003; Hellison, 1995; Larson, 1994; Martinek *et al.*, 1999; Pedersen and Seidman, 2004; Shields and Bredemeier, 1995; Ryckman and Hamel, 1995; Siegenthaler and Gonzalez, 1997). Sport participation also correlates with lower likelihood of school dropout, improved grade point averages, and higher rates of college attendance for low-achieving and working class males (Eccles *et al.*, 2003; Marsh and Kleitman, 2003; McNeal, 1995). On the surface, it looks like sport can result in numerous different life skills; however, without experimental research to validate these claims it is not clear whether sport can "teach" these skills, or whether young people are attracted to sport in order to demonstrate competence (of skills they already have).

It is also unclear whether all sports are correlated with these numerous skills (i.e. sport is a homogenous experience which results in the same outcomes) or whether each sport is a separate entity that may be suited to teaching a specific subset of life skills. Reed Larson and his colleagues first proposed that different activities could result in different experiences. Larson and colleagues (Dworkin *et al.*, 2003; Hansen *et al.*, 2003; Larson *et al.*, 2006) presented an analysis of domains of learning experiences that may be associated with positive youth development. Internal domains consisted of: (a) exploration and identity work for identity formation; (b) development of initiative; and (c) emotional self-regulation. Social/interpersonal growth domains were: (a) developing peer relationships and knowledge; (b) teamwork and social skills; and (c) acquiring adult networks and social capital. These domains of learning represent some of the processes through which adolescents can learn positive developmental outcomes through their involvement in structured programmes. Hansen and Larson (2002) developed the Youth Experience Scale (YES) to measure these developmental experiences. They used the results from focus groups (i.e. Dworkin *et al.*, 2003) where 55 high school students described their growth experiences in the organised activities in which they participated.

In addition to these focus groups, the development of the Youth Experiences Scale (YES; Hansen and Larson, 2002) involved analysis of literature on organised activities, vetting potential items with diverse youth and with a set of adult experts, and assessing item properties (Hansen and Larson, 2002). Hansen and Larson (2005) revised the YES to create a shorter instrument that had stronger psychometric properties. The goal of this process was to reduce the number of items in each scale but retain the scale's conceptual and measurement integrity. Validity data for the YES 2.0 (Hansen and Larson, 2005) showed that the correlations between the positive and negative scales were low, which suggests there are two broad dimensions or first-order factors (i.e. positive developmental and negative experiences). The positive scales of the YES 2.0 are moderately intercorrelated. Three of the 15 positive scales are correlated at 0.62 or higher, and the remaining 15 ranged in correlation between 0.50 and 0.60. The negative scales are also intercorrelated, with a range of correlations between scales of 0.46 to 0.77. Hansen and Larson (2002) reported that high intercorrelations among the negative scales are a concern; however, they may be indicative of a shared programme and individual factors that influence responses to all of these scales (e.g. the effect of negative adult behaviour on youth experience) rather than a lack of conceptual differentiation. Hansen and Larson (2005) also conducted confirmatory factor analyses to examine the factor structure of the YES 2.0 positive and negative scales. The results indicated that the six positive and the five negative scales were better conceptualised as distinct dimensions of positive or negative experience. Specifically, the separate scales provided distinct contributions to their overall dimensions, positive or negative, and researchers should not treat the combination of subscales as one conceptual dimension.

Hansen *et al.* (2003) used the YES 2.0 to explore adolescents' reports of the different developmental experiences in organised youth activities, including extracurricular and community-based activities. Participants in the study included 450 ninth-, eleventh-, and twelfth-grade students (55.8 per cent female, 44.2 per cent male) from a small city in Central Illinois, with below average education levels, above average families living below the poverty line, and low median household income. Results showed that these youth reported higher rates of positive experiences in organised activities in comparison to academic class work and hanging out with friends. Youth activities were specifically related to initiative, identity work, emotional learning, developing teamwork, and forming ties with community members. Results also highlighted the differences between organised activities. Specifically, service, faith-based, community, and vocational activities were associated with experiences related to identity work, prosocial norms, and links with adults. Sports were associated with experiences related to identity work and emotional development.

Larson *et al.* (2006) also examined the developmental experiences of a more diverse sample of adolescents. A sample of 2,280 (51 per cent female, 49 per cent male) eleventh-grade students from 19 diverse high schools responded to a survey of youth experiences. Results revealed that youth in faith-based activities reported higher rates of experiences related to identity, emotional regulation, and interpersonal development, in comparison to other organised activities. Sports and arts programmes stood out as providing more experiences related to the development of initiative. Sport was also related to high levels of stress. Service activities were associated with experiences related to the development of teamwork, positive relationships, and social capital. Finally, all organised activities were associated with higher rates of developmental experiences when compared to academic class work.

These findings demonstrated that different youth activities result in different developmental outcomes. Even though Larson and colleagues only report sport as one activity, it is plausible that sport does not provide a homogenous experience for all young people. Rather, the different rules, structures, coaching styles, motivational climates, and organisational nuances observed across sports may provide young people with diverse developmental experiences and positive youth development outcomes. Larson *et al.* (2006, p. 861) suggested that the field needs research that evaluates "the mediating processes responsible for differences not only between but within categories of organised activities".

Holt and Jones (2008) concluded that sport is not a panacea for youth development, but rather each sport presents different opportunities for learning specific skills. Specifically, scholars and practitioners cannot take sport as a homogeneous experience that teaches the same set of skills to all people. The individual nuances that differentiate sports can result in athletes learning entirely different skills. Take, for example, a young golfer and an American Footballer. The nature of American Football means that athletes will be exposed to skill-building activities related to teamwork and communication, whereas the golfer will be exposed to skill-building activities related to sportsmanship (i.e. calling your own fouls) and focus. Similarly, two football players with different coaches, who espouse different values, may learn different skills. In line with this theory, and the suggestion of Larson *et al.* (2006), future research is required to establish whether different sports, coaching styles, and competitive levels make unique contributions to the development of athletes.

To date, it is not entirely clear which life skills can be developed through playing sport. It is clear that sport can teach something valuable; however, what is learned seems to be dependent on (but might not be limited to) the structure of the sport, the coaching, and the organisational structure. It is important for scholars and practitioners to recognise that the learning of a predetermined set of life skills is not guaranteed, and that young people may be attracted to certain sports because they have a prerequisite skills base (but these skills may not be initially apparent). Moreover, a guiding principle of the positive youth development framework is that youth is a strength-based conception built upon the development of competencies (rather than the sole removal of risk and maladaptive behaviours). As such, even though young people may enter a sport with certain skills, practitioners can still facilitate development so that athletes improve existing skills. It is also important to recognise that the structure of the coaching and the types of practices young people experience play a critical role in the skills they develop.

"Teaching" life skills?

A common phrase observed in the sport and exercise psychology literature is that life skills are "taught not caught". This suggests that athletes do not simply acquire life skills by being in a sporting environment, but rather coaches and practitioners need to teach athletes in order for them to gain positive benefits (Danish *et al.*, 1993; Gould *et al.*, 2005). Without systematic teaching, the development of life skills will be coincidental rather than intentional. Danish and Nellen (1997) suggested that life skills are learned in the same way as sport skills, namely through demonstration, modeling, and practice. The practice of teaching life skills in this respect usually involves taking young people out of the sporting context and teaching the skills separately (i.e. in the classroom or on the sidelines). Schön (1987) illustrated this point by comparing this type of teaching to charging a battery with electricity so that the battery can discharge energy in an electrical device, stating that this type of direct teaching is like trying to charge up an athlete with information in the classroom so that they can discharge that information in another life domain.

The notion that adults need to teach life skills to young people has led to the development of several life skills programmes that formally teach life skills. The Life Development Intervention (LDI) provides the theoretical foundation to the majority of existing life skills interventions. The LDI is a counselling approach to sport psychology (i.e. it is concerned with non-sport related areas of coping and growth in addition to performance concerns; Danish *et al.*, 1993). The purpose of the LDI is to prepare people to cope with critical life events (and non-events) – for example, adjusting to transitions, coping with injuries, coping with non-selection, changing jobs, retirement from sport, and retirement from work. Danish and Nellen (1997) stated that the LDI is appropriate for developing life skills through participation in sport because the LDI approach uses sport as a model for promoting personal growth.

The LDI assumes that there is something valuable in sport; however, sport by itself does not enhance personal growth. The LDI suggests some mediating variables are needed (e.g. specially designed adult or peer-led life skills programmes) to charge young people up with information and knowledge. The GOAL programme is a ten-hour, ten-session programme taught by carefully selected high school students, designed to teach middle school or junior high school students a sense of personal control and confidence about their future. Programme organisers select older high school students as the most appropriate leaders because they provide strong role models for what younger students can become. Additionally, these students have grown up in the same neighborhoods, attended the same schools, and confronted and overcome similar obstacles. As such, these older students are in the perfect position to be effective teachers. Danish and Nellen (1997) suggested that the major findings of unpublished research (Meyer *et al.*, 1996; Meyer and Danish, 1996; both cited in Danish and Nellen, 1997) conducted on the GOAL programme were that participants learned the information that GOAL teaches, were able to achieve the goals they set, found the process easier than they expected, and thought they had learned about how to set goals; participants had better school attendance (as compared with a control group); and male participants did not report the same increase in health-compromising behaviours such as alcohol and drug abuse, smoking, and violence as was found in the control group who reported increases in these behaviours. Participants thought the GOAL programme was fun, useful, important, and something that would be helpful for their friends.

In addition to these unpublished findings, O'Hearn and Gatz (1999, 2002) conducted two studies, using the GOAL programme, with mostly Hispanic students in the United States. In the first study (O'Hearn and Gatz, 1999), participating students increased their knowledge of goal-setting when compared to a control group. Furthermore, the participants were able to attain the goals they set. The second study (O'Hearn and Gatz, 2002) found that participants also improved their problem-solving skills. Danish (2002) did not design the GOAL programme to be a sport-based life skills programme; thus, GOAL does not integrate sport skills into life skills education. Rather, GOAL attempts to use terms and sport-specific metaphors that may reflect sport events, such as "goalkeeper" (Danish, 2002). Importantly, adults take young people out of the sporting context to learn life skills. As a result, scholars and practitioners have developed additional programmes that integrate the LDI with aspects of sport practice and performance.

The Sport United to Promote Education and Recreation programme (SUPER; Danish *et al.*, 2002) was the product of the series of pilot sports-based life skills programmes developed by Danish and colleagues at the Life Skills Center at Virginia Commonwealth University that linked sports and life skills. SUPER is taught as a series of 18 sports clinics, with participants involved in three sets of activities: learning the physical skills related to a specific sport; learning life skills related to sports in general; and playing the sport. As with the GOAL programme, young people learn life skills separately from actual participation in sport. Adults remove young people from playing sport to a different area where they learn life skills, with the aid of a participant's workbook. Young people then practise skills when playing sport (i.e. charged and discharged).

Papacharisis *et al.* (2005) evaluated an abbreviated version of SUPER. Greek schoolchildren aged between 10 and 12 participated in one of two studies using an eight-session version of SUPER. The first study involved 40 female volleyball players on two teams; the second study involved 32 male soccer players on two different teams. In each study, one team served as the experimental group, and was taught the abbreviated version of SUPER; the other team served as the control group, and received no life skills instruction. In both studies, the researchers took measurements of physical skills, knowledge of the SUPER programme, and self-beliefs about ability to set goals, to problem solve, and to think positively. Participants who were taught the SUPER programme showed improvements between pre- and post-test in physical skills and programme knowledge compared to the control group.

In a subsequent study, Goudas *et al.* (2006) examined the effectiveness of teaching life skills as part of physical education lessons. Goudas *et al.* assigned 73 seventh-grade students to either an experimental or a wait-list control group. The experimental group received life skills instruction focused on setting goals, making plans for achieving goals, and positive thinking. Participants were assessed on physical fitness tests (i.e. sit and reach, and push-ups), knowledge about life skills, and beliefs about effective use of life skills. Results showed gains and retention on physical fitness, knowledge, and self-beliefs regarding goal-setting in comparison to the control group. Goudas *et al.* concluded that school-based physical education is an effective context for life skills education, and the SUPER programme is an effective method for teaching life skills.

Brunelle *et al.* (2007) reported a similar evaluation of a life skills programme based on the LDI. Brunelle and colleagues taught an abbreviated five-session version of SUPER to 100 adolescent golfers at a week-long national golf academy. The life skills component included five 45-minute SUPER sessions alongside sport skill instruction. After completion of the training camp, participants returned to their home sites and initiated one year of community service. This service involved assisting golf professionals and home site leaders in the instruction of a life skills programme. Six months after the camp, 42 study participants had the opportunity to be involved in the community service portion of the programme. The remaining participants either were unable to complete their community service, or failed to return follow-up survey data. Results showed that the scores of social interest, social and personal responsibility, and goal knowledge from participants in the SUPER programme significantly increased from pre- to post-test. Furthermore, involvement in the community service experience continued to enhance the prosocial values of the participants (Brunelle *et al.*, 2007). These results suggest that while the life skill intervention had the potential to increase awareness of prosocial values and begin the process of developing these attitudes, maintained use depends upon having the opportunity to put them into practice (Brunelle *et al.*, 2007).

An interesting extension of this study would be to examine positive (and negative) outcomes at several other time-points post-intervention and post-community service. A criticism levied at all of the LDI evaluation research is that even though a limited number of evaluations do exist, no evaluations have attempted to address whether young people maintain life skills over time. In essence, existing research has examined life skills at one point in time; however, positive development is comprised of well-being across time, also known as "thriving" (Lerner *et al.*, 2006). Lerner and colleagues coined the term "thriving" to describe the process of positive development across time that results in idealised personhood.

A different criticism is that few studies have evaluated whether young people can transfer life skills learned in sport into other life domains. As previously noted, researchers broadly define life skills in terms of transferability from one life domain to another. If athletes do not (or cannot) use life skills in life domains outside of sport (e.g. work, school, relationships), the skill is a sport skill and not a life skill. Thus, future research must consider the applicability of the positive outcomes associated with sport in other life domains. Moreover, researchers must also consider the possibility that some of the positive outcomes associated with sport may be life skills that athletes have transferred into sport from other life domains.

Researchers have also conducted several studies that highlighted the role of the coach in developing life skills. McCallister *et al.* (2000) interviewed 22 volunteer youth coaches to understand how they developed life skills in their athletes. McCallister *et al.* regarded the coach to be the most significant individual in instilling outcomes of positive youth development such as fair play, respect for others, cooperation, decision-making, leadership, and moral development, because coaches are in positions of authority and influence. Furthermore, coaches' principles and philosophies regarding the value of sport will directly influence the experiences of the children and adolescents in their charge. Results suggested that many of these coaches experienced considerable difficulty regarding how they taught life skills to their players, and they assumed that life skills would be an automatic by-product of participation.

Gould *et al.* (2005) also investigated how coaches had taught life skills to their athletes. Gould and colleagues interviewed a sample of award-winning coaches recognised for their achievements in developing good citizens, productive individuals, and successful athletes. The aim of the study was to understand the strategies coaches use to develop life skills in actual sports programmes. Results suggested these coaches did not rely on one strategy or technique; rather, they talked about a continual process guided by a philosophical base, trust, and strong coach–player relationships. In addition, these coaches implemented specific strategies and follow-up procedures to help their players develop. Having a coaching philosophy related to positive youth development was critical. Gould and colleagues suggested a win-at-all-costs philosophy could be detrimental to development, whereas a philosophy based on advancing psychosocial development would best serve young sports people. Having strong relationship skills, such as communication, empathy, and rapport-building, facilitated a strong coach–athlete relationship, and developing a strong coach–athlete relationship is one of the most important elements for developing life skills (Petitpas *et al.*, 2005). Employing strategies such as treating players with respect, and team-building, augmented life skills development. Finally, utilising resources and environmental considerations such as parents, peers, and societal norms allowed life skills to be cultivated. Gould and colleagues' approach suggested a slight diversion from the systematic teaching strategies of the LDI to a more integrated model of sport and life skill development. Specifically, the SUPER programme differentiates between time spent learning life skills and the time spent playing sport, whereas Gould and colleagues found that the high school football coaches did not think of life skills development strategies as differing from their general coaching. Instead, they fused the two.

In a subsequent study, Gould *et al.* (2006) investigated the needs of high school coaches and their perceived role in developing life skills. Gould *et al.* surveyed 154 North American high school coaches from seven sports on demographics, coaching objectives, the role of sport in character development, problems in sport today, the role of coaches, and coach influences on athletes. The survey was comprised of 99 items, with most items requiring Likert rating responses. Coaches ranked "helping young people develop psychologically and socially" as the most important coaching objective, and "having a winning team" as least important. Coaches felt that sport teaches many skills, and coaches strongly agreed that teamwork, the value of hard work, time management, and goal-setting are developed through sport participation. Interestingly, coaches did not agree that sport could teach fairness, accepting defeat gracefully, and not holding grudges after competitions (i.e. moral character development).

Conroy and Coatsworth (2006) highlighted the area of coach education as an avenue for life skills development by examining education programmes to teach coaches the skills to promote life skills. A review of efficacy trials of Coach Effectiveness Training (CET; Barnett *et al.*, 1992; Smith *et al.*, 1979, 1995; Smoll and Smith, 1984; Smoll *et al.*, 1993) and the Penn State Coaching Training programme (Coatsworth and Conroy, 2006; Conroy and Coatsworth, 2004) revealed that coach education has the potential to change coach behaviour – particularly increases in reward and reinforcement. Coach education resulted in changes in youths' perceptions of coaches. In particular, young people perceived CET-trained coaches as offering more reward and reinforcement, mistake-contingent encouragement, and general technical instruction. CET-trained coaches were more likely to have participants report that they liked their coach more and they believed the coach liked them more. Finally, coach education programmes can enhance athletes' self-esteem, reduce youth's anxiety, and optimize achievement goals in youth sport participants. Conroy and Coatsworth concluded that the evidence base indicates that coach education, with an emphasis on psychosocial education, is an efficacious method for promoting positive development (e.g. life skills) through sport.

Holt *et al.* (2008) described how coaches structure an environment to teach life skills. They collected interview and observation data over a single season with 12 Canadian high school-aged student athletes. Results revealed the high school student athletes felt they learned skills associated with initiative, respect, teamwork, and leadership through sport. Interestingly, the coach did not directly teach athletes these skills, but rather structured an environment whereby athletes were required to demonstrate these skills. For example, the coach created boundaries and expectations that allowed for the expression of skills. Thus, the student athletes learned through experience. Participants did not believe respect and initiative transferred to other life domains; only teamwork and leadership were transferable. Holt and colleagues concluded that sport might provide a context that teaches specific life skills (e.g. teamwork) rather than a range of skills.

Rutten *et al.* (2007) also investigated prosocial and antisocial behaviour in adolescent athletes. The sample comprised 260 male and female soccer players and competitive swimmers between 12 and 18 years of age. Researchers recruited participants from 25 sports teams in the Amsterdam and Utrecht areas of The Netherlands. The participants completed questionnaires on social desirability, anti- and prosocial behaviour, sociomoral atmosphere of the sporting environment, sociomoral reasoning about sport dilemmas, and coach–athlete relationship quality. Multilevel regression analysis revealed that characteristics of the sporting environment accounted for 8 per cent of the variance in antisocial behaviour and 7 per cent of the variance in prosocial behaviour. Results suggested that coaches who maintain good relationships with their athletes reduce antisocial behaviour, and that exposure to relatively high levels of sociomoral reasoning within the immediate context of sporting activities promotes prosocial behaviour. Results highlight the importance of the coach in promoting specific life skills. In this study, coaches structured an environment that encouraged prosocial behaviour and reduced antisocial behaviour.

In addition to coaches, other social agents may also play a key role in the teaching of life skills. Mahoney and Statin (2000) investigated the influence of structure on the antisocial behaviour of Swedish adolescents. Mahoney and Statin discovered that when adolescents participated in structured activities (such as sport), they were more likely to engage in more prosocial activities, were more likely to have more friends in after-school contexts, and were less likely to engage in antisocial behaviour. Peers, parents, and youth activity leaders provided structure. Mahoney and

Statin suggested that structure of activities was related to skills building experiences that built complexity and challenge, regular participation, rule-guided engagement, direction by one or more skilled adults, sustained active attention, and clear feedback on performance. Adults did not directly teach young people about prosocial behaviour; rather, the structure of the activities encouraged them to "catch" these skills.

In closing, it may be more important to show coaches how to structure the environment rather than how to teach skills directly. By learning how to provide opportunities for young people that place them outside their comfort zones, it may be possible that coaches can help young people develop life skills.

"Catching" life skills

Schön (1987) criticised the teaching model of charging up a young person with information so that he or she can discharge that information in a different life domain. Schön suggested that this is an inappropriate practice in a dynamic world. He suggested the positivist epistemology of technical rationality (battery charging) is an inaccurate representation of how people think and act. As such, Schön presented an alternative epistemology in which people gain knowledge through experience. In this respect, young people do not necessarily learn life skills directly from a teacher, but rather teachers give young people the opportunity to practise skills and learn from trial, error, and experience. Essentially, this is an athlete-led, rather than coach/teacher-led, approach to developing life skills.

The problem with the coach- or teacher-led approaches to life skills development is the omission of the athlete as an agent of his or her own development. Dworkin *et al.* (2003) reported that the young people believe that that they are agents of their own development and change. Agency took the form of deliberate exploration, or involved trial and error where adolescents evaluated how things could have gone better and taught themselves from their mistakes. Organised activities were arenas in which youth could explore and conduct trial-and-error experiments. The young people did not learn because of direct teaching strategies, but rather learned because of their own experiences.

The systematic teaching of life skills is an adult-led approach to youth development that allows an adult to impart knowledge to the young people participating in the programme (Larson and Walker, 2006). Young people in adult-driven situations are in a passive, dependent role and do not have ownership of learning, which can reduce motivation (Larson and Walker, 2006). Simply following leader instructions may compromise reflection, creativity, and independent decision-making skills of young people participating in the activity.

Larson and Angus (2010) found that young people responded to environments (e.g. organised activities) as active agents in the dialectic process of development. Young people made choices, pursued goals, and changed how they thought about and acted on the world. Importantly, young people were active producers of their own development, and adults did not systematically teach skills, values, and/or virtues. Young people responded to challenges by developing insights that allowed them to reach goals. Although adults did not systematically teach young people skills, they did play a role. Adults provided a resource upon which young people could draw. Young people actively drew on adults' knowledge to develop their own knowledge, and to find their way in adult worlds. For example, in terms of developing personal responsibility, young people developed through successful experiences in taking on responsibility. Over time, they progressively changed their self-concept to that of being a responsible person.

Lerner *et al.* (2006) noted that the basic unit of analysis within the developmental system involves a mutually influential relationship between a developing person and a multilevel and changing ecological context. These bi-directional relations between the athlete and the context constitute developmental regulation. Adaptive developmental regulations (i.e. positive outcomes such as life skills) emerge when the interactions between the individual and the context advance the well-being of both components (Lerner *et al.*, 2005). As such, a teacher-led approach may not constitute adaptive developmental regulation, given the power hierarchy between the coach/teacher and the athlete, and the unidirectional knowledge exchange from one to the other. On the other hand, an experiential, athlete-led approach to life skills development will more likely benefit both athlete and the context (i.e. coaching, team, and/or organisation) because athletes are central to their own development and the context will function better as a consequence of improved individuals. Readers can observe an example of this concept in the results of Brunelle *et al.* (2007). In the community aspect of the intervention, the young people were able to develop their life skills (individual benefit) while providing free coaching to young people at their home clubs (context benefit).

Although it may be true that athletes do not simply catch life skills by being in a sporting environment, it does not mean that coaches and practitioners need to provide highly structured systematic teaching strategies in order for young people to learn skills (Gould and Carson, 2008). It could be that the teaching of life skills is more about creating boundaries and structures so that young people learn skills by doing, through a process of trial and error. Clearly, from a safety and ethical perspective there are certain mistakes that practitioners cannot afford young people to make, so the coach can ensure that athletes experiment in a safe environment. To illustrate this point, we can take the example of Brazilian street kids playing soccer. It is clear that in many cases these children do not have access to coaching, or to any adult supervisor who could "teach" them life skills, because of their socio-economic circumstances. It is a disheartening prospect that without supervision these young people will not learn how to work in teams or to communicate with one another, and that young people do not have the agency and initiative to develop. However, this may not be the case. In this example, it could be that the co-active nature and the influence of peer interaction associated with team sports facilitates communication and teamwork and allows young people to learn through trial and error (i.e. experimenting with non-verbal communication, developing social cohesion, forming new groups). A coach or practitioner may facilitate this process by setting up games and training activities that require communication and teamwork so that young people begin to practise these skills in a more deliberate manner. In this respect, coaches teach life skills by structuring an environment to facilitate implicit learning. This idea aligns with the research on coaching life skills previously described (e.g. Gould *et al.*, 2005).

In a study of perceived life skills development, Jones and Lavallee (2009b) found that athletes could develop life skills through a process of experiential learning. Jones and Lavallee interviewed a single athlete several times in order to understand the meaning of experiences in relation to her life skill development. The results suggested that life skill development was the culmination of dispositional factors (e.g. a disposition for hard work), the experience of sport requiring the practice of certain skills, and the family supporting and reinforcing key life skills away from the field of play. In this case, the experience of playing tennis required the athlete to practise certain skills because the situation required them. She experienced situations that required her to communicate with other players and to organise her school schedule in order to practise and compete. Over a prolonged period, the athlete learned to communicate effectively and to organise her schedule through the process of trial and error. No coach, parent, or teacher ever taught her which skills to learn and how to learn; rather, the athlete talked about learning through experience. The athlete recognised that her coach and her parents often conditioned her tennis experience so that she had to practise particular skills. For example, when entering tournaments, her parents delegated responsibility for finding tournaments, requesting paperwork, and filling in tournament registrations. If she did not organise these aspects of tournament tennis, she would not be able to compete. As such, she soon learned how to organise herself because she valued playing in tennis tournaments. There were inevitably mistakes made along the way but the result was a process of organisation that worked for her.

Jones and Lavallee (2009b) suggested that the organisation of the sport, coaching styles, parent styles, and other aspects of the developmental climate all contribute to the skills learned by the athlete. This multi-agent, multilevel approach to development provided support for Fraser-Thomas *et al.*'s (2005) model of sport programming for positive youth development. Their model incorporated talent development research (e.g. Côté, 1999; Côté and Hay, 2002) into a larger framework of positive youth development. Their model suggests that successful positive youth development programmes consider youths' intellectual, physical, psychological, and social stages of development. Practitioners should conduct programmes in appropriate settings, and they should foster developmental assets. Furthermore, Fraser-Thomas *et al.* highlighted the importance of policy-makers and sports organisations. Fraser-Thomas *et al.* (2005) suggested sports organisations need to ensure accessibility of youth sport programmes to all youth, and to ensure that programmes are designed to improve youth holistically rather than simply producing better-skilled individuals. Finally, Fraser-Thomas and colleagues proposed that it is the responsibility of policy-makers and organisations to provide coaches and parents with opportunities to learn and teach internal assets through training, education, and experience so that young people can use parents and coaches as a resource (i.e. external assets). In sum, they promote a multi-agent approach in supporting positive youth development through sport.

In closing, having the key social agents structure an environment so that young people can experiment and discover what needs to be done may be an approach that can supplement existing life skills programmes. Athletes then become agents of their own development while allowing social agents to guide the process and to provide boundaries so that athlete exploration and trial and error is experienced in a physically and psychologically safe environment.

Applied implications

Rather than just systematically teaching life skills to young people (i.e. via life skills workshops), adults may better serve young people by also structuring sport experiences so that they have opportunities for experimentation and self-reflection. This does not mean that adults leave young people unsupervised. Adult leaders provide scaffolding for learning in multiple ways. For example, adults structure practice, provide motivational support, offer encouragement, provide challenge, and steer young people away from potentially frustrating situations (Larson and Walker, 2005). This approach to cooperative learning (e.g. Dyson *et al.*, 2004) facilitates meaningful participation in learning. Athletes may work together to master the content (i.e. application of life skills), but athletes are not only responsible for learning the material; they also help their group-mates learn (i.e. personal and social responsibility; Hellison, 1995).

Larson *et al.* (2005) postulated that balancing techniques from adult- and youth-led perspectives helps young people develop. By using a balance of adult supervision and experiential learning, adults can help young people stay on track while maintaining a young person's investment and motivation in the activity (Larson *et al.*, 2005).

Like Gould *et al.*'s (2005) high school coaches, Miller and Kerr (2002) stated that "The ideal sport model will not be attained until life skills development occurs within and as a result of the sport experience" (p. 150). As such, both sport skills and life skills need to integrate seamlessly so that coaches do not need to remove athletes from the sporting field in order to learn life skills. Holt *et al.* (2007) proposed the Teaching Games for Understanding Model (Werner *et al.*, 1996) as a practical method for structuring physical education experiences to foster positive development. Teaching Games for Understanding is a model whereby learners begin by playing a modified game, and then develop game knowledge and skill proficiency within representative game activities. The model is designed to create more knowledgeable and proficient game players, and to motivate participants. Young people learn skills because they are required in order to succeed in that context. As they become more proficient within the adapted games context, young people can begin to introduce skills across domains. Holt and colleagues described situational and personal factors that practitioners could use to create an environment in which young people can learn about positive youth development. Situational factors include providing young people with choices and decision-making responsibilities within appropriate lesson boundaries and expectations. Personal factors include the promotion of reflection, strategic thinking, and planning activities that are conducive to demonstrating good character (e.g. respect for rules, respect for teammates). Overall, the structured environment promotes skills learning, as opposed to the teacher directly teaching skills.

Aligned with the suggestions of Holt *et al.* (2007), Hellison (1995) featured reflective practice in other positive youth development programmes (e.g. the personal and social responsibility model). Reflection may be a key skill in the development of life skills, because Danish *et al.* (1993) stated that one of the barriers to life skill development might be that athletes are not aware of the skills they have learned by playing sport. Specifically, young people may be executing skills in practice, but skills will not necessarily be transferable because the young people are unaware of what they are doing. Danish and colleagues suggest several factors and characteristics that can encourage development and transfer of life skills. Young people could develop and transfer life skills to other life domains if they are able to increase their awareness of the skills they have acquired through their experiences in sport, knowledge of how and in what context they learned life skills, and awareness that these skills are valued in other life domains (Danish *et al.*, 1993). Employing reflective practice and enhancing self-awareness of life skills could be an essential element of life skill development in athletes, and should be actively encouraged by practitioners.

Reflective practice is at the opposite end of systematic teaching strategies (e.g. LDI). Schön's (1987) theory of reflective practice suggested people learn in two different ways: reflection *in* action, and reflection *on* action. First, people gain knowledge through what he called “reflection in action”. Reflection in action, also known as thinking on your feet, involves developing new understandings to inform our actions in the situation that is unfolding. Schön suggested that when individuals go about the spontaneous, intuitive performance of actions of everyday life (e.g. participating in sport), they demonstrate specific knowledge. However, often this knowledge cannot be articulated; individuals cannot say what they know, they do what they know (i.e. knowledge is in action). For example, a child may be able coordinate the multiple bodily movements involved in throwing a ball and judging the distance of a target; however, it is unlikely that the child will be able to articulate how he or she does this.

Overall, reflection in action is non-cognitive knowing (Van Manen, 1999) in which knowledge resides in the actions that are lived and experienced by individuals. As such, when young people are involved in organised sport they are exposed to a range of skill-building experiences related to the nature and structures of the sport (e.g. team sports and teamwork). However, young people may be unaware of the knowledge in action that they have acquired during their sporting experiences. As such, it is also important to make knowledge in action readily useable across contexts. Athletes can use reflection *on* action to increase their awareness of the skills they have developed in action.

Young people can use reflection on action to explore why they acted as they did, what was happening in a situation and why, what they have learned, and how they can use this knowledge in the future. The outcome of reflection on action is a repertoire of thoughts and ideas, based on successful response strategies, and outcomes that one can draw upon when confronted with new scenarios. Schön (1987) posited that this repertoire is central to reflective thought. Specifically, when individuals make sense of a situation they perceive to be unique, they relate it to previous experiences. The familiar experience (i.e. one learned through sport, such as anxiety management) functions as a precedent, a metaphor, or an exemplar for the unfamiliar one (e.g. anxiety management for an exam), therefore allowing one to function when in unfamiliar scenarios (Schön, 1987).

Coaches and practitioners could integrate reflective practice into coaching sessions using group discussion and discourse, or by using reflection journals whereby the journal prompts athletes to think about their sport experiences and which skills could be used in other life domains. Jones *et al.* (2011) recently tested a reflective practice programme to develop life skills in a sample of university athletes. Jones *et al.* (2011) developed the ELITE (Enhancement of Leadership, Intercommunication, Teamwork, and Excellence) life skills reflective practice programme to improve two targeted life skills (specifically, communication and self-organisation). Three male field hockey players and two female tennis players from a British university participated in the intervention over a period of eight weeks. Jones *et al.* targeted each life skill separately in two four-week phases. Each week, Jones and colleagues met with the athletes and encouraged them to reflect on different aspects of their sporting experiences. The first session involved reflecting on life skills practised in the context of training by answering a series of questions – for example, "describe the communication/organisation skills you used in your last training session." The second session progressed by focusing on life skills practised in competition – for example, "describe a competition in which communication/organisation skills helped your performance." The third session advanced into anticipatory reflection (i.e. planning) – for example, questions included "which scenarios in the future do you anticipate you will need good communication/organisation skills"? During the third session, the first author actively encouraged the participants to think about non-sport scenarios that would also require good communication/organisation skills, and to consider how principles of good sport communication/organisation applied to these non-sport scenarios. The fourth session gave participants the opportunity to practise the skills they had been discussing in the previous weeks (i.e. reflecting in action). The participants put the principles of effective communication/organisation into practice in a series of interactive games and activities that required the participants to use the skills they had previously discussed. For example, when practising communication skills, participants were given team-building activities that required clear communication to accomplish the task. Similarly, when practising organisation skills, participants were asked to pattern, prioritise, and plan (Petrie and Denson, 1999) their academic and training commitments to produce a study timetable for a forthcoming exam period.

Jones *et al.* (2011) used a series of single-subject, multiple baselines, with minimal meaningful harm and benefit criteria and SMD_{all} effect sizes (i.e. mean difference between baseline and intervention) to evaluate the ELITE intervention. The results revealed no meaningful harm from participating in the programme, and the tennis players showed meaningful benefits. SMD_{all} effect sizes demonstrated that the intervention had a positive effect. Post-intervention interviews also indicated that participants valued the targeted life skills, and the programme was enjoyable. Jones and colleagues concluded that coaches and practitioners might wish to expand the ELITE life skills programme to other life skills. Practitioners could apply the ELITE procedures (i.e. reflection on training and competition, anticipatory reflection, and reflection in action) to any life skill. Coaches and practitioners would just need to adjust the stem of the reflection question. For example, rather than asking about communication in training and competitions, scholars and practitioners could encourage athletes to reflect on respect or discipline practised in training and competition.

Conclusion

This chapter has presented some of the key issues for developing life skills with athletes. Practitioners need to be aware of several important concepts that may hinder or promote development in young people. First, life skills are only life skills if they are transferable into other life domains. As such, any intervention should actively encourage and evaluate (if possible) the use of specific skills in non-sport scenarios. Second, to date, research has shown that sport correlates with several positive outcomes (i.e. not a causal relationship). This is important because practitioners need to be mindful that young people may choose activities that suit their skill base, these skills may not be initially apparent, and young people can improve their existing skills. Third, sport is not a homogenous experience or a panacea for life skill development. Not all sports will develop the same skills in the same way. Adaptive developmental regulations only occur when the needs and assets of the individual match the needs and assets of the context. Thus, it could be possible that two individuals, on the same team, receiving the same coaching, may not develop the same skills (if they do not have the same needs and assets). Practitioners can help match individual and contextual needs and identify individual and contextual assets so that adaptive developmental regulations are supported. Fourth, scholars and practitioners could use both direct systematic teaching strategies and experiential learning strategies to develop life skills; however, research has shown that young people are agents of their own development, and may benefit from more athlete-centred approaches where adult leaders promote learning by providing guidance, support, and agency. Finally, practitioners can play an important role in educating coaches, parents, and peers so that social agents are given opportunities to understand their role in the development of young people. Furthermore, practitioners are in a unique position to facilitate adaptive coaching strategies (e.g. autonomy supportive coaching styles) and reflective practice interventions with young people so that they increase their self-awareness of the skills they develop through the process of trial-and-error experimentation.

In closing, the development of life skills in athletes is a complex undertaking that involves several components of a broad developmental system. An awareness of the existing research from sport psychology and developmental science, combined with some practical strategies, can provide practitioners with a knowledge base from which to intervene in and facilitate the development of life skills.

References

Barber, B. L., Eccles, J. S., and. Stone, M. R. (2001). Whatever happened to the "Jock," the "Brain," and the "Princess"? Young adult pathways linked to adolescent activity involvement and social identity. *Journal of Adolescent Research*, 16, 429–455.

Barnett, N. P., Smoll, F. L., and. Smith, R. E. (1992). Effects of enhancing coach–athlete relationships on youth sport attrition. *The Sport Psychologist*, 6, 111–127.

Brunelle, J., Danish, S. J., and Forneris, T. (2007). The impact of a sport based life skills program on adolescent prosocial values. *Applied Developmental Science*, 11, 43–55.

Brustad, R. J. (1992). Integrating socialisation influences into the study of children's motivation in sport. *Journal of Sport and Exercise Psychology*, 14, 59–77.

Coatsworth, J. D. and Conroy, D. E. (2006). Enhancing the self-esteem of youth swimmers through coach training: Gender and age effects. *Psychology of Sport and Exercise*, 7, 173–192.

Conroy, D. E. and Coatsworth, J. D. (2004). The effects of coach training on fear of failure in youth swimmers: A latent growth curve analysis from a randomised controlled trial. *Journal of Applied Developmental Psychology*, 25, 193–214.

Conroy, D. E. and Coatsworth, J. D. (2006). Coach training as a strategy for promoting youth social development. *The Sport Psychologist*, 20, 128–144.

Côté, J. (1999). The influence of the family in the development of talent in sport. *The Sport Psychologist*, 13, 395–417.

Côté, J. and Hay, J. (2002). Children's involvement in sport: A developmental perspective. In J. M. Silva and D. E. Stevens (eds), *Psychological foundations of sport* (pp. 484–502). Boston, MA: Allyn and Bacon.

Craven, P. (2006). Inclusive sport. Retrieved 19 November 2009, from www.efds.net/content/publications/incsports/Inclusive%20Sport%20summer%2006.pdf.

Danish, S. (2002). *Going for the goal: Leader manual* (4th edn). Richmond, VA: Life Skills Associates.

Danish, S. J. and Donohue, T. (1995). Understanding media's influence on the development of antisocial and prosocial behaviour. In R. Hampton, P. Jenkins and T. Gullota (eds), *Preventing violence in America* (pp. 133–156), Thousand Oaks, CA: Sage.

Danish, S. J. and Nellen, V. C. (1997). New roles for sport psychologists: Teaching life skills through sport to at risk youth. *Quest*, 49, 100–113.

Danish, S. J., Petitpas, A. J., and Hale, B. D. (1993). Life development intervention for athletes: Life skills through sports. *The Counseling Psychologist*, 21, 352–385.

Danish, S. J., Fazio, R., Nellen, V. C., and Owens, S. (2002). Community-based life skills programs: Using sport to teach life skills to adolescents. In J. Van Raalte and B. W. Brewer (eds), *Exploring sport and exercise psychology* (pp. 269–288). Washington DC: American Psychological Association.

Dworkin, J. B., Larson, R. W., and Hansen, D. (2003). Adolescents' accounts of growth experiences in youth activities. *Journal of Youth and Adolescence*, 32, 17–26.

Dyson, B., Griffin, L. L., and Hastie, P. (2004). Sport education, tactical games and cooperative learning: Theoretical and pedagogical considerations. *Quest*, 56, 226–40.

Eccles, J. S. and Barber, B. L. (1999). Student council, volunteering, basketball, or marching band: What kind of extracurricular activity matters? *Journal of Adolescent Research*, 14, 10–43.

Eccles, J. S., Barber, B. L., Stone, M., and Hunt, J. (2003). Extracurricular activities and adolescent development. *Journal of Social Issues*, 59, 865–889.

Fox, K. R. (2004). Tackling obesity in children through physical activity: A perspective from the United Kingdom. *Quest*, 56, 28–40.

Fraser-Thomas, J. L., Côté, J., and Deakin, J. (2005). Youth sport programs: An avenue to foster positive youth development. *Physical Education and Sport Pedagogy*, 10, 19–40.

Goudas, M., Dermitzaki, I., Leondari, A., and Danish, S. (2006). The effectiveness of teaching a life skills program in a physical education context. *European Journal of Psychology of Education*, 21, 429–438.

Gould, D. and Carson, S. (2008). Life skills development through sport: Current status and future directions. *International Review of Sport and Exercise Psychology*, 1, 58–78.

Gould, D., Collins, K., Lauer, L. and Chung, Y. (2005). Coaching life skills: A working model. *Sport and Exercise Psychology Review*, 2, 4–12.

Gould, D., Chung, Y., Smith, P., and White, W. (2006). Future directions in coaching life skills: Understanding high school coaches' views and needs. *Athletic Insight*, 8, Retrieved 24 December 2010, from www.athleticinsight.com/Vol.8Iss3/CoachingLifeSkills.htm.

Hansen, D. M., Larson, R. W., and Dworkin, J. B. (2003). What adolescents learn in organised youth activities: A survey of self-reported developmental experiences. *Journal of Research on Adolescence*, 13, 25–55.

Hellison, D. (1995). *Teaching responsibility through physical activity*. Champaign, IL: Human Kinetics.

Holt, N. L. and Jones, M. I. (2008). Future directions for positive youth development and sport. In N. L. Holt (ed.), *Positive youth development through sport* (pp. 122–131), London, UK: Routledge.

Holt, N. L., Tamminen, K., and Jones, M. I. (2007). Promoting positive youth development through teaching games in physical education. *Health and Physical Education* (Special Edition), 8–13.

Holt, N. L., Tink, L. N., Mandigo, J. L., and Fox, K. R. (2008). Do youth learn life skills through their involvement in high school sport? *Canadian Journal of Education*, 31, 281–304.

Jones, M. I. and Lavallee, D. (2009a). Exploring the life skills needs of adolescent athletes. *Psychology of Sport and Exercise*, 10, 159–167.

Jones, M. I. and Lavallee, D. (2009b). Exploring perceived life skills development and participation in sport. *Qualitative Research in Sport and Exercise*, 1, 36–50.

Jones, M. I., Lavallee, D., and Tod, D. (2011). Developing communication and organisation skills: The ELITE life skills reflective practice program. *The Sport Psychologist*, in press.

Larson, R. W. (1994). Youth organisations, hobbies, and sports as developmental contexts. In R. K. Silberiesen and E. Todt (eds), *Adolescence in context* (pp. 46–65). New York, NY: Teachers College Press.

Larson, R. W. (2000). Toward a psychology of positive youth development. *American Psychologist*, 55, 170–183.

Larson, R. and Angus, R. (2010). Pursuing paradox: The role of adults in creating empowering settings for youth. In M. Aber, K. Maton, and E. Seidman (eds), *Empowerment settings and voices for social change* (pp. 65–94). New York, NY: Oxford University Press.

Larson, R. W. and Walker, K. (2005). Processes of positive development: Classic theories. In P. Witt and L. Caldwell (eds), *Recreation and youth development* (pp. 131–148). State College, PA: Venture.

Larson, R. W. and Walker, K. C. (2006). Learning about the "real world" in an urban arts youth program. *Journal of Adolescent Research*, 21, 244–268.

Larson, R. W., Walker, K., and Pearce, N. (2005). A comparison of youth-driven and adult-driven youth programs: Balancing inputs from youth and adults. *Journal of Community Psychology*, 33, 57–74.

Larson, R. W., Hansen, D., and Moneta, G. (2006). Differing profiles of developmental experiences across types of organised youth activities. *Developmental Psychology*, 42, 849–863.

Lerner, R. M., Almerigi, J. B., Theokas, C., and Lerner, J. V. (2005). Positive youth development: A view of the issues. *Journal of Early Adolescence*, 25, 10–16.

Lerner, R. M., Lerner, J. V., Almerigi, J., Theokas, C., Phelps, E., Naudeau, S. *et al.* (2006). Toward a new vision and vocabulary about adolescence: Theoretical and empirical bases of a "positive youth development" perspective. In L. Balter and C. S. Tamis-LeMonda (eds), *Child psychology: A handbook of contemporary issues* (pp. 445–469). New York, NY: Taylor & Francis.

Life Skills Center (n.d.). *What are life skills?* Retrieved 15 April 2010, from www.lifeskills.vcu.edu/lskills.htm.

Mahoney, J. L. and Stattin, H. (2000). Leisure activities and adolescent antisocial behaviour: The role of structure and social context. *Journal of Adolescence*, 23, 113–127.

Marsh, H. W. and Kleitman, S. (2003). School athletic participation: Mostly gain with little pain. *Journal of Sport and Exercise Psychology*, 25, 205–228.

Martinek, T., McLaughlin, D., and Schilling, T. (1999). Project effort: Teaching responsibility beyond the gym. *Journal of Physical Education, Recreation, and Dance*, 70, 59–65.

McCallister, S. G., Blinde, E. M., and Weiss, W. M. (2000). Teaching values and implementing philosophies: Dilemmas of the coach. *Physical Educator*, 57, 35–45.

McNeal, R. B. (1995). Extracurricular activities and high school dropouts. *Sociology of Education*, 68, 62–81.

Miller, P. S. and Kerr, G. A. (2002). Conceptualising excellence: Past, present and future. *Journal of Applied Sport Psychology*, 14, 140–153.

O'Hearn, T. C. and Gatz, M. (1999). Evaluating a psychological competence program for urban adolescents. *Journal of Prevention*, 20, 119–144.

O'Hearn, T. C. and Gatz, M. (2002). Going for the goal: Improving youth problem solving skills through a school-based intervention. *Journal of Community Psychology*, 30, 281–303.

Papacharisis, V., Goudas, M., Danish, S., and Theodorakis, Y. (2005). The effectiveness of teaching a life skills program in a school-based sport context. *Journal of Applied Sport Psychology*, 3, 247–254.

Pedersen, S. and Seidman, E. (2004). Team sports achievement and self-esteem development among urban adolescent girls. *Psychology of Women Quarterly*, 28, 412–422.

Petitpas, A. J., Cornelius, A. E., Van Raalte, J. L., and Jones, T. (2005). A framework for planning youth sport programs that foster psychosocial development. *The Sport Psychologist*, 19, 63–80.

Petrie, T. A. and Denson, E. L. (1999). *A student athlete's guide to college success: Peak performance in class and life.* Belmont, CA: Wadsworth Publishing Co.

Rogge, J. (2004). *IOC and UNAIDS join forces to engage sport community in fight against aids.* IOC Press Release, 1 June.

Rutten, E. A., Stams, G. J. J. M., Biesta, G. J. J., Schuengel, C., Dirks, E., and Hoeksma, J. B. (2007). The contribution of organised youth sport to antisocial and prosocial behaviour in adolescent athletes. *Journal of Youth and Adolescence*, 36, 255–264.

Ryckman, R. M. and Hamel, J. (1995). Male and female adolescents' motives related to involvement in organised team sports. *International Journal of Sport Psychology*, 26, 383–397.

Schön, D. (1987). *Educating the reflective practitioner.* San Francisco, CA: Jossey-Bass.

Shields, D. L. L. and Bredemeier, B. J. L. (1995). *Character development and physical activity.* Champaign, IL: Human Kinetics.

Siegenthaler, K. L. and Gonzalez, G. L. (1997). Youth sports as serious leisure. *Journal of Sport and Social Issues*, 21, 298–314.

Smith, R. E., Smoll, F. L., and Curtis, B. (1979). Coach effectiveness training: A cognitive behavioural approach to enhancing relationship skills in youth sport coaches. *Journal of Sport Psychology*, 1, 59–75.

Smith, R. E., Smoll, F. L., and Barnett, N. P. (1995). Reduction of children's sport performance anxiety through social support and stress-reduction training for coaches. *Journal of Applied Developmental Psychology*, 16, 125–142.

Smoll, F. L. and Smith, R. E. (1984). Leadership research in youth sports. In J. M. Silva and R. S. Weinberg (eds), *Psychological foundations of sport* (pp. 371–386). Champaign, IL: Human Kinetics.

Smoll, F. L., Smith, R. E., Barnett, N. P., and Everett, J. J. (1993). Enhancement of children's self-esteem through social support training for youth sport coaches. *Journal of Applied Psychology*, 78, 602–610.

UNICEF. (n.d.). *Definition of terms.* Retrieved 12 April 2007, from www.unicef.org/lifeskills/index_7308.html.

Van Manen, M. (1999). The practice of practice. In M. Lange, J. Olson, H. Hansen, and W. Bÿnder (eds), *Changing schools/changing practices: Perspectives on educational reform and teacher professionalism.* Luvain, Belgium: Garant.

Werner, P., Thorpe, R., and Bunker, D. (1996). Teaching games for understanding: Evolution of a model. *Journal of Physical Education, Recreation and Dance*, 67, 28–33.

World Health Organisation (1999). Partners in life skills education. Geneva, Switzerland: World Health Organisation, Department of Mental Health.

11 Practitioner–client relationships in applied sport psychology practice

David Tod and Mark B. Andersen

Abstract

Sport psychology researchers have directed much effort to examining the typical interventions consultants use when helping athletes (e.g. goal-setting, imagery), but have not extensively studied other factors that may influence service delivery outcomes, such as the quality of the working relationships between practitioners and clients. In contrast, a substantial body of research in clinical and counselling psychology has demonstrated that a variety of process factors and, most critically, the therapist–client relationship predicts therapeutic outcome. Although researchers have not often examined the sport psychologist–athlete alliance directly, a review of the literature reveals that investigators have considered service delivery relationship issues, most often in association with other topics, such as effective consultants' characteristics and practitioner development. In this chapter, we review the current understanding of the practitioner–athlete relationship. We begin by providing an overview of relevant clinical and counselling psychology theory and research, before reviewing the sport psychology literature in which relationship issues have been mentioned, such as transference and countertransference. Later, we present practical implications sport psychologists may find helpful for developing their relationship-building skills; for example, the value of personal counselling and supervision. Finally, we suggest areas of research that may extend current knowledge, such as examining the factors that may influence practitioner–athlete relationships, including athletes' attachment styles and practitioners' levels of self-disclosure.

Keywords: athlete–practitioner relationship, working alliance, real relationship, applied sport psychology, service delivery, transference, countertransference, practitioner development

Introduction

When considering approaching a sport psychologist, athletes may ask themselves, "will this person be able to help me, and will we get on well?"

Sport psychologists, particularly trainees, may consider similar questions, such as "have I got something worthwhile to offer?" and "will I be able to build rapport with this client?" Such questions provide glimpses into two of the, arguably, most influential ingredients contributing to effective applied sport psychology practice: psychological knowledge, and the ability to establish positive working relationships. Typically, psychological theory and interventions help practitioners understand clients' situations and work with them to find ways to resolve their issues. Also, forming salubrious relationships with athletes facilitates consultants' attempts to help clients address their issues. According to some sport psychologists, the effectiveness of applied sport psychology interventions is dependent on the quality of the relationships that athletes and practitioners share (e.g. Andersen, 2006). Largely, however, investigators have focused on the psychological (and typically cognitive-behavioural) interventions practitioners have at their disposal, and have not devoted similar amounts of attention to investigating the relationships consultants develop with athletes (or others). Such a research emphasis may create the impression among trainees that effectively assisting athletes usually involves teaching them how to set goals, imagine success, utter positive (motivational, instructional) statements, and breathe deeply. Although cognitive-behavioural interventions do help many athletes, they are not the sole, or perhaps even the primary, basis of effective applied sport psychology (cf. Murphy, 2000). Such interventions are just some of the ingredients in the mix. Some applied sport psychology investigators have examined client–practitioner relationships, often through case study approaches (e.g. Stevens and Andersen, 2007a), but such research is relatively rare. Further relationship inquiry may contribute to building a solid foundation of interpersonal skills and understanding upon which to base future training and professional development to enhance service delivery effectiveness for both students and seasoned consultants.

Tod *et al.* (2009) recently described service delivery competence as a multidimensional constellation of knowledge, skills, and processes in which sport psychologists: (a) meet clients' needs and expectations, (b) develop and maintain mutually beneficial relationships, (c) understand psychological interventions and apply them to assist athletes in specific situations, (d) empathise with athletes' circumstances and interpret them through the lenses of suitable theories and models, and (e) reflect on how they (the practitioners) have influenced the interactions and outcomes of service provision. It would be difficult to write a single chapter providing an in-depth understanding of the various components mentioned in the above description. Authors contributing to this book, however, have focused on some of these specific aspects (see, for example, Chapter 12 on reflective practice, or Chapter 1 on models of service delivery). Also, several authors in this book have written about how to help athletes with specific issues, such as injury rehabilitation or life skills development. In the current chapter we review a component mentioned in the above description of service provision competence; specifically, we focus on the role relationships play when practitioners interact with athletes. We start by reviewing the counselling and clinical psychology literature focused on therapeutic process factors that influence therapy outcomes, from which an examination of the practitioner–client relationship will emerge. Then we present relevant sport psychology literature, before identifying possible research avenues and implications for training and practice.

Drawing from counselling and clinical psychology

Similar to their sport counterparts, counselling and clinical psychology researchers have examined the influence of specific factors or interventions on service delivery outcomes. In contrast to their sport colleagues, however, counselling and clinical psychology investigators have also conducted much research into the associations other process variables (including practitioner–client relationships) have with therapeutic outcomes. Orlinsky *et al.* (1994) published a systematic review in which they examined nearly 500 studies where authors had investigated relationships between psychotherapy process variables (including relationship factors) and outcomes conducted between 1950 and 1992. These authors identified 11 process variables associated with psychotherapeutic outcomes, seven of which were client-focused. The client variables included: (a) suitability for treatment, (b) cooperativeness versus resistance, (c) contribution to the therapeutic bond, (d) interactive collaboration, (e) expressiveness, (f) affirmation of the therapist, and (g) openness versus defensiveness. The remaining four variables were: (a) global therapeutic bond, (b) therapists' and clients' reciprocal affirmations, (c) treatment duration, and (d) therapeutic realisations. In a follow-up review, Orlinsky *et al.* (2004) examined a further 279 studies published between 1993 and 2001, and concluded that the latest research provided further support for the 1994 review conclusions, indicating that no major changes needed to be made to their interpretations of the earlier findings. Orlinsky *et al.* (2004) summarised the results from both reviews, writing that "both relationship variables and intervention procedures, patient participation and therapist influences, contribute jointly and variously to shaping the outcome of therapy" (p. 363). A body of sport psychology process-oriented literature equivalent to that in psychotherapy does not exist. There are, however, pockets of similar ideas between the two knowledge bases. Evidence, for example, indicates that athletes, coaches, and practitioners recognise that relationship factors, client variables, and interventions contribute to sport psychology consulting outcomes (Anderson *et al.*, 2004a; Meyers *et al.*, 1996).

In addition to identifying factors related to therapeutic results, some clinical and counselling psychology researchers have sought to identify which variables are the active ingredients, or explain the most variance, in service delivery outcomes. With respect to identifying the active ingredients involved in therapy, some investigators believe the major psychotherapies are (roughly) equally helpful (Imel and Wampold, 2008). According to these researchers, although results from numerous meta-analyses indicate psychotherapy assists clients, there is little convincing evidence that any specific therapeutic approach is more effective than any other (Ahn and Wampold, 2001; Shapiro and Shapiro, 1982; Smith and Glass, 1977; Wampold *et al.*, 1997). These researchers suggested that therapeutic outcomes are due primarily to factors common to the various psychotherapies, rather than those specific to each approach (Lambert and Barley, 2002; Lambert and Ogles, 2004; Wampold, 2001). Specific factors include the techniques and interventions associated with each model of therapy. There is less agreement, however, regarding the variables that constitute the common factors. Grencavage and Norcross (1990) reviewed 50 publications and found that the number of common factors proposed per article ranged from 1 to 20, with a total of 89 variables identified. The most frequently occurring common factors included: development of the therapeutic alliance, opportunity for catharsis, acquisition and practice of new behaviours, and clients' positive expectations. Tracey *et al.* (2003) found that experienced psychologists viewed common factors along two dimensions: feeling versus thinking, and therapeutic activity. Along the first dimension, common factors may be placed along a continuum as emphasising either the more cognitive (e.g. persuasion) or emotional dimensions of people's experiences (e.g. anxiety reduction). According to the second dimension, common factors represent either activities occurring within sessions (e.g. feedback) or attributes individuals bring to therapy (e.g. clients' positive expectations). In addition to the two dimensions, a cluster analysis yielded three groups of common factors. The *bond cluster* appeared to represent the relationship or working alliance. The *information* or *explanation cluster* appeared to indicate the value of providing clients with an explanation for their problems or complaints. The *role cluster* appeared to signpost the value of structuring therapy in ways that help clients make sense of the therapeutic process. Although variation exists regarding the common factors, the bond or relationship the parties' involved share stands as one of the most studied and accepted factors influencing therapeutic outcomes (Lambert and Barley, 2002).

Defining key terms: the tripartite psychotherapeutic relationship model

Many applied psychologists consider that the success of any therapeutic endeavour depends on open, trusting, and collaborative relationships between clients and practitioners (e.g. Spinelli, 2002). In contrast, client non-compliance, premature termination, and poor outcome may result from a lack of a connection (Sexton and Whiston, 1994). In addition, therapists' theoretical orientations influence how they conceptualise the therapeutic relationship, and how the practitioner–client bond influences therapeutic outcomes (Gelso and Hayes, 1998). Some rational-emotive behaviour therapists believe that the relationship contributes to, but is not necessary for, client change (e.g. Ellis, 2000). Many existential therapists, in contrast, argue psychotherapeutic relationships are the mechanisms by which clients change and grow (Spinelli, 2002; Yalom, 1980).

Gelso and colleagues (Gelso, 2009; Gelso and Carter, 1985, 1994; Gelso and Hayes, 1998; Gelso and Samstag, 2008) have developed a tripartite model for understanding psychotherapeutic relationships, consisting of the working alliance, the transference–countertransference configuration, and the real relationship. Recently, Gelso and Samstag (2008) defined the relationship as the "feelings and attitudes the therapy participants have toward one another and the manner in which these are expressed" (p. 268). Gelso's model builds on Greenson's (1967) earlier psychodynamic-based conceptualisation of the relationship, and he traced the three components back to Freud's original works (e.g. Freud, 1912/1958). For example, according to Gelso, Breuer and Freud (1893–1895/1966) were the first individuals to argue for the need to engage the patient as a collaborator in the therapeutic process – a concept that underpins the working alliance.

Gelso and Carter (1994) defined the working alliance as "the alignment or joining of the reasonable self or ego of the client and the therapist's analysing or 'therapising' self or ego for the purpose of the work" (p. 297). Gelso (2009) defined the real relationship as "the personal relationship existing between two or more people as reflected in the degree to which each is genuine with the other and perceives the other in ways that befit the other" (pp. 254–255). Genuineness and realistic perceptions are the two key features of the real relationship. Genuineness occurs when therapists and clients are authentic, open, and honest with each other. The realistic perceptions therapists and clients have about their interactions are, however, separate from the transference–countertransference configuration. Magnitude and valence are two additional concepts associated with the real relationship. Magnitude pertains to the strength of the real relationship. Valence represents a continuum where real relationships can range from being quite negative to highly positive.

Transference refers to client material, and Gelso and Cater (1994) defined it as "the repetition of past conflicts with significant others, such that feelings, attitudes, and behaviours belonging rightfully in those earlier relationships are displaced onto the therapist" (p. 297). An athlete, for example, may respond to an older female sport psychologist in ways that resemble her interactions with her mother. If she's not close to her mother because she doesn't believe her mum loves her unconditionally, the athlete may find herself hesitant to share personal information with her sport psychologist, even though she realises that doing so might help her attain positive outcomes from her interactions with the practitioner. Gelso and Carter (1994) defined countertransference as "the therapist's transference to the client's material, both to the transference and non-transference communications presented by the client" (p. 297). For example, a male sport psychologist who does not have children (but wishes he did) may find he acts towards young athletes in paternal ways. According to Gelso and Hayes (1998), transference and countertransference could help, hinder, or have little influence on psychotherapy. Gelso and Hayes (1998) also suggested that transference and countertransference material is present in most therapies (and human relationships), regardless of whether or not therapists and clients recognise these phenomena.

Theorists (e.g. Greenberg, 1994; Hatcher, 2009; Horvath, 2009; McCullough, 2009; Patton, 1994) have critiqued Gelso and colleagues' (e.g. Gelso, 2009; Gelso and Carter, 1994) framework on a number of grounds. One major criticism has been the inherent vagueness of the components. For example, therapists may struggle to determine whether clients' responses reflect transference or the real relationship. Theorists have also criticised the concept of the real relationship for being redundant and unnecessary. These individuals have also argued that there is no objective way to establish what is real or not in a relationship. In response, Gelso and colleagues have argued that research indicates that the real relationship adds to the understanding of the therapeutic connection beyond what is addressed by the other components. Also, the criticisms regarding vagueness and the lack of objectivity could be levelled at any construct in the human psychosocial sciences. The various components are not concrete entities, but labels for processes that occur when therapists and clients interact (Gelso and Samstag, 2008). The components merge together to become the psychotherapeutic relationship, although the configurations and relative influences of the components may vary as therapy unfolds over time. Gelso and Hayes (1998) proposed that "the temptation to reify the constructs is great; as we theorise, it so easily seems like the processes we are labelling take on a substance and life of their own. But the temptation to reify must be avoided" (p. 136).

Of Gelso's psychotherapeutic relationship components, the working alliance has received the most attention from investigators. According to Gelso and Hayes (1998), no construct in psychotherapy research has been as vigorously examined as the working alliance. Perhaps one reason why the working alliance has been such a central focus is because researchers consider it a common factor across most of the major psychotherapies (Gelso and Hayes, 1998). A second, although more sceptical, reason the working alliance has been studied extensively is the availability of reliable, valid, and easily administered questionnaires (Gelso and Hayes, 1998). Researchers have used more than 24 alliance scales in examining the construct, and investigators have found medium to high correlations among the most commonly used inventories (Horvath and Bedi, 2002). Factor analytic investigations have indicated that the leading measures assess, to varying degrees, (a) the interpersonal bond among parties, (b) individuals' collaborative involvement in treatment, and (c) collaboration or agreement on the goals and tasks in therapy (Horvath and Bedi, 2002). These factors correspond to the major components of Bordin's (1994) working alliance theory, which we discuss next.

Among the various frameworks, researchers have drawn on Bordin's (1979, 1983, 1994) working alliance model most often, and it still has high currency among investigators. According to Bordin (1994), clients' distresses often reflect their lifelong searches for safety and self-realisation, and, ideally, they collaborate with therapists in the change process. Working alliances consist of the interpersonal bonds between therapists and clients, along with their negotiations about therapeutic change goals and tasks. Therapeutic change goals refer to planned client outcomes, such as enhanced anxiety management. The process of change-goal negotiation between clients and therapists itself may result in positive outcomes. For example, assisting clients, who are feeling anxious, to identify the specific stressors they have difficulty coping with and the changes they can make to deal with them may help reduce their anxieties. Bordin (1994) argued that clients' commitment to therapy would be enhanced when they contributed directly to therapeutic change goals.

Working alliance tasks refer to those activities designed to help clients achieve their goals. Working alliances may be strengthened when there is a shared understanding of the tasks and roles for which each individual is responsible. For example, athletes might be responsible for attempting to complete agreed upon out-of-session exercises. Practitioners might be expected to provide opportunities for athletes to express and explore their thoughts and feelings surrounding their issues. Often, clients' contributions to identifying working alliance tasks may assist them in understanding their relevance. Also, the interpersonal bonds of the working alliance between clients and practitioners develop from their shared experiences in therapy, and are expressed in terms of their liking, trusting, and respecting each other. Usually, seeking to clarify a common understanding of tasks and roles from the outset of a therapeutic engagement can positively influence a client's commitment and engagement.

According to Bordin (1994), therapists and clients benefit by learning from the relationship strains they experience in service delivery. Strains refer to difficulties arising in therapy that weaken or rupture working alliances. Just as an untreated wound may turn gangrenous and lead to the loss of a body part, unaddressed strains and ruptures may result in the termination of once productive working alliances (Stiles, 2006). Although Bordin (1994) did not identify specific strains in his writing, he referenced Safran *et al.* (1990), who listed possible strain markers. Strain indicators included clients': (a) negative sentiments towards therapists, (b) disagreements with practitioners over goals and tasks, (c) begrudging or hasty compliances with goals or tasks, (d) avoidance behaviours, (e) defensive self-esteem enhancing statements, and (f) non-responsiveness to interventions. Although strains may give rise to therapists and clients feeling ineffective and guilty, Bordin (1994) believed ruptures and tensions present opportunities to develop strong working alliances and help clients along the change process. For example, Bordin (1994) discussed how, during therapy, clients may find themselves acting in maladaptive ways that are similar to those behaviour patterns that led them to seek psychological assistance. Examination of these therapy-related maladaptive behaviours may help clients understand their actions in other situations and learn new ways of behaving, leading to both improved working alliances with their therapists and improved functioning. An athlete who is having difficulty accepting and sharing personal information with his sport psychologist may come to realise that his lack of trust in others is a reason why he finds it difficult to fit into a new team. As he begins to challenge and work through his inability to trust others, he may find he builds a strong working alliance with the practitioner, and that trust begins to spill over into his sport, with him becoming comfortable in his team environment.

Researchers have investigated associations between the working alliance and therapeutic outcomes, and the findings from these studies have been subject to multiple meta-analyses. The overall effect sizes (*r*) from three meta-analyses were 0.26 (Horvath and Symonds, 1991), 0.22 (Martin *et al.*, 2000), and 0.21 (Horvath, 2001; Horvath and Bedi, 2002), indicating small to moderate, but consistent, effects. Horvath and Bedi's (2002) work is the most recent alliance–outcome meta-analysis of which we are aware, was based on 90 studies, and was published as part of the results from the American Psychological Association Division of Psychotherapy's Task Force on empirically supported therapy relationships. According to the results, neither the therapists' theoretical orientations nor the working alliance measures influenced the alliance–outcome relationship. Although client- and observer-rated alliances seemed more related to outcomes than therapist-assessed alliances, the large standard deviations indicated considerable overlap. In addition, therapist-rated outcomes were marginally more related to alliances compared with observer- and client-rated outcomes, although, again, large standard deviations indicated overlap. The alliance–outcome relationship was also not influenced by whether the same person or different people had rated the alliance and outcome variables. Regarding time of assessment, Horvath and Bedi (2002) observed that alliance measures were more related with outcome when assessed early or late in treatment, as opposed to assessment at some midpoint (although differences were small). The authors speculated that the strain and stress of working through issues during therapy may have a dampening effect leading to a weaker relationship from early to mid-therapy. The rise in the alliance–outcome relationship late in therapy might be confounded by treatment benefits. Horvath and Bedi's (2002) meta-analysis, along with the others, complements the major findings from psychotherapy process-outcome research indicating that relationship factors are associated with psychotherapy effectiveness. For example, although considerable overlap was apparent, and the lack of independence among the effect sizes precluded the use of statistical tests, Horvath and Bedi's (2002) finding that clients', rather than therapists', alliance ratings may have stronger associations with outcome is conceptually coherent with Orlinsky and colleagues' reviews discussed above (Orlinsky *et al.*, 1994; Orlinsky *et al.*, 2004).

In addition to examining psychotherapeutic outcome, Horvath and Bedi (2002) also reviewed research regarding associations between the working alliance and other therapy-related variables. Regarding client characteristics, for example, therapists may have difficulty developing working alliances with individuals who have personality disorders, or are delinquent, homeless, or drug-dependent. Clients with fearful, anxious, dismissive, and preoccupied attachment styles may also have difficulties developing working alliances early in treatment. With respect to example therapist variables, practitioners who adopt open communication styles, display empathy, and are willing to explore client material find it easier to establish working alliances than practitioners who exhibit closed communication styles, lack empathy, and do not examine client material. It is no surprise that therapists who display well-developed communication skills, and involve clients in the therapeutic process, usually have strong working alliances. Regarding example therapist–client interaction variables, hostile, negative, or competing interactions may threaten working alliances. In addition, collaboration and cooperation contributes to strong working alliances and positive therapeutic outcomes. Examining associations between the working alliance and collaboration, however, might lead to inflated correlations because they are similar and potentially overlapping variables. Research on the process variables associated with working alliances may have potential application for service delivery. For example, therapists might benefit from learning about communication styles associated with enhanced working alliances.

Although much research has been undertaken with respect to the working alliance, there are areas where future investigation could expand understanding and contribute to practice. For example, few experimental studies exist in which the working alliance has been manipulated to reveal causal relationships with other variables, in particular therapy outcomes (Horvath and Bedi, 2002; Kazdin, 2007). Such research, however, would be fraught with ethical problems. For example, a design where a therapist remained cool and aloof with six clients but was warm and engaging with six others would never get past an internal review board, for obvious reasons. In addition, psychotherapy researchers still need to conduct research demonstrating how the working alliance might lead to change, or the mechanisms underpinning its effects (Horvath and Bedi, 2002; Kazdin, 2007). Conducting experiments to provide evidence that working alliances lead to service delivery outcomes may also be problematic because of the difficulty in establishing suitable control groups (i.e. where no working alliance has been established). Researchers might be able to compare different types of alliances, however, to reveal that those that are strong are related to better outcomes than those that are weak. Also, investigators examining the reasons why the working alliance influences therapeutic outcomes may provide information that assists practitioners in reflecting on ways they can build strong relationships with clients.

Despite the difficulties in conducting experimental investigations, professionals still have an understanding of how psychotherapeutic relationships lead to change and what the mediating variables may be, although such explanations are typically influenced by authors' theoretical orientations (Gelso and Hayes, 1998). According to psychodynamic therapists, for example, through trusting, loving alliances clients begin to internalise therapists' rational, caring worldviews. That internalisation leads to clients beginning to behave, think, and feel in ways similar to their therapists. As Andersen (2011) suggested:

> All the mechanisms by which change is made are too complex to describe here, but the one most relevant ... is the internalisation of the psychologist. Athletes often take the qualities of the psychologist and make internal representations of how the psychologist acts, thinks, feels, and behaves. These internal representations act as guides for the athlete to change or alter his or her thinking, emotional reactions, and behaviours. When athletes say to their sport psychologists, "I was at the tournament and getting nervous, and then I heard your voice in my head..." we know that the internalisation of the psychologist is on its merry and helpful way.

The relationship in applied sport psychology

A body of literature is emerging in which sport psychology professionals are discussing and examining practitioner–athlete relationships (Andersen, 2006; Poczwardowski *et al.*, 1998; Tod and Andersen, 2005). Much of the literature includes discussion and opinion pieces, but there have been some attempts to study actual practitioner–athlete relationships. In their discussion paper, for example, Petitpas *et al.* (1999) paralleled the tripartite model when they discussed the working alliance, the transference–countertransference configuration, and facilitative conditions, drawing on Rogers' (1957) person-centred therapy. In the clinical and counselling psychology literature, many individuals have equated the real relationship with Rogers' facilitative conditions, although doing so provides an incomplete and misleading representation (Sexton and Whiston, 1994). The facilitative conditions focus on the counsellor, whereas the real relationship includes the interactions between practitioner and client. Nevertheless, based on their discussion, Petitpas *et al.* (1999) identified ways trainees could be taught to recognise and manage relationship issues in practice, such as being clients themselves, having their athlete interactions observed, and keeping training logs. In addition to the sparse literature focused on the practitioner–athlete alliance, there are a number of related threads of work in which relationship-based themes have emerged. We present overviews of the most relevant of these related threads in the following section.

Research examining practitioner–client interactions

In one of the few studies focused specifically on practitioner–client relationships, Tod *et al.* (2005) explored athletes' and trainee consultants' views regarding their early working alliance experiences. The investigators underpinned the research with Bordin's (1994) working alliance theory. Each of the four female and three male trainees met with an athlete (four males and three females) on three occasions to assist with an identified presenting issue. Consultations lasted between 30 and 90 minutes. The researchers conducted individual semi-structured interviews with participants after the first and third consultations. Paralleling working-alliance theory, participants differentiated between the friendly (or interpersonal bond) and the professional (goals and tasks) elements of their relationships. Both the athletes and trainees valued the collaborative efforts of the other parties. Participants did not consider a similar sporting background necessary for positive working alliances. The athletes, however, perceived that similar backgrounds helped the trainees relate to them and speak a similar language. Trainees believed they could empathise with their athletes, and felt confident they understood the psychological demands of the sport. Having played similar sports seemed to assist trainees in managing their anxieties regarding their ability to help clients. Although participants generally considered the consultations to have been positive experiences, some minor relationship strains emerged. The strains occurred when trainees (a) imposed their values on athletes, (b) had difficulty managing their anxieties and acted in ways that annoyed athletes, (c) did not explain fully their roles as consultants, and (d) did not appear to be listening to their athletes. Evidence that transference and countertransference influenced the relationships also emerged in both positive and negative ways.

In a related study, although not focused on the relationship specifically, Lloyd and Trudel (1999) analysed ten consultations that an experienced sport psychologist, Terry Orlick, had with five clients. Lloyd and Trudel's

(1999) aims were to examine the verbal behaviours and the content of the sessions. Data included frequencies of different verbal behaviours, and participants' responses during semi-structured interviews. Regarding verbal behaviours, the athletes spoke for about 59 per cent of the sessions, the consultant for about 40 per cent, and approximately 1 per cent was spent in silence. The most frequent verbal behaviours included an athlete's response to a consultant question (27 per cent), an athlete's initiation of a subject for discussion (26 per cent), and a consultant explanation of a topic (15 per cent). In the interviews held after the consultations, the athletes suggested that Orlick was a good listener, asked helpful questions, shared information at suitable moments, and assisted them in organising their thoughts. Lloyd and Trudel (1999) also compared the topics discussed in the practitioner–athlete consultations with those that Orlick (1989, 1996) suggested he focused on during service delivery in two of his previous articles. The topics discussed in the consultations were similar to those Orlick had suggested previously.

To date, there exist few studies in which sport psychologist–athlete in-session interactions have been examined in ways similar to Tod and colleagues' (2005) and Lloyd and Trudel's (1999) investigations. In such studies, it is likely that recording consultation sessions influence participants' behaviours, although it is difficult to determine the extent to which their responses are changed. Athletes may not disclose pertinent information, and consultants might be on their best professional behaviour. Despite the limitations, continued research examining in-session behaviours might have educational value. For example, identifying the typical relationship strains that occur during consulting, along with the ways such ruptures are repaired, may help future consultants avoid such issues, recognise them when they take place, or fix the damage that has occurred. Practitioners might also take comfort in realising that they are not alone in making mistakes, and such breakdowns do not necessarily signal the end of productive working alliances.

Characteristics of effective practitioners

Investigators have explored, both qualitatively and quantitatively, athletes', coaches', and sport science and medicine administrators' perceptions about the qualities of effective sport psychologists (Anderson *et al.*, 2004a; Dunn and Holt, 2003; Gentner *et al.*, 2004; Gould *et al.*, 1991; Lloyd and Trudel, 1999; Lubker *et al.*, 2008; Orlick and Partington, 1987; Partington and Orlick, 1987a, 1987b; Weigand *et al.*, 1999). Helpful consultants are perceived to have well-developed interpersonal skills, such as being likeable, trustworthy, and empathetic, and they are also able to fit into team environments. Conversely, practitioners with poor interpersonal skills, such as being inflexible, insensitive, or overbearing, alienate clients. In addition to having good social skills, highly rated sport psychologists are perceived to be technically competent, providing clients with specific, practical, and concrete strategies. Service delivery style is another technical competence component, and sports participants believe effective consultants adopt athlete-centred approaches and focus on identifying individuals' strengths, weaknesses, and needs. Technically competent consultants also provide a variety of services, including assistance with competition preparation, help with mental skills development, and general counselling services for both sport and non-sport related issues.

In addition to listing effective consultants' attributes, athletes and coaches have identified factors that may impede sport psychologists' effectiveness. For example, practitioners are less effective if they are unable to meet with athletes often enough to resolve client issues. Also, intimidating coaches may interfere with sports psychologists' abilities to develop trust with athletes. Athletes may also refrain from seeking assistance if they believe intimidating coaches will pressure practitioners to divulge clients' personal information.

Practitioners have also provided their views about effective sport psychologist competencies (Gould *et al.*, 1989, 1991; Sharpe and Hodge, 2011; Lubker *et al.*, 2008; Partington and Orlick, 1991; Sedgwick and Zaichkowsky, 2003; Simons and Andersen, 1995; Statler, 2003; Straub and Hinman, 1992; Sullivan and Nashman, 1998). Similar to coaches and athletes, practitioners consider that effective consultants have outstanding interpersonal skills. Also, helpful consultants understand sporting environments, and have the psychological knowledge necessary to assist athletes in practical ways. For example, helpful practitioners understand the training and performance demands placed on athletes. In addition, effective consultants are able to address clients' individual needs. Caring sport psychologists are committed to helping athletes achieve their goals and experience their sporting participation as rewarding. Effective practitioners examine their own behaviours, thoughts, and feelings, and are aware of their strengths and limitations as consultants. They also interact with colleagues and engage in peer supervision.

The research reviewed above reveals the attributes a range of individuals perceive effective and ineffective practitioners to exhibit during consultancy relationships. These studies do not, however, provide data about the relationships that consultants, effective or otherwise, form with athletes. Neither do these studies provide evidence that practitioners' attributes have causal relationships with service delivery outcomes. The attributes are somewhat similar to Rogers' (1957) facilitative conditions: they detail the competencies that most likely allow practitioners to establish helpful alliances with clients. Further research is needed to provide data on the relationships, helpful and unhelpful, that practitioners form with athletes. Direct examination of the consultant–athlete relationship, for example, might reveal how these competencies interact with athletes and situational factors to influence service delivery outcomes.

Findings from longitudinal counsellor development research

Some researchers have examined ways that practitioners develop over time, and have observed that, with experience, consultants come to recognise and appreciate the role relationships play in the helping process more than they did as beginning consultants (e.g. Tod and Bond, 2010). Tod *et al.* (2009, 2011), for example, followed a cohort of Australian sport psychologists, interviewing them four times over a six-year period beginning immediately prior to their postgraduate training. These participants reported how their understanding and appreciation of the consulting relationship had broadened and deepened with experience, as illustrated by one male consultant who said: "I always had a sense that the relationship was massively important, but it becomes a lot more significant when you are doing that [professional practice] day to day, week in and week out." Often, especially through experiencing difficult situations, practitioners developed greater appreciation for the relationship than they had during training. For example, the practitioner in Tod and Bond's (2010) case study discussed how she was running a team meeting when one of the athletes stormed out of the room. She did not follow him to check what was happening because she felt it was her responsibility to continue chairing the session. She reported the athlete did not want to meet with her afterwards because she had not left to the meeting to look after him. In reflecting on the situation, the practitioner said:

> If you haven't got a good relationship then it's very difficult and I don't think clients are going to trust you; when that relationship with the [player] broke down, I wasn't really able to work with him ... I definitely understand it [the relationship] better than I did, and feel more strongly; if I didn't feel the relationship was strong enough, I don't think I could be effective and therefore it's kind of pointless and unethical.
>
> (p. 41)

To date, longitudinal research on practitioner development has not included examination of actual consultant–athlete relationships. Examination of real working relationships would provide another source of data on how practitioners develop, and also provide information on how their client interactions evolve with experience.

Transference, countertransference, and the erotic

Transference and countertransference

As mentioned above, in the psychotherapy literature transference and countertransference have been conceptualised in various ways according to professionals' theoretical orientations (Gelso and Hayes, 1998). Typically, sport psychology authors have adopted a slightly broader perspective on transference and countertransference compared with Gelso and Hayes' (1998) definitions presented earlier, which were focused on the repetition of past conflicts. According to the definitions writers use most often in the sport psychology literature, transference refers to when clients respond cognitively, behaviourally, or emotionally, either consciously or unconsciously, to therapists in ways resembling patterns of response to significant others, real or imagined, in their lives (Andersen, 2004). Countertransference refers to when therapists respond to clients in similar ways they have with significant others (Andersen, 2004). Similar to Gelso and Hayes (1998), sport psychology authors have acknowledged that transference is not limited to service delivery, but is a phenomenon present in human relationships generally. Also, transference and countertransference may help or hinder service delivery outcomes. A male athlete, for example, whose father died just prior to him becoming a teenager, might miss his dad greatly. He may carry a disappointment that he was never able to form a friendship with his dad, and that they had only shared a father–child relationship. He may respond to an older male sport psychologist as though the practitioner were a stand-in for the father he missed. With the help of his practitioner, the athlete might examine his reactions to his sport psychologist and begin to understand the relationships he had experienced with his previous and current coaches (who were older males) and his behaviour towards them. He might have, unconsciously, expected them to be friendly father figures, and could have been frustrated and disappointed when they did not respond as he had hoped. An increased self-awareness from examining transference might help the athlete manage his responses and emotions with his current coach.

There is just a small body of sport psychology literature in which transference and countertransference are examined, and much of it consists of discussion papers. Most often, transference and countertransference are mentioned briefly in relation to other topics, such as cross-gender consulting (Henschen, 1991; Yambor and Connelly, 1991), service delivery (Andersen, 2000a; Giges, 1998; Poczwardowski *et al.*, 1998), psychodynamic therapy (Conroy and Benjamin, 2001; Hill, 2001), training and supervision (Andersen and Williams-Rice, 1996; Van Raalte and Andersen, 2000), and the therapeutic relationship (Petitpas *et al.*, 1999). These issues are also mentioned with respect to erotic transference, a topic detailed in more depth below.

Works focusing on transference and countertransference in greater depth than previously have begun to appear in the literature in the past 10–15 years. Strean and Strean (1998), along with Andersen (2006), for example, described how transference and countertransference influence service delivery, and illustrated their arguments with case examples. Building on Andersen's (2005a) chapter, Stevens and Andersen (2007b), in their review of erotic transference, revealed how therapists from several schools of thought conceptualised transference and countertransference, including psychodynamic theory, humanistic psychology, person-centred approaches, cognitive-behavioural therapy, social psychology, and feminist theories. These authors (Andersen, 2005a; Stevens and Andersen, 2007b; Strean and Strean, 1998), along with others (e.g. Giges, 1998), have also discussed how transference and countertransference may be applied in the sport psychology service delivery process. For example, monitoring their countertransferences may help practitioners ensure they are providing athletes with the help needed to resolve issues. To assist consultants in recognising and monitoring their countertransference, Calhoun *et al.* (2005) outlined several specific types of countertransference that are possible, including over-identification, alignment, disavowal, disdain, envy, defensive normalisation, and idealisation.

Moving beyond the level of opinion and review papers, some authors have briefly reflected on the influences transference and countertransference have had on their athlete interactions (Katz, 2009; Price and Andersen, 2000; Tod, 2007a). Tod (2007a), for example, speculated that his own deficiencies as an athlete and unrealised wish of having had the guidance of a mentor, along with his client's (John's) similar desire for such a guide, may have contributed to the positive working alliance they shared. With additional reflection, perhaps Tod's (2007a) interpretation was naive and overly positive. The power imbalance associated with a mentor–mentee relationship may have combined with the inequality inherent in psychological service delivery to influence Tod's (2007a) interactions with John. For example, Tod (2007a) did observe that occasionally John seemed to want direct guidance when Tod was encouraging him to identify solutions himself. Tod's (2007a) explicit reference to mentoring may also reveal he over-identified with the mentor John desired and he missed as an athlete. A more cautious interpretation may be that at least the transference–countertransference configuration did not prevent positive service delivery outcomes from occurring. The reinterpretation of Tod's (2007a) article highlights the complexities and subjectivities associated with applied sport psychology working alliances, and perhaps provides one reason why this has not been subject to much empirical investigation. The components involved in transference and countertransference are often difficult to recognise, conceptualise, and measure.

The earliest published quantitative study on countertransference we can find appeared in 2006, and the investigators surveyed UK practitioners about the importance of, and the mechanisms they used to support and develop, their self-awareness and countertransference management (Winstone and Gervis, 2006). In the first two subscales of the questionnaire the researchers used, respondents indicated their perceived importance of self-insight, described as the degree to which practitioners were aware of and understood the basis of their feelings; and self-integration, or consultants' sense of, and security in, self. Participants indicated that self-awareness was important, and the highest-scoring items included "have capability to reflect on your feelings", and "understand how your feelings influence and motivate you in your client work". Respondents also reported that self-integration was important to "distinguish between client's needs and your needs" and "recognise boundaries between yourself and others" (the two highest-scoring items). With respect to countertransference management, participants indicated that their personal and professional issues seldom, or occasionally, affected their practice. When issues did arise, participants would most likely attempt to resolve them on their own or talk with colleagues. Respondents were less likely to seek supervision or engage in individual counselling. Across the sample, 50 per cent had had one to five supervision sessions in the previous 12 months. A further 31 per cent indicated they had not received any supervision. These results parallel other findings suggesting that sport psychologists do not regularly engage in supervision (Watson *et al.*, 2004). The findings also indicate that practitioners may be hesitant to seek counselling for their own issues. Individual counselling and supervision are the two strategies professionals suggest are suitable for recognising and managing countertransference, and for consultant development more generally (Petitpas *et al.*, 1999; Van Raalte and Andersen, 2000; Winstone and Gervis, 2006). Research investigating the reasons why practitioners do not engage in regular supervision or seek individual counselling, when these activities are likely to offer benefits, may help to identify ways to encourage consultants to include these strategies as part of their professional development.

Erotic transference

Perhaps even more so than transference and countertransference, there has been limited discussion and few investigations on erotic transference in the literature. Until recently, erotic transference and sexual/romantic exchanges between sport psychologists and athletes, if acknowledged, were typically mentioned as subtopics of broader areas such as the transference–countertransference configuration or ethics, and generally there has been a heterosexual flavour to the material (Henschen, 1991; Yambor and Connelly, 1991). For example, Petitpas *et al.* (1994) included items related to sexual attraction to clients and romantic involvement with them after discontinuing a professional relationship in their ethics survey of Association of Applied Sport Psychology (AASP) members. Few respondents admitted to being sexually attracted to clients or becoming involved with them after terminating the professional relationship. Also, participants identified both items as controversial behaviours. In a later survey of AASP members, males and certified consultants were more likely to admit to being sexually attracted to clients than were females and non-certified practitioners (Etzel *et al.*, 2004). The group means, however, indicated that most participants suggested they were rarely attracted to their clients. Results also suggested that participants considered being sexually attracted towards clients was a controversial topic, and becoming involved with athletes before or after finishing a professional relationship was a rare behaviour.

As the primary focus of interest, literature on erotic transference and sexual interactions has begun to appear (sporadically) in the past 15 years. Petrie and Buntrock (1995) published a conference abstract of a study among AASP members, and 4 per cent of male respondents admitted to having been sexually involved with a client (the figure was much lower for females). More recently, Petrie *et al.* (2005) found that about 35 per cent of female and 45 per cent of male sport psychologists had been sexually attracted to clients. Few participants had acted on those attractions or had sought supervision to help them manage their feelings. It is probable that results from the various surveys underreport the extent to which practitioners are attracted to clients. Andersen and Stevens (Andersen, 2005a; Stevens and Andersen, 2007b), for instance, have detailed why erotic transference and sexual attraction and behaviour will likely occur in applied sport psychology. Consultants have close, and sometimes intimate, contact with athletes, and, as a population, their clients are young, athletic, attractive, and outgoing. In addition, athletes may find that practitioners are the only caring and non-judgemental individuals involved in their sports, which itself can be attractive. It is encouraging, however, that there is a huge difference between the numbers of consultants admitting to attraction and those acting on their desires. The different percentages between being attracted towards clients and acting on those emotions may provide evidence that most practitioners avoid giving their desires free reign, although such indiscretions do occur.

To illustrate erotic transference in the sport psychology context, Stevens and Andersen (2007a) have published case studies of two practitioners. These two case studies revealed how practitioners may either deny and repress their erotic feelings, or become overwhelmed and act out on their desires. Although it may be easy to accuse practitioners of unethical and dangerous behaviour, Stevens and Andersen (2007a) observed that often consultants may be unable to recognise and manage their erotic thoughts and feelings. Although there is a lack of research, it is likely that erotic material is seldom discussed in training or supervision, beyond the citing of ethical codes that prohibit sexual conduct among practitioners and clients (Whelan, n.d.). Supervisors, teachers, and practitioners may avoid discussing erotic material with others. Sport psychology professionals may fear that discussing their sexual attraction towards clients will raise suspicions about their ethics, motives, and behaviours (Andersen, 2005a). Emotions of anxiety, guilt, and confusion may also be present. In a culture of denial and avoidance, new practitioners may leave their training programmes unprepared for a phenomenon that seems likely to occur sooner or later.

Professional practice literature

Professional practice literature, in which authors reflect on their consulting experiences, provides another source from which knowledge about sport psychology working alliances may be gleaned (e.g. Tod, 2009). For example, a number of case studies have been published in texts such as *Doing Sport Psychology* (Andersen, 2000b) and *Sport Psychology in Practice* (Andersen, 2005b). Most authors contributing to these books presented dialogue from actual practitioner–client interactions, along with their interpretations. By documenting consultant–athlete interactions, readers are able to compare authors' interpretations with their own (Murphy, 2000). The chapters illustrated many relationship-related issues arising in service delivery, often not well addressed in other types of articles. For example, Marchant (2000) presented, in a diary format, the process by which he used goal-setting in professional Australian Rules football. The case study illustrated how good working alliances assisted goal-setting intervention effectiveness. Other factors that influenced goal-setting implementation included clients' personalities and resistances, along with consultants' characteristics, including (a) their abilities to manage their overall workloads, (b) their confidence to be open and honest with athletes about sensitive information, and (c) their capacities to respond to athletes' pressing issues.

In many professional practice articles, authors do not specifically examine the relationships, thoughts, feelings, and behaviours that have occurred during athlete interactions. Instead, authors often describe their consulting experiences and present lessons they have learned. Examples include the articles focused on services delivered at the Seoul and Calgary Olympic Games, published in the 1989 third issue of *The Sport Psychologist*. Additional examples include the articles published in the 1990 fourth issue of *The Sport Psychologist*, where the focus was on consultation experiences with professional athletes. Morris and Thomas (2004) examined the articles in the 1989 and 1990 issues of *The Sport Psychologist*, and observed that practitioners typically adopted educational stances and taught athletes psychological skills for performance enhancement purposes. Crisis intervention and personal counselling occupied subsidiary roles for practitioners. In addition, the majority of practitioners did not use standardised psychological tests, and described themselves as following flexible approaches to helping athletes rather than adhering to structured models. Also, although a number of the practitioners suggested that psychological skills needed to be integrated with training and mastered before athletes reached elite levels, they seldom detailed how psychological skills were applied in competition. Neither did authors discuss how they resolved any service delivery challenges they encountered.

Although to date applied sport psychologists have not written a great deal about their working alliances, the professional practice literature may be a potentially rich source of information about practitioner–athlete relationships, as illustrated in Andersen's (2000b, 2005b) edited books along with Hay's (2009) recent text on performance psychology. Practitioners who write and reflect on their client relationships provide stories that may assist others in examining their own service delivery practices. For example, readers may become aware of the possible obstacles to effective working alliances, or increase their awareness of their own countertransferences.

Implications for professional practice

Orlinsky *et al.* (2001) surveyed over 4,000 mainstream practitioners from more than 14 countries about the people, events, and objects that influenced their professional development. The influences considered to have made the greatest contributions to development included (in descending order of the importance attached to them by the practitioners): client interactions, supervision, personal therapy, life experience, collegial interactions, workshops and courses, theory and research, and being a supervisor. The ordering of the list seems to make intuitive sense. Most of the influences involve interactions with other people, except the items relating to (a) workshops and courses, and (b) theory and research. Items higher up the list have greater similarities with service delivery activities than those further down the list. Using Orlinsky *et al.*'s (2001) list of influential sources as subheadings, we present ideas below that may assist practitioners and trainees as they focus on developing relationship-building skills.

The extent to which the ideas presented below might contribute to practitioners' knowledge and abilities to develop and maintain effective athlete relationships may be enhanced through reflective practice. In recent years, literature on reflective practice in sport psychology has blossomed, and evidence is accumulating that such behaviour contributes to professional competence (Anderson *et al.*, 2004b; Cropley *et al.*, 2007; see also Chapter 12 in this volume). The accumulating evidence in sport psychology literature has parallels with similar observations present in educational and counselling psychology research, in which self-reflection and active experimentation together contribute to learning (Kolb *et al.*, 2001; Rønnestad and Skovholt, 2003). Anderson *et al.* (2004b) presented a series of questions, under the headings of *description of consulting experience, reflection, consequences of actions, alternative tactics*, and *learning*, to help practitioners reflect on their consulting experiences. The questions Anderson *et al.* (2004b) presented may help consultants reflect on their athlete relationships, either in supervision or by keeping a reflective journal.

Client interactions

Among an array of other benefits, both practitioners and educators have identified that client interactions help individuals learn about the role of relationships in applied sport psychology and aid in developing interpersonal skills (Tod *et al.*, 2007). Considerable variation exists across organisations and countries with respect to the amount of practical client experience needed to obtain professional qualifications (Morris *et al.*, 2003; Tod and Lavallee, 2011). Counsellor- and expertise-development models indicate that thousands of hours of practice, typically across several years, are needed for individuals to become highly adept at the helping process (Jennings *et al.*, 2005; Rønnestad and Skovholt, 2003). Given the tremendous variation that exists in humans, and the interactions they have with each other, it is understandable that it may take considerable experience before sport psychologists have the abilities to build and maintain effective working alliances with the different athletes with whom they will work and types of issues with which clients present.

In some situations practitioners may not be ready or able to engage in actual client interaction, such as when trainees are having difficulty controlling their anxieties about working with athletes; when practitioners do not have the necessary knowledge and skills to help individuals with specific issues; and when consultants' own issues interfere with their abilities to assist (Andersen *et al.*, 2000; Tod *et al.*, 2009). In these circumstances, role-plays may help practitioners begin to control their emotions or develop their needed competencies. Opportunities for practitioners to examine and develop their counselling and relationship-based skills and attributes arise when they participate fully in role-plays. Consultants and educators have reported that individuals may become so immersed in role-plays that their own needs and typical ways of responding begin to surface (Tod *et al.*, 2007). In reflecting on such situations, for example, practitioners might identify ways their own countertransference material may arise when working with athletes. Awareness of the psychotherapy process literature may assist practitioners, supervisors, and educators in setting up role-plays in which relationships issues and strains are likely to emerge as participants become immersed in their roles. Third parties, such as supervisors or other practitioners, may view role-plays in action, and consultants might find the prospect of being evaluated anxiety-provoking. Possible ways to help individuals manage their anxieties and other emotions are available, such as reducing the number of observers or allowing breaks during role-plays (Tod, 2007b).

Supervision

Supervision provides opportunities for practitioners to gain understanding about how they relate to athletes and coaches, and how their needs, desires, and histories influence working alliances (Van Raalte and Andersen, 2000). Supervisors may help supervisees use many of the strategies discussed in this section to assist in the development of relationship-building skills and knowledge, such as suggesting suitable literature and training workshops, setting up role-plays, and providing opportunities for self-reflection. The extent to which practitioners are able to explore professional relationship issues may depend on the supervision model supervisors adopt. For example, the relationship between the supervisee and supervisor is a central issue in psychodynamic supervision approaches (Van Raalte and Andersen, 2000). Psychodynamic adherents believe that how supervisees relate to their supervisors may have some connections to their relationships with athletes. Examining the supervisor–supervisee relationship may help unearth what practitioners bring to their client interactions and provide insight into the dynamics of their service delivery relationships. The discussion in this type of supervision, however, is typically on the practitioner–athlete relationship and how supervisees relate to their clients. Other supervision models may emphasise relationship issues less, such as in cognitive-behavioural approaches, when the discussion may be more technique-based and focused on helping supervisees' master interventions they will use with athletes.

Practitioner development research provides evidence that trainees are initially focused on learning interventions they perceive will help provide solutions to clients' issues, such as goal-setting, relaxation, or imagery (Tod *et al.*, 2009). Such a focus may reflect their doubts about their abilities to help clients beyond psychological skills training, and their need to find justification for their involvement with athletes. Once practitioners have mastered a range of interventions, they may then be in positions to focus on examining how their own issues influence working alliances (e.g. countertransference) and learning relationship-building skills. Psychodynamic models of supervision may be better suited to advanced trainees or qualified practitioners (Van Raalte and Andersen, 2000).

Personal therapy

A number of authors have advocated the various benefits practitioners gain when they undertake personal counselling, in terms of both resolving their own issues and developing professional competencies (Andersen *et al.*, 2000; Petitpas *et al.*, 1999; Tod, 2010; Winstone and Gervis, 2006). Petitpas *et al.* (1999), for instance, suggested that by being a client, practitioners gain a greater understanding of the consultant–athlete relationship and a better appreciation for how their values, needs, and concerns influence client interactions. Longitudinal studies of practitioners provide support for this suggestion. For example, in a recent two-year case study, a female practitioner discussed how, through personal counselling, she had learned a great deal about empathy and what it was like to sit in the client's chair (Tod and Bond, 2010). She also had learned about how she influenced working alliances with her clients.

The number of sport psychology training programmes that require or strongly encourage students to undertake personal therapy is unknown, but they are likely to be relatively few (Andersen *et al.*, 2000). Also, the number of practitioners who have sought counselling for personal issues or to enhance self-knowledge has not been studied directly, but indirect evidence indicates that the proportion could be low (Winstone and Gervis, 2006). Many sport psychologists have been competitive athletes themselves, and perhaps some have been influenced by the "tough guy" attitudes present in the sporting context. If so, these individuals may have difficulty in seeking personal therapy, despite working in a helping discipline. Making counselling an encouraged option, as part of training, the attainment of professional qualifications (e.g. licensure, accreditation, registration), or continued professional development, may help to communicate the value of personal self-examination.

Reflecting on life experiences

Both mainstream and sport psychology professionals have indicated that social interactions outside of service delivery can contribute to professional competence (Tod *et al.*, 2007). Potentially, any interaction with another person provides practitioners with opportunities to learn about relationships, how they react to others, how other people view them, and ways of connecting to clients. For example, being cut from a sports team, as a player or the sport psychologist, affords practitioners a chance to reflect on the ways they react to their own and others' disappointments. From such reflections, practitioners may enhance their empathy and other facilitative characteristics that allow them to connect deeply with clients. In other interpersonal interactions, practitioners might practise or experiment with relationship-building skills, such as active listening and empathetic reflection. These experiences do not need to be sport related. Athletes present with a wide range of issues that non-athletes experience, such as mental health problems, death of loved ones, interpersonal and relationship difficulties, racism, sexism, homophobia, and other forms of discrimination. Reflections on their experiences with these issues outside of sport will likely assist practitioners when athletes raise them in service delivery.

Collegial interactions

Junior and senior sport psychologists have identified numerous benefits that collegial interactions have for their professional competence and motivation (Simons and Andersen, 1995; Tod *et al.*, 2009). With respect to their athlete relationships, practitioners can discuss cases with peers to help them reflect and identify ways to develop and maintain working alliances. In addition, practitioners might also establish peer supervision dyads or groups. In peer supervision, examining how consultants interact with each other might yield insights into how they react to clients, and how athletes might react to them.

Workshops, seminars, and training courses

In addition to providing training about service delivery issues (including relationships), workshops, seminars, and other short courses may offer practitioners opportunities to engage in role plays and other types of simulated service delivery. These simulations are typically conducted in group settings where other practitioners may be present. Evidence indicates that applied psychologists perceive such situations to be useful because they are able to share and compare ideas, learn alternative ways of interacting with clients, and get feedback on their own behaviours (Kolb *et al.*, 2001; Tod and Bond, 2010).

Theory and research

Orlinsky *et al.*'s (2001) results indicated that practitioners typically consider theory and research to be less influential than the other sources of information discussed above, a finding that has also emerged in sport psychology investigations (Tod and Bond, 2010). Practitioners may doubt the relevance of much research for their situations, such as laboratory studies or when samples consist of undergraduate students (Stewart and Chambless, 2007; Tod *et al.*, 2007). Also, researchers do not often present their findings in ways that assist practitioners in applying them to their situations, such as reporting results in meaningful metrics (Andersen *et al.*, 2007). Practitioners do appear to value literature that they can apply to their specific circumstances (Tod *et al.*, 2009), and there are books, chapters, and articles that deal with relationships in service delivery. Examples include Norcross' (2002) edited book, *Psychotherapy Relationships that Work*, which emerged from an American Psychological Association Division of Psychotherapy Task Force commissioned to identify, operationalise, and disseminate information on evidence-based therapy relationships. The Task Force also published their findings in issue 4, volume 38 of *Psychotherapy* (2001).

Practitioners have indicated they also find non-research literature helpful in developing relationship-building abilities. In Tod *et al.* (2009), for example, inexperienced practitioners reported finding helpful textbooks and articles that discussed frameworks and suitable ways to communicate with clients (e.g. Egan, 2009). Once these practitioners had gained some client experience, they began to read literature on case studies of actual service delivery taking place, which was helpful in reflecting on their own client interactions (e.g. Andersen, 2000b; Yalom, 1999).

Being a supervisor

Practitioners who have suitable experience and qualifications may find that supervising others stimulates professional growth (Rønnestad and Skovholt, 2003). Supervising other consultants may help practitioners reflect on their own client relationships and interpersonal skills. Such reflection might assist practitioners in uncovering blind spots about their own relationship-building knowledge and skills.

Possible future research directions

As illustrated above, despite isolated exceptions: (a) there is a small body of literature in which authors discuss the sport psychologist–athlete relationship; (b) much of the existing work consists of opinion, discussion, and review papers, rather than traditional scientific or experimental reports; and (c) investigations have proceeded along several different lines of inquiry. There are benefits to developing the area, such as providing practitioners, trainees, educators, and supervisors with information they can use to help them develop their own, or others', service delivery practices. Given the scattered and unreplicated avenues along which investigators have proceeded to date, researchers might advance current understanding by establishing sustained research programmes that result in a series of related studies being published on a topic. Individuals might find it easier to establish research programmes if they draw on relevant theory to underpin their work. For example, sport psychology researchers can draw on Bordin's (1994) theory to guide investigations on the working alliance. Similarly, psychotherapy theory on the real relationship or the transference–countertransference configuration may provide foundations for researchers examining these topics in an applied sport psychology context.

In addition to drawing on relevant theory, understanding the types of process research that clinical and counselling psychology investigators undertake may help professionals in sport psychology design rigorous and sound methods with which to answer their research questions (e.g. Barkham, 2003; McLeod, 2003). For example, some researchers conducting psychotherapy process studies observe variables related to therapist–client interactions. Orlinsky *et al.* (1994) proposed one taxonomy of such variables, with six categories labelled *therapeutic contracts, therapeutic operations, therapeutic bonds, participant self-relatedness, in-session impacts,* and *sequential flow.* Therapeutic contract variables involve the aims, tasks, formats, and settings of psychotherapy. Examples of therapeutic contract variables include the goals of therapy, the duration of sessions, and the frequency of consultations. The therapeutic operations category involves factors related to therapists' and clients' actions during therapy; examples include problem presentation, therapist interventions, and patient cooperation. Therapeutic bond variables involve the interpersonal connections between practitioners and clients. Examples of such variables include personal role investment, interactive coordination, and mutual affect. The participant self-relatedness category involves variables associated with the ways individuals respond to their own cognitions and emotions; examples include: therapist self-congruence, patient openness, and client self-acceptance. In-session impact variables are connected with the ways participants are influenced during psychotherapy; examples include insight, catharsis, and hope. Sequential flow variables reflect how sessions or courses of treatments develop over time. Examples of sequential flow variables include: session development, stages in psychotherapy, and treatment duration.

When designing process-oriented studies, investigators often observe actual psychotherapeutic service delivery. Researchers consider a variety of observable events, temporal units, participants, and psychotherapy data collection methods when designing studies to understand the process of service delivery (Orlinsky, 2001). In addition to measuring events that occur during psychotherapy, such as verbal statements and non-verbal behaviours, researchers assess those that take place before and after therapeutic consultations. Examples include clients' pre-therapy expectations and perceptions of therapists' helpfulness. Regarding temporal units, investigators measure events that occur quickly (e.g. facial expressions) and those that take place more slowly (e.g. clients' responses to therapists' interventions). Process-oriented researchers gather data from therapists, clients, independent observers (e.g. supervisors), or any combination of the three. Although self-report questionnaires are frequently used, investigators also electronically record therapy sessions (with participants' permission). Understanding how process-oriented psychotherapy research is conducted can assist applied sport psychology investigators in designing studies on the thoughts, feelings, and behaviours occurring when practitioners interact with athletes.

With guidance from clinical and counselling psychology theory, along with an appreciation of process research, sport psychology investigators may be well positioned to answer a range of questions related to the athlete–practitioner relationship. One group of questions focuses on practitioner–athlete interaction outcomes. For example, in what ways do athlete–practitioner relationships shape and influence service delivery outcomes? How do specific components, such as the working alliance, transference, countertransference, and the real relationship, influence consulting outcomes, such as enhanced client happiness, interpersonal functioning, and well-being, both independently and in interaction with each other? A second group of questions deals with the antecedents that predict or influence practitioner–athlete relationships. Example variables that could be measured include attachment style, athletes' presenting issues, self-awareness, and consultant self-disclosure. A third group of questions focuses on understanding the relationship components. For example, researchers might explore how transference and countertransference is expressed and managed in sport psychology consulting. Documenting the typical relationship strains that occur and are repaired may also advance understanding.

The small number of individuals who label themselves as sport psychologists is one possible obstacle to conducting research. In comparison with related practitioners, such as counselling psychologists, and sport-related professions such as athletic trainers, and strength and conditioning specialists, there are relatively few full-time sport psychologists (Andersen, 2009). If researchers, however, focused instead on psychology practitioners who work with athletes, a different possibility emerges, because there are many professionals from a number of mental health care professions who assist sport participants (Hanrahan and Andersen, 2010). Adopting a broader definition of practitioner may also allow insights into the similarities between sport and other types of applied psychology work.

Conclusions

If applied sport psychology were likened to a meal, then the literature gives the impression that the main course represents the interventions used in service delivery, and the relationships consultants build with clients are the condiments that add flavour and depth. An inspection of the literature, however, reveals divided opinion regarding the evidence that the typical applied sport psychology interventions (i.e. psychological skills training) enhance competitive performance (Gardner and Moore, 2006; Martin *et al.*, 2005). Also, enhancing performance is not the only goal athletes have when seeking assistance from sport psychologists. As an alternative and broader perspective, effective service delivery results from moving away from an overemphasis on interventions and giving greater consideration to the other components: the consulting relationship, along with practitioners' and athletes' intra- and interpersonal attributes. Although there are few set recipes for managing relationships and working alliances, there are chefs, cookbooks, and cooking classes available to assist sport psychologists in developing their competencies so they can connect with athletes in ways that help clients resolve their issues and attain positive service delivery results.

References

Ahn, H. and Wampold, B. E. (2001). Where oh where are the specific ingredients? A meta-analysis of component studies in counselling and psychotherapy. *Journal of Counselling Psychology*, 48, 251–257.

Andersen, M. B. (2000a). Beginnings: Intakes and the initiation of relationships. In M. B. Andersen (ed.), *Doing sport psychology* (pp. 3–16). Champaign, IL: Human Kinetics.

Andersen, M. B. (ed.), (2000b). *Doing sport psychology*. Champaign, IL: Human Kinetics.

Andersen, M. B. (2004). Transference and countertransference. In G. S. Kolt and M. B. Andersen (eds), *Psychology in the physical and manual therapies* (pp. 71–80). Edinburgh, UK: Churchill Livingstone.

Andersen, M. B. (2005a). Touching taboos: Sex and the sport psychologist. In M. B. Andersen (ed.), *Sport psychology in practice* (pp. 171–191). Champaign, IL: Human Kinetics.

Andersen, M. B. (ed.), (2005b). *Sport psychology in practice.* Champaign, IL: Human Kinetics.

Andersen, M. B. (2006). It's all about sport performance ... and something else. In J. Dosil (ed.), *The sport psychologist's handbook: A guide for sport-specific performance enhancement* (pp. 687–698). Chichester, UK: Wiley.

Andersen, M. B. (2009). Performance enhancement as a bad start and a dead end: A parenthetical comment on Mellalieu and Lane. *The Sport and Exercise Scientist*, 20, 12–14.

Andersen, M. B. (2011). Who's mental? Who's tough? and Who's both?: Mutton constructs dressed up as lamb. In S. Gordon and D. Gucciardi (eds), *Mental toughness in sport: Developments in research and theory* (in press, pp. 66–85), London, UK: Routledge.

Andersen, M. B. and Williams-Rice, B. T. (1996). Supervision in the education and training of sport psychology service providers. *The Sport Psychologist*, 10, 278–290.

Andersen, M. B., McCullagh, P., and Wilson, G. J. (2007). But what do the numbers really tell us? Arbitrary metrics and effect size reporting in sport psychology research. *Journal of Sport and Exercise Psychology*, 29, 664–672.

Andersen, M. B., Van Raalte, J. L., and Brewer, B. W. (2000). When sport psychology consultants and graduate students are impaired: Ethical and legal issues in training and supervision. *Journal of Applied Sport Psychology*, 12, 134–150.

Anderson, A. G., Knowles, Z., and Gilbourne, D. (2004b). Reflective practice for sport psychologists: Concepts, models, practical implications, and thoughts on dissemination. *The Sport Psychologist*, 18, 188–203.

Anderson, A. G., Miles, A., Robinson, P., and Mahoney, C. (2004a). Evaluating the athlete's perception of the sport psychologist's effectiveness: What should we be assessing? *Psychology of Sport and Exercise*, 5, 255–277.

Barkham, M. (2003). Quantitative research on psychotherapeutic interventions: Methods and findings across four research generations. In R. Woolfe, W. Dryden and S. Strawbridge (eds), *Handbook of counselling psychology* (2nd edn, pp. 25–73). London, UK: Sage.

Bordin, E. S. (1979). The generalisability of the psychoanalytic concept of the working alliance. *Psychotherapy: Theory, Research and Practice*, 16, 252–260.

Bordin, E. S. (1983). A working alliance based model of supervision. *The Counselling Psychologist*, 11, 35–42.

Bordin, E. S. (1994). Theory and research on the therapeutic working alliance: New directions. In A. O. Horvath and L. S. Greenberg (eds), *The working alliance: Theory, research, and practice* (pp. 13–37). Chichester, UK: Wiley.

Breuer, J. and Freud, S. (1893–1895). Studies on hysteria'; trans. J. Strachey (1966). *The standard edition of the complete psychological works of Sigmund Freud* (Vol. 2, pp. 3–335). London, UK: Hogarth Press.

Calhoun, J. W., Herring, K. M., and Iadevito, T. L. (2005). Systemic issues involved in working with professional sports teams. *Clinics in Sports Medicine*, 24, 929–942.

Conroy, D. E. and Benjamin, L. S (2001). Psychodynamics in sport performance enhancement consultation: Application of an interpersonal theory. *The Sport Psychologist*, 15, 103–117.

Cropley, B., Miles, A., Hanton, S., and Niven, A. (2007). Improving the delivery of applied sport psychology support through reflective practice. *The Sport Psychologist*, 21, 475–494.

Dunn, J. G. H. and Holt, N. L. (2003). Collegiate ice hockey players' perceptions of the delivery of an applied sport psychology program. *The Sport Psychologist*, 17, 351–368.

Egan, G. (2009). *The skilled helper: A problem-management and opportunity-development approach to helping* (9th edn). Belmont, CA: Wadsworth.

Ellis, A. (2000). Rational emotive behaviour therapy. In R. J. Corsini and D. Wedding (eds), *Current psychotherapies* (6th edn, pp. 168–204). Itasca, IL: F. E. Peacock.

Etzel, E. F., Watson, J. C., II, and Zizzi, S. (2004). A web-based survey of AAASP members' ethical beliefs and behaviours in the new millennium. *Journal of Applied Sport Psychology*, 16, 236–250.

Freud, S. (1912). The dynamics of transference'; trans. J. Strachey (1958). *The standard edition of the complete psychological works of Sigmund Freud* (Vol. 12, pp. 99–108). London, UK: Hogarth Press.

Gardner, F. and Moore, Z. (2006). *Clinical sport psychology*. Champaign, IL: Human Kinetics.

Gelso, C. J. (2009). The real relationship in a postmodern world: Theoretical and empirical explorations. *Psychotherapy Research*, 19, 253–264.

Gelso, C. J. and Carter, J. A. (1985). The relationship in counselling and psychotherapy: Components, consequences, and theoretical antecedents. *The Counselling Psychologist*, 13, 155–243.

Gelso, C. J. and Carter, J. A. (1994). Components of the psychotherapy relationship: Their interaction and unfolding during treatment. *Journal of Counselling Psychology*, 41, 296–306.

Gelso, C. J. and Hayes, J. A. (1998). *The psychotherapy relationship: Theory, research, and practice*. New York, NY: Wiley.

Gelso, C. J. and Samstag, L. W. (2008). A tripartite model of the therapeutic relationship. In S. D. Brown and R. W. Lent (eds), *Handbook of counselling psychology* (4th edn, pp. 267–283). Hoboken, NJ: Wiley.

Gentner, N. B., Fisher, L. A., and Wrisberg, C. A. (2004). Athletes' and coaches' perceptions of sport psychology services offered by graduate students at one NCAA Division I university. *Psychological Reports*, 94, 213–216.

Giges, B. (1998). Psychodynamic concepts in sport psychology: Comment on Strean and Strean (1998). *The Sport Psychologist*, 12, 223–227.

Gould, D., Murphy, S., Tammen, V., and May, J. (1991). An evaluation of US Olympic sport psychology consultant effectiveness. *The Sport Psychologist*, 5, 111–127.

Gould, D., Tammen, V., Murphy, S., and May, J. (1989). An examination of US Olympic sport psychology consultants and the services they provide. *The Sport Psychologist*, 3, 300–312.

Greenberg, L. S. (1994). What is "real" in the relationship? Comment on Gelso and Carter (1994). *Journal of Counselling Psychology*, 41, 307–309.

Greenson, R. R. (1967). *The technique and practice of psychoanalysis* (Vol. 1). New York, NY: International Universities Press.

Grencavage, L. M. and Norcross, J. C. (1990). Where are the commonalities among the therapeutic common factors? *Professional Psychology: Research and Practice*, 21, 372–378.

Hanrahan, S. J. and Andersen, M. B. (2010). Preface. In S. J. Hanrahan and M. B. Andersen (eds), *Routledge handbook of applied sport psychology: A comprehensive guide for students and practitioners* (pp. xiii-xv). London, UK: Routledge.

Hatcher, R. L. (2009). Considering the real relationship: Reaction to Gelso's "The real relationship in a postmodern world: Theoretical and empirical explorations". *Psychotherapy Research*, 19, 269–272.

Hays, K. F. (ed.), (2009). *Performance psychology in action: A casebook for working with athletes, performing artists, business leaders, and professionals in high-risk occupations.* Washington, DC: American Psychological Association.

Henschen, K. (1991). Critical issues involving male consultants and female athletes. *The Sport Psychologist*, 5, 313–321.

Hill, K. L. (2001). *Frameworks for sport psychologists: Enhancing sport performance.* Champaign, IL: Human Kinetics.

Horvath, A. O. (2001). The alliance. *Psychotherapy*, 38, 365–372.

Horvath, A. O. (2009). How *real* is the "real relationship"? *Psychotherapy Research*, 19, 273–277.

Horvath, A. O. and Bedi, R. P. (2002). The alliance. In J. C. Norcross (ed.), *Psychotherapy relationships that work: Therapist contributions and responsiveness to patients* (pp. 37–69). New York, NY: Oxford University Press.

Horvath, A. O. and Symonds, B. D. (1991). Relation between working alliance and outcome in psychotherapy: A meta-analysis. *Journal of Counselling Psychology*, 38, 139–149.

Imel, Z. E. and Wampold, B. E. (2008). The importance of treatment and the science of common factors in psychotherapy. In S. D. Brown and R. W. Lent (eds), *Handbook of counselling psychology* (4th edn, pp. 249–266). Hoboken, NJ: Wiley.

Jennings, L., Hanson, M., Skovholt, T. M., and Grier, T. (2005). Searching for mastery. *Journal of Mental Health Counselling*, 27, 19–31.

Katz, J. (2009). Role development and delivery of sport psychology at the Paralympic Games. In B. Hemmings and T. Holder (eds), *Applied sport psychology: A case-based approach* (pp. 183–201). Oxford, UK: Wiley.

Kazdin, A. E. (2007). Mediators and mechanisms of change in psychotherapy research. *Annual Review of Clinical Psychology*, 3, 1–27.

Kolb, D. A., Boyatzis, R. E., and Mainemelis, C. (2001). Experiential learning theory: Previous research and new directions. In R. J. Sternberg and L. F. Zhang (eds), *Perspectives on thinking, learning, and cognitive styles* (pp. 227–247). Mahwah, NJ: Erlbaum.

Lambert, M. J. and Barley, D. E. (2002). Research summary on the therapeutic relationship and psychotherapy outcome. In J. C. Norcross (ed.), *Psychotherapy relationships that work: Therapist contributions and responsiveness to patients* (pp. 17–32). New York, NY: Oxford University Press.

Lambert, M. J. and Ogles, B. M. (2004). The efficacy and effectiveness of psychotherapy. In M. J. Lambert (ed.), *Bergin and Garfield's handbook of psychotherapy and behaviour change* (5th edn, pp. 139–193). New York, NY: Wiley.

Lloyd, R. J. and Trudel, P. (1999). Verbal interactions between an eminent mental training consultant and elite level athletes: A case study. *The Sport Psychologist*, 13, 418–443.

Lubker, J. R., Visek, A. J., Geer, J. R., and Watson, J. C., II (2008). Characteristics of an effective sport psychology consultant: Perspectives from athletes and consultants. *Journal of Sport Behaviour*, 31, 147–165.

Marchant, D. B. (2000). Targeting futures: Goal setting for professional sports. In M. B. Andersen (ed.), *Doing sport psychology* (pp. 93–103). Champaign, IL: Human Kinetics.

Martin, D. J., Garske, J. P., and Davis, M. K. (2000). Relation of the therapeutic alliance with outcome and other variables: A meta-analytic review. *Journal of Consulting and Clinical Psychology*, 68, 438–450.

Martin, G. L., Vause, T., and Schwartzman, L. (2005). Experimental studies of psychological interventions with athletes in competitions: Why so few?' *Behavior Modification*, 29, 616–641.

McCullough, L. (2009). The challenge of distinguishing figure from ground: Reaction to Gelso's work on the real relationship. *Psychotherapy Research*, 19, 265–268.

McLeod, J. (2003). Qualitative research methods in counselling psychology. In R. Woolfe, W. Dryden, and S. Strawbridge (eds), *Handbook of counselling psychology* (2nd edn, pp. 74–92). London, UK: Sage.

Meyers, A. W., Whelan, J. P., and Murphy, S. M. (1996). Cognitive behavioural strategies in athletic performance enhancement. In M. Hersen, R. M. Eisler, and P. M. Miller (eds), *Progress in behaviour modification* (Vol. 30, pp. 137–164). Pacific Grove, CA: Brooks/Cole.

Morris, T. and Thomas, P. (2004). Applied sport psychology. In T. Morris and J. Summers (eds), *Sport psychology: Theory, applications and issues* (2nd edn, pp. 236–277). Milton, QLD, Australia: Wiley.

Morris, T., Alfermann, D., Lintunen, T., and Hall, H. (2003). Training and selection of sport psychologists: An international review. *International Journal of Sport and Exercise Psychology*, 1, 139–154.

Murphy, S. M. (2000). Afterword. In M. B. Andersen (ed.), *Doing sport psychology* (pp. 275–279). Champaign, IL: Human Kinetics.

Norcross, J. C. (ed.), (2002). *Psychotherapy relationships that work: Therapist contributions and responsiveness to patients*. New York, NY: Oxford University Press.

Orlick, T. (1989). Reflections on sportpsych consulting with individual and team sport athletes at summer and winter Olympic games. *The Sport Psychologist*, 3, 358–365.

Orlick, T. (1996). The wheel of excellence. *Journal of Performance Education*, 1, 3–18.

Orlick, T. and Partington, J. (1987). The sport psychology consultant: Analysis of critical components as viewed by Canadian Olympic athletes. *The Sport Psychologist*, 1, 4–17.

Orlinsky, D. E. (2001). Psychotherapy process research. *International encyclopedia of the social and behavioural sciences* (Vol. 18, pp. 12499–12504). Oxford, UK: Elsevier.

Orlinsky, D. E., Botermans, J. F., Rønnestad, M. H., and The SPR Collaborative Research Network (2001). Towards an empirically grounded model of psychotherapy training: Four thousand therapists rate influences on their development. *Australian Psychologist*, 36, 139–148.

Orlinsky, D. E., Grawe, K., and Parks, B. K. (1994). Process and outcome in psychotherapy – noch einmal. In A. E. Bergin and S. L. Garfield (eds), *Handbook of psychotherapy and behaviour change* (4th edn, pp. 270–376). New York, NY: Wiley.

Orlinsky, D. E., Rønnestad, M. H., and Willutzki, U. (2004). Fifty years of psychotherapy process-outcome research: Continuity and change. In M. J. Lambert (ed.), *Bergin and Garfield's handbook of psychotherapy and behaviour change* (5th edn, pp. 307–389). New York, NY: Wiley.

Partington, J. and Orlick, T. (1987a). The sport psychology consultant evaluation form. *The Sport Psychologist*, 1, 309–317.

Partington, J. and Orlick, T. (1987b). The sport psychology consultant: Olympic coaches' views. *The Sport Psychologist*, 1, 95–102.

Partington, J. and Orlick, T. (1991). An analysis of Olympic sport psychology consultants' best-ever consulting experiences. *The Sport Psychologist*, 5, 183–193.

Patton, M. J. (1994). Components of the counselling relationship – An evolving model: Comment on Gelso and Carter (1994). *Journal of Counselling Psychology*, 41, 310–312.

Petitpas, A. J., Brewer, B. W., Rivera, P. M., and Van Raalte, J. L. (1994). Ethical beliefs and behaviours in applied sport psychology: The AAASP ethics survey. *Journal of Applied Sport Psychology*, 6, 135–151.

Petitpas, A. J., Giges, B., and Danish, S. J. (1999). The sport psychologist-athlete relationship: Implications for training. *The Sport Psychologist*, 13, 344–357.

Petrie, T. and Buntrock, C. (1995). Sexual attraction and the profession of sport psychology. *Journal of Applied Sport Psychology*, 7(Suppl.): S98.

Petrie, T., Tebbe, C., and Greenleaf, C. (2005). Sport psychologists' sexual and nonsexual boundary violations with client-athletes. In T. Morris, P. Terry, S. Gordon, S. J. Hanrahan, L. Ievleva, G. Kolt, and P. Tremayne (eds), *ISSP 11th world congress of sport psychology: Promoting health and performance for life, CD-ROM*. Sydney, NSW, Australia: International Society of Sport Psychology.

Poczwardowski, A., Sherman, C. P., and Henschen, K. P. (1998). A sport psychology service delivery heuristic: Building on theory and practice. *The Sport Psychologist*, 12, 191–207.

Price, F. L. and Andersen, M. B. (2000). Into the maelstrom: A five-year relationship from college ball to the NFL. In M. B. Andersen (ed.), *Doing sport psychology* (pp. 193–206), Champaign, IL: Human kinetics.

Rogers, C. R. (1957). The necessary and sufficient conditions of therapeutic personality change. *Journal of Consulting Psychology*, 21, 95–103.

Rønnestad, M. H. and Skovholt, T. M. (2003). The journey of the counsellor and therapist: Research findings and perspectives on professional development' *Journal of Career Development*, 30, 5–44.

Safran, J. D., Crocker, P., McMain, S., and Murray, P. (1990). Therapeutic alliance rupture as a therapy event for empirical investigation. *Psychotherapy*, 27, 154–165.

Sedgwick, W. A. and Zaichkowsky, L. B. (2003). *Personal components in the development of expert applied sport psychologists*. Paper presented at the XIth European Congress on Sport Psychology, Copenhagen, Denmark, July.

Sexton, T. L., and Whiston, S. C. (1994). The status of the counselling relationship: An empirical review, theoretical implications, and research directions. *The Counselling Psychologist*, 22, 6–78.

Shapiro, D. A. and Shapiro, D. (1982). Meta-analysis of comparative therapy outcome studies: A replication and refinement. *Psychological Bulletin*, 92, 581–604.

Sharp, L., and Hodge, K. (2011). Sport psychology consulting effectiveness: The sport psychology consultant's perspective. *Journal of Applied Sport Psychology*, 23, 360–376.

Simons, J. P. and Andersen, M. B. (1995). The development of consulting practice in applied sport psychology: Some personal perspectives. *The Sport Psychologist*, 9, 449–468.

Smith, M. L. and Glass, G. V. (1977). Meta-analysis of psychotherapy outcome studies. *American Psychologist*, 32, 752–760.

Spinelli, E. (2002). The therapeutic relationship as viewed by existential psychotherapy: Re-embracing the world. *Journal of Contemporary Psychotherapy*, 32, 111–118.

Statler, T. A. (2003). *The art of applied sport psychology: Interviews with North America's outstanding consultants*. Paper presented at the Association for the Advancement of Applied Sport Psychology, Philadelphia, PA, October.

Stevens, L. M. and Andersen, M. B. (2007a). Transference and countertransference in sport psychology service delivery: Part II. Two case studies on the erotic. *Journal of Applied Sport Psychology*, 19, 270–287.

Stevens, L. M. and Andersen, M. B. (2007b). Transference and countertransference in sport psychology service delivery: Part I. A review of erotic attraction. *Journal of Applied Sport Psychology*, 19, 253–269.

Stewart, R. E. and Chambless, D. L. (2007). Does psychotherapy research inform treatment decisions in private practice? *Journal of Clinical Psychology*, 63, 267–181.

Stiles, W. B. (2006). The client–therapist relationship. In C. Feltham and I. Horton (eds), *The Sage handbook of counselling and psychotherapy* (2nd edn, pp. 64–72). London, UK: Sage.

Straub, W. F. and Hinman, D. A. (1992). Profiles and professional perspectives of 10 leading sport psychologists. *The Sport Psychologist*, 6, 297–312.

Strean, W. B. and Strean, H. S. (1998). Applying psychodynamic concepts to sport psychology practice. *The Sport Psychologist*, 12, 208–222.

Sullivan, P. A. and Nashman, H. W. (1998). Self-perceptions of the role of the USOC sport psychologists in working with Olympic athletes. *The Sport Psychologist*, 12, 95–103.

Tod, D. (2007a). Reflections on collaborating with a professional rugby league player. *Sport and Exercise Psychology Review*, 3, 4–10.

Tod, D. (2007b). The long and winding road: Professional development in sport psychology. *The Sport Psychologist*, 21, 94–108.

Tod, D. (2009). Reflections on working with a powerlifter. In U. Johnson and M. Lindwall (eds), *Svensk Idrottspsykologisk Förenings Årsbok 2008* (pp. 49–60). Stockholm, Sweden: Andrén and Holm.

Tod, D. (2010). Training and professional development in applied sport psychology. In S. J. Hanrahan and M. B. Andersen (eds), *Routledge handbook of applied sport psychology: A comprehensive guide for students and practitioners* (pp. 21–29). London, UK: Routledge.

Tod, D. and Andersen, M. (2005). Success in sport psych: Effective sport psychologists. In S. Murphy (ed.), *The sport psych handbook* (pp. 305–314). Champaign, IL: Human Kinetics.

Tod, D. and Bond, K. (2010). A longitudinal examination of a British neophyte sport psychologist's development. *The Sport Psychologist*, 24, 35–51.

Tod, D. and Lavallee, D. (2011). Taming the Wild West: Training and supervision in applied sport psychology. In D. Gilbourne and M. B. Andersen (eds), *Critical essays in applied sport psychology* (pp. 193–215). Champaign, IL: Human Kinetics.

Tod, D., Marchant, D. B., and Andersen, M. B. (2005). United we stand, divided we fall. In T. Morris, P. Terry, S. Gordon, S. J. Hanrahan, L. Ievleva, G. Kolt, and P. Tremayne (eds), *ISSP 11th world congress of sport psychology: Promoting health and performance for life, CD-ROM*. Sydney, NSW, Australia: International Society of Sport Psychology.

Tod, D., Andersen, M. B., and Marchant, D. B. (2009). A longitudinal examination of neophyte applied sport psychologists' development. *Journal of Applied Sport Psychology*, 21(Suppl. 1), S1–S16.

Tod, D., Andersen, M. B., and Marchant, D. B. (2011). 6 years up: Applied sport psychologists surviving (and thriving) after graduation. *Journal of Applied Sport Psychology*, 23, 93–109.

Tod, D., Marchant, D., and Andersen, M. B. (2007). Learning experiences contributing to service-delivery competence. *The Sport Psychologist*, 21, 317–334.

Tracey, T. J. G., Lichtenberg, J. W., Goodyear, R. K., Claiborn, C. D., and Wampold, B. E. (2003). Concept mapping of therapeutic common factors. *Psychotherapy Research*, 13, 401–413.

Van Raalte, J. L. and Andersen, M. B. (2000). Supervision I: From models to doing. In M. B. Andersen (ed.), *Doing sport psychology* (pp. 153–165). Champaign, IL: Human Kinetics.

Wampold, B. E. (2001). *The great psychotherapy debate: Models, methods, and findings.* Mahwah, NJ: Erlbaum.

Wampold, B. E., Mondin, G. W., Moody, M., Stich, F., Benson, K., and Ahn, H. (1997). A meta-analysis of outcome studies comparing bona fide psychotherapies: Empirically, "all must have prizes". *Psychological Bulletin*, 122, 203–215.

Watson, J. C., II, Zizzi, S. J., Etzel, E. F., and Lubker, J. R. (2004). Applied sport psychology supervision: A survey of students and professionals. *The Sport Psychologist*, 18, 415–429.

Weigand, D. A., Richardson, P. A., and Weinberg, R. S. (1999). A two-stage evaluation of a sport psychology internship. *Journal of Sport Behavior*, 22, 83–104.

Whelan, J. (n.d.). *Ethics code: AASP ethical principles and standards.* Retrieved 27 November 2010, from http://appliedsportpsych.org/about/ethics/code.

Winstone, W. and Gervis, M. (2006). Countertransference and the self-aware sport psychologist: Attitudes and patterns of professional practice. *The Sport Psychologist*, 20, 495–511.

Yalom, I. D. (1980). *Existential psychotherapy.* New York, NY: Basic Books.

Yalom, I. D. (1999). *Momma and the meaning of life: Tales of psychotherapy.* New York, NY: Basic Books.

Yambor, J. and Connelly, D. (1991). Issues confronting female sport psychology consultants working with male student-athletes. *The Sport Psychologist*, 5, 304–312.

12 Reflective practice

Key issues for applied sport psychologists

Brendan Cropley and Sheldon Hanton

Abstract

The purpose of this review is to situate the concept of reflective practice within the professional training and development of applied sport psychology (ASP) practitioners – in particular, to: (a) consider the potential value of reflective practice as a mechanism to assist ASP practitioners in developing the effectiveness of their practice; and (b) provide an insight into how the process of reflective practice can be facilitated. The review initially attempts to frame the current environment in which neophyte consultants are trained and professional practitioners work before progressing to consider reflective practice, its definitions and relationship with professional practice. The use of reflective practice within sport psychology is then considered, with the final section of the chapter focusing on providing guidance on how practitioners can engage in reflective practice.

Keywords: reflective practice, effectiveness, knowing-in-action

Framing reflective practice within applied sport psychology

The field of applied sport psychology (ASP) has experienced significant developments in recent years as it has progressed into professional status. As a result, ASP practitioners have become increasingly accountable for the evaluation and development of the effectiveness of their service delivery (Cropley *et al.*, 2010a; Martindale and Collins, 2007). In line with this, professional body training and development programmes (e.g. The British Association of Sport and Exercise Sciences [BASES] Accreditation programme; The British Psychological Society's Division of Sport and Exercise Psychology [BPS-DSEP] Chartership programme; The Association for Applied Sport Psychology [AASP] Certification programme) have begun to embrace frameworks that encourage both neophytes and professionals to develop knowledge through engagement in processes of experiential learning. Growing evidence has suggested that in order to be effective ASP practitioners must develop and apply the types of knowledge that allow them to better deal with the problems of real-world practice (e.g. Anderson *et al.*, 2004; Cropley *et al.*, 2010a; Tod and Bond, 2010). It is suggested, therefore, that if practitioners are to hone their skills, learn about themselves, and better serve the needs of their athlete-clients, frameworks that engage practitioners in a process of learning from experience are essential (Van Raalte and Andersen, 2000).

It has been acknowledged for some time that, due to the complex and multifaceted nature of ASP support that centers on human interaction, practice is unlikely to be effective through simple application of theory to practice alone (Anderson *et al.*, 2004). Thus, traditional positivistic frameworks of professional knowledge developed through empirical, quantifiable science may not furnish practitioners with the understanding and applied "know-how" to act effectively in dynamic consultancy environments. For example, Martens (1987) recognised that the largely positivistic-based knowledge he used as an academic sport psychologist was not enough to enable him to practise sport psychology effectively. Consequently, Anderson *et al.* (2004) suggested that ASP practitioners need to draw on a more integrated *knowledge-in-action* approach. Also known as *practice-based* (Cropley *et al.*, 2010a), *tacit* (Anderson *et al.*, 2004), and *craft* (Knowles *et al.*, 2001) knowledge, it has been proposed that in professional practice this knowledge-in-action is made up of social norms, values, prejudices, experiences, and different sources of knowledge, such as ethics, aesthetics, and empirical evidence (Anderson *et al.*, 2004; Compagnucci and Cardós, 2007). Through the development of knowledge-in-action it is thought that practitioners begin to combine and integrate these different sources of knowledge, allowing them to better understand how to practise more effectively in the specific context of the consultancy environment. These definitions of knowledge-in-action perceive such knowledge as a characteristic of the competent and effective practitioner, with its origins embedded within experience (Cropley *et al.*, 2010b; Schön, 1987).

At this juncture, it is important to note that the presumption that learning is an automatic process associated with merely having an experience may be incorrect. Aitchison and Graham (in Criticos, 1993) suggested that we do not habitually learn from experience, but instead experience has to be examined, analysed, and considered in order to shift it to knowledge. Recent research that attempted to further understanding of the concept of "experience" in sport found that for experience to be gained, knowledge has to be acquired through learning from reflecting on the incident itself (Hanton *et al.*, 2007). Effective learning from experience, and thus the generation of knowledge-in-action is, therefore, only likely to be recognised and applied if the learner actively engages in processes that result in the excavation of the knowledge embedded within the experience (Andresen *et al.*, 2000).

One such process that has gained acceptance in recent years within the field of ASP is that of reflective practice. Reflective practice has been reported as a mechanism to enable practitioners to better understand themselves, the effectiveness of the service they provide, and actually learn about "doing" sport psychology by generating practice-based knowledge (cf. Andersen, 2000; Anderson *et al.*, 2004; Cropley *et al.*, 2007; Tod and Bond, 2010; Woodcock *et al.*, 2008). Moreover, practitioners from the educare professions (e.g. nursing, education) have suggested consistently that reflective practice is of paramount importance within professional practice (Larrivee, 2008; Yip, 2006). Mirroring developments in these related fields, practitioners who provide supervision to neophytes during the practicum experience element of their training within ASP have also recognised the need to provide supervisees with the essential skills for understanding their own practice through reflective processes (Knowles *et al.*, 2007). Additionally, through examining potential learning experiences that contribute to service delivery competence in ASP, Tod *et al.* (2007) emphasised the need for a greater focus on reflective practice to assist practitioners in developing knowledge and skills. As a consequence, reflection is considered integral to ASP practice, as it facilitates experiential learning and helps to improve the effectiveness of service delivery (Cropley *et al.*, 2011). It is important to appreciate, however, that reflective practice is not solely reserved for neophytes, but should be embraced by all practitioners at every level of professional development. This is because reflective practice can be used for a number of purposes (e.g. to improve self-awareness; to increase the practitioner's accountability) and represents a commitment to lifelong learning and development.

Despite the growing support for reflective practice many misconceptions within the field of ASP remain: such as (a) what reflective practice actually is, (b) who reflective practice is for, (c) how we engage in reflective practice, and (d) what the outcomes of reflective practice should be. To illustrate, many practitioners share the common perception that reflective practice consists of simply thinking or mulling over what has happened during an experience, whereas closer examination of the phenomenon demonstrates that it encompasses a much more complex process (Knowles and Saxon, 2010). Drawing on the growing reflective practice research base within the field of ASP, as well as research evidence from related fields (e.g. coaching, nursing), this chapter aims to facilitate the development of conceptual clarity with regard to the perception and applied process of reflective practice. The chapter initially focuses on exploring what reflective practice actually is, before examining how reflective practice fits into ASP service delivery. The chapter then places specific emphasis on how practitioners can develop their reflective skills and engage in the process more effectively, and concludes with a consideration of future research within the area.

What is reflective practice?

One of the challenges of reviewing the literature on reflection is that it emanates from many different sources, and, due to the complex nature of reflective practice, as evidenced by the number of typologies that exist, a simple definition is elusive (Ghaye and Lillyman, 2000). For example, in the endeavour to provide a better understanding of reflective practice, Boyd and Fales (1983) suggested that "Reflection is the process of internally examining and exploring an issue of concern, triggered by an experience, which creates and clarifies meaning in terms of self and results in a changed conceptual perspective" (p. 100). Alternatively, Raelin (2002) proposed that reflection is:

> The practice of periodically stepping back to ponder the meaning of what has recently transpired to ourselves and to others in our immediate environment. It illuminates what the self and others have experienced, providing a basis for future action. In particular, it privileges the process of inquiry, leading to an understanding of experiences that may have been overlooked in practice.
>
> (p. 66)

Whilst both definitions contain similar aspects, the differences are particularly apparent. For example, Raelin's definition implies that the outcome of reflective practice is a basis for future action, whereas Boyd and Fales indicated that the outcome relates to a changed conceptual perspective. Whilst both may be correct, the inconsistencies fuel conceptual confusion. Also, Raelin suggested that reflection occurs periodically. However, Boyd and Fales's definition, along with those of other authors (e.g. Barnett and O'Mahoney, 2006), suggests the process is initiated when individuals become aware of or concerned with an incident or problem. Although reflecting on problems is important, it should not be done at the expense of other aspects of our working lives, such as reflecting on experiences where behaviour has been effective (Ghaye, 2010; Loughran, 2006). This represents a movement away from traditional conceptualisations of reflective practice (e.g. Dewey, 1933) that suggested reflection is driven by the occurrence of problems, and emphasises the utility of reflection for human flourishing by focusing on practice-based strengths (Ghaye *et al.*, 2008). Certainly, reflective practice is about building on achievements and being creative in our work in an attempt to learn from experience, develop novel practice, and work around the problems associated with ASP service delivery.

In attempts to provide more context-specific insights into what reflective practice actually is, Anderson *et al.* (2004) and Knowles *et al.* (2007) were in agreement that reflection offers an approach to practice that requires ASP practitioners to be open and questioning. For example, Knowles and colleagues stated that reflective practice is:

> An approach to practice that involves creating opportunities to access, make sense of and learn from the tacit knowledge-in-action we use in

> our daily work. This tacit, knowledge-in-action, which incorporates values, prejudices, experiences, analysis and social norms, is integral to practice.
>
> (p. 109)

This definition draws on the premise that reflective practice offers ASP practitioners a framework to access, make sense of, and learn from the relevant knowledge-in-action that emanates from experience. However, Anderson *et al.* warned that, in order for this to happen, practitioners must make space and time to examine practice in detail, as attending to and questioning thoughts, feelings, and emotions associated with an experience can lead to feelings of discomfort and vulnerability. If practitioners are to really understand their experiences and understand the context of their practice, then Anderson and colleagues suggest that practitioners must be willing to challenge such emotions. Hence, it is widely accepted that reflection is a complex process involving the whole person (Cropley *et al.*, 2010a; Ghaye and Lillyman, 2000).

These definitions provide us with a better understanding of the concept of reflective practice. However, in line with the work of several authors who proposed benefit in viewing reflective practice holistically through landscape maps (e.g. Ghaye and Lillyman, 2000), it is suggested that examining reflective practice through its inherent characteristics will help to clarify its nature and processes further. By attempting to elucidate reflective practice in this way we can become more aware of what the process entails. Consequently, we should be able to label the cognitive processes associated with reflective practice more accurately, as well as helping to extend the necessary information required for developing reflective skills.

Characteristics of reflective practice

Reflective practice is often seen as representing a choice for practitioners to be reflective or not about their work, but in reality all practitioners engage in reflection about the professional service they provide (Bright, 1995). The thought processes often labeled as reflection, however, are seldom representative of reflective practice (Cropley *et al.*, 2010a). For example, contemplating an experience or event is not always purposeful and does not necessarily lead to new ways of thinking or behaving in practice, which, in agreement with the constructs inherent within many definitions, lie at the core of effective reflective activity (Andrews *et al.*, 1998). Consequently, by drawing on the common factors apparent within definitions of reflective practice across different fields, the characteristics of reflection become apparent. For example, there appears to be significant agreement that in order to engage in reflective practice the process must be *purposeful* and result in *change* to beliefs, values, understanding and/or behaviour (Anderson *et al.*, 2004). This also supports Dewey's (1933) contention that reflective practice must be *deliberate*. Other commonalities that appear to exist in definitions of reflective practice are that it is a *cognitive* process that involves the *self* and is triggered by the *questioning* of actions, values, and beliefs. Finally, it is commonly agreed that reflective practice is a *complex* and *skilled* activity that requires an ability to analyse practice actions and make judgements regarding effectiveness (Anderson *et al.*, 2004; Cropley *et al.*, 2010b). This would suggest that practitioners can improve their ability to reflect on their experiences by developing certain cognitive skills.

These characteristics clearly separate reflective practice from other modes of thinking (e.g. contemplation, deliberation, evaluation), and are thought to present ASP practitioners with a more apt understanding of what the process entails. Although there has been a greater focus on reflective practice within ASP, understanding of the concept still appears equivocal. This seems particularly true for practitioners who became professionally qualified prior to recent changes in training programmes (e.g. BASES, 2009; BPS-DSEP, 2007) where reflective practice was not included as a formal aspect of professional training (Cropley *et al.*, 2010a, b). If the benefits of reflective practice so widely acknowledged in other fields are to be recognised, then ASP practitioners must ensure that they engage in processes more characteristic of reflection.

Timing of reflective practice

The timing and context in which practitioners engage in reflection is also a consideration in helping to define the process itself. Schön (1983) considered two distinct time phases in which reflection may occur: *reflection-on-action* and *reflection-in-action*. Reflection-on-action refers to the retrospective reflective practices a person engages in following the completion of an event. Conversely, reflection in action takes place during an activity, allowing the practitioner to make in vivo decisions regarding how to potentially alter a situation in line with the interpretation of what is happening in attempts to act more effectively. Schön argued that being able to reflect in action is central to the art by which professionals handle and resolve their difficulties and concerns in practice.

There has been considerable debate regarding the notion and validity of reflection-in-action (see Van Manen, 1991), with Schön himself raising inconsistencies in his definition. However, in agreement with Schön's (1987) later writings, it is thought that reflection-in-action refers to the reflective thinking that occurs at any time during a particular experience, even if the practitioner has a "stop and think" moment. This is because the reflection that the practitioner engages in has the potential to influence the client in that specific situation (Schön, 1987). Once the practitioner cannot influence the situation any more (i.e. the consultation has finished) any reflection that occurs is deemed as reflection-on-action, and this is the aspect that is primarily focused upon in our chapter.

Summary: defining reflective practice

In attempts to understand the concept of reflective practice more comprehensively and be able to frame reflection within the practice of ASP, it appears more valuable to consider the principles associated with reflective practice, rather than the multitude of context specific definitions available within the literature. Reflective practice is characterised by complex, skilled, cognitive processes involving the whole person (Ghaye and Lillyman, 2000). The process is instigated by deliberate questioning of actions, values, and beliefs associated with an experience with a view to developing knowledge that should lead to change. It is important to note, however, that while the outcome of reflective practice is labeled as "change", this could actually represent: (a) a change in behaviour, values, or beliefs; (b) confirmation or rejection of a particular theory or practice; and/or (c) a change in knowledge of the self, the context of practice, or the environment in which the consultant is working (cf. Knowles and Saxton, 2010).

It is our view that reflective practice refers to many processes and modes of thinking, and we would argue that as long as the process that practitioners engage in results in positive outcomes that ultimately lead to the development of more effective practice, then we should not be hampered by definitions of these processes. However, if practitioners are to consistently benefit from reflecting on their practice, then it is important that their modes of thinking are more characteristic of *reflective practice*. This is in agreement with Dewey (1933), who implied that reflection involves not simply a sequence of ideas but a consequence, which is viewed as a consecutive ordering of ideas in such a way that each of these ideas in the sequence determines the next idea as its proper outcome. With other modes of thinking, successive portions of a reflective thought do not necessarily grow out of one another and support one another; as a result, they tend to come and go in medley without a developing outcome.

Reflective practice: an applied sport psychology review

Reflective practice in experienced and neophyte ASP practice

The product of reflective practice has been suggested to have the potential to offer a rich resource highlighting the knowledge-in-action required to do sport psychology (Anderson *et al.*, 2004), and thus answer calls from practitioners for the reporting of real-life consulting experiences (Andersen, 2000). As a result, growing research interest within ASP has been afforded to this concept. It is thought that the use of reflective accounts to outline specific issues concerning ASP practice has the potential not only to inform the supervision of trainee sport psychologists but also to enhance the effectiveness of sport psychologists' professional practice (Jones *et al.*, 2007; Knowles and Gilbourne, 2010). For example, self-reflections on neophyte practice have identified key issues (e.g. self-awareness, role of supervision) related to the process of sport psychology service delivery, provided a sense of what aspiring professionals can expect during their initial training experiences, and outlined relevant practice-based knowledge to aid in the growth of sport psychology consultants in training (e.g. Cropley *et al.*, 2007; Holt and Strean, 2001; Jones *et al.*, 2007; Tammen, 2000; Tod and Bond, 2010; Tonn and Harmison, 2004; Woodcock *et al.*, 2008).

Reflective accounts reported by professionally trained practitioners have traditionally been less readily available, particularly within the peer-reviewed literature. Examples of these papers (e.g. Bull, 1995; Friesen and Orlick, 2010) offer insights into many aspects of practice, outline recommendations to those embarking on extended periods of ASP support, and provide additional support for the use of reflective practice in learning from experience. However, these articles tend to lack emphasis on the reflective processes the professional consultants engaged in. This lack of attention is representative of many narratives (e.g. McCann, 2000) available by both neophyte and experienced practitioners, and has compounded the confusion experienced over the integration of reflective processes into the practice of ASP consultants. This is also exemplified in the special issue of the BPS *Sport* and *Exercise Review* (BPS, 2006), which presented experienced practitioners' reflective accounts of providing in-event support at the 2004 Athens Olympics. This narrative analysis of "Athens" provided recommendations for those "in-event" psychologists working towards the Beijing Olympics, and substantiates claims over the value of reflection in providing a source for learning and development within ASP. It is therefore thought that the potential learning opportunities provided by honest and insightful reflections outweigh the many possible limitations caused by a lack of consideration on the reflective processes adopted.

Anderson *et al.* (2004) have provided the most substantial understanding of reflective practice and its role within ASP to date. Anderson and colleagues presented a case for the value of reflective practice as an approach to professional training and development that can assist practitioners in effectively managing themselves in practice. By drawing on the types of knowledge that are valued within ASP, and considering the work of Schön (1987), Anderson *et al.* proposed that "Through reflective practice, sport psychology practitioners can access, make sense of, and learn from the relevant knowledge-in-action that contributes to actually doing sport psychology" (p. 191). Such proposals are in agreement with those made in other sport related fields (e.g. sports coaching; Knowles *et al.*, 2001), and raise awareness of the utility of reflective practice in helping practitioners to understand their work and themselves. This is consistent with Petitpas *et al.*'s (1999) view that greater emphasis on self-knowledge and adaptability is required to prepare applied sport psychologists to practise more effectively. Further, Poczwardowski *et al.* (1998) contented that "By paying attention to the self, thoughtfully analysing consultations and being aware of limitations, self-interests, prejudices and frustrations; practitioners will be in a better position to manage themselves and their practice effectively" (p. 199). In addition, Poczwardowski *et al.* suggested that reflecting on each consulting experience is essential for maximal personal growth and development.

Enhancing self-awareness in applied sport psychologists

The relationship between reflective practice and self-awareness is a common theme emanating from the ASP literature. Specific accounts of practitioner's reflections on practice have highlighted reflection to be a valuable process in examining the "self" and uncovering more effective ways of "being" (e.g. Anderson, 1999; Cropley *et al.*, 2007; Holt and Strean, 2001). For example, Tonn, in Tonn and Harmison's (2004) account of neophyte practice, revealed that reflecting on her experiences allowed the enhancement of self-awareness regarding how she provided sport psychology services to athletes in a team setting. Tonn and Harmison additionally suggested that trainees can benefit tremendously from the process of self-reflection regarding their practicum experience by gaining a deeper insight into practice and self-awareness. Support for these recommendations has been provided by Tod *et al.* (2007), who interviewed participants regarding potential learning experiences within ASP. The participants in this study revealed a belief that the benefits of practical experience are enhanced with self-reflection, which leads to enhanced self-awareness. This is a contention further corroborated in related fields, such as nursing (Conway, 1998) and education (Scanlan and Chernomas, 1997). Similarly, Tod and Bond's (2010) exploration of a neophyte practitioner's development focused on the ways in which service delivery perceptions and practices changed following formal education (e.g. university courses). The practitioner identified that one benefit of reflective learning was increased awareness that resulted in a greater appreciation of the ways in which practitioners influenced the support they provided to athletes and a broadening theoretical orientation.

Building on the notion that reflective practice enhances self-awareness, Winstone and Gervis (2006) outlined the potential importance of reflection in combating countertransference in ASP practice. Countertransference refers to the direction of the transference from practitioner to client, and occurs when thoughts and feelings in the sport psychologist are evoked by the client (Winstone and Gervis; see also Chapter 11 in this volume). Strean and Strean (1998) highlighted that if practitioners are not aware of negative feelings toward clients, or have no way of talking about them and working with them, they are likely to repress them. The danger is that without self-awareness of potential countertransference the sport psychologist/athlete relationship will be compromised, which in turn will have a significant impact on the effectiveness of the support provided. Winstone and Gervis outlined that despite the intuitive value of reflective practice in helping practitioners to resolve this issue, little research attention has considered this relationship in any detail. However, Candy *et al.* (1985) suggested that if people are aware of what they are presently doing and can be encouraged to reflect on it and to consider alternatives, they are in a position to adjust their feelings and behaviours. It seems imperative, then, that practitioners are able to enhance self-awareness and act upon it appropriately.

Developing and understanding professional philosophy

Self-awareness gained through reflecting "on" practice has been highlighted as an important contributor to the understanding, development, and integration of professional philosophy within ASP (Friesen and Orlick, 2010). Understanding the philosophical underpinnings of approaches to ASP has the potential to enhance the effectiveness of service delivery within ASP (Poczwardowski *et al.*, 2004). Lindsay *et al.* (2007) explained, however, that a lack of congruence between chosen methods and practitioner beliefs and values may become apparent if ASP practitioners do not examine and become familiar with their own personal philosophy. Further, Poczwardowski *et al.* (2004) suggested that questions relating to core beliefs and values should be addressed through a practitioner's ongoing self-reflection and training to foster and develop knowledge of the self. Lindsay and colleagues therefore presented autoethnographic accounts informed by reflection on consultancies by an ASP practitioner in attempts to explore one practitioner's journey towards congruence in professional philosophy. Lindsay *et al.* disclosed that the process of formal reflection-on-action adopted by the practitioner in the study was central to making changes to his practice, and thus establishing an approach and act in a manner that was far more congruent with his underpinning values. This supports suggestions in other fields that reflection offers a focus to become more self-aware of the contradictions that exist between how we would like to practise, and how we actually do (Driscoll and Teh, 2001). Drawing on Poczwardowski *et al.*'s (2004) conceptual framework of professional philosophy, Friesen and Orlick (2010) also contended that reflecting on practice offers practitioners the opportunity to examine the philosophies of practising sport psychologists in attempts to better understand how their beliefs and values influence the provision of a holistic service. In order to enhance this potential learning opportunity, the authors concluded that "Future studies should include reflective narratives or case studies from other consultants exemplifying how they deliver holistic sport psychology services" (p. 242).

Enhancing the effectiveness of ASP through reflective practice

Research available within the field of ASP that focuses on reflective practice has regularly alluded to its links with the development of effective service delivery. For example, Tod *et al.* (2007) indicated that practitioners enhance their understanding of their client interactions and themselves with self-reflection, and such knowledge might help them become more effective consultants. In attempts to explore this potential relationship more explicitly and add to the evidence base that provides specific support for reflective practice, recent research has examined how reflective practice may aid the development of characteristics associated with effective ASP consultants. Specifically, Cropley *et al.* (2007) examined the value of a neophyte practitioner engaging in structured reflection-on-practice with a view to developing the competence and effectiveness of his service delivery. Content analysis procedures were applied to the trainee's reflections in an attempt to identify links between the process of reflection and the development of consultant characteristics associated with effectiveness (e.g. good communicator, provider of a good practical service). The findings of Cropley *et al.*'s study indicated that by adopting reflective practice during an ASP accreditation programme, the trainee practitioner was able to analyse the interaction of his thoughts, feelings, and behaviours, and the context in which they occurred. The trainee suggested that as a result of this he was better able to deal with issues that emerged from experience as he became more aware of, and was able to develop, a number of the characteristics associated with effectiveness. Consequently, he reported the emerging ability to recurrently consider the effectiveness of himself and his practice. These findings support the earlier work of Anderson (1999) and Holt and Strean (2001), who reported that the practitioners in their studies were able to access and make sense of their knowledge-in-action through reflective practice. Both Holt and Strean and Anderson also highlighted how accessing this knowledge-in-action facilitated self-evaluation learning, and ultimately increased the effectiveness of practice.

Despite growing support for the apparent connections between reflective practice and effectiveness within ASP, there is still currently a lack of empirical support for such associations. Indeed, Newman (1999) warned against accepting the value of such a reflective approach to practice without questioning the evidence upon which claims are based. In light of this, a series of research projects by Cropley *et al.* (2010b; 2011) has attempted to explicate the proposed links between effective and reflective practice more thoroughly. First, Cropley *et al.* (2010b) developed a definition of effective practice within ASP before examining the reflective practice experiences of neophyte and professionally accredited sport psychologists. The emerging definition suggested that effective practice in ASP is a multidimensional process of agreeing, setting, and achieving goals that includes the active use of reflective practice to assist sport psychologists in learning from their experiences. Additionally, drawing on the knowledge of neophyte and accredited (BASES) practitioners, Cropley *et al.* uncovered that reflective practice is: (a) thought to be an integral aspect of ASP practice; (b) helps to move competent practice towards effective practice; (c) more effective when using structured approaches to reflection, and embracing opportunities to reflect with others; and (d) key to developing the knowledge required to practise effectively. Building on these findings, Cropley *et al.*'s (2011) later study presented a staggered single-subject multiple baseline across individuals designed to examine whether the development of skills in reflective practice enhanced the effectiveness of ASP service delivery. In agreement with the previous suggestions of Husu *et al.* (2008), the findings of this investigation supported the notion that reflective practice is a genuine way of fostering change in practitioner's professional actions. Specifically, the intervention administered had a positive experimental impact on the levels participants were able to reflect at (e.g. descriptive to critical), and this consequently had a positive influence on the effectiveness of participants' practice. The relationship between higher levels of reflection and effectiveness was demonstrated, in part, through quantitative measures of effectiveness (e.g. consultant evaluation forms, performance profiles). However, these were deemed as inconclusive due to the suitability of the measures, given the nature of the ASP support being provided by the participants (e.g. counselling-based approaches rather than mental skills training). Nevertheless, social validation procedures provided significant support for the relationship, with the participants reporting that they were better able to access the types of information required to excavate knowledge and thus learn from their experiences. This was suggested to better help them understand the context of their practice and how best to "work with" their clients.

It is important to note that the participants in both of Cropley and colleagues' (2010b, 2011) investigations also outlined some issues of concern with regard to the way in which the field of ASP may have accepted reflective practice without question. For example, it was argued that there is currently not enough support to help practitioners understand what reflective practice is, how they can engage in reflective practices, and how they make these practices successful. Further, the participants indicated that, without guidance and support, confusion remains as to how reflective practice is distinct from other modes of thinking, and therefore practitioners tend to think they are engaging in reflective practice when actually they're not. Finally, participants in both studies recognised the extensive time and effort required to engage in higher levels of reflective practice. Andrews *et al.* (1998) warned that effective reflection requires considerable investment of time. However, in agreement with Holt and Strean (2001), there is no substitute for taking the time to think through important issues, and therefore practitioners should afford specific time for reflection when planning a period of ASP support.

Facilitating the supervision of neophytes through reflective practice

Van Raalte and Andersen (2000) described the applied sport psychology supervision process as a long-term interpersonal relationship designed to develop competent, knowledgeable, and ethical practitioners to ensure the welfare of athlete-clients. It is suggested that quality supervision can maximise developmental opportunities through organising appropriate self-reflection, fostering a developmental approach through an optimal supervisory relationship, and responding to perceived failings and neophyte anxiety in a way that is supportive but also stimulates learning and development (Woodcock *et al.*, 2008). Thus, support is provided for the thoughts of Anderson *et al.* (2004), who proposed that reflective practice may offer a framework to facilitate the effective supervision of trainee practitioners. For example, it has been acknowledged that trainee practitioners are initially dependent on the guidance of their supervisors because they lack sufficient service delivery knowledge (Tod and Bond, 2010). By developing an environment where the sharing of experiences is encouraged and learning through reflection on our experiences is embraced, supervisors are likely to encourage their supervisees to learn from the relevant knowledge-in-action embedded within their consultancy experiences (Knowles *et al.*, 2007).

In relation to a number of anecdotal accounts that have reported the value of a supervision process underpinned by reflective practice (e.g. Holt and Strean, 2001; Jones *et al.*, 2007; Woodcock *et al.*, 2008), Knowles *et al.* (2007) further explored the value of this approach to supervision in professional training programmes. Over a three-year period of supervision, the supervisee in the study outlined that "The combination of experiences increased my capacity to make sense of my applied experiences, to critically evaluate my own practice, and to manage my own professional and personal development" (p. 119). Knowles and colleagues also reported the value of a shared approach to reflection that assisted the supervisee in better understanding new approaches to practice. The value of this approach was also outlined in Woodcock and colleagues' (2008) account of neophyte development. Woodcock *et al.* indicated that although the trainee engaged in solitary reflection, reflective conversations with a supervisor provided greater insight into learning experiences, which furthered the practitioner's understanding of important factors related to service delivery.

It must be noted that the potential success of employing a reflective practice approach to supervision may lie in the ability of the supervisor to engage in a shared reflective process. In Knowles *et al.*'s (2007) investigation, the supervisor was experienced in the research and application of reflective practice, thus it cannot be assumed that by merely applying a process of reflection the benefits stated in previous research will be achieved. Indeed, Andrews *et al.* (1998) outlined that supervisors not only need to be skilled in reflecting, but also need to be competent in facilitating reflectiveness in others. This may mean that in order to teach reflectively we have to become reflective ourselves (cf. Scanlan and Chernomas, 1997).

Intervening with reflective practice

It would appear that the benefits associated with reflection on practice as reported by ASP practitioners also help to develop the performance of athletes, and as such become an appropriate aspect of holistic ASP interventions. This particularly holds true in light of recent reports that have advocated the development of more humanistic approaches to consultancy. Here, practitioners work on developing a working alliance with their clients to facilitate them in becoming more independent through enhancing the self-awareness and problem-solving skills required for self-regulation (Andersen, 2009; Anderson *et al.*, 2004; Holt and Strean, 2001). Although the value of reflective practice in this setting appears clear, only a few practitioners have reported its use as an intervention with athletes.

Faull and Cropley (2009) presented a case study with an elite, senior-level triathlete with the aim of outlining how a structured approach to reflective practice, introduced by the sport psychologist, could be incorporated as a method of advancing the athlete's evaluative skills and improving their self-awareness. The athlete was encouraged to reflect, using a structured approach, on the critical incidents experienced during each day of a four-week international training camp. Following this, the sport psychologist met with the athlete in order to evaluate their experiences of adopting a reflective learning approach. The athlete reported that reflective practice had assisted them in the decisive assessment and understanding of their performance, which consequently helped the athlete to make more informed decisions about how to improve performance. Additionally, the athlete reported becoming more self-aware as both an athlete and a person, and in this sense it was agreed that a structured approach to reflection had assisted in the holistic development of the athlete. Indeed, helping athletes to become self-aware has been demonstrated to aid athletes in more effective arousal control (Sherman and Poczwardowski, 2005), improved self-confidence (Weinberg and Gould, 2007), more successful goal-setting (Zimmerman, 2002), and self-actualisation (Hogg, 1995). The athlete in Faull and Cropley's case study also reported several key issues that should be considered by ASP practitioners before considering the integration of reflective practice into athlete-centered interventions. First, the athlete's initial impression of reflective practice was a negative one. This remained the case until formal education was introduced regarding the understanding and the process of reflection, which highlights the importance of the sport psychologist being able to "teach" reflective practice and get their clients to buy into the process. Second, the athlete tended to reflect primarily on negative experiences, and whilst this aided the athlete in better understanding their performance, it is recommended that positive incidents are given equal thought so that strength-based behaviours can be maintained and built upon (cf. Allen *et al.*, 2010).

Other research has reported similar benefits of engaging athletes in reflective practice. For example, Hanrahan *et al.* (2009) and Allen *et al.* (2009) both presented intervention studies, where the experimental groups were asked to complete structured self-reflection following a dance performance, and a "performance evaluation sheet" after competing in a golf-putting task, respectively. Specifically, Hanrahan *et al.* examined the impact of structured self-reflection on the achievement goals' orientations, levels of intrinsic motivation, and perceived performance of recreational dancers, whereas Allen *et al.* examined the influence of positive reflection-on-action on athlete's attributions, emotions, and self-efficacy following a golf-putting competition. Hanrahan *et al.*'s findings suggested that structured self-reflection benefited the participants by assisting in the acquisition of physical skills, changing their approach to dancing, improving focus on their own performance (task orientation), and enhancing self-awareness. Moreover, Allen *et al.* concluded that positive reflection can be sufficient in promoting more internal and controllable attributions. Both Hanrahan *et al.*'s and Allen *et al.*'s investigations offer recommendations to ASP consultants to encourage athletes to reflect on their performances. However, the findings of these studies must be considered with caution, as little attempt to elucidate potential cause-and-effect relationships between the reflective processes adopted and the development of the associated characteristics was made. Additionally, the apparent understanding and use of reflection appeared little more than a structured evaluation of performance, and should not, therefore, be considered as reflective practice. Thus, it is questionable as to whether the participants engaged in processes that really enabled them to excavate knowledge from their experiences and learn how to positively alter behaviour.

Critiquing reflective practice

Reflective practice appears to have become more prominent within the field of ASP, with both researchers and practitioners promoting the value of reflection in the personal and professional development of ASP consultants. However, before the field embraces fully the concept of reflective practice it is important to raise a number of issues concerning its integration into ASP practice.

First, in some instances understanding of the concept of reflective practice is still equivocal in ASP. This may be due to the field taking its understanding of reflection from the educare professions and applying it without due consideration for the milieu of ASP practice. For example,

Martindale and Collins (2007) acknowledged that there is little guidance concerning *what* ASP practitioners should actually be reflecting on. Thus, the benefits so widely acknowledged in other fields may not be recognised. A greater awareness of the way in which reflective practice can be adopted by both trainee and qualified consultants is therefore required within the ASP literature.

Second, reflective practice is recognised as a highly skilled activity (cf. Andrews *et al.*, 1998), and it appears as though these skills may be taken for granted, with assumptions within ASP being made that reflecting requires little effort. Such notions are compounded by the fact that professional ASP organisations have placed little emphasis on the development of reflective skills, and offer little guidance on its use (cf. Knowles *et al.*, 2007). Although some organisations (e.g. BASES) have now made reflective practice workshops a compulsory component of professional training, we may still be in danger of labelling reflection as "something to be done", rather than a mechanism for developing effective practice, due to the lack of understanding and support provided by trainees' supervisors with regard to the process of engaging in reflective activities. Indeed, little guidance or training in reflective practice is currently available for supervisors. Additionally, with the exception of the work by Cropley *et al.* (2011), little evidence exists in the ASP literature that suggests how or even if reflective practice skills can be taught (cf. Ghaye and Lillyman, 2000).

Third, despite the intuitive appeal and narrative reports that support the value of reflective practice, little empirical evidence exists to suggest that practice development actually occurs as a direct result of reflective practice (Cropley *et al.*, 2010b). Most studies have used self-report feedback as a means of assessing the effectiveness of reflective practice (e.g. Cropley *et al.*, 2007; Tammen, 2000; Tonn and Harmison, 2004), and only one study has attempted to use objective measures of performance to determine improvements in applied practice (e.g. Cropley *et al.*, 2011). The relationship between reflective practice and effectiveness could therefore be questioned.

Fourth, reflective practice literature within ASP, in many cases, contains little detail about the approaches to reflection adopted by the practitioners within the study. It is therefore difficult to empathise with the authors and learn from their experiences with complete confidence. For example, although Tonn and Harmison (2004) advocate the value of engaging in reflective practice for the development of ASP practice, they do little to explicate the approaches adopted that resulted in such perceptions. As the reporting of reflective narrative becomes a more accepted method of investigation, it is hoped that researchers will be more lucid in their explanations of their reflective approach to practice (cf. Knowles and Gilbourne, 2010).

Finally, Anderson *et al.* (2004) suggested that reflective practice could be used to self-evaluate practice, and increase sport psychologists' accountability to their client, themselves, and their profession. Whilst using reflection to examine and justify practice, and taking personal responsibility for monitoring practice and striving to increase effectiveness is clearly beneficial to the development of ASP practice, reflective practice as a means of being accountable to the profession may be problematic. The monitoring of practitioners by professional bodies (e.g. AASP, BPS) through reflection may result in practitioners engaging in a socially desirable practice in order to meet the requirements associated with the training syllabus (cf. Cropley *et al.*, 2010b). Certainly, honest reflections of what "actually" happened during practice would undoubtedly raise ethical issues about a practitioner's actions and behaviours (Ghaye, 2007).

Summary

The reflective practice literature within ASP has tended to be, until recently, characterised by anecdotal accounts of neophyte practitioners reflecting on their practicum experiences (e.g. Holt and Strean, 2001; Tonn and Harmison, 2004). Whilst these accounts provide a valuable insight into issues of professional development and the utility of reflective practice in helping trainees to learn from their experiences, it could be argued that the lack of emphasis placed on the reflective processes adopted in these accounts, as well as the lack of discussion of some of the issues associated with reflective practice, has resulted in equivocal understandings of definitions, processes, benefits, and applications of reflective practice for sport psychologists. Further, the paucity of reflective accounts by experienced sport psychologists and the lack of an empirical evidence base that supports the claims made by practitioners in the field may suggest that the field has "jumped on the bandwagon" of reflective practice. However, as support has grown for the use of reflective practice, calls for a greater and more diverse evidence base have been made apparent, which a number of authors have started to answer. This research has begun to establish links between reflective and effective practice (Cropley *et al.*, 2007, 2010b, 2011); considered the utility of reflective approaches to supervision (Knowles *et al.*, 2007); examined how knowledge concerning the delivery of holistic ASP services can be accessed and developed through reflection (Friesen and Orlick, 2010); and examined the value of reflective practice as an approach to the development of athletic performance (Faull and Cropley, 2009).

Facilitating reflection: the what, when, and how guide to professional practice

Several pertinent issues that remain with regard to reflective practice within ASP relate to the actual engagement in the process. Despite the apparent growth in the ASP reflective practice literature, in many cases manuscripts fail to present detailed information about the approaches to reflection adopted by the practitioners within the study. This has resulted in recent publications questioning the available guidance on "what" we should actually be reflecting on (Martindale and Collins, 2007), and the value of group versus individual reflection (Husu *et al.*, 2008). Moreover, understanding about "when" reflection on practice should occur and how practitioners can engage in effective processes remains equivocal (Cropley *et al.*, 2010a; Sparrow, 2009). This section of the chapter therefore aims to address these issues, and attempts to provide guidance on approaches to conducting reflection-on-practice.

What to reflect on?

When attempting to understand "what" practitioners should reflect on, it is important to appreciate that the issue can be examined from both a macro- (e.g. what types of situation should I reflect on?) and a micro- (e.g. what aspects of our practice should we consider?) perspective.

Macro-perspective

Traditionally, reflective practice was deemed to be initiated by an experience of concern or a problem associated with practice (Boyd and Fales, 1983; Dewey, 1933). However, this implies that we only learn from those situations that have created doubt or where things have not gone as planned. Ghaye *et al.* (2008) voiced concerns over this approach by suggesting that when trying to improve work and working lives through reflective practice, thinking can get stuck in vocabularies of human deficit and thus fail to explore the creative potential of those involved. Thus, it would seem more beneficial for reflection-on-practice to be instigated by the occurrence of events both positive and negative in nature through more affirmative methods of inquiry, where seeking for what is right in work is appreciated (Shepherd, 2006). This supports the comments of the ASP practitioners who participated in Cropley *et al.*'s (2010b) study. These participants advocated that neophytes and experienced psychologists alike must learn from all incidents (positive and negative), so that positive aspects of practice can be appreciated, maintained, and built upon and negative aspects of practice can be understood so that appropriate changes can be made.

Although many practitioners would probably argue that they reflect on everything they do, it is likely that much of their "thinking" is not representative of the process of reflective practice. As reflective practice is considered such a complex process, and depending on the approach to reflection adopted, it is improbable that practitioners would afford the time to reflect in depth and effectively on all of their experiences (Andrews *et al.*, 1998; Dewey, 1933). Ghaye and Lillyman (2000) suggested that we are unable to reflect on every aspect of what we do, and should therefore consider "significant" aspects of practice or "critical" situations. This supports the work of some practitioners who have advocated the adoption of a *critical incident* approach to selecting those experiences for in-depth reflective practice (e.g. Faull and Cropley, 2009; Holt and Strean, 2001; Tripp, 1993). This approach allows the focus to be placed on any issue that is deemed important to the individual and their practice. Holt and Strean (2001) suggested that "Critical incidents do not exist independently of an observer, they are created by the way professionals look at situations" (p. 192). Hence, a critical incident is a subjective interpretation of the significance of an event (Tripp, 1993). Reflection-on-practice should be initiated once a person experiences an event that has personal significance to them, as these experiences are likely to be the most beneficial in terms of learning and impacting practice.

Micro-perspective

From a micro-perspective, research from the field of education has attempted to further understanding of the issues of what aspects of an event we should reflect on. Bain *et al.* (1999), for example, proposed four different foci for reflection, which could be generalised to focus on (a) the activity being undertaken, (b) the self, (c) professional issues, and (d) the context in which the activity takes place. Although these suggestions help to clarify the main factors to be taken into consideration, practitioners must also be aware of the purpose for engaging in reflection on practice. James and Clarke (1996) indicated that reflection can serve technical (e.g. developing the mechanical aspects of practice), practical (e.g. understanding personal meaning within a situation), and critical (e.g. challenging habitual practices) purposes (see Anderson *et al.*, 2004). Depending on which purpose is pertinent to the situation the practitioner finds themselves in, the reflection itself should consider different aspects of the event in different levels of detail (Sparks-Langer and Colton, 1991). For example, if a practitioner reflected for a practical purpose, then the reflector should explore personal meaning within the situation by addressing the influence of their own experiences, perceptions, and understandings of the context of their own and their client's feelings and actions. James and Clarke (1996) recommended that truly reflective practitioners would operate at all three levels of reflection. However, recent research has indicated that being critically self-aware is an acquired skill that comes with experience and intellect, and consequently not all practitioners will be able to reflect at this higher level (Cropley *et al.*, 2011). Additionally, it may not be necessary to reflect at a critical level if the practitioner is simply reflecting on practice to serve a technical purpose as a means of increasing their accountability to their client or the profession.

When to reflect on practice

The timing at which reflection-on-action occurs following an experience requires particular attention. In order to engage in reflective practice, the "self" must be considered in terms of thoughts, feelings, emotions, and associated behaviours and discourses. However, it is unlikely that we can gain clarity in our understanding of these factors and how they impacted upon the situation being reflected upon if we engage in reflective practices under the sway of the emotions associated with the experience itself. Boud (2001) suggested that in order to facilitate a level of engagement in reflective practice that satisfies the need for practitioners to use intellect, feelings, and senses in learning opportunities, we should: (1) revisit the experience, paying particular attention to negative and positive feelings; (2) re-evaluate the experience from an emotionally removed position; and (3) make a commitment to change. It is therefore suggested that we must be "in the right mind" to reflect from a position where thinking can be guided by the emotions associated with an experience and not manipulated by these.

Whilst waiting for the opportunity to reflect from an emotionally removed position is important, the issue of memory decay and recall is also brought into question. Certainly, reflective practice is a process reliant on memory (Cropley *et al.*, 2010b; Wallace, 1996). As a result, it is recommended that reflection-on-action occurs within a time-frame that allows for the fine details that comprise the fabric of an experience to be accounted. Research in ASP has considered this time-frame to be within 48 hours of the experience (e.g. Cropley *et al.*, 2007; Woodcock *et al.*, 2008). This is not, however, always realistic, and in some situations it may take longer to appraise and understand the emotion associated with our experiences. As a result, both Knowles *et al.* (2001) and Knowles *et al.* (2007) have advocated that a dual-staged process of reflective practice whereby both immediate and *delayed* reflection-on-action occurs. This process requires practitioners to frame their experiences immediately following the incident by making notes regarding the relevant issues, associated feelings, and conclusions. These notes can then be used at a later time to help the practitioner to relive the experience and ensure that the factors that shaped the situation are considered in reflective thought. Support for this process is apparent in the ASP literature, with Cropley *et al.* (2007) reporting that the dual-staged process improved the quality and depth of reflections because the practitioner had already started to make sense of the experience before formally engaging in reflective practice. Woodcock *et al.* (2008) also noted that the practitioner in their research recorded all internship experiences in a daily diary, followed by a 24-hour delayed reflection that focused on examining the meaning of the experiences, with the outcome of the process being significantly augmented learning.

Despite some support for the aforementioned approaches, there appears little evidence to suggest that practitioners should reflect at a particular time post-incident, or that one approach is particularly better than another. It is recommended that practitioners become aware of the issues associated with reflecting on their experiences and make informed decisions about how they engage in reflective practices based on their personal situation and the context in which they currently find themselves working. In any sense, it is clear that ASP practitioners must reserve time for reflective practice when planning a period of support (Cropley *et al.*, 2010b). For example, time should be factored in for preparation, service provision, collection of feedback, and structured reflection. A number of researchers have professed to the considerable investment of time required to engage in reflection, but suggest that if practitioners are committed to lifelong learning and professional development, then taking time to fully engage in reflective practices will be worthwhile (Holt and Strean, 2001; Telfer and Knowles, 2009).

How to reflect on practice

Considerations of the specific reflective processes practitioners have engaged in are scarce within the ASP literature, making it difficult to inform decisions about how to integrate reflection in ASP practice. Anderson *et al.* (2004) suggested that the practicalities of engaging in reflective practice are flexible, but in a field where reflective practice is in its infancy an evidence-base of models of best practice may enhance the adoption of systematic reflection-on-action and thus aid practitioners to elicit the proposed benefits of reflecting on their experiences. Reflective processes are usually triggered through the questioning of practice. However, asking the right reflective questions at the right moment is a skilled activity (Ghaye, 2009). Moreover, Johns (1994) argued that reflective practice is a profoundly difficult thing to do, and therefore guidance to support practitioners' reflections is important. It is also thought that learning through reflection is more potent if there is an understanding of frameworks that encourage a structural process to guide the act of reflection (Platzer *et al.*, 1997). Indeed, Cropley *et al.*'s (2011) recent study uncovered that by educating sport psychologists in the use of a specific reflective framework, their motivation to reflect increased, they were better able to access clarity and make sense of their experiences, and their ability to learn from their experiences improved.

Much attention has been given to the value of recording events and experiences in written form, particularly through the use of reflective diaries and journals (Telfer and Knowles, 2009). This is because it is thought that the exercise of diary-writing promotes the qualities (e.g. open-mindedness) and skills (e.g. self-awareness, critical analysis, problem-solving) required for reflection, as well as the motivation for engaging in a formal reflective process (Anderson *et al.*, 2004; Cropley *et al.*, 2011). To engage in journal writing, a reflection guide or model might be used to structure the post-experience writing process. Models range from very structured, such as Johns' structured approach to reflection (Johns, 1994), to models that are far less structured, such as Boud's model of reflective thought and action (Boud, 2001). Such a guided approach has been successfully adopted within ASP by Lindsay *et al.* (2006), who proposed that the cyclical approach of Gibbs's (1988) model facilitated the continual development of the practitioner as they progressed through each stage of the model's process. In addition, the focus of the model on practical action plans meant that the practitioner was able to generate behavioural solutions to issues that they faced in their practice. Additional reports of the use of specific reflective methods have been provided by Anderson (1999) and Cropley *et al.* (2007), who reported the benefits of using a modified version of Johns' (1994) structured model (see Anderson *et al.*, 2004). In light of the way in which Anderson (1999) adhered to Johns' ideas that suggested we shouldn't blindly follow reflective frameworks but should instead adapt them to suit our own needs and the context in which we are reflecting, it is important that practitioners make an informed decision about the method that is most appropriate for them. This decision may be influenced by who you are reflecting for, or what you are actually reflecting on. It may also be determined by your ability to engage in reflective practice. For example, it is suggested that neophyte reflective practitioners are guided by more structured models so that they access the types of information that allow them to systematically reflect on their experiences, rather than simply mulling them over (Knowles *et al.*, 2001).

Despite support for the use of structured reflective writing, personal reflection can be limited by our own knowledge and understanding. Additionally, structured models have been criticised, as they are thought to create recipes for reflective thinking that lead practitioners into certain thought processes, thus removing the spontaneity and "art" of reflecting on action. In attempts to overcome such problems, it is thought that the sharing of experiences with others publicly may create a forum to facilitate an interchange of views (Knowles *et al.*, 2001). Certainly, engaging in reflective conversations with others presents the practitioner with the opportunity to access the knowledge of a colleague and thus make more informed decisions about developments to future practice in light of the current experience. Indeed, Johns (2000) considered that through sharing reflections on learning experiences greater understanding of those experiences could be achieved than by reflection as a lone exercise. Evidence from the sport psychology literature has demonstrated the potential benefit of engaging in a process of shared reflection, usually with a professional practice supervisor, followed by solitary written reflection (e.g. Cropley *et al.*, 2011; Woodcock *et al.*, 2008). In these situations, the shared reflection acts as an initial process whereby trainee practitioners can work through their experiences with a more knowledgeable other.

This helps to shed light on experiences that may be novel in nature, and therefore provide the trainee with a valuable resource to draw upon when reflecting on their own.

Johns (1994) suggested that a supervisor could provide a supportive environment that will encourage reflective practitioners to develop a deeper, more critical understanding of their work. This clearly lends itself well to the supervised experience framework for practitioner development within ASP, where the professional practice supervisor could encourage the use of reflective practice by engaging their supervisees in reflective conversations. However, Johns proposed that although the practitioner's supervisor may be appropriate to fulfill this role, it is important that a relationship of mutual respect and understanding is developed between the supervisor and practitioner. This is indicative of the concept of the "safe learning environment", which is proposed to be essential to learning the skill of reflection (Cropley *et al.*, 2011). A safe environment is one in which students are free to examine and reflect on their work thoughtfully and honestly without fear of judgement or reprisal. Indeed, Telfer and Knowles (2009) acknowledged that reflective conversations open the practitioner to "outside gaze" but can sometimes feel threatening, especially in the early stages of practice. Without a safe learning environment, it is likely that the experience of discomfort and feelings of threat will increase. Supervisors must therefore be aware that such conditions must be met.

Importantly, Anderson *et al.* (2004) suggested that becoming a reflective practitioner is more than a collection of techniques, and instead involves an all-encompassing attitude to practice that requires the practitioner to commit to professional and personal development. It is also a process that requires certain skills that can be developed through guidance and practice. Research by Cropley *et al.* (2011) revealed the potential value of mentoring and the provision of feedback in helping practitioners to better understand the process of reflection and the types of questions they should consider, and in developing critical skills in reflective practice. As a result of this support, the participants in Cropley *et al.*'s study reported a developing ability to also reflect "in" action, as a direct result of better understanding the types of information they needed to access in order to make more informed decisions regarding their experiences. It must be recognised, however, that the ability to provide such support will depend upon the practitioner's supervisor or critical friend, and their understanding of and ability to engage in reflective practices.

Chapter summary and future directions for reflective practice within applied sport psychology

The purpose of this review was to situate the concept of reflective practice within the professional training and development of ASP practitioners – in particular, to consider the potential value of reflective practice as a mechanism to assist ASP practitioners to develop their effectiveness. Due to the complex nature of ASP and the recent movements towards more athlete-centred approaches to practice, greater emphasis has been placed on the need for practitioners to access, make sense of, and develop the knowledge-in-action (tacit knowledge) required to actually "do" sport psychology (Anderson *et al.*, 2004). As a result, greater value has been placed on frameworks that facilitate experiential learning. In light of this, reflective practice has grown in credence over recent times. Although discipline-specific research is still in its infancy, reflective practice has been consistently highlighted to be a process that has the potential to aid ASP practitioners in enhancing their self-awareness, making sense of practice, and addressing issues concerning effective practice, and should therefore be considered as an integral aspect of professional practice. Understandings of definitions, processes, benefits, and applications of reflective practice for sport psychologists are improving, but greater consistency in the approaches to learning from experience and the use of the term "reflective practice" is required. Reflective practice literature within ASP is also largely anecdotal, with little empirical evidence available to substantiate claims regarding the potential value of reflection for the field. Additional research is therefore required in order to address a number of concerns emanating from the extant literature.

Some support is evident to suggest that through reflecting on action, ASP practitioners can become better able to develop a questioning approach to practice and to engage in activities representative of reflection-in-action (Cropley *et al.*, 2011; Telfer and Knowles, 2009). Nevertheless, it is suggested that this developmental process is examined more closely in future research in attempts to uncover the specific mechanisms underpinning such significant behavioural changes. This research would potentially uncover valuable information that could be used to guide training programmes and encourage practitioners to develop in vivo decision- and judgement-making skills that have been closely linked to effective practice (Petitpas *et al.*, 1999). Further, the value of engaging in solitary reflection and in shared reflection is well documented within the literature (e.g. Anderson *et al.*, 2004; Ghaye and Lillyman, 2000; Johns, 1994). Nevertheless, in agreement with Woodcock *et al.* (2008), future research should consider the implications of shared reflection versus private reflection, and their impact on features surrounding professional development. Findings of this research would have the potential to improve understanding of the most effective methods of engaging in reflective practice and clarify further beneficial processes for professional training and development in ASP. Finally, future research should examine the developmental processes associated with practitioners becoming eligible to act as mentors for reflective practice. Little evidence of criteria exists that would help define the "expert" reflector and, consequently, someone who is suitable to act as a mentor. This would potentially lead to the development of mentor training programmes, and ensure consistency and quality across mentoring schemes. In general, the reflective practice literature in ASP would benefit from reflective accounts from professionally trained practitioners, as well as additional empirical research that attempts to establish the impact of reflection on service delivery. Due to the potential impact that reflective and effective practice may have on the professional status of ASP, it is suggested that all lines of enquiry deserve attention.

References

Allen, M., Jones, M., and Sheffield, D. (2010). The influence of positive reflection on attributions, emotions, and self-efficacy. *The Sport Psychologist*, 24, 211–226.

Andersen, M. B. (2000). Introduction. In M. B. Andersen (ed.), *Doing sport psychology* (pp. xiii–xvii). Champaign, IL: Human Kinetics.

Andersen, M. B. (2009). Performance enhancement as a bad start and a dead end: A parenthetical comment on Mellalieu and Lane. *The Sport and Exercise Scientist*, 20, 12–14.

Anderson, A. (1999). Reflections of a budding sport psychologist: First meetings. In H. Steinberg and I. Cockerill (eds), *Sport psychology in practice: The early stages* (pp. 30–37). Leicester, UK: British Psychological Society.

Anderson, A., Knowles, Z., and Gilbourne, D. (2004). Reflective practice for applied sport psychologists: A review of concepts, models, practical implications and thoughts on dissemination. *The Sport Psychologist*, 18, 188–203.

Andresen, L., Boud, D., and Cohen, R. (1999). Experience-based learning: Contemporary issues. In G. Foley (ed.), *Understanding adult education and training* (pp. 225–239). Sydney, NSW, Australia: Allen and Unwin.

Andrews, M., Gidman, J., and Humphreys, A. (1998). Reflection: Does it enhance professional nursing practice? *British Journal of Nursing*, 7, 413–417.

Bain, J. Ballantyne, R., Packer, J., and Mills, S. (1999). Using journal writing to enhance student teachers' reflectivity during field placements. *Teachers and Teaching*, 5, 51–73.

Barnett, B. G. and O'Mahoney, G. R. (2006). Developing a culture of reflection: Implications for school improvement. *Reflective Practice*, 4, 499–523.

Boyd, E. and Fales, A. (1983). Reflective learning: Key to learning from experience. *Journal of Humanistic Psychology*, 23, 99–117.

Bright, B. (1993). What is reflective practice? *Curriculum*, 6, 69–81.

British Association of Sport and Exercise Sciences (BASES) (2009). *Supervised experience and accreditation guidelines*. Retrieved 20 January 2010, from www.bases.org.uk/supervisedexp.asp.

British Psychological Society (BPS) (2006). Reflections on Athens. *Sport and Exercise Psychology Review*, 2, 1–72.

British Psychological Society (BPS) (2007). *Division of Sport and Exercise Psychology chartership guidelines*. Retrieved 10 October 2007, from www.bps.org.uk/spex/spex_home.cfm.

Boud, D. (2001). Using journal writing to enhance reflective practice. *New Directions for Adult and Continuing Education*, 90, 9–16.

Bull, S. (1995). Reflections on a 5-year consultancy programme with the England woman's cricket team. *The Sport Psychologist*, 9, 148–163.

Candy, P., Harri-Augstein, S., and Thomas, L. (1985). Reflection and the self-organised learner: A model of learning conversations. In D. Boud, R. Keogh, and D. Walker (eds), *Reflection: Turning experience into learning* (pp. 100–117). London, UK: Kogan Page.

Compagnucci, E. and Cardós, P. (2007). The development of professors' professional knowledge in psychology. *Orientación y Sociedad*, 7, 1–11.

Conway J. (1998). Evolution of the species "expert nurse". An examination of the practical knowledge held by expert nurses. *Journal of Clinical Nursing*, 7, 75–82.

Criticos, C. (1993). Experiential learning and social transformation for a post-apartheid learning future. In D. Boud, R. Cohen, and D. Walker (eds), *Using experience for learning* (pp. 159–165). Buckingham, UK: Open University Press.

Cropley, B., Miles, A., Hanton, S., and Anderson, A. (2007). Improving the delivery of applied sport psychology support through reflective practice. *The Sport Psychologist*, 21, 475–494.

Cropley, B., Hanton, S., Miles, A., and Niven, A. (2010a). The value of reflective practice in professional development: An applied sport psychology review. *Sports Science Review*, 19, 179–209.

Cropley, B., Hanton, S., Miles, A., and Niven, A. (2010b). Exploring the relationship between effective and reflective practice in applied sport psychology. *The Sport Psychologist*, 24, 521–541.

Cropley, B., Hanton, S., Miles, A., and Niven, A. (2011). Developing the effectiveness of applied sport psychology service delivery: A reflective practice intervention. *Psychology of Sport and Exercise*, in press.

Dewey, J. (1933). *How we think*. Boston, MA: DC Heath and Co.

Driscoll, J. and Teh, B. (2001). The potential of reflective practice to develop individual orthopedic nurse practitioners and their practice. *Journal of Orthopedic Nursing*, 5, 95–103.

Faull, A. and Cropley, B. (2009). Reflective learning in sport: A case study of a senior level triathlete. *Reflective Practice*, 10, 325–339.

Friesen, A. and Orlick, T. (2010). A qualitative analysis of holistic sport psychology consultant's professional philosophies. *The Sport Psychologist*, 24, 227–244.

Ghaye, T. (2007). Is reflective practice ethical? (The case of the reflective portfolio). *Reflective Practice*, 8, 151–162.

Ghaye, T. (2009). Reflection: Principles and practices. In C. Heaney, B. Oakley, and Rea, S. (eds), *Exploring sport and fitness* (pp. 5–11). London, UK: Routledge.

Ghaye, T. (2010). In what ways can reflective practices enhance human flourishing? *Reflective Practice*, 11, 1–7.

Ghaye, T. and Lillyman, S. (2000). *Reflection: Principles and practice for healthcare professionals*. Dinton, UK: Quay Books.

Ghaye, T., Melander-Wikman, A., Kisare, M., Chambers, P., Bergmark, U., Kostenius, C., and Lillyman, S. (2008). Participatory and appreciative action and reflection (PAAR) – democratising reflective practices. *Reflective Practice*, 9, 361–397.

Gibbs, G. (1988). *Learning by doing: A guide to teaching and learning methods*. Oxford, UK: Oxford Brookes University, FE Unit.

Hanrahan, S. J., Pedro, R., and Cerin, E. (2009). Structured self-reflection as a tool to enhance perceived performance and maintain effort in adult recreational salsa dancers. *The Sport Psychologist*, 23, 151–169.

Hanton, S., Cropley, B., Neil, R., Mellalieu, S. D., and Miles, A. (2007). Experience in sport and its relationship with competitive anxiety. *International Journal of Sport and Exercise Psychology*, 5, 28–53.

Hogg, J. M. (1995). *Mental skills for competitive swimmers*. Edmonton, Alberta: Sport Excel Publishing.

Holt, N. and Strean, W. (2001). Reflecting on initiating sport psychology consultation: A self-narrative of neophyte practice. *The Sport Psychologist*, 15, 188–204.

Husu, J., Toom, A., and Patrikainen, S. (2008). Guided reflection as a means to demonstrate and develop student teachers' reflective competencies. *Reflective Practice*, 9, 37–51.

James, C. R. and Clarke, B. (1996). Reflective practice in nursing: Issues and implications for nurse education. In T. Ghaye (ed.), *Reflection and action for health care professionals* (pp. 35–48). Newcastle Upon Tyne, UK: Pentaxion Ltd.

Johns, C. (1994). Guided reflection. In A. Palmer, S. Burns, and C. Bulman (eds) *Reflective practice in nursing* (pp. 110–130). Oxford, UK: Blackwell Science.

Johns, C. (2000). *Becoming a reflective practitioner*. London, UK: Blackwell Science.

Jones, L., Evans, L., and Mullen, R. (2007). Multiple roles in an applied setting: Trainee sport psychologist, coach, and researcher. *The Sport Psychologist*, 21, 210–226.

Knowles, Z. and Gilbourne, D. (2010). Aspiration, inspiration and illustration: Initiating debate on reflective practice writing. *The Sport Psychologist*, 24, 504–520.

Knowles, Z. and Saxon, J. (2010). Needs analysis and reflective practice: Two important components of case studies. *The Sport and Exercise Scientist*, 25, 23.

Knowles, Z., Gilbourne, D., Borrie, A., and Neville, A. (2001). Developing the reflective sports coach: A study exploring the processes of reflection within a higher education coaching programme. *Reflective Practice*, 2, 185–207.

Knowles, Z., Gilbourne, D., Tomlinson, V., and Anderson, A. (2007). Reflections on the application of reflective practice for supervision in applied sport psychology. *The Sport Psychologist*, 21, 109–122.

Larrivee, B. (2008). Development of a tool to assess teachers' level of reflective practice. *Reflective Practice*, 9, 341–360.

Lindsay, P., Breckon, J. D., Thomas, O., and Maynard, I. (2007). In pursuit of congruence: A personal reflection on methods and philosophy in applied practice. *The Sport Psychologist*, 21, 335–352.

Loughran, J. J. (2006). A response to "Reflecting on the self". *Reflective Practice*, 7, 43–53.

Martens, R. (1987). Science, knowledge and sport psychology. *The Sport Psychologist*, 1, 29–55.

Martindale, A. and Collins, D. (2007). Enhancing the evaluation of effectiveness with professional judgment and decision making. *The Sport Psychologist*, 21, 458–474.

McCann, S. C. (2000). Doing sport psychology at the really big show. In M. B. Andersen (ed.), *Doing sport psychology* (pp. 209–222). Champaign, IL: Human Kinetics.

Newman, S. (1999). Constructing and critiquing reflective practice. *Educational Action Research Journal*, 7, 145–161.

Petitpas, A. J., Giges, B., and Danish, S. J. (1999). The sport-psychologist–athlete relationship: Implications for training. *The Sport Psychologist*, 13, 344–355.

Platzer, H., Snelling, J., and Blake, D. (1997). Promoting reflective practitioners in nursing: A review of theoretical models and research into the use of diaries and journals to facilitate reflection. *Teaching in Higher Education*, 2, 103–121.

Poczwardowski, A., Sherman, C. P., and Henschen, K. P. (1998). A sport psychology delivery heuristic: Building theory on practice. *The Sport Psychologist*, 12, 191–207.

Poczwardowski, A., Sherman, C., and Ravizza, K. (2004). Professional philosophy in the sport psychology service: Building theory on practice. *The Sport Psychologist*, 18, 445–463.

Raelin, J. (2002). I don't have time to think! versus the art of reflective practice. *Reflections*, 4, 65–79.

Scanlan, J. M. and Chernomas, W. M. (1997). Developing the reflective teacher. *Journal of Advanced Nursing*, 25, 1138–1143.

Schön, D. (1983). *The reflective practitioner*. New York, NY: Basic Books.

Schön, D. (1987). *Educating the reflective practitioner*. San Francisco, CA: Jossey Bass.

Shepherd, M. (2006). Using a learning journal to improve professional practice: A journey of personal and professional self-discovery. *Reflective Practice*, 7, 338–348.

Sherman, C. P. and Poczwardowski, A. (2005). Integrating mind and body. Presenting mental skills to young teams. In M. B. Andersen (ed.), *Doing sport psychology* (pp. 17–45). Champaign, IL, Human Kinetics.

Sparks-Langer, G. M. and Colton, A. B. (1991). Synthesis of research on teachers' reflective thinking. *Educational Leadership*, 48, 37–44.

Sparrow, J. (2009). Impact of emotions associated with reflecting on the past. *Reflective Practice*, 10, 567–576.

Strean, W. and Strean, H. (1998). Applying psychodynamic concepts to sport psychology practice. *The Sport Psychologist*, 12, 208–222.

Tammen, V. V. (2000). First internship experiences. In M. B. Andersen (ed.), *Doing sport psychology* (pp. 181–192). Champaign, IL: Human Kinetics.

Telfer, H. and Knowles, Z. (2009). The how to of reflection. In C. Heaney, B. Oakley and S. Rea (eds), *Exploring sport and fitness* (pp. 36–48). London, UK: Routledge.

Tod, D. and Bond, K. (2010). A longitudinal examination of a British neophyte sport psychologist's development. *The Sport Psychologist*, 24, 35–51.

Tod, D., Marchant, D., and Andersen, M.B. (2007). Learning experiences contributing to service-delivery competence. *The Sport Psychologist*, 21, 317–334.

Tonn, E. and Harmison, R. J. (2004). Thrown to the wolves: A student's account of her practicum experience. *The Sport Psychologist*, 18, 324–340.

Tripp, D. (1993). *Critical incidents in teaching: Developing professional judgement*. London, UK: Routledge.

Van Manen, M. (1991). *The tact of teaching: The meaning of pedagogical Thoughtfulness*. Albany, NY: SUNY Press.

Van Raalte, J. and Andersen, M. B. (2000). Supervision I: From models to doing. In M.B. Andersen (ed.), *Doing sport psychology* (pp. 153–162). Champaign, IL: Human Kinetics.

Wallace, D. (1996). Using reflective diaries to assess students. *Nursing Standard*, 10, 44–47.

Weinberg, R. S. and Gould, D. G. (2007). *Foundations of sport and exercise psychology* (5th edn). Champaign, IL: Human Kinetics.

Winstone, W. and Gervis, M. (2006). Countertransference and the self-aware sport psychologist: Attitudes and patterns of professional practice. *The Sport Psychologist*, 20, 495–511.

Woodcock, C., Richards, H., and Mugford, A. (2008). Quality counts: Critical features for neophyte professional development. *The Sport Psychologist*, 22, 491–506.
Yip, K. (2006). Self-reflection in reflective practice: A note of caution. *British Journal of Social Work*, 36, 777–778.
Zimmerman, B. J. (2002). Becoming a self-regulated learner: An overview. *Theory into Practice*, 41, 64–70.

Index

Page numbers in *italics* denote tables, those in **bold** denote figures.

28058580R00206

Printed in Great Britain
by Amazon